Wild in the City

Exploring The Intertwine

The Portland-Vancouver Region's Network
of Parks, Trails, and Natural Areas

SECOND EDITION

Edited by Michael C. Houck and M. J. Cody

OREGON STATE UNIVERSITY PRESS
CORVALLIS, OREGON

AUDUBON SOCIETY OF PORTLAND
PORTLAND, OREGON

Library of Congress Cataloging-in-Publication Data
Wild in the city : exploring the intertwine, the Portland-Vancouver region's
network of parks, trails, and natural areas / edited by Michael C. Houck and
M. J. Cody. — 2nd ed.
      p. cm.
Includes index.
ISBN 978-0-87071-612-6 (alk. paper) — ISBN 978-0-87071-634-8 (e-book)
1. Natural history—Oregon—Portland Region—Guidebooks. 2. Portland
Region (Or.)—Guidebooks. I. Houck, Michael C. II. Cody, M. J. (Mary Jane),
1946-
QH105.O7W563 2011
508.795'49—dc23
                              2011025706

William Stafford's poem on page 91 is published with permission of the Confluence Press.
Portions of Bill Monroe's essay on page 107 first appeared in a different form in *The Oregonian*.

Oregon State University Press
121 The Valley Library, Corvallis, Oregon 97331-4501
Phone: 541-737-3166   Fax: 541-737-3170
Web: osupress.oregonstate.edu

Contents

The publication of this volume is made possible by the financial support of:

and additional financial support from:

NATIONAL PARK SERVICE'S RIVERS AND TRAILS CONSERVATION ASSISTANCE PROGRAM

PORTLAND PARKS & RECREATION'S CITY NATURE PROGRAM

TUALATIN BASIN'S CLEAN WATER SERVICES

TUALATIN HILLS PARK & RECREATION DISTRICT

VANCOUVER-CLARK PARKS & RECREATION

WEST MULTNOMAH SOIL & WATER CONSERVATION DISTRICT

Foreword

By Richard Louv

WILD IN THE CITY: EXPLORING THE INTERTWINE is your roadmap to nature just outside the back door, down the road, or beyond the next hill. Its contributors have given us a wise and useful guide to the natural glories in the greater Portland-Vancouver region. With this book in hand, anyone can plan an enjoyable outing. When it's time to relax, open to the essays that offer insight into local wonders, ranging from the Anna's hummingbird's successful colonization of the Northwest to an idiosyncratic view of Johnson Creek.

That's the thumbnail description of *Wild in the City*, which only hints at the vein of gold that runs through this book. Individuals will toss it in the daypack or the car to have it available for quick reference. But groups can make special use of it too. The Intertwine regional trail network gives form to our kinship with neighbors, friends, strangers, and fellow species. Together, we're healthier and stronger and more interesting than if we lived our lives apart. By definition, The Intertwine suggests a shared appreciation of nature: bicyclists and walkers who use the trails; moms who push strollers under big-leaf maples in the fall; grandparents who take kids in hand, and lean close for a look at minnows in a slow-moving stream; backpackers who take urban-area hikes to prepare for a week in the mountains; and kayakers who explore the city's waterways. In addition to ad hoc expeditions, group organizers can mark out a plan to visit every site that is listed, perhaps choosing when to do so by types of terrain or the rainy-season mud factor. Schools, hiking clubs, botany groups, birding partners, and others can add this volume to their reference shelves.

Everyone can use this book. A growing body of scientific evidence strongly suggests that all of us are starved for nature time, and our society suffers from what I've called "nature-deficit disorder." And yet, we know that human beings, especially in their formative years, are happier, healthier, and smarter when they spend time outdoors in natural settings. This is why *Wild in the City* is so important a resource, especially to families with children. With guidance from this book, family nature clubs can be created in any neighborhood—inner city or suburban. If this approach becomes the norm in every community, we'll be well on our way to true cultural change and the benefits of nature will be added to our everyday lives.

Richard Louv is the author of *The Nature Principle* and *Last Child in the Woods: Saving Our Children from Nature-Deficit Disorder* and chairman of the Children & Nature Network, www.childrenandnature.org.

Preface

WHAT STARTED AS A SERIES of natural history essays in "The Urban Naturalist," an Audubon Society of Portland publication during the 1980s, grew into our first book, *Wild in the City: A Guide to Portland's Natural Areas*, which was published in 2000.

Eleven years later, *Wild in the City: Exploring The Intertwine* represents a new collection of lively essays, wonderful sites, and rambles to experience nature nearby, and narratives on efforts to better integrate the built and natural environments. Since that first edition, Metro and local park providers have brought more than 12,000 acres of natural areas into the public realm. Seventy miles of streamside habitat has been protected; and many miles of trails have been added to the Portland-Vancouver regional trail network.

When Portland Audubon launched its Urban Naturalist program in 1980, urban wildlife was considered an oxymoron by many. They asserted that the region's urban growth boundary was intended to focus on development inside and to protect nature "out there" beyond the boundary. Thirty years later, access to nature in the city is a critical element of modern urban planning and design.

Wild in the City: Exploring The Intertwine is more than an indispensable guide to the Portland-Vancouver parks, trails, and natural areas. It's an expression of the philosophy that nature not only belongs in the city, but is also essential to creating and sustaining our quality of life in this splendid place.

By Mike Houck and M. J. Cody, co-editors

Acknowledgments

To

The more than one hundred contributors to *Wild in the City: Exploring The Intertwine*—writers and illustrators, all of whom are dedicated to celebrating urban nature, and without whom this book would not exist.

And To

The Audubon Society of Portland for being a pioneer in the field of urban ecology, beginning with the protection of its wildlife sanctuary on Cornell Road in the 1930s, and continuing today with its urban conservation and urban nature programs; and, for providing a forum for a community that shares a passion to ensure that everyone in the Portland-Vancouver region has access to nature.

The local park providers and countless nonprofit groups without whose wealth of information and expertise *Wild in the City: Exploring The Intertwine* would not be the region's most valuable guide to parks, trails, and natural areas.

The Metro Council for launching Connecting Green in 2007 and for taking on a lion's share of the financial investment and staff talent that birthed The Intertwine and The Intertwine Alliance; and for continued support of The Intertwine vision.

Portland's Bureau of Environmental Services and Tualatin Basin's Clean Water Services, who constantly remind us that The Intertwine is not only about parks and trails, but also about healthy watersheds, without which the region's diversity of plants and animals would not continue to thrive; and whose assistance included both financial support and written contributions from their talented pools of ecologists, landscape architects, planners, and engineers.

Thank you all for helping to create this book, which celebrates nature nearby.

From

The *Wild in the City* creative team: Martha Gannett, Rafael Gutierrez, Bob Wilson, Bob Sallinger, M. J. Cody, and Mike Houck.

The Intertwine

THE INTERTWINE is the network of parks, trails, natural areas, and special places in the Portland-Vancouver metropolitan region. At its core, it is about providing people with connections to nature, to their communities, and to one another across urban and rural landscapes.

The concept of an interconnected system of parks, trails, and natural areas is not a new one. In his 1903 report to the Portland Park Board, John Charles Olmsted recommended a "system of public squares, neighborhood parks, playgrounds, scenic reservations, rural or suburban parks, and boulevards and parkways" built around features that are today's landscape icons: Forest Park, Mount Tabor, Washington Park, Macleay Park, and the Terwilliger Parkway.

THE INTER TWINE

In a 1938 address to Portland's City Club, Lewis Mumford advocated for a Vancouver-Portland open space plan as well as establishing a bi-state Columbia Gorge Commission. Forty years later another regionalist, William H. Whyte, in his book *The Last Landscape*, argued that ample access to parks and urban nature should complement higher density, compact cities, and regional planning and "take its cue from the patterns of nature itself—the water table, the floodplains, the ridges, the woods, and above all, the streams."

Our first regional open space and park plan was created in 1971 by the Columbia Regional Association of Governments (CRAG), which advocated a vision in which "Man and nature" were one and foresaw "creeks, streams, and rivers as a total greenway system, a public front yard for an ever widening circle of people, the canals of Holland and Venice, but natural and on a grand scale."

Since then, there have been several iterations of a vision for a comprehensive, interconnected parks and open space system for our region. The 40-Mile Loop, inspired by Olmsted's parkway and boulevard plan, is today a nearly 150-mile continuous loop trail through Multnomah County and Portland with connections to Vancouver and Clark County.

Thanks to CRAG's successor, Metro, along with Clark County, local park providers, and local stormwater management agencies, the idea of a parks and trails network has expanded to embrace a much broader initiative to integrate the built and natural environments at all scales, from the streetscape to large natural areas. We now understand that creating trail networks linking urban and rural landscapes with natural areas not only provides recreation but also preserves interconnected green-spaces, improves watershed quality, protects wildlife, and enhances human health, both physical and psychological. We share this landscape with myriad other life forms, and what we do has profound implications for their survival, as well as our own. That understanding is fueling The Intertwine vision of an exceptional interconnected system of parks, natural areas, trails, and open spaces that is an essential element of the greater Portland-Vancouver metropolitan area's economic success, ecological health, civic vitality, and overall quality of life.

Wild in the City invites you to hike, bike, and paddle as you explore The Intertwine.

By Bob Sallinger and Mike Houck

A Regional Treasure
By Tom Hughes

AS METRO COUNCIL PRESIDENT, it is my honor and privilege to work with more than one hundred contributors to *Wild in the City: Exploring The Intertwine*, which introduces us—both new and long-time residents, and those just passing through—to The Intertwine's interconnected system of parks, trails, and natural areas. The Intertwine is a collection of assets of immeasurable economic, recreational, and natural value, and one of the most endearing and enduring parts of our region's sense of place. *Wild in the City* also challenges us to expand and nurture The Intertwine so it continues to function as our region's heart, lungs, and soul.

Look at any tourism brochure for our region, or any travel article photo spread, and you'll see The Intertwine. People enjoy our restaurants and culture, of course, but it is our landscape—our rivers, urban streams and wetlands, mountains and trees, right in the heart of our cities—that draws them to the Portland-Vancouver region and makes their visit memorable. This dramatic setting is both awe inspiring and humbling.

Our trails link parks and natural areas and connect us to the larger regional landscape. When our trails network is completely built, we will be able to walk, cycle, or paddle from home to work, from school to play, from river to winery. We will lead healthier, safer, and more serene lives, in tune with the seasons and better connected to our neighbors.

Other benefits of The Intertwine include healthy ecosystems, clean air and water, and access to nature, all of which contribute directly to a vibrant regional economy. After asking hotel staff for a recommended place to eat, visitors next ask for the best place to hike or ride a bike. Companies want to establish themselves where they can have a healthy and happy work force. Even when the economy is in a downswing, people continue to move here. Why? Because they value access to nature where they live, work, and learn. Our region's quality of life attracts creative, well-educated citizens who are just as dedicated to protecting our region's natural assets as long-term residents.

Wild in the City: Exploring The Intertwine invites us all to acquaint, or reacquaint, ourselves with the diversity of plants and animals that share this special place with us. What we experience we appreciate, and what we appreciate we nurture. I hope you will join me in exploring and will come to appreciate the amazing, ever-growing system of parks, trails, and natural areas that is The Intertwine.

Tom Hughes is the Metro Council president.

A Personal View
By Wim Wiewel

BEFORE MOVING TO PORTLAND I lived for twenty-five years in Chicago, where the motto is *Urbs in Horto*: "City in the garden." I often wondered at the perverse Latinist who thought of the environment of Chicago as a garden. Originally it was flat prairie, which does have a certain natural beauty, but today it's an asphalt oasis surrounded by monocultures of corn and soybeans.

Portland is just the opposite. Here, you can't say it's a city in the garden if only because the environment immediately surrounding the city is too wild to properly be called a garden. It took me awhile to realize that nature existed within the city almost as much as it surrounded the city. This awareness was helped by the fact that it's green all year, as opposed to many northern climes where, from November to March, the landscape appears brown, gray, and dead. In our verdant environs, you notice nature on even the grayest days in winter.

Early on, I began to enjoy the Saturday farmers' markets on the South Park Blocks at Portland State University. What more eloquent way of bringing nature into the city could there be?

Then I began to explore farther: Forest Park, Tryon Creek State Natural Area, the Johnson Creek Watershed, and Springwater Corridor trail, and the abundance of streams, trees, and flowers on the hills of the west side of the city and the more isolated hillocks to the east. And that's not even to speak of the *two* seemingly ever-present (no matter where I was) majestic rivers. If only I could figure out which bridge got me out of the Rose Garden and back downtown . . .

In the University District Framework Plan we will continue to visually connect Portland State, a campus (in the academic sense) focused on sustainability, to this idea of being an urban *campus* (from the Latin, meaning "field") deeply imbedded in our natural environment.

This book contains multiple contributions that expand on the theme of our profound connections, as urban dwellers, to our geography, geology, and ecology, as well as the spiritual and physical interweaving of city and nature. Portland has a glorious history in this regard, but the work will never be done. *Wild in the City* shows it's a worthwhile quest, where even small victories are real and over time add up to major change.

Wim Wiewel is the president of Portland State University.

How To Use This Book

WILD IN THE CITY: EXPLORING THE INTERTWINE is a selection of natural history essays interspersed with rambles and sites that represent the best sampling of *The Intertwine*—the network of parks, trails, and natural areas within the Portland-Vancouver metropolitan region. The sites we have selected embody a wide variety of The Intertwine's ever-growing, bi-state, regional trail network that, when complete, will comprise over 950 miles of trails.

In addition to specific sites, twenty-two rambles—unique walking, biking, and paddling excursions—encompass more than one site. Nature respects no political boundaries. Accordingly, we've arranged the site descriptions, rambles, and accompanying essays by watersheds, which are the basic organizing unit for understanding the natural history of our region. Progressing down a stream or through a watershed provides a more vivid understanding of how parks, trails, and natural areas interact with and contribute to the region's ecological health.

Because of the nature of nature in the Pacific Northwest, we cannot guarantee that you will find the sites exactly as described in this book. Adverse weather, development, or maintenance may lead to closures or restrictions, or make areas impassable. Although care is taken to maintain many of the paths or trails, many of these greenspaces are not manicured parks, but wild places where nature comes first. It is recommended that you bring gear appropriate for your excursion and attempt only hikes, bike trips, or paddles for which you have adequate knowledge, skill, and physical conditioning.

In preparing rambles and sites, we relied on maps and data from a collection of federal, state, and local agencies, as well as online resources such as Google Maps. Since we have limited space, the maps, especially the rambles, do not have as much detail as we would like. And site conditions, rules, and regulations are subject to change without notice. As you explore The Intertwine, we encourage you to use additional resources, such as those found at the end of this section, which can provide more specific information.

Nearly every natural area, park, trail, and refuge can be reached by public transit. Specific routes accompany site guides, but it is advisable to contact TriMet or C-Tran for up-to-date routing.

The following references provided the animal and plant citation standards: *Flora of the Pacific Northwest: An Illustrated Manual*, C. Leo Hitchcock and Arthur Cronquist

continued on page xx

Regional Watersheds and Site Locations

Sites

1 Graham Oaks Nature Park
2 Canemah Bluff Natural Area
3 Camassia Natural Area
4 Mount Talbert Nature Park
5 Tryon Creek State Natural Area
6 Bryant Woods Nature Park
7 Elk Rock Island
8 Oaks Bottom Wildlife Refuge
9 Tanner Springs Park
10 Marquam Nature Park
11 Hoyt Arboretum
12 Washington Park
13 Pittock Acres Park
14 Audubon Society of Portland Sanctuaries
15 Mount Tabor Park
16 Cooper Mountain Nature Park
17 Jenkins Estate
18 Tualatin River National Wildlife Refuge
19 Jackson Bottom Wetlands Preserve
20 Fernhill Wetlands
21 Hyland Forest Park
22 Lowami Hart Woods
23 Commonwealth Lake Park
24 Jordan Park
25 Tualatin Hills Nature Park
26 Koll Center Wetlands
27 Vista Brook Park and the Fanno Creek Trail
28 Deep Creek Canyon and the Cazadero Trail
29 Gresham Buttes
30 Gresham Woods and Butler Creek Greenway
31 Clatsop Butte Park and Natural Area
32 Powell Butte Nature Park
33 Leach Botanical Garden
34 Zenger Farm
35 Beggars-Tick Wildlife Refuge
36 Reed College Canyon
37 Crystal Springs Rhododendron Garden
38 Nadaka Nature Park
39 Whitaker Ponds Nature Park
40 Heron Lakes Golf Course
41 Smith and Bybee Wetlands Natural Area
42 Kelley Point Park
43 Government Island
44 Howell Territorial Park and Howell Lake
45 Oak Island Trail
46 Wapato Access Greenway State Park Trail
47 Warrior Rock Lighthouse Trail
48 Ridgefield National Wildlife Refuge
49 Oxbow Regional Park
50 Sandy River Delta
51 Lacamas Lake Regional Park
52 Columbia Springs
53 Cottonwood Beach
54 Steigerwald Lake National Wildlife Refuge
55 Water Resources Center Wetlands
56 La Center Bottoms

Rambles

A Upper Willamette Narrows Paddle
B Lower Willamette River Loop Ramble
C Lower Willamette River Paddle
D Springwater on the Willamette Trail Ramble
E Ross Island Paddle
F The Willamette Greenway Ramble
G A Cheapskate's Ramble
H Exploring North Portland Ramble
I Storming Downtown Portland Ramble
J Storming East Portland Ramble

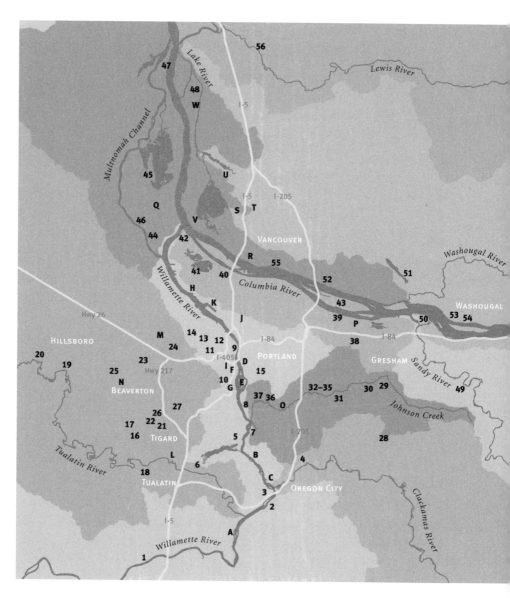

(University of Washington Press, 1973); *Birds of Oregon: A General Reference*, David B. Marshall, Matthew G. Hunter, Alan L. Contreras (Oregon State University Press 2003); and online sources.

Our primary responsibility is to be good stewards of these natural areas. Please be considerate of private property as well. Be smart. Travel safe. Have fun!

Key to map icons

P Parking

 Wildlife Viewing/Scenic Viewpoint

i Information/Interpretive Sign

 Restrooms

 Canoe/Kayak Launch

Picnic Area

Additional References

Since scale for the ramble maps is limited, we encourage you to use these additional resources which can provide more detailed information for navigation.

Portland

Portland Bureau of Transportation Maps
(www.gettingaroundportland.org):

North Portland Bike/Walk Map

Mapa del Norte de Portland para Ciclistas y Peatones

Mapa del Noreste de Portland pars Ciclistas y Peatones

Southeast Portland Bike/Walk Map

Southwest Portland Bike/Walk Map

Northwest and Downtown Bike/Walk Map

Downtown Portland by Bicycle

Portland by Bicycle Citywide Bike Map

Walking Routes

Vancouver

Vancouver-Clark Parks Pedestrian and Cycling Map
(www.cityofvancouver.us/parks-recreation)

Regional

The Intertwine Alliance
(www.theintertwine.org)

Metro *Bike There!*

Metro *Walk There!*

City of Beaverton: Beaverton Bikeway Map
(www.beavertonoregon.gov)

Washington County: Let the Journey Begin, Washington County Bike Map
(www.VisitWashingtonCountyOregon.com)

Clackamas County Bike It Maps
(www.clackamas.us)

Multnomah County Bike Map and Brochure
(www.sustainableportland.org)

Clark County Bike Map
(www.sustainableportland.org)

Transit

TriMet Transit Guide (www.trimet.org)

RideSmart Wilsonville (www.ridesmart.com)

C-Tran Transit Guide (www.ctran.com)

A SENSE OF PLACE

Hometown

WILDNESS IS AS MUCH PERCEPTION AS REALITY. As we enter the twenty-first century in this City of Portland, its 580,000 inhabitants (1.6 million in the tri-county area) think of places like Forest Park, Oaks Bottom Wildlife Refuge, Tryon Creek State Natural Area, or Elk Rock Island as wild. Surely these are undeveloped havens for wild creatures and for people seeking the natural world.

But these places are not the "howling wilderness" described by the pioneer settlers. All of them have been altered since the first developers, Francis Pettygrove and Asa Lovejoy, in 1845 platted sixteen blocks near today's Tom McCall Waterfront Park and cleared four streets of Douglas fir and western redcedar that were two to six feet through. They whitewashed the stumps because they were traffic hazards.

In 1850, Charles and Sarah Talbot took up 640 acres of Donation Land Claim in the West Hills. It took them three days to pack their possessions from the Willamette River upward through the primal forest to Council Crest. Here they built their cabin, burned and hewed forest into pasture, garden, and orchard, and raised their family.

The Talbots, now recalled by SW Talbot Road and Talbot Terrace, knew the howl of timber wolves on Portland Heights. They used the beaten trails of Roosevelt elk, lost some of their sheep to black bear and cougar (they called them panther), and hunted black-tailed deer and blue grouse in what's now an upscale residential district.

A daughter, Ella, was among the first fifty pupils at St. Helens Hall. She sped down the hill path three miles to school on her black pacing pony. Her parents sent their shepherd dog to discourage any panther.

That was wild in the city like we will never know.

But we still want to observe and celebrate the mysteries of the natural world, the passage of the seasons, and that sense of participation in an ancient ritual of renewal near our doorstep.

These experiences, in modified form, await in all the special places described in this book. They can even take place over the downtown high rises where adaptable red-tailed hawks and peregrine falcons hunt the rock pigeon.

Boys in the City

As boys growing up before World War II in a Portland that was more overgrown hometown than city, we had unlimited freedom to roam on our bicycles. The one parental admonition was, "Be sure you're home by dinnertime."

Our passion was birding. The connection began in the Portland Public Schools when "Nature Study" was part of the curriculum. There were terrariums, aquariums, plant presses, and small animal cages for the specimens we collected for study and display. It was a hands-on period for young naturalists.

Oregon Audubon Society (now Audubon Society of Portland) supplied the schools with nickel leaflets about each bird, including glorious color prints matched by an outline page that could be hand-colored.

David went to Glencoe Grade School and Tom to Laurelhurst Grade School, but we connected at Multnomah County Library lecture hall where Audubon members heard from noted area naturalists like William L. Finley, Stanley G. Jewett, Leo Simon, and Alex Walker. They were keen to encourage youthful interests, and they set the course for our careers.

In 1936, David could walk to school listening to western meadowlarks in the old pasture between 49th and 53rd Avenues on SE Belmont. David's earliest field trips were after school into Mount Tabor Park. It was fine habitat for California quail, Cassin's and Hutton's vireos, and orange-crowned, yellow-rumped, black-throated gray, and Wilson's warblers.

David showed Tom his first MacGillivray's warbler and lazuli bunting on the brushy west slope of Mount Tabor. The city reservoirs were a stopover for perky bufflehead ducks. In later years, removal of the natural understory made the park less attractive to a variety of birds. Today, a better understanding of the important role that our local buttes play in bird migration has caused the city to begin to restore habitat on Mount Tabor.

During spring lunch breaks at Laurelhurst, Tom walked into the old apple orchard and pasture between Glisan Street and Sullivan's Gulch (an ice-age flood channel that now holds Interstate 84). Rooster pheasants crowed, house wrens scolded, and his first western bluebird was there on a fence post. It was as sky-blue as in the Audubon pamphlet. Another exciting first in that orchard was a migrant northern shrike. We called it "butcher bird" because it impaled its prey on thorns. Providence Portland Medical Center now covers that area.

Birding was not sophisticated in the 1930s. Keyed field guides, powerful binoculars, spotting scopes, and tape-recorded bird calls were all to come. Tom had 4X field glasses, and David scored when his dad bought him 6 × 30 World War I surplus artillery binoculars with solid brass frames.

Our guides were *Birds of the Pacific States* by Ralph Hoffman and *Birds of the Pacific Coast* by Willard Ayres Eliot and illustrated with paintings by Bruce Horsfall, now displayed at Audubon's center on NW Cornell Road. Eliot and Horsfall were Portland Audubon members.

Our territory expanded with narrow-tired Columbia bicycles and New Departure two-speed gearshifts. There were no bike lanes, but traffic wasn't a problem.

Left to right:
Albert Marshall, William
Telfer, Tom McAllister,
and David Marshall
circa 1940

We were joined by another lad, Bill Telfer. As a trio we camped and birded around Portland and rode to the Pacific beaches and Cascade Mountains on our bikes. This continued until we went our separate ways in the Army, Navy, and Air Force in World War II.

Exploring

The edge of town was 82nd Avenue. Beyond were cultivated fields and extinct volcanic buttes. Short-eared owls, which resembled giant bouncing moths, and harriers swept the fields for voles. Vesper and Savannah sparrows nested in the grass, and seasonal flocks of horned lark and pipit rose from underfoot.

In the tall timber and margins of hazelnut, alder, and dogwood on Kelly and Powell Buttes and Mount Scott, the blue grouse hooted, and ruffed grouse drummed when the red-flowering current bloomed.

Mocks Bottom, now displaced by Swan Island Industrial Park, drew an array of wintering waterfowl. Showy hooded mergansers gathered here for courtship display. The southwest-facing bluff gets the winter sun, and it attracted flocks of yellow-rumped warblers and sometimes a Townsend's warbler. The oak woodland was a perfect niche for slender-billed nuthatches.

If there was one wildest spot for us in that boyhood interlude, it was the Columbia lowlands drained by the Columbia Slough, and especially North Portland Peninsula converging at Kelley Point, where the Willamette and Columbia Rivers meet. Lakes, sloughs, seasonal ponds, Oregon ash and black cottonwood forests, sedge meadows, and willow and red osier thickets intertwined and confused a sense of direction.

After ditching the bikes, we hiked and waded through a holdover of what naturalist John Kirk Townsend experienced while collecting out of Fort Vancouver in the 1830s. Western painted turtles lined floater logs to absorb the solar heat. A blue heron rookery that filled the cottonwoods was a cacophony of clacking, clicking, and squawking. We called it the "heron factory." Deer, raccoon, mink, otter, and beaver left fine track impressions along silty margins. Wood duck pairs squealed and twisted upward through the hardwoods. Green herons crouched in the bank shadows.

Bullock's orioles brought a splash of tropical color to the green mansions. We focused on a new bird song of rising, falling phrases, as if in conversation, and got our first red-eyed vireo. Bill recorded one of the last yellow-billed cuckoos in this region. This once-common cuckoo summered in the understory willow thickets and dined on tent caterpillars. The cuckoo's willow habitat, which tolerated prolonged, deep flooding, faded with the taming of the Columbia and Willamette Rivers and an invasion of hybrid reed canarygrass and Himalayan blackberry.

In June, prior to its harnessing, the Columbia River, fresh and swollen from melting snowpack far in the Rocky, Teton, Bitterroot, and Wallowa Mountains, shut us briefly out of our lowland haunts.

Young ears are tuned to sound in all registers. We had a game of running down every natural sound and attaching it to bird, amphibian, or animal call. We could camp and make a breeding bird list by lying in our sleeping bags and listening to the morning chorus. Night ended with screech- and pygmy-owl calls and the dawn song of violet-green swallows and purple martins.

David's brother, Albert, who later played in the Portland Symphony, brought his flute and called pygmy-owls to us when we camped in Audubon's Pittock Sanctuary.

By August, the lowland lakes shrank and exposed mud flats and beds of smartweed and wapato. The best place was Ramsey Lake, for its assembly of shorebirds en route from tundra nesting grounds. Pectoral sandpipers spread through the sedges to pick insects. Flocks of long-billed dowitcher, least and western sandpiper, and dunlin probed the lakebed before it dried. Watchful yellowlegs waded belly deep. The sound of their downscale whistle alarm took the smaller shorebirds with them.

To catch the shorebird show on Ramsey meant an early arrival. By the time the sun burned off the morning cloud cover the flocks were away, the pectoral sandpipers to the pampas of Argentina. Ramsey Lake is now part of the Port of Portland's Rivergate Industrial District. But adjoining Smith and Bybee Lakes have been encompassed into nearly two thousand acres of protected urban wetland.

Changes

What are the most notable changes in seventy years of city birding? Certainly there's the loss of the nighthawks that hunted insects in the neon-lit sky over SW Broadway when we came out of the movie theaters. The wing rush and boom as the male nighthawk dove toward a rooftop where the female laid her two eggs was part of a downtown Portland June or July night.

David's Grandmother Marshall lamented the disappearance of the western bluebirds that used her birdhouses and the mountain quail that ran through her yard on SW Summit Drive.

The yellow warbler's incisive songs from the tops of the elms lining our residential streets were pure summer music. Those waves of migrating warblers we anticipated each spring are sadly diminished. The largest of our warblers, the yellow-breasted chat, hid in the tightest cover and was common in the spirea thickets west of Rocky Butte. Its staccato burst of chucks, chortles, and hews could be heard anytime night or day, and especially on moonlit nights. That cover is gone, and so is the chat.

When we ranged the city on our bikes, the "sip-three-beers" call of the olive-sided flycatcher rang from the tallest fir tops, native brush rabbits grazed at wooded road margins, and Swainson's thrushes filled the summer twilight with song.

House finches extended their range north and within a few years displaced one of our finest songsters, the purple finch. David found the first house finch nest in 1939. Soon they frequented every bird feeder in town. The starling invasion followed.

One of our trio's best days was the discovery of a spring-fed marsh off SE Linwood Avenue. It held nesting sora and Virginia rails, pied-billed grebes, and an eastern kingbird feasting on dragonflies. Don't look for that marsh; it's filled and gone.

Birds now regularly seen along the Willamette and Columbia that we considered a rarity are Caspian tern, bald eagle, peregrines, and osprey. The bald eagle, peregrine, and osprey all made dramatic comebacks from declines caused by the pesticide DDT.

Another range extender, now found citywide, is the western scrub-jay. We found it only in an isolated northern colony on Sauvie Island around the stately oaks.

Anna's hummingbird was not on our Oregon bird list as boys. In the 1970s, it was nesting and residing year-round in Portland following a rapid range extension north from California where it lived on chaparral slopes.

Today, nesting Canada geese are all along the waterways where none used to reside year-round in western Oregon. Adaptable raccoon and coyote have found city sanctuary (no hunting) and food sources from direct handouts to fruiting ornamentals, unsecured garbage, and dog food.

Nature is dynamic and the flora and fauna change, too often with finality, in response to building, filling, paving, and draining. Climate fluctuates, food sources alter, and distribution patterns advance and shrink. The introduction of exotic species has had a dramatic impact on natives. Examples in Portland are English ivy, carp, fox squirrels, starlings, and bullfrogs.

Bringing the wild into our city life, whether through yard plantings, recreating stream corridors and wetlands, or setting aside tracts of natural parkland and trail corridor, will continue those pleasures of discovery and connection with nature that we knew in our hometown.

By Tom McAllister and David Marshall

Portland Parks:
The Legacy of Colonel L. L. Hawkins

COLONEL LESTER LEANDER HAWKINS' ROLE in the beginnings of the Portland Parks system was an important one, though hardly well known. When my great-uncle "LL" came to Portland in the late 1870s, the city had only five parks: the Park Blocks, the Plaza Blocks, Terwilliger Park, Holladay Park, and City Park—all established between 1852 and 1871. While the city was to expand enormously in the next few decades, the total percent of parkland area compared poorly with that of other cities in the country. By the 1890s, when Portland was only fifty years old and was celebrated as the "metropolis" of the Northwest, it greatly needed a park system to match its proud ambitions and magnificent setting. At this time, LL retired as president of the Ainsworth National Bank, which he had helped found, giving him considerable time to aid the city in this effort.

Exactly when LL's interest in parks began can only be speculated. It may, however, have started in his student days at the University of California, when in 1870 he organized a major outing into Yosemite Valley under his teacher, Joseph Le Conte, professor of geology, botany, and natural history. Le Conte waxed eloquent about the future park in his "Ramblings of the University Excursion Party." He also had high praise for LL, whom he described as "strong, thick, almost herculean in build" and the "soul of the party." The success of the excursion party was partly influenced by the fact that they met and befriended the remarkable John Muir, who was then living in the valley and later founded the Sierra Club. Muir spoke passionately about the unique qualities of the natural world, its benefits and the need to protect them. When Muir later came to Portland to lecture, LL would introduce him to his friends in the newly formed Mazamas mountaineering club. That group's founder was William Gladstone Steel, a major force in making Crater Lake a National Park in 1902. When LL was president of the Mazamas in 1895, he helped Muir coordinate the Sierra Club's and Mazamas' efforts to retain the Cascade Range Forest Reserve. Acts like these encouraged the early conservation movement to create our national park system. Our country's awakening to the need for parks then resulted in the extraordinary national, state, and city parks we share today.

LL's conservation interests developed into a passion for city parks. In 1897, Donald Macleay gifted 130 acres of heavily timbered land at the foot of Balch Creek to Portland, but as time passed there was no inclination at City Hall to improve the park.

Colonel Hawkins, fellow Mazama member Rodney Glisan, and others residing nearby were determined to keep Macleay Park intact without development. As a result,

LL instigated and helped build the first scenic trail in Macleay Canyon, as well as an extensive trail up to City Park (Washington Park), which was a great success. And not content with merely opening the way and promoting these parks, he provided a tally-ho coach-and-four (horses), and took out visitors from abroad, allowing them to see the "wondrous beauties of Portland's matchless location."

It was with his fellow mountain climbers, Dr. Thomas Lamb Eliot and Ion Lewis, that he joined ranks to establish a Portland Board of Parks Commissioners in 1900. Together, the newly appointed commission continued promotion of Portland parks, though it was becoming apparent that their efforts needed a considerable boost from a more authoritative source. Fortuitously for the commission, both Ion Lewis and Dr. Eliot had many connections in the Boston area, where Dr. Eliot sought out the Olmsted Brothers, a well-known landscape design company at the time. Returning to Portland, Dr. Eliot and LL urged the city to have the Olmsted firm do an expert survey of parks plans and suggest future improvements.

Tallyho! To Future Parks

John C. Olmsted, partner in the firm and stepson of Frederick L. Olmsted, the "father" of landscape architecture in the U.S., was invited to come to Portland. Making his journey more feasible was the fact that Seattle and Spokane would also engage the firm in similar projects. Portland could only afford a written report but had the added incentive of needing a preliminary layout plan for what was to be the Lewis and Clark Centennial Exposition of 1905. Ion Lewis was general architect for the plan, and it was decided that he would facilitate Olmsted's recommendations. To make it all more cost effective, LL agreed to take John Olmsted around the city, showing him all the possible park sites from the Columbia River in the north to Sellwood in the south, and from Rocky Butte in the east to the summit of the west Tualatin Hills.

This impressive trip was made in LL's tallyho, "Jupiter," and lasted over three weeks. LL planned the itinerary, provided the latest maps of the city, or contour maps where available, and suggested locations for parks and scenic drives. Today, many of these suggestions, which were noted by Olmsted in his diary and letters home, have come to realization. They include the "South Hillside Boulevard" (later Terwilliger Boulevard); "Northwest Hillside Parkway" (only the Vista Avenue component was built); Duniway and Marquam Parks; Skyline Boulevard; and the western treed hillside of the city (Forest Park) as well as a lengthy series of interconnected hiking trails along it. Further, LL's hiking and biking friend, Henry Pittock, saw to it that his newspaper, *The Oregonian*, published Olmsted's "Report of the Park Board, 1903."

LL died young (age fifty-seven) in 1906. At his passing, a parks board resolution stated: "We recall his indefatigable zeal in behalf of good parks, the beautifying of the city … or the development of its great natural features of beauty and for every kind of human good."

Reminders of L.L. Hawkins can be found throughout Portland in the form of more than forty giant sequoias. They were first suggested, then planted, by LL as park improvements when he first came on the park commission. As Dr. Roland Grant stated at the time of his memorial service, "The Sequoia Gigantia [*sic*] about the city will grow to be his nature monuments and may his benediction fall on us, who tarry at the base of the mountain he has climbed. I say this in loving remembrance of one of the rarest of men, a true disciple of nature."

The sequoias are large now, over one hundred years in age. As such, they are the more lasting memorial of LL's contribution—Herculean in size, much as he would have liked.

By William J. Hawkins III

Deep History

PORTLAND'S LUSH AND VARIED LANDSCAPE is one reason why many of us live here. It includes forested uplands extending from the foothills of the Cascade and Coast Ranges all the way into the heart of Portland, as well as broad alluvial plains, volcanic buttes, and patches of bare bedrock scoured by Ice Age floods. The area is drained by a profusion of streams ranging from small intermittent creeks to one of the largest rivers in North America. As bicyclists and pedestrians are keenly aware, ours is a region of considerable topographic relief, ranging from near sea level along the Willamette and Columbia Rivers to more than one thousand feet in the Tualatin Mountains, Mount Scott, and the Chehalem Mountains. The remarkable range of habitats and regional biodiversity are a direct result of this physical landscape.

How did this geographic diversity come to be? What combination of processes and events resulted in our varied landscapes? Unlike arid regions, where the bedrock is spectacularly exposed and the geologic history laid bare, Portland's geology is hidden beneath a thick mantle of soil and luxuriant vegetation. As a consequence, our region's geologic origins remain a mystery to most people. It has taken geoscientists many decades to reconstruct the geologic history of the Portland area, and the work continues. This is but a thumbnail sketch of the geology as presently understood.

Spatial and temporal scales go together. We begin with the large regional scale of the metropolitan area, which reflects some of the earliest and broadest forces affecting the landscape, and progress toward smaller, local scale features, which are generally the most recent manifestations of geologic processes.

Early History: Setting the Stage

The entire Portland region is nestled in a broad lowland between the Cascade Range to the east and the more subdued Coast Range to the west. This regional setting reflects one of the oldest geologic forces directly shaping our region: the subduction of the Pacific Plate beneath the North American Plate. This converging of continental plates resulted in the uplift of the Coast Range (composed of marine sedimentary and volcanic rocks) and, beginning about 40 million years ago, the volcanism and uplift that formed the Cascade Range. The lowland between these two mountain ranges, which extends from Eugene north to Puget Sound, is known as the Puget-Willamette Trough (or in our area, the Willamette Lowland). The ancient Willamette Lowland became the crucible for the subsequent geologic and hydrologic processes that resulted in much of our modern landscape.

The metropolitan area lies where the Willamette Lowland is crossed by the Columbia River. For at least 16 million years, the Columbia has drained a large part of the continental interior, transecting our region through gaps cut through both the Cascades and the Coast Range. As the Willamette Lowland developed, local river systems evolved in response. Streams from the surrounding uplands began to flow toward the lowland interior to form what we now know as the Willamette River. The Willamette and Columbia have had a major influence on the geologic history of our region, and it is the confluence of these two major rivers that is largely responsible for its settlement.

Roughly 12 to 16 million years ago, as the Willamette Lowland was developing, basaltic lava flows of enormous volume were erupting on the other side of the Cascade Range in far eastern Washington and Oregon. These lavas, known as the Columbia River Basalt Group, eventually covered much of central Washington and north-central Oregon. The largest of these lava flows followed the Columbia River channel through the Cascades and into the Willamette Lowland, eventually covering the ancestral Willamette Valley from the Salem area north to Clatskanie. Some of the basalt flows made it through the Coast Range to the Pacific Ocean where they now form headlands along the northern Oregon Coast such as Cape Lookout and Yaquina Head.

Beginning of the Modern Landscape

The nascent Willamette Lowland was still actively forming when the Columbia River Basalt flooded the region, and the once-flat lava flows were caught up in the continuing structural deformation driven by plate tectonics. As a consequence, the basalt was folded and faulted to eventually form the series of uplands and basins that are now some of the most visible elements in our present landscape. Many of the major uplands west and south of Portland, such as the Tualatin Mountains, Chehalem Mountains, Parrett Mountain, Cooper and Bull Mountains, as well as the hills bounding the northern Willamette Valley such as the Eola Hills and the Red Hills of Dundee, are all folded or faulted masses of Columbia River Basalt. These uplands form the boundaries defining the major geographic sub areas in our region such as the Portland-Vancouver area, the Tualatin Basin, and the northern Willamette Valley.

Even though it forms major uplands in our region, the Columbia River Basalt is mostly hidden beneath thick soil and vegetation. It is revealed only in scattered road cuts and canyons, for example: along West Burnside Street near the entrance to Washington Park, above 23rd Avenue and Burnside, along Leif Erikson Drive in Forest Park, at the base of the Tualatin Mountains along Highway 30, and at West Linn and Oregon City along the Willamette River. Our humid climate has weathered the basalt to form the red Jory soil, prized by viticulturists in the northern Willamette Valley. For a really good look, the basalt is exposed in all of its glory in the Columbia River Gorge and areas to the east.

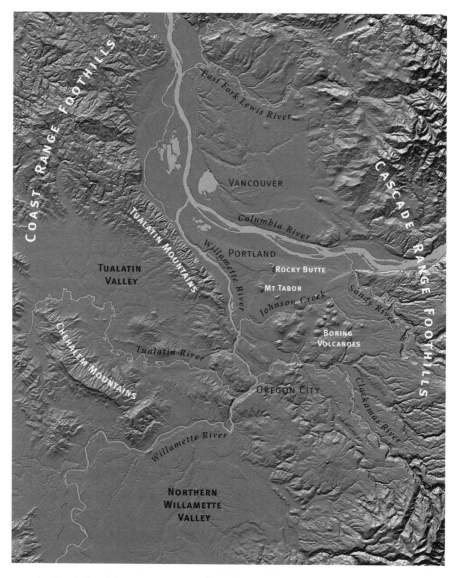

As the Columbia River Basalt lava flows were being folded and faulted to form the broad template of our landscape, rivers were busily carrying vast amounts of silt, sand, and gravel from surrounding uplands, rapidly filling subsiding low areas. The ancestral Sandy and Clackamas Rivers created a series of broad alluvial surfaces extending from Estacada and Sandy northeast into the Portland-Vancouver area. These deposits include the Troutdale Formation and Sandy River Mudstone. The ancestral Tualatin and its tributaries carried sediment from the Coast Range into the Tualatin Basin. Streams from both the Cascades and the Coast Range filled the northern Willamette Valley with sediment. While local streams deposited sediment derived from the adjacent mountain ranges, the Columbia, in contrast, carried sediment derived predominantly from the distant terrains of eastern Washington, Idaho, Montana, and Canada. The distinctiveness of sediment from different sources has allowed geologists to reconstruct the geologic history of drainages in the region. The stream deposits in the Portland region contain a remarkable record of changes in sea level, major glaciations, volcanic eruptions, and floods.

Homegrown Volcanoes

Our area is, of course, much more than a featureless alluvial plain subdivided by basalt uplands. Over the past five hundred thousand years, the geologic evolution of the metropolitan area was punctuated by volcanic eruptions that dotted the landscape with cinder cones, lava flows, and small shield volcanoes. The products of these eruptions, collectively known as the Boring Volcanics, now form the prominent hills in and around Portland such as Mount Tabor, Rocky Butte, Kelly Butte, Powell Butte, and Mount Scott. Several of these volcanic hills are now locations of major parks and greenspaces. Cinder deposits from one of the more recent eruptions can be seen in the amphitheater in Mount Tabor Park. The eruptions didn't only result in isolated hills; widespread lava flows from this series of eruptions also form the broad plateau above and southeast of Oregon City.

The Finishing Touches

Large basalt uplands and volcanic hills notwithstanding, much of our landscape consists of broad surfaces with relatively low relief. Examples include the floors of the northern Willamette Valley and Tualatin Basin, most of east and north Portland, and much of Vancouver north to the Lewis River. Ride a bike the length of the Springwater Corridor trail and you will see just how pleasantly flat Portland can be. Although this gently sloping terrain resulted primarily from the action of streams emanating from adjacent uplands, most of the surficial deposits and modern topography in lowland areas are the result of the Missoula Floods, cataclysmic Ice Age torrents that repeatedly inundated the area approximately fifteen thousand years ago.

The Missoula Floods resulted from the failure of a glacial ice dam, which blocked the Clark Fork River in western Montana. This ice dam impounded and released a volume of water roughly half that of Lake Michigan. When the ice dam failed, which it did repeatedly, water coursed across central Washington, down the Columbia River Gorge through the Cascades, and through the Coast Range to the Pacific Ocean. Because of topographic constrictions in the Coast Range, floodwaters backed up in the Willamette Valley to an elevation of about four hundred feet, nearly to Eugene. In the Portland area, rushing floodwaters carved large channels around Rocky Butte, Mount Tabor, and north of Prune Hill near Vancouver, creating such features as Alameda Ridge and Sullivan's Gulch (where Interstate 84 and the MAX line nestle side-by-side). Floodwaters deposited huge gravel bars in Southeast Portland that now form subtle terraces. In the topographic constrictions between the Portland Basin, Tualatin Basin, and northern Willamette Valley, the rushing floodwaters were an erosive force, scouring the terrain down to the Columbia River Basalt bedrock. Such scoured areas include the Tonquin Scablands between Sherwood and Wilsonville, and areas of thin rocky soils near West Linn such as the The Nature Conservancy's Camassia Natural Area.

Sea level has risen nearly four hundred feet since the last Ice Age, causing the Columbia River valley to fill with sand and silt. The subsequent action of the Columbia on its floodplain has created most of the familiar landscape features near the river including Blue Lake, Smith and Bybee Lakes, Vancouver Lake, Sauvie Island, and countless sloughs and side channels. Similar processes along the Willamette have created Oaks Bottom and Ross Island.

The barren and flood-ravaged Ice Age landscape provided a ready sediment supply for winter's east winds. These winds left a blanket of sediment known as the Portland Hills Silt on many of the uplands around the Portland Area. This massive windblown silt (or loess) is unstable and prone to sliding when saturated with water and over-steepened by excavation, for example by road cuts. The inherent instability of the Portland Hills Silt thwarted early real estate development in the Tualatin Mountains and is one of the reasons that Forest Park is a park.

Epilogue: The Story Continues

Our landscape continues to evolve. The infrequent earthquakes jostling the Portland metropolitan area are subtle reminders that the forces that created the Tualatin Mountains are still in play. Oral and written histories include accounts of a landslide that blocked the Columbia River as well as numerous volcanic eruptions. Occasional floods continue to do their best to rearrange stream channels and confound those with riverfront property, in spite of our best engineering efforts.

By Marshall Gannett

ACKNOWLEDGMENTS: *This narrative relied heavily on recent work by Russ Evarts, Jim O'Connor, Terry Tolan, Ian Madin, and the late Marv Beeson, among others. I would like to especially thank Jim O'Connor for his thoughtful review.*

No Vacancy?

IN NATURE, THE NO VACANCY SIGN is always posted. Biology tends to fill its niches. Ecologists speak in terms such as "species packing" and "carrying capacity" to describe how a piece of habitat enrolls as many species, and as many individuals of those species, as its resources can support. Of course, disequilibria may occur through extinction or overpopulation. But adjustments may be expected, with adaptive aliens or native generalists moving into the vacated habitat, and busts will follow booms. The resulting biota may well be simplified and less stable than the old, but it is rare for habitat to remain vacant—unless the habitat itself is replaced by something else, like strip malls or parking lots.

Yet "vacancy" can have a different meaning, one imbued with charm, fascination, and invitation. My favorite oxymoron is "vacant lot." To a curious kid, what is less empty than a vacant lot? On a recent trip to the Southeast, I was entranced by the many species of trilliums, violets, and swallowtails, if saddened by the proliferation of sprawl and "palace projects": one- to five-acre subdivisions of enormities thrown up by developers for people with too much money and an edifice complex. Yet habitat remained, in between. One of the best things I saw was a wooded branch stream with the wonderful name Thicketty Creek, which was still just that.

Fortunate is the child who grows up close to a thicket, a good ditch, "crick," or watercourse of any kind, or an undeveloped field. These are the kinds of humble places where most people make their first deep connection with nature, if they ever do at all. Once, folks lived near great mountains, meadows, forests—and some still do. But with most of the bloated population now huddled in the cities and suburbs, the vacant lot takes on heroic proportions. It becomes the job of the overlooked rough, the fragments of secondhand lands, and all such hand-me-down habitats to provide initiation for kids who would know more of the world than walls and malls afford. Richard Louv's essential book *Last Child in the Woods: Saving Our Children from Nature Deficit Disorder* has shown us the baleful consequences of the loss of such places.

A woman told me recently how lucky she was to grow up in Minnesota on a family lot of five acres surrounded by farms. She could walk out and find grouse bursting from the dust, and sometimes even spy the rare lady slipper orchid. Lucky, indeed. For me, it was an old irrigation ditch on the Colorado plains that furnished my escape hatch from the grid, and that of countless other Denver kids over the ages. I worry that fewer and fewer kids grow up with even a back lot or an uncut alley to explore. And when they do have some rough ground nearby, it is likely to be off limits. After a reading in Denver, someone handed me a clipping about two boys arrested and booked—not for stealing cars or vandalism, but for digging a foot-deep hole in Jefferson County Open Space! Somehow they thought that, on land with such a name, they could make a fort. Whither the culture whose kids no longer go forth to make forts? In *Having Everything Right*, Kim Stafford described his "Separate Hearth":

> Two blocks from home the human world dwindled to a path threading through nettle and alder. A spider web across the path meant no one was there before me. I crawled under its fragile gate to solitude and was gone.... The Woods was a wild tract developers had somehow missed in their swathe through old Oregon. It probably stretched about three miles long by two miles wide, and was surrounded by the city of Portland and its suburbs. Raccoon, beaver, salmon, deer, awesome pileated woodpeckers, and exotic newts were among the secret lives of the place.... A huge tree had fallen, and where the root-mass tore out from the earth a hollow was left that no one could see, roofed over with the arched limbs of fir, woven by my hands with sword fern and moss, with leaf litter, until the roof became a knob of the earth itself. Like Ishi, I approached by a different way each time, so as not to wear a path others might see, and I covered the entrance to my den with boughs broken, not cut in a human way.

I often ask of audiences how many had such a place. Almost everyone's hand goes up. Not that many embraced their "cricks" and trees and forts with the fervor and completeness that Stafford devoted to his secret spot, but I find most people can remember an outdoors-place that made a difference in how they view the world. Yet when I ask how many could return and find that place substantially unchanged, few hands rise and faces drop. It seems most folks know the betrayal of special places ruined. And what difference does it make?

In *The Thunder Tree: Lessons from an Urban Wildland*, I describe the "extinction of experience," whereby people become more disaffected from nature the more that common species and elements are lost from their immediate vicinities. When experience of everyday nature dries up within one's radius of reach—which is smaller for the very old, young, poor, and disabled, one tends to see less, know less, thus care less. And when caring flees, conservation heads out the back door, and further losses ensue: a truly insidious cycle.

Now there is a timely corollary that worries me almost as much as the extinction of experience itself. Cities are beginning to address growth management in a meaningful way, and this is unquestionably a good thing. If urban growth boundaries can be maintained, sprawl can be contained. But the UGB has a tricky sister named infilling. When growth is contained but not stemmed, pressure increases to fill in the last blank spots on the planners' maps. Infilling is touted as a progressive remedy for more livable cities. Maybe so, when densities increase in poorly used zones to the benefit of both community function and the outlying lands. But sparing the rural perimeter should not be the only goal of urban growth management. Every time infilling takes a vacant lot, either through direct development or conversion to formal parkland, something precious is lost in the heart of the living city.

Portland, and every other city, needs to maintain a generous ration of what British nature writer Richard Mabey calls the unofficial countryside: undedicated, unmanaged, undeveloped ground where unplanned, unsupervised, unstructured play can take place—along with unexpected discovery. Realtors refer to such places as raw land, and others call it waste ground. But in my view, nothing is less wasted than ground where the hand of man has held back and the minds of boys and girls can engage with plants and animals and water and dirt, nothing more sacred than land that is yet raw, real, and ripe with surprise.

The big urban wilds—Tryon and Forest Parks, Oaks Bottom, the rivers, sloughs, and islands—are extraordinarily important. But the little places, the corners and crannies and ravines, the urban greenspaces writ small, claim their own significance. In England, ancient Commons may still be found, benisons among the urban landscape. But we have no such city commons. If we are to remain a people who love the land, we must champion the bits of wild land within reach of the children as well as the wilderness, the remnants along with the whole bolts. When kids actually put down the mouse and go outdoors, they must find more than a No Vacancy sign where once their parents played.

By Robert Michael Pyle

River City

I POKE AROUND PORTLAND BY BOAT, catching the sights and smells here at the confluence of two great rivers. At water level I get a new angle on the city. Familiar arrangements can appear to be marvelous.

One summer Saturday I headed up the Columbia and into the Willamette, where the natural and the human gave every sign of getting along. Herons and kingfishers worked the water near the growl and diesel whiff of a working tug. Men in small boats, fishing for steelhead, were catching and tossing back shad. Ocean-going ships took on lumber, gave up Toyotas. In the foreground, an osprey lifted a wide-eyed shad to a nest atop pilings. Behind that, a crane lifted buckets of gravel from a barge. In the background, Forest Park.

Spring Chinook already had passed, but a great sustaining notion of this place is that salmon and steelhead still surge through the heart of a metro area of 1.6 million people. One of America's great fishing holes lies within view of a Merrill Lynch office. Here is a heron rookery within paddling distance of NBA basketball. I can dock the boat and stroll to the world's best bookstore.

Where else on the continent—on the planet—do the great intentions of nature and people come braided so closely together?

It's what sets us apart, and always has. Captain John Couch, a city founder, had his eye on commerce. Seafaring ships could probe this far, and no farther, into the Willamette. But what really got Couch—what he wrote East about—was that he could shoot ducks from his front porch.

Although Portlanders are now a fully urbanized people, the rivers still make us who we are. Never too deeply buried in the urban ethos is an imaginative truth, that not so long ago we emerged to a riverside clearing, the sons and daughters of pioneers, self-selected for rugged individuality.

Oddly, the view from a boat suggests how we insulate ourselves, with bridges and sea walls, from the river. In a darker mood I think we might be as estranged from natural rhythms as any other urban folk. We wrap ourselves in the River City myth but measure our well-being in economic terms. The danger of a working river rises to consciousness only occasionally, when we have to break out the sand bags. Or, ludicrously, when a gravel barge runs over a dozen rugged individualists from Nike rowing an unlit dragon boat at night.

As a people we Euro-Americans came here busting woods and taming rivers. Now that we've mostly done that, our sense of identity hinges on what we have left of woods and rivers. We could easily lose what is unique and beautiful about this place. Or we could learn to coexist with the creatures and features of the wild.

The encouraging thing is that we got here too late to have completely screwed things up. And in the last couple of decades, the notion of responsibility toward the habitat has begun to penetrate city life. Kids these days are alert to the connectedness of things—of woods to salmon, and of rivers to our sense of spirit and well-being.

We're getting wiser.

Will we be wise enough in time?

More and more people are coming. As my species crowd the river, the threat is more subtle, more quietly insidious, than toxic outflow from a paper plant. It's the threat of losing in small increments the surrounding greenspaces to asphalt and condos, of leaching small poisons from driveways and lawns. From a boat the river looks and smells clean to me, but I am haunted by warnings: Do not eat the bottom-fish. In the paper I read sickening reports of one-eyed fish with crooked spines, and of river otters with withered penises, shrunken testicles.

Another time, on another outing, I anchored overnight near the edge of city limits.

When the morning sun rose high enough to catch the bank, a small river otter emerged from willow roots and slid down into the water. Then another slid the mud bank. And another. Five, in all, liquid black and glossy, climbed up the bank and went skidding down again, nosing into the water without a splash.

The otters started wrestling in the water. They made of themselves an otterball. Heads over tails over heads over tails, the otterball went churning along the surface, throwing up spray. When that got old, they dived and surfaced separately. One little show-off came up near the boat with a crawdad between his teeth. He cracked and ate the crawdad.

When I glanced up, I saw the otters' parents. They had come out to watch, and to watch me watching.

I felt, for my own crowding species, on the spot.

By Robin Cody

Scattered Eden

"Kipuka" is the name in the Hawaiian language for a ridge or hill left alive when molten lava flows past and around, burning and burying all else in its path. With scorched flanks, this lucky eminence preserves the original matrix of soil, plant, insect—the old ways of the place. After the lava cools, birds return to the kipuka, and in this green island of life as it was, native plants and other small beings carry on.

"Gore" is the name in the English language for an anomaly of land left outside the surveyor's grid, through an error in transected lines. These patches of yet-free land may be crooked triangles or tapering ribbons wild between owned forests and tilled fields. These oddments may become inhabited by a squatter, who then lives outside the grid by eminent domain. Hibberts Gore in Lincoln County, Maine, for example, is just under a square mile, and has one inhabitant. Avery's Gore, in Vermont, is over seventeen square miles with no inhabitants. Such a place is a kind of "common," not part of any town or county.

"Volunteer" is the name we give a plant that plants itself. Birds carry seed, or wind answers the seed's wispy yearning. Then, in a niche at some shadowed margin of the city's busy ways, up comes the little green flag of the volunteer.

"Wild" is that quality of life by which a creature lives in its own way, by its own wits, either inside the city, or out.

The concepts of kipuka and gore and common and volunteer and wild have come to inform my perception of tiny wildernesses in the city formed not by design but by the gift of our neglect. When settlement in Stumptown began to plat ownership, then to skin the hills and swales, to obliterate and then to pave what had been wild, certain places remained as they had been. Whether by elevation or other quirky obstacle to development's volcanic overlay, places like Rocky Butte, Powell Butte, Mount Tabor, and scattered gulches, ravines, or soggy bottomlands were spared early, though not all for long. Any such anomaly over a certain size within the city will eventually become a place for house, business, street, or park—as these are the ways we understand earth where we live in density.

Over time, only small remnants may remain as kipuka and gore. But the habits of the volunteer can restore crumbs of the wild almost anywhere in a paved realm. One example in my neighborhood is a curving ribbon of land between SW Terwilliger Boulevard and SW 5th Avenue, between Interstate 5 on the north and SW Taylor's Ferry Road on the south. Varying in width between ten and thirty feet, and several blocks in length, this swathe does not appear to be property or park. It sustains a pleasing diversity of flowers, trees, vines, birds, green by day and dark by night. Yes, the neighbors tend to use this river of green as a place to dump their garden cuttings, and these cast-offs often root and grow. There are hyacinths in spring, and Himalayan blackberry, sassy thistle, fat iris. Still, the predominant life of the place is native. Maple, Douglas fir, cascara, poison oak, sword fern, winterberry, and native huckleberry hold their own against ivy and dandelion. Cars whiz past, to be spewed onto the freeway just beyond. But from this cleft as I walk along, I hear the quizzical call of the towhee, shy and safe in the happy gloom of this forgotten commons.

Schooled by my local example of this effect, I begin to see what I would call Scattered Eden everywhere. A frost-cracked seam in pavement raises leaves of grass. An untrodden shadow behind a phonebooth becomes a haven for tendrils of native blackberry. The frontage strip before an abandoned storefront begins to welcome seedlings of cottonwood, leaves swiveling in sunlight. Such small places keep the faith of old ways, remind us of what we have over run, but ways on which, in the end, we rely.

When a store in my neighborhood fails, and stands empty, any patch of earth, in the zone of that store's purview begins to go wild. The first year, the offering will be random weeds. But generally by the second spring, young trees planted by the birds, volunteers re-inhabiting kipuka, reach up: alder, fir, cedar, and of course ailanthus, "tree of heaven," the world wanderer. The old florist shop two blocks from my house went under, was torn down and a clothing store half built before the developer's funding stalled everything. And now, in the strip along the sidewalk, this vacancy is growing lush with willowy grasses and magnificent Queen Anne's lace. I could see these as invaders, but I choose to recognize the return of earth. We are going back in time. The whole Eden of this place, as it was before, begins to gather in a citywide mosaic pattern of return.

By observing this return of the local wild not yet tamed, I experience a parallel in my mind, my dreams, my sense of the possible. I experience what I call my lizard brain—that interior set of thoughts that come out of nowhere in response to the old stimuli of breath, sky, joy, sorrow, perception—the growth of ideas and stories not subdued by the obligations of city life: wild ideas, volunteer intuitions, a kipuka of interwoven dreams, a gore of true identity.

This interior effect is, to my mind, the benefit of this way of seeing. If that stem of primordial horsetail can push up through blacktop, I can escape my own limitations in spite of all.

As I walk or ride through my beloved native city, I see these green beckonings in forgotten places. There seems to be a song coming toward me in the ripened sunlight or soft rain:

We green were here before. We send you breath. Suffer us to remain, to prosper in our own old ways. We green and you in spirit will keep this place alive, after.

By Kim Stafford

Lashed To Our La-Z-Boys

IT STARTS WHEN WE'RE YOUNG, with seeing. A songbird perhaps. Or a riot of rhododendron. Maybe a butterfly on the breeze. And as our infant eyes explode with wonder, some mysterious flame touches the tinder, igniting a lifelong love affair.

With the wild.

The infatuation at the heart of the human experience is not with the managed, or the massaged. Not with the planned, permitted, and packaged, the burnished and branded and tamed.

It's with the wild.

Every child, including all those children so soon confined by the constraint of being grown, intuitively grasps the magic in the meadowlark, the sorcery in the salmon, the tallness of Doug fir's tale.

Determined to foster this impulse, people spent years isolating pockets of wild in our city, surrounding them, preserving, protecting, and polishing them, beating back the barbarians at the built environment gate. All that was nice, of course, but it wasn't enough. Something key was missing. We had the warp but not the weft. We'd lost the connections that weave together the places that hold the story of our place.

It is little secret that we exist in a profoundly sick society. Hundreds of thousands of us nested here in the metropolitan area are all but addicted to prescription drugs. And the terrible truth is that a massive number of our maladies are self-inflicted. By drinking. By smoking. By overeating. Mostly, of course, by being sedentary. Lashed to our La-Z-Boys, leashed to the infernal combustion engine, we ride a sad spiral toward bankruptcy of both pocket and spirit.

Yet all is not lost. Early in this new century, there's a move afoot to spur something called "active transportation." Taking root among us is a multi-pronged assault on everything from congestion and climate change to air quality and obesity. Active transportation may sound obtuse, but it's really nothing more than a matrix within which people of all ages can comfortably do something as basic as walk and ride, aided by bikes and mass transit, to everywhere they live and labor, buy and sell, pray and play … yes, even in nature.

The call, compelling for far more than its cost-effectiveness, is not just for another park trail here or bike path there. Advocates are insisting on nothing less than the retrofitting of our entire urban environment, including taking back sections of our most valuable civic assets—the public rights of way—and repurposing them for a higher, for a healthier, purpose. Our glorious ecosystem, radiating its sylvan spokes from the confluence of the Columbia with the Willamette, has long been hailed for being so fertile that "even its fence posts bear fruit." It's more than an intriguing opportunity; it's a downright invitation to excellence. Our land at Eden's gate now faces the opportunity to be a world leader in fostering the urban wild.

We must grasp this chance to make walking and bicycling fundamental pillars of an urban transportation system that seamlessly integrates with The Intertwine, the region's emergent network of parks, trails, and natural areas. That will not happen as a result of geography, climate, or historical happenstance. It will happen only if we carefully plan, and fully fund, this path.

The challenge before us is indeed considerable. So, too, is our responsibility. For it now falls to us to honor this remarkable corner of our planet. To craft at last a city worthy of its setting. To nurture our neighbors. And to nourish these places we share, and call home.

By Jonathan Nicholas

Mr. Pish and the Horse Chestnut

THERE ARE A GOOD MANY fine, old horse chestnuts in Northwest Portland. One of the finest stood in the parking strip by our driveway—a tree like a cathedral. When it flowered it was illuminated by great, sweet-scented candles. Standing just east of our property line, towering up over the street and sidewalk, it was a neighborhood landmark.

An old man who lived some way up the street, not even in sight of the tree, took a dislike to it. I will call him by my daughter's childish mispronunciation of his name: Mr. Pish. I don't know what motivated Mr. Pish to make war on the big tree—maybe its size—most reasons for making war seem to have to do with exhibiting power, proving oneself "bigger." Anyhow, he spread rumors that the tree was "sick," and that its slight lean toward the street was "dangerous." The city sent people out to look at it, causing alarm, so that my daughter, then about eleven, went and stood with her back to it all afternoon, defying the authorities and the chainsaws. But the fuss seemed to die down. It was much later, and the children all in school, and there were new owners of the property where the tree stood, when the men with chainsaws suddenly arrived.

I was in my study at the back of my house when I realized that the horrible whining sound I'd been trying to ignore was right out front. The butchery was half done when I came down our steps, distraught, crying, "Why?"

The men doing the job had no answer; they told me the tree was solidly rooted and in splendid health. But it was the job they had to do. They did it with professional skill and speed, cleaned up, and went away.

The neighborhood was shocked, grieved, aggrieved. For days, people walking past would demand, "Why did you cut down your tree?" We had to explain, again and again, that it hadn't been our tree, or our desire, but the new owners had consented to the city's decision to yield to Mr. Pish's obsessive, meddling animosity.

We mourned. To relieve my heart I wrote the poem "The Aching Air." After a while, we took a sort of revenge by planting a European beech in nearly the same place, but in our front yard, on our property, where the Pishes of the world would have to go to far more trouble to make trouble. The beech obligingly grew very fast to a very respectable size—sooner, in fact, than we expected. Never believe it when they tell you a tree is slow-growing. The only tree we ever planted that didn't get three times as big as we expected, twice as fast as it was supposed to, was a crab apple, which went in for being stunted and gnarly, though charming. Our beech is quite a big tree now, though it can't match the enormous old copper beech just down the street. And, thanks to recent city policies of planting in parking strips, farther down the hill the street is lined with handsome young maples.

But still, every autumn when the horse chestnuts turn gold, every spring when they light their candelabra, we remember the tree that was ours by right of love, and I remember a child standing with her back against the huge trunk, defending it.

By Ursula K. Le Guin

Lower Willamette River Watershed

OVERHEAD, A FLOCK OF CEDAR WAXWINGS makes its way across the river, surging upward after insects that are elusive to the human eye, but a veritable feast for the small birds. Up and down the waxwings zip about, searching out the watery expanse at the confluence of the Molalla and Willamette Rivers—making this place also a meeting of predator and prey. Here, some thirty-six miles upstream from where the Willamette joins the Columbia, life abounds.

River confluences hold a richness of fish, birds, and mammals, all sustained by the variety of conditions they create—from the structure of the river bottom to the intermingling of differing waters and their dynamic rise and fall. Here the sediments and rocks of the Molalla meet the deeper, wider Willamette.

The Willamette and the Molalla could not be more different. The small Molalla River descends from the Cascades, unimpeded by dams. The bigger Willamette's major tributaries are dammed, which both alters the natural flow and virtually eliminates the passage of native fish from the Pacific to their high-mountain spawning grounds. The Molalla's water is relatively clean, whereas thousands of square miles of runoff from cities and agricultural operations compromise the Willamette's water quality.

The Molalla is also relatively unchallenged by sewer waste, though it has one pipe in its lower reach from a municipal treatment plant. In stark contrast, the Willamette receives tons of untreated waste from an aging sewer system. The good news is that Portland has invested $1.4 billion in upgrading its sewer system, which will soon make combined sewer overflows a thing of the past.

Canoeing the lower Willamette takes you through one of the most pollution-challenged stretches of the river, including the area below Willamette Falls. There the imprint of industry has been felt for decades from pulp and paper mills that have poured thousands of gallons of polluted liquors into the river. Today these mills reuse their waste, making them more efficient and much cleaner.

For tens of thousands of years, the falls were the historic meeting place of the Kalapuyan and Chinookan peoples, who lived on the lower Willamette and the Columbia. At the falls—a significant natural dividing line between the upper and lower Willamette—native peoples built cantilevered platforms and netted spring and fall Chinook salmon that would leap up the lower channels, heading upstream to spawn. They also harvested lamprey from the rocks. From time to time, Native Americans still harvest lamprey here, working their way across the slippery rocks in the summer months to grasp the eel-like lamprey where they cling with their sucker-shaped mouths.

Below the falls, the Willamette works its way through suburban and heavily urbanized landscapes. The river soon courses northward, hemmed in occasionally by basalt outcrops and islands, evidence of long-ago volcanic flows that coated the Columbia Basin. Here and there the relics of industry can be seen, from the iron-smelting furnace at Lake Oswego's George Rogers Park, to the abundance of wood pilings that used to secure barges and massive log rafts awaiting their turn at the mill. Today, the pilings hold to the riverside shadows and provide habitat for smallmouth bass—a warmwater game fish not native to the Willamette.

Portland's relationship with the Willamette is one that is historically rich. Yet we have dug the river deeper, scooped out its fine, rich, brown sediments to create seawalls and terminals, and filled in the many wetlands and backwaters. Today, in places where native black cottonwoods might have stood, there are creosote-imbued pilings, some holding buildings and docks still in use, and others abandoned relics of the earlier industrial era. The inlets are artificial indentations in the shoreline known as "slips"—the parking places for ships.

The Portland Harbor is now a Superfund site, but thankfully the tide is slowly turning. Today, we are writing a new chapter for the river, one that includes an increased level of shared stewardship, both institutional and individual. The river's reach between downtown Portland and the Columbia may be the most seriously polluted, yet progress is being made as the city decreases the runoff from streets and yards, reduces inputs from sewers, and cleans up the harbor.

Though our scientific understanding of these impacts has grown, the challenge is in marshalling the wisdom to act. The same notion must be applied to the historic loss of habitat and recent trends to restore it. This is another kind of confluence—one of scientific understanding and action that will make the river whole again, diminishing the stark contrast between the Willamette and its smaller, free-flowing sister upstream.

By Travis Williams

Graham Oaks Nature Park

LOCATION: 1.5 miles W of I-5 on Wilsonville Road; entrance is across from Willamette Way W, Wilsonville, OR **ACTIVITIES:** Hiking, Biking, Wildlife viewing **FACILITIES:** Restrooms, Parking, Paved and unpaved trails, Picnic area, Visitor center, Wildlife viewing structure, Interpretive signs/info **FEES AND REGULATIONS:** No fees, Open 6 am to sunset, No pets—Exception: pets on leash on Tonquin Trail only **HIKING DIFFICULTY:** Easy **HIGHLIGHTS:** Stunning views of Mount Hood and the Cascades; Trails through oak woodland, emergent wetland, oak savannah, Douglas fir and western redcedar forest **PUBLIC TRANSIT:** Westside Express (WES); SMART Bus from the station

The 250-acre Graham Oaks Nature Park includes oak savannah, oak woodland, conifer forest, bottomland forest, emergent wetland, and shrub habitats, as well as the salmon-bearing Legacy Creek. The trail network links visitors to all the habitats with viewpoints and benches at strategic locations.

The Missoula Floods deposited silts here; the main flows probably occurred to the east of Graham Oaks, though the park may have been part of huge deltas at times. Graham Oaks' open, flatter sections were farmed for many years, thanks in part to an underground tile system. As the drain tiles age and fail, historic springs and wet areas reappear.

Arrowhead Creek crosses the northeast part of Graham Oaks. Decades ago, a three-thousand-foot-long stormwater pipe was built from Dammasch State Hospital (at present-day Villebois village) to Legacy Creek. The increased flow caused deep channel cuts and slope failures along Legacy Creek. At about the same time, several acres of fill material were placed in the Arrowhead Creek bed. The creek cut a narrow incision through the fill, visible from the bridge on the Arrowhead Trail. The stormwater pipe was modified recently and Arrowhead Creek will get most of its water back. Downstream development has made it impossible to return all of the creek's former flow.

The Gateway and Tonquin trails take visitors through a young oak savannah planted in 2007. The small oak trees will take hundreds of years to achieve the mushroom-shaped crown of the single large oak visible just off the trail. Coyotes, black-tailed deer, Savannah sparrows, northern harriers, turkey vultures, and red-tailed hawks are common sights in the savannah. Native prairie wildflowers grown from locally gathered seed are planted in clusters around some oaks. They will begin to spread through the grassland, creating a colorful landscape in spring, as well as feeding pollinators.

Most of the oak woodland is only a few years old, but the north section of the Coyote Way Trail provides views into a five-acre patch of mature oak woodland. Profuse camas blooms appear in the wetter areas in springtime. The oak trees here have a narrow, vertical shape typical of woodland oaks that grow close together. Many songbirds, including white-breasted nuthatches, are common in this woodland.

The Legacy Creek Trail brings visitors to some of the nicest stands of Douglas fir and western redcedar at Graham Oaks. The shady trail is a great escape from the heat in summer. Where English ivy was once knee-deep on the forest floor, abundant trillium, wood violet, and other wildflowers bloom in spring, and shrubs provide habitat complexity. Pileated woodpeckers are heard year-round, and young steelhead and cutthroat trout inhabit Legacy Creek.

Winter is the best time to view the emergent wetland where waterfowl loaf and feed. The surrounding shrubs leaf out in spring and provide nesting habitat for redwinged blackbirds and common yellowthroats. Sharp-eyed visitors may see American pipits and shorebirds in wetland and savannah habitats during migration.

Unexpected Pleasures

Graham Oaks is full of surprises. On a cold, damp February morning, a crew was planting trees and shrubs in ankle-deep water and marking them with slender bamboo stakes. Western bluebirds followed the planting crew, perching on the stakes and circling out to grab insects that were disturbed by the planters' activity. The bluebirds would get within a few feet of the preoccupied planters as they moved across the wet ground, unaware of the hungry, feathered mob following them. Visitors at the main trailhead on a calm, clear June morning may be treated to views of colorful hot air balloons rising several miles to the north while the morning chorus of songbirds rises from the woods. The Coyote Way trail offers a chance for quiet visitors to see these nimble hunters pouncing on rodents in the tall grass.

The Tonquin Trail

The Tonquin Trail is still being planned at the time of publication. The already built portions of the Tonquin Trail through Graham Oak Nature Park will be part of a twelve to sixteen mile regional trail connecting Graham Oaks and the Willamette River with the Tualatin River National Wildlife Refuge and Tigard's Cook Park on the Tualatin River to the north.

—Jane Hart

In addition to installing more than 145,000 native plants and controlling English ivy on sixty acres of forests, Metro pulled several miles of perimeter fence around the agriculture fields to remove barriers to wildlife movement across the site. Acres of invasive English hawthorn were removed to make way for the young native plants along the Arrowhead Trail. The broad view of oak savannah to the west of the main trailhead became possible after an old filbert orchard was removed.

While the oak trees in the savannah and oak woodland will take many decades to grow, other plants will develop more quickly. Willamette Valley ponderosa pine, a variety native to the valley, will be visible above the grasses in less than ten years. Most of the trees and shrubs along the Arrowhead Trail and the northern part of the Tonquin Trail will take on their mature character in ten to twenty years. Regular visitors can see an ever-changing landscape—watching new habitats emerge and new wildlife appear.

Access

The Tonquin Trail crosses the site—a wide, paved trail suitable for walking, running, and cycling. Other trails connect the nature park to surrounding neighborhoods and provide a loop through the mature forest on the west side of the park. These crushed-rock trails have a gentle grade and vary from four to six feet in width.

How to Get There

By car: From Portland: Interstate 5 south to exit 283; west 1.5 miles on SW Wilsonville Road. Just past SW Willamette Way the parking lot is on the right. **Public transit:** Westside Express (WES) stops at Wilsonville Station near Barber Street. From there, proceed about 1.75 miles by foot or bicycle, or take the SMART Bus, which has a stop at the main entrance. Proceed west on Barber, south on Kinsman to Wilsonville Road, then west to the nature park entrance. If planning to ride SMART, check the schedule for days and hours of operation.

By Elaine Stewart and Adam Stellmacher

More information: Metro

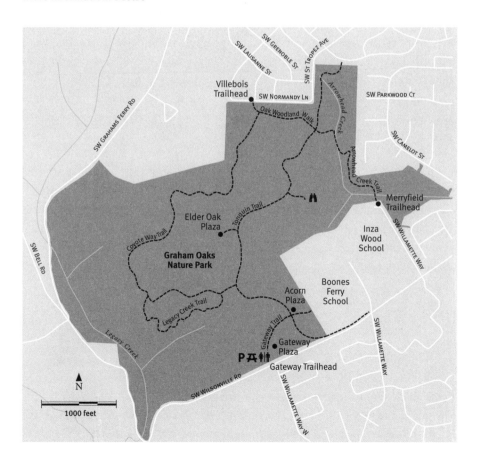

Upper Willamette Narrows

I find the four-mile round-trip paddle upstream to the Willamette Narrows one of the most scenic paddles in the entire region. **Old West Linn's Willamette Park** (not to be confused with Portland's Willamette Park near downtown!) is in the historic village of Willamette and is a great place for family picnics and activities. Naturalists will appreciate the nice little wetland with a boardwalk across from the city's **Bernert Landing boat ramp** and access to the Willamette River above Willamette Falls.

My favorite time to go is on a weekday when it's unlikely there will be motorized activity (motorized boating is clearly a priority at the boat ramp). Most boat launches have minimal parking for cars without boat trailers. This one has no parking for cars without boat trailers. After offloading your kayak or canoe you have to park at another parking lot a short distance to the south, across from Willamette Park. The local constabulary will issue citations if you use the spaces designated for vehicles with trailers. This is one of the great inequities between the way human-powered watercraft and motorized boaters are treated by the state marine board. One hopes that as the paddling community expands, the state will accord equal facilities to all.

Once I have managed to launch my kayak, I like to poke around at the mouth of the **Tualatin River**, just upstream from the boat ramp. Don't count on exploring the lower reach of the Tualatin however, as it is inaccessible to canoes or kayaks due to its generally low level, fast current, and abundant rocks.

The prime attraction on this paddle is the set of islands and scenic passages the river has carved through the basalt, creating winding, narrow, and intimate nooks and crannies that contrast dramatically from the main channel, which I try to avoid. I've found it's much more pleasant to hug the west bank, both to avoid wakes from passing motorized craft and to be closer to the adjacent forests that in early spring and summer are alive with bird calls and songs. Once past the ostentatious McMansions on the west bank, frontage riprap gives way to a well-vegetated, shady riparian forest.

The highlight for me is picking my way behind basalt islands that create the narrows. I stay to the right side of the main channel, in the thin, shady channel as I approach The Nature Conservancy's twelve-acre **Little Rock Island**, just over a mile upstream from Willamette Park. This is also the quietest part of the trip, even on hot summer days when the motorized traffic can be heavy. The basalt islands with their thin soils are reminiscent of the Camassia Preserve and Elk Rock Island downstream. The thin soils dry out quickly and support dry-site species like Oregon white oak and Pacific madrone. In spring, the islands are festooned with wildflowers. A variety of saxifrages, *Lomatium*, white *Delphinium*, *Eriogonum*, *Brodiaea*, *Sedum*, and yellow composites grow on the small island's steep faces. As testament to the ecological importance of the **Willamette Narrows** portion of the Willamette Greenway, Metro Regional Parks and Greenspaces purchased over 450 acres on the west side of the Willamette. Oregon State Parks owns **Coalca Landing** on the river's east bank, which has an informal put-in for paddlers, just upstream of sixty-seven-acre **Rock Island**.

The birding in this stretch of the river is particularly rewarding, owing to the narrow channel and relatively pristine forest habitat. I let my kayak drift a bit and sit for long stretches, listening for pileated woodpeckers, northern flickers, Wilson's warblers, purple finches, Swainson's thrushes, and cedar waxwings. Once out on the main channel, turkey vultures, red-tailed hawks, and osprey soar overhead while spotted sandpipers flutter

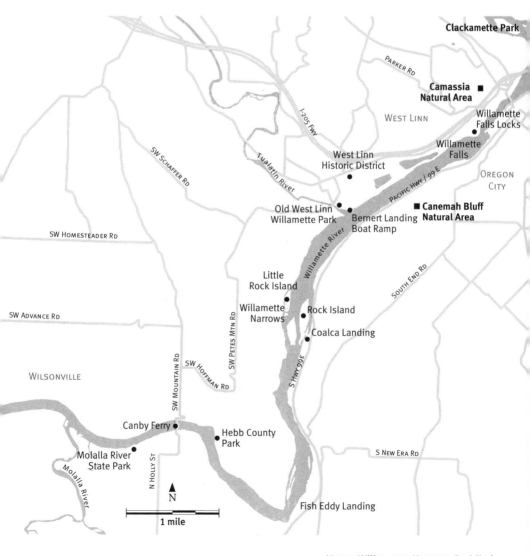

up- and downstream in front of your craft. The banks to the right in spring and summer are covered with *Sedum*, yellow sunflowers, and other wildflowers.

I find the overhead power lines and buoys in the middle of the river a reliable marker, at about river mile thirty, to gauge when I should start paddling east across the river to start my return to Willamette Park. I aim for a point just upstream of **Rock Island**. When the river is running high enough, I love to jet through the narrow, very fast moving channels between the basalt outcroppings of Rock Island. There is a very tricky channel to negotiate at the start of this downstream leg. You need to thread your canoe or kayak between rocks at this point, but once inside the quiet backwater, it's smooth sailing. When I've passed through this miniature gorge, I prefer to cut back across the river, using one of the upstream channels of Little Rock Island, and return to Willamette Park along the west bank to avoid motorized traffic in the main channel.

Guides to the Willamette

> *Wild on the Willamette, Exploring the Lower Willamette River* (Urban Greenspaces Institute and Audubon Society of Portland, 2003)

> *The Willamette River Field Guide*, by Travis Williams (Timber Press, 2009)

> *Canoe and Kayak Routes of Northwest Oregon*, by Philip N. Jones (The Mountaineers Press, 1997)

Also check out the *Willamette Water Trail Guide*, printable online.

If I want to extend the trip to a longer, approximately ten-mile paddle, I continue upstream as far as **Molalla River State Park** and the **Canby Ferry**, which adds another six miles, round trip, to the four-mile Little Rock Island out-and-back.

Once back to Bernert Landing, I sometimes paddle on downstream to **Willamette Falls Locks**, making sure I hug the river's north bank to avoid getting anywhere near the falls. If I am planning to continue downstream through the locks, which is a great experience, I call ahead to the U.S. Army Corps of Engineers (503-656-3381) to let them know I'm headed their way. (For more on the Locks see page 56.) It's a thrill to sit in your small paddle craft as the water rushes out of the lock in front of you, lowering you in four steps back to the Willamette at Oregon City. If you've arranged for a shuttle, you can then continue downstream to one of several pull-out spots on the lower Willamette, the nearest being **Clackamette Park**.

Access

Bernert Landing boat ramp, owned by West Linn Parks and Recreation, is adjacent to West Linn's Willamette Park. There are two launch sites. The preferable one, if it is not a hot, busy weekend full of motorboats, is the formal boat ramp to the left of the park at the end of 12th Street. There is another informal ramp at the foot of 14th Street at the west end of the park. You can also park along the road and carry your canoe or kayak down a short embankment to a crumbling ramp at the mouth of the Tualatin River.

The formal boat ramp is a fully developed facility with restrooms and two docks. One of the launch areas has a gangplank down to a floating dock, which is better to use if there is a lot of motorized boat activity. A second dock is adjacent to a concrete boat ramp. If there are no parking spaces and the ramp is busy you can drive to the other end of the park at the foot of, or along, 14th Street.

How to Get There

BY CAR: From Interstate 205 west of Oregon City take West Linn's Historic Willamette District (10th Street) exit and head south on 10th Street. Get into the right lane, and turn right (west) at the stop sign onto Willamette Falls Drive, and then immediately left on 12th Street. Keep straight at the stop sign at Tualatin Avenue and head down the hill on 12th, which is one-way at this point. The park is on your right and the formal boat ramp is to the left. It's also possible to take a scenic route paralleling the Tualatin River, in which case you would take the Stafford Road exit off Interstate 205. Head north on Stafford Road to Wankers Corner and turn right onto SW Borland Road. Follow Borland southeast until it becomes Willamette Falls Drive and turn right on 12th into Willamette Park.

By Mike Houck

More information: West Linn Parks Department

Canemah Bluff Natural Area

LOCATION: Adjacent to Canemah City Park, 914 4th Avenue, Oregon City, OR **ACTIVITIES:** Wildlife, Wildflower and oak/madrone viewing, Willamette River views, Hiking, photography, Metro education programs **FACILITIES:** Parking at Canemah City Park—redevelopment plans include benches, a native plant demonstration garden, and possibly restrooms **FEES AND REGULATIONS:** Open dawn to dusk, No fees, No dogs or bikes, For programs contact Metro for permit information **HIKING DIFFICULTY:** Moderate **HIGHLIGHTS:** Excellent example of a partially restored oak woodland and prairie and exposed basalt bedrock; Wildflowers from March to May; Spectacular Willamette River and Willamette Falls views **PUBLIC TRANSIT:** No direct service

The Canemah Bluff Natural Area is located adjacent to the Canemah Historic District of Oregon City. The 271-acre parcel was purchased by Metro with funds from 1995 and 2006 bond measures. The site is valued for its rich diversity of habitats dating back to prehistoric times, including conifer forests, ash bottomlands, prairies, and Oregon white oak-madrone woodlands, which support a wide variety of wildlife.

The area overlooks the Willamette River approximately a half mile upriver from Willamette Falls, a major traditional fishing and gathering location for Native American populations. The town of Canemah was also an early focus of settlement in the Willamette Valley. It reached its peak from 1850 to 1870 and included homes (some of which can still be seen) of wealthy tradesmen and sea captains, commercial buildings, and a landing for riverboats. Canemah Bluffs offers spectacular vistas of Willamette Falls and views of West Linn from across the Willamette River. The rocky outcrops and forested canopy of Canemah Bluffs can be seen from the west side of the Willamette and travelers driving along Interstate 205.

Careful observation offers many clues to the "recent" geological events and human management that helped shape the modern landscape. The bluffs are part of a rock bench sandwiched between the Willamette River and the higher plateau to the east. The underlying geologic formation is Columbia River Basalt, the top of the bluff overlain with the more recent Troutdale formation and Boring Lava deposits. During the Missoula Floods, Canemah's steep bluffs and bench were exposed, scoured, and steepened as floodwaters repeatedly spilled into and out of the Willamette Valley. These cataclysmic events, combined with regular burning by Native Americans, created a mosaic of unique habitats similar to The Nature Conservancy's Camassia preserve, Elk Rock Island, and the Willamette Narrows.

One of Canemah's outstanding features is the combination of wildflowers, oak woodland, and prairie habitat areas and associated wildlife. Camas and *Brodiaea* lilies, white larkspur, rosy *Plectritis*, and many other native wildflowers bloom from March to May. Birders should keep an eye out for chipping sparrows, red-breasted sapsuckers, white-breasted nuthatches, and orange-crowned warblers. Hawks and eagles frequently soar over the nearby Willamette River.

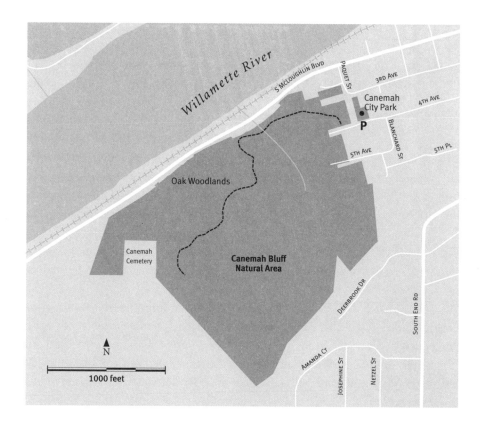

Canemah Bluff is not the place for a vigorous hike at a brisk pace. Take your time over a couple of hours to meander along the small trails that lead into the wildflower meadows and then into the oak woodlands and upland conifer–dominated forests. Absorb and enjoy what the site has to offer.

Canemah is fragile so please stay on trails and keep your dogs at home.

How to Get There

By car: From Oregon City, head south on McLoughlin Boulevard (Highway 99E). At the first light after the tunnel, turn left onto South 2nd Street. Curve one block to a stop sign and turn right onto High Street (which turns into South End Road). Follow South End Road for one-quarter mile and veer right onto 5th Avenue. Follow 5th (which turns into Miller Street) to a stop sign on 4th Avenue and turn left. Go to the end of 4th Avenue and park at Canemah City Park. Follow the gravel path through the park to Canemah Bluff Natural Area. **Public transit:** No direct service

By Brian Vaughn and Jonathan Soll

More information: Metro

Camassia Natural Area

LOCATION: Behind West Linn High School, off SE Sunset Avenue at the end of Walnut Street, West Linn, OR **ACTIVITIES:** Hiking, Wildflower viewing **FACILITIES:** Parking, Unpaved trails, Interpretive signs **FEES AND REGULATIONS:** Open dawn to dusk, No pets, No bikes, No picnics, Keep to trails, No wildflower collection **HIKING DIFFICULTY:** Easy **HIGHLIGHTS:** Oak-madrone woodland, Camas prairie, 400 plant species, perhaps Portland's finest wildflower natural area **PUBLIC TRANSIT:** No direct service

One of the strangest and most enticing natural areas in the Portland area is the mixture of oak-madrone woodland and prairie that is The Nature Conservancy's Camassia Natural Area. Setting foot in this delicate preserve is like stepping into another world.

Certainly that is how naturalist Murray Miller must have felt when he explored this area in the 1950s. Impressed by Camassia's unique values he persuaded The Nature Conservancy to acquire the property, and in 1962 it became the conservancy's first Oregon preserve and remains one of the loveliest spots in the region.

The approach to Camassia is through a hardwood forest thickly populated by Oregon white oak, which is an important and threatened ecosystem in its own right. But it doesn't prepare the visitor for what lies ahead. After a short distance the ground rises and the trail opens into what is the most striking aspect of Camassia: a tangled bluff-top landscape of scattered Pacific madrone and oak trees, ash swales, wet meadows, and rocks.

The rocky appearance of Camassia can be credited to the great Missoula Floods of fifteen thousand years ago. At that time, glacial ice dammed many of the Northwest's rivers creating huge glacial lakes such as Lake Missoula along the Idaho-Montana border. When the lake's ice dam broke, as it did periodically, a vast volume of water came cascading down the Columbia, pouring through the Willamette Valley, and scouring the existing landscape down to bare rock. At the same time, huge boulders floated in on ice rafts. As the ice melted, these "erratics"—many from hundreds of miles away— were deposited throughout Washington and northwest Oregon. At Camassia both the gray of the native basalt and the "salt and pepper" of the erratics are readily visible.

Another dominant feature of the Camassia Natural Area is an oak and madrone savannah. This landscape was once a common feature of the Willamette Valley, but it required regular burning (something Willamette Valley Native Americans did frequently to preserve its character). When European settlers displaced the Indian population, the burning stopped and fire suppression began, permitting encroachment from the coniferous forest. Oak-madrone woodlands are becoming scarce in northwest Oregon, but at Camassia, The Nature Conservancy is working to restore this significant habitat type by removing Scot's broom, Himalayan blackberry, and other invasives, and limiting the incursion of Douglas fir.

The woodland is dominated by two trees. Oregon white oak is extremely important for habitat, but for looks it cannot compare to its arresting companion the Pacific madrone. The madrone is a native tree, the only native broadleaf evergreen in this part of the world. Its coppery bark, peeling to reveal a cinnamon, satin-smooth interior layer, gives it an exotic look. And in April, it bears spectacular clusters of creamy-white flowers. April is also the season for an even more extraordinary flower display, which takes place in the wet meadows interspersed between the trees.

Perhaps the most important food plant for the Indian tribes of the Northwest was the camas, a beautiful, blue lily with six petals (technically tepals). Its bulbs were roasted or boiled and eaten, or dried and ground into flour. Camas prairies were major meeting grounds for the various tribes and wars over the rights to these prairies were common. Due to development of all sorts, the sight of a wet meadow turned blue with the springtime camas bloom is becoming an increasingly uncommon sight.

But camas, Camassia Natural Area's namesake, still can be found here in abundance, reaching its peak bloom in mid to late April. At that same time, the meadows of Camassia are also carpeted with the purple-blue blossoms of large *Collinsia* and the flush of rosy *Plectritis*—an unforgettable sight.

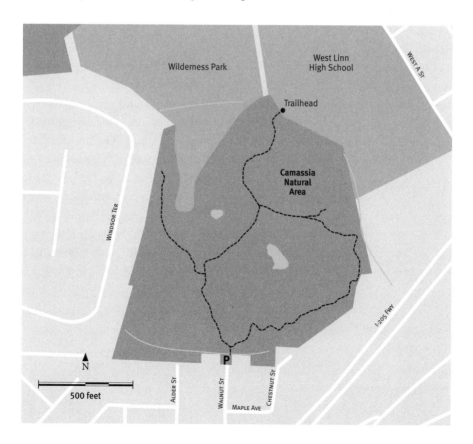

And as if that weren't enough, nearly four hundred other flowering plants can be found at Camassia, many of which are rare in the Willamette Valley. Birds and other animals find a haven here too. Camassia is used as one of the sites for Audubon Society of Portland's annual springtime Bird Song Walks, where birds found have included cedar waxing, Hutton's and warbling vireo, western tanager, American and lesser goldfinch, as well as—more rarely—California quail, lazuli bunting, and chipping sparrow.

A visit to Camassia is not a hike in the ordinary sense. The natural area is small and the trails are limited, rocky, and uneven in places. They are also bordered by poison oak, requiring considerable alertness from walkers and providing a continuing reminder to stay on the trails.

But hiking isn't the main point anyway. Visitors to Camassia are repaid in beauty rather than in miles walked . . . and reminded of how fortunate we are to have this natural wildflower garden in our city.

Access

A walking park only, the trail system consists of a short loop trail with a couple of spurs. The trail varies from damp (although boardwalks are in place through most of the wettest and most sensitive areas) to dry and rocky, with uneven terrain in some places. Camassia is a fragile site, so please observe the regulations conscientiously.

How to Get There

BY CAR: From Portland's west side head south on Oregon Highway 43. (Alternatively, from the east side take Interstate 205 to Highway 43 exit 8; leave the freeway and proceed south on Highway 43.) Continue south on Highway 43 until shortly before the Oregon City–West Linn Arch Bridge; bear right onto Willamette Falls Drive. After 0.3 miles, bear right onto Sunset Avenue; in another 0.2 miles (just after Sunset crosses I-205 turn right onto Walnut Street. The Camassia Natural Area is 0.1 mile ahead, at the end of the street. From Oregon City, cross the bridge and bear left onto Willamette Falls Drive, then follow directions above. While Walnut Street is the official access point, if you're on your bike there is informal access via a gate at West Linn High School's football field and track. The Oregon City Bridge may have closures with ongoing construction. (For more information: ODOT Arch Bridge Shuttle timetable.) **PUBLIC TRANSIT:** No direct service

By Bob Wilson

More information: The Nature Conservancy

Mount Talbert Nature Park

LOCATION: Just southeast of the intersection of I-205 and Sunnyside Road (10695 SE Mather Road), Clackamas, OR **ACTIVITIES:** Hiking, Wildlife viewing **FACILITIES:** Mather Road Trailhead—Parking, Restrooms, Drinking fountain, Picnic shelters, Interpretive signs **FEES AND REGULATIONS:** Open daily half an hour before sunrise to half an hour after sunset, No dogs or bikes **HIKING DIFFICULTY:** Easy, Moderate **HIGHLIGHTS:** A 216-acre forest in a sea of residential and commercial development with nothing comparable nearby; Outstanding spring migration birding; Spring wildflowers; Fantastic foliage color and abundant mushrooms in the fall **PUBLIC TRANSIT:** MAX Green Line; TriMet bus 156

Mount Talbert is the largest undeveloped butte in a series of extinct volcanoes and lava domes that stretch southward from Powell Butte to the Clackamas River. The 216-acre nature park is owned and managed by Metro and North Clackamas Parks and Recreation.

Nearby Interstate 205, Clackamas Town Center, development on Mount Scott, rapidly growing Happy Valley, and housing creeping up the slopes of Mount Talbert all provided the impetus to purchase this property in 1996 with bond measures in order to protect remaining habitat. The park opened to the public in 2007, and local residents are now thrilled to have this large, natural area in their backyard.

More than four miles of trails are almost all under forest cover—from conifers on the north side to the oak woodlands on the southern slope. Most areas have a mix of conifers and deciduous trees, which makes for fabulous fall color. The trail system is basically an outer loop and an inner loop with trails coming into the loops from the trailheads. The outer loop is appropriately named the Park Loop Trail and is accessed from all the trailheads. From the Park Loop Trail you can make an inner loop that includes the 750-foot summit, by taking the West Ridge and Summit Trails. The summit is forested with only a partial view to the south.

Every trail junction is marked with very clear "map posts" that make it challenging to get lost on Mount Talbert. Interpretive signs along the trails provide information about the plants and animals that can be seen in the park and explain the ongoing oak woodland restoration. The quality of the native plant communities present is exceptional. The number of non-native, invasive plants on Mount Talbert is relatively low because most major disturbances occurred before many of the worst weeds were introduced from outside the region. The natural, native plant associations are still in place and maintaining this healthy condition is a major management goal for the nature park.

An exciting management experiment is taking place on about twenty acres of Mount Talbert, where there are healthy stands of Oregon white oak. Oak woodlands are now a rare habitat in the northern Willamette Valley. The region's Native Americans managed oak woodlands with fire for thousands of years to favor the oaks and other plants and to improve hunting. The burning killed young Douglas firs growing among the oaks, which would otherwise grow much taller than the oaks, shade them out, and eventually replace them. Once Native American burning stopped, oak woodlands, and the plants associated with them, began to die out.

Within some of the healthiest oak woodlands on Mount Talbert, Metro has removed most of the Douglas firs and some of the other competing trees and shrubs to "release" the oaks from the suppression by shade. By favoring the Oregon white oaks in this way, managers hope to revitalize and reestablish the oak woodlands, as is being done on Cooper Mountain, Graham Oaks, and other natural areas. This management will also favor the other plants and animals that thrive in oak woodlands. Possibly the most well-known of these is the western gray squirrel—see a carved statue of this oak woodland icon at the Mather Road Trailhead.

During spring migration in late April and in May, you can see large numbers of warblers and other neotropical migrants in the restored oak woodlands when they stop to feed on their way north. At last count, seventy-five species of birds have been seen at Mount Talbert, including some that require a sizeable chunk of forest for nesting such as great horned owl, Cooper's hawk, red-tailed hawk, and hairy woodpecker. For the experienced birder, the most exciting news from Mount Talbert might be the resident nesting population of Hutton's vireos. Since the Hutton's vireo is about the plainest little gray bird in the state, few will appreciate the thrill of seeing one as much as an avid birdwatcher.

Other common wildlife besides the western gray squirrel is the black-tailed deer, whose trails through the forest are easy to see. There are also two non-native tree squirrels—émigrés from the East Coast—the fox and the eastern gray squirrels. Other mammals include coyotes, raccoons, opossums, bats, voles, moles, and shrews. Rough-skinned newts and Pacific chorus frogs are apparent when it's wet and garter snakes will be active when it's sunny and warm. A very lucky sighting would be the unique rubber boa, by far the most northern of all the boas. Mount Scott Creek, which supports cutthroat trout, coho salmon, and steelhead trout, roughly follows the northern border of the park.

Access

The main park entrance is on SE Mather Road. A secondary trailhead comes into the park from the north, at Southeast 117th Avenue and Sunnyside Road. Parking here is limited and the trail is not universally accessible. There are also four walk-in trailheads from neighborhood streets. There are 4.2 miles of forested hiking trails that loop around and through the park and lead to the summit. Trails are moderate and can be rough or muddy in spots. Poison oak is common on the south side of the park; be sure you can recognize this plant.

How to Get There

BY CAR: From Interstate 205 east on Sunnyside Road to 117th. Or from SE Sunnybrook Boulevard turn south on 97th Avenue and stay on it as it turns east and becomes

Mather Road. The park entrance is on the left. **PUBLIC TRANSIT:** TriMet bus 156 (weekdays only) goes from the MAX Green Line station at Clackamas Town Center to Mather Road and goes by the main entrance to the park at the Mather Road Trailhead.

By James Davis

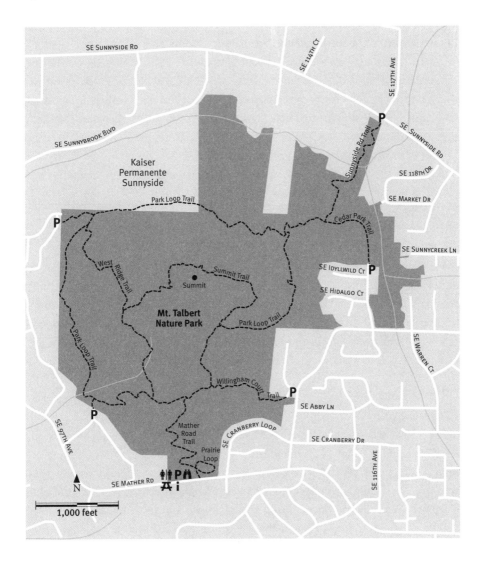

Lower Willamette River Loop
Sellwood Riverfront Park to Oregon City Falls

Before setting out on this twenty-five-mile loop ride, Sellwood Riverfront Park ❶ is worth a brief look. When I visited the site with Portland Park staff in the early 1980s, it was a heap of Himalayan-blackberry-covered sawdust, having once been an old mill site. It's a tribute to the landscape architects who transformed a truly ugly landscape into a fine neighborhood park and a great place to access the Willamette. The funky little wetland feature in the park's northeast corner, abutting the black cottonwood forest, has a short boardwalk from which you can see native wetland plants like spirea, blue elderberry, creek dogwood, willow, and wapato, and kids can catch polliwogs. Green heron sometimes skulk about looking for frogs, one of which is the rare northern red-legged frog (*Rana aurora*).

From the park, I jump on the Springwater on the Willamette trail and head out to Milwaukie and the **Jefferson Street Boat Ramp** ❷, where there are great views of the **Johnson Creek confluence with the Willamette River** ❸ and a distant view of **Elk Rock Island**. The route south is along the paved bicycle-pedestrian path that winds riverward of the Kellogg Creek Wastewater Treatment Plant. The short path abruptly dumps you onto SE 19th Avenue and SE Eagle Street. Ride straight south to SE Sparrow Street. All the streets in this quiet neighborhood are named after birds. At the end of Sparrow Street is the entrance to Milwaukie's **Spring Park** ❹ and access to Elk Rock Island.

What was a garbage-dumping site not too many years ago is now a pleasant playground and picnic area, thanks to neighborhood activists and volunteers. I generally lock my bike here and take an unpaved path (very muddy when it rains) out to Elk Rock (see page 62). I've always found Elk Rock to be alluring simply because you cannot always get to it. It's a small, basalt outcropping with gnarled Pacific madrone and thick stands of Oregon white oak, juxtaposed with the nearby cliffs across the river. This little island tempts you to bring a picnic lunch and just sit, staring out at the Willamette and beautiful cliffs and, in early spring, the profusion of wildflowers.

Continuing South
After collecting your bike, be sure to gear way down as the ride up SE Sparrow is steep. Take a sharp right-hand turn onto **SE River Road** ❺ and you're on the way to Oregon City.

My next favorite stop is **Meldrum Bar Park**, well worth the half-mile side trip for excellent views of the Willamette River downstream and upstream to nearby Goat

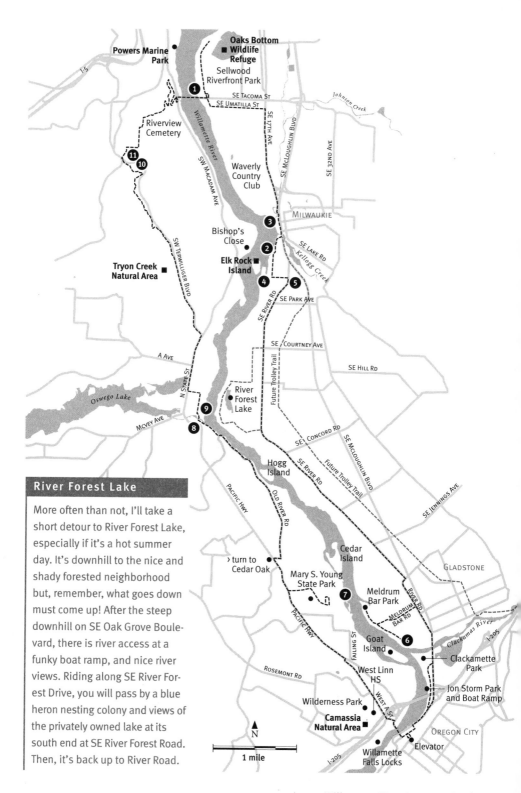

River Forest Lake

More often than not, I'll take a short detour to River Forest Lake, especially if it's a hot summer day. It's downhill to the nice and shady forested neighborhood but, remember, what goes down must come up! After the steep downhill on SE Oak Grove Boulevard, there is river access at a funky boat ramp, and nice river views. Riding along SE River Forest Drive, you will pass by a blue heron nesting colony and views of the privately owned lake at its south end at SE River Forest Road. Then, it's back up to River Road.

Island, which has a large great blue heron colony that you can observe from Meldrum Bar's rocky beach. There have been recent attempts at promoting native habitat restoration near a huge community garden plot, although mountain bikes and ORVs have chewed up the surrounding forest. If you take another short side trip on **Dahl Beach Road** ❻ (an out and back) to the south, you'll find a nice sandy beach should you be ready for a swim at the mouth of the Clackamas River.

Heading back to River Road and across the Clackamas River is the access to **Clackamette Park**. After some birding and a short dip in the Clackamas, it's time to mount up and head to Oregon City via Clackamette Drive and the bicycle path paralleling SE McLoughlin Boulevard into Oregon City. It's worth a short stop at **Jon Storm Park** and then on to the new bicycle and pedestrian path to downtown Oregon City.

Having grown up in Estacada when a trip to Oregon City for Chinese food was a big deal and a trip up the **elevator** was a must, I always make time for a ride up the elevator to the bluff above. Incredibly, there's still an elevator operator that runs it. The elevator provides interpretive signs and great views of the Oregon City Falls and the Willamette Falls Locks across the Willamette River. There's even a cycle shop at the elevator's base in the event you've broken a chain or need a repair you can't handle yourself.

It's time to head back north, with a little less than half the route completed at this point. Gear down again after crossing the Oregon City/West Linn Bridge to pump hard up the steep hill to West Linn High School and **The Nature Conservancy's Camassia**

The Trolley Trail

The once-remote and isolated communities of Gladstone, Jennings Lodge, Oak Grove, and Milwaukie experienced great change with the addition of the streetcar. In the mid to late 1800s, one primary dirt road for pedestrians and horse-drawn carriages paralleled the east shore of the Willamette River. By 1890, that route would become the Portland to Oregon City streetcar line—one of the first interurban railways in the country and the first to run on hydroelectric power.

In 1958, streetcar passenger service ceased due to the rapid spread of the automobile; however, freight movement on the interurban line continued for ten more years before it was abandoned as well. A campaign to protect the right-of-way eventually led to a joint property acquisition in 2001 by Metro and North Clackamas Parks and Recreation District.

While the six-mile right-of-way is walkable today, construction of an accessible, multi-use trail won't begin until well into 2011, and beyond. When completed, the trail will meander through historic and suburban residential areas and a series of natural drainage basins that are home to myriad birds, mammals, and aquatic life. Wetlands along the way will continue to provide important wildlife habitat and also filter pollutants before entering the Willamette River.

—Toby Forsberg

Natural Area (see page 38). I prefer to walk my bike past the tennis courts, baseball field, and onto the track that runs around the football field. There are two stiles through the chain link fence that provide access to the preserve. Camassia is a highlight of the trip, a walk through an elfin oak wonderland, especially in the spring when blue camas, pink *Plectritis*, and other native flowers are blooming. The trails are quite soggy in spring, given that the underlying basalt causes water to pool, which is why many of the plants are growing here. If you cut out any of the stops during your loop this should not be one of them.

The Willamette Falls Locks

Another great side trip includes the historic Willamette Falls Locks. There is a walkway on which you must walk your bicycle down to the locks. The access road is off limits to bikes and pedestrians. There are interpretive signs at the locks and a wonderful small museum. See page 56.

On to Mary S. Young State Park

Back on the bike, go north past the high school and take the very busy Oregon Highway 43 to Mary S. Young State Park. While the park is a state property, it's actually managed by the City of West Linn. This is a great place for a hike in the forest, and if you want to take a dip in the Willamette there are **great beaches** ❼. There are also wonderful views upstream on the Willamette, including Meldrum Bar, Clackamette Park, and the distant heronry on Goat Island. There's a short side trip to Cedar Island across a metal bridge. Lots of interpretive signs and trail maps will help orient you to the 133-acre natural area park. There are multiple trails down to the river, some paved and some unpaved. This is a great spot for lunch, sitting on a bench overlooking the Willamette and enjoying the spectacular river views

Old River Road to George Rogers Park

Another highlight of the ride is the shady, flat route along **Old River Road**. I frequently miss it, but if you have sharp eyes and quick reflexes you can access Old River Road by riding between two barriers to the right off Oregon Highway 43. If your reflexes are a bit slow the next opportunity is at Cedar Oak. Old River Road is the most pleasant riding experience of the entire trip. The road undulates and winds through cool forested landscape along the west shore of the Willamette River for about two miles to the entrance of George Rogers Park in Lake Oswego. I like to stop frequently to take in the views of small basalt islands.

Just as the road makes a sharp turn to the left, there's a **footbridge** ❽ on the right that passes over Oswego Creek and into George Rogers Park ❾. Albert and Miriam Durham settled here in 1847 and established a mill on

Oregon City Bridge Closure

The historic bridge from Oregon City to West Linn will be closed for repairs and is expected to reopen to traffic in late 2012. A shuttle service will accommodate bicycle and pedestrian travel throughout construction.

More information: ODOT Arch Bridge Shuttle timetable

what was then Sucker Creek, which flowed out of Sucker Lake (now Oswego Lake). The real draw to the park is the newly refurbished 1865 iron furnace, the first to be built west of the Rockies by a few of Portland's most prominent civic leaders: W. S. Ladd, Henry Failing, and H. W. Corbett. George Rogers—born Jorge Rodrigues on Portugal's Madeira Island—a local grocery store owner and Lake Oswego city councilman, started the campaign to save the furnace. The twenty-six-acre park was eventually purchased in 1945, and in 1969 the bicycle path was added. There's a spacious sandy beach here if you're up for another dip.

On to Tryon Creek Park

Back in the saddle, ride north on Oregon Highway 43 to SW Terwilliger Boulevard and take the bike path that parallels Terwilliger for a 2.5-mile ride—and thanks to the numerous tree roots, a very bumpy one—to **Tryon Creek Natural Area**. If you're looking for another forest walk it's hard to top Tryon Creek (see page 51). There's a large nature center, restrooms, and soft walking paths. However, if it's "horse to the barn" time continue on the bike path past **Lewis and Clark Law School ❿** to Terwilliger.

From Terwilliger it's time to gear down once again to ride up **SW 2nd Avenue ⓫** to SW Palatine Hill Road and to the Riverview Cemetery entrance just past SW Viewpoint Terrace. From there it's a relaxing downhill ride through the cemetery. As you ride through be considerate of those who may be visiting relatives. Some cyclists in recent years have been extremely disruptive, leading to threats by the owners to shut the cemetery down to cycle use. There are cyclist logos painted on the roadways with one-way arrows. Follow them downhill, eventually arriving at SW Macadam Avenue. From there it's back across the Sellwood Bridge to complete the loop.

By Mike Houck

Sellwood Bridge Crossing

Getting to the Sellwood Bridge and across it is the trickiest part of the ramble. Cross SW Macadam Avenue at the traffic light. Take the north-bound traffic lane that passes under the bridge heading to Portland. Once you are under the bridge a turnout to the right allows access to the spiral access ramp. Take the spiral access to the sidewalk on the north side of the bridge to complete the loop across the Willamette. There are signs on the bridge that advise you to walk your bicycle across the bridge, owing to the narrow sidewalk and a significant drop into the oncoming lane of traffic. At the east end of the bridge there is bike-pedestrian access on the left to SE Spokane Street and back down the hill to Sellwood Riverfront Park. Of course, all of this will be moot once the Sellwood Bridge replacement is finished, but that will take awhile.

Tryon Creek Watershed

IN 1850, SOCRATES HOTCHKISS TRYON proved a donation land claim for 645 acres at the confluence of a rushing stream and the Willamette River south of Portland. The native word for the place was unknown, and his own formidable moniker was condensed to name it—Tryon Creek.

The creek originates in seeps and springs above Portland's hilly Multnomah Village, and it first appears as a blue line on the map near Portland's Arnold Park. From there it runs seven steep miles down to the Willamette River. Tryon's major tributaries are Arnold and Falling Creeks. The entire Tryon Creek Watershed covers a little over four thousand acres in Clackamas and Multnomah Counties. With all its branches, it comprises about twenty-seven miles of open channel, and three miles of pipes.

Tryon is one of only a few free-flowing streams that drain Portland's West Hills, and one of the city's last urban streams to support a small steelhead run. But even in living memory, the fish were once much more plentiful; one elderly watershed resident remembers childhood outings with her father to collect spawned-out salmon by the wheelbarrow-load for garden fertilizer.

Like the fish, the big trees once seemed inexhaustible. Socrates Tryon Jr. sold his father's land to the Oregon Iron Works, which cut and burned the enormous old-growth cedars and Douglas firs to make charcoal. Major logging concluded in 1961 but some massive stumps are still visible along trails in Tryon Creek State Natural Area. Now, more than half the Tryon Creek watershed is developed with single-family homes. About 21 percent is protected in parks and open space, most of that in Tryon Creek State Natural Area.

Nearly a quarter of the watershed is paved and, like other urban streams with a great deal of paving, the creek has become increasingly "flashy" in the hydrologic sense. Asphalt doesn't allow water to sink into the ground, so runoff is swift and groundwater recharge lower now than in the past. As a result, flow in Tryon Creek can vary by a factor of more than five thousand between the last dry September days and the wettest winter storms a few months later.

Despite the pollution and altered flows, resident cutthroat trout persist in Tryon, and some migratory steelhead still manage to make their way up to spawn. In the past few years, a few endangered coastal coho and spring Chinook juveniles have also been observed in Tryon Creek State Natural Area. The most lamentable barrier from the fish standpoint is the two-hundred-foot culvert under Highway 43, near Tryon's confluence with the Willamette. Several public agencies have worked to restore stream banks from the Willamette up to the 1920s-era culvert opening and "remodel" the culvert itself with new baffles to make fish passage easier. Complete replacement with a bridge is contemplated and would greatly assist with restoring threatened and endangered fish in the Tryon system. Other projects, such as storm water planters in Multnomah Village, deal with polluted runoff and also help to restore the system.

The state park in the lower watershed was developed as a result of citizen advocacy, and the area maintains a tradition of resident engagement; the state park has a strong Friends group, and a watershed council also advocates for stream health. The continued interest and engagement by local residents is reassuring: the salmon and the big trees may remain in living memory.

By Jonna Papaefthimiou

Tryon Creek Stormwater Innovation

Today, standing on SW 30th Avenue and SW Dolph Court, it's hard to imagine that Tryon Creek was once buried and forgotten. The 2.7-acre Headwaters Development Project site was once a forested wetland—a headwaters tributary of nearby Tryon Creek. Before construction of Pilusoís Restaurant and Night Club in the 1940s, the site was contaminated with gasoline, oil, and cleaning fluids. When the site was developed, nine hundred feet of the creek was piped and buried. Pilusoís had a dance floor that retracted to reveal an indoor swimming pool, which often featured synchronized swimming exhibitions. The building later housed an Elks Lodge and the site was covered with 99,000 square feet of hard, impervious surfaces.

The Headwaters Project in the Upper Tryon Creek Watershed transformed the site. Creek banks are planted with native trees, shrubs, and grasses, and the creek now connects a forest wetland upstream with a downstream rain garden that manages stormwater runoff from streets and parking areas.

As you walk around the site, off of SW Barbur Boulevard (99W) on SW 30th Avenue between SW Marigold Street and SW Dolph Court, look for stormwater management strategies such as ecoroofs, planters, restored creek channels, green streets, and a rain garden.

—Amin Wahab

Tryon Creek State Natural Area

LOCATION: 11321 SW Terwilliger Boulevard, Portland **ACTIVITIES:** Hiking, Biking, Jogging, Horseback riding **FACILITIES:** Restrooms, Parking, Wheelchair accessible trail and facility, Nature Center, Small picnic area/shelter, Drinking water **FEES AND REGULATIONS:** Pets on leash **HIKING DIFFICULTY:** Easy, Moderate **HIGHLIGHTS:** All-abilities interpretive trail; Annual Trillium Festival and native plant sale in early spring; Second-growth forest habitat with small canyon and creek; Nature Center programs and events for all ages offered by the Friends of Tryon Creek State Park **PUBLIC TRANSIT:** TriMet bus 39

Located within a dense, residential, suburban area straddling the Portland and Lake Oswego border just steps from Lewis & Clark College, Tryon Creek State Natural Area presents a tranquil sanctuary for communing with nature year-round. The 677-acre nature park, originally owned by homesteader Socrates Tryon was sold to the Oregon Iron Works to be logged for its then-plentiful Douglas firs, used initially to make the charcoal needed to run the iron furnace and then logged sporadically until the 1960s. Tryon Creek now stands as a healthy, second-growth forest teeming with wildlife and offering opportunities to explore a complex forest-and-creek habitat.

In 1970, with a large-scale residential development plan firmly in place, neighbors organized to raise community awareness of the potential loss of this urban jewel and formed the Friends of Tryon Creek Park. Governor Tom McCall, along with support from Transportation Commission Chair Glen Jackson, stepped in to purchase what was at the time Oregon's only urban state park. In the 1990s, the name was officially changed to Tryon Creek State Natural Area to recognize its unique ecological attributes and to differentiate it from state parks with campsites and other recreational amenities. The nonprofit Friends of Tryon Creek's professional staff, in a unique partnership with Oregon Parks and Recreation Department, now develops a range of programs throughout the year for people of all ages and helps manage ongoing restoration efforts and invasive species removal.

The forest now boasts stands of big-leaf maple, red alder, and one hundred-year-old western redcedar and Douglas fir. Many of the loop trails lead to the namesake creek, which is crossed by a number of picturesque bridges, the Stone Bridge on Iron Mountain Trail being one of the most scenic. Birds are often hard to find in the thick canopy, but it is not unusual to spot pileated and downy woodpeckers, barred and great horned owls, Cooper's hawks, brown creepers, along with a range of songbirds including Pacific wrens, black-capped chickadees, and nesting Wilson's warblers. Banana slugs are popular residents along with six species of salamander, brush rabbits, and black-tailed deer.

Spring is a wonderful time to visit when the forest fills with white trillium blooms (usually mid-March to mid-April). The beautiful, triangular-shaped flower has come to personify spring at Tryon Creek and is celebrated at the annual Trillium Festival (usually the first weekend in April), which is coordinated by the Friends. The festival includes a native plant sale, guided hikes, and activities for children.

The park is popular with runners and dog walkers (on leash only!), who appreciate the well-kept trail system and forested setting. Make sure to stop in at the Tryon Creek Nature Center, another contribution from the Friends, for trail maps, information on ranger-led hikes, classes and workshops, and public events. The paved all-abilities Trillium Trail, with native plants identified along its loops, make the park accessible to all nature lovers.

Robins Awake!

Trillium is what we usually call them here because their petals, sepals, and leaves all come in threes. But the ancient name, "wake-robin," also works well for this lily since, as one of our earliest bloomers, trilliums pop up at just about the time American robins begin their incessant morning song. By late March, trilliums are abundant, and Portland-area forests seem to glow in the light of their creamy blossoms.

Tryon Creek State Natural Area schedules its annual Trillium Festival in early April to coincide with the peak of the bloom, but come much later, and the flowers—purple-petaled now—will be senescent, subsiding until the time comes to wake next year's crop of robins.

—Bob Wilson

Access

The fourteen miles of trails include a paved bicycle path that stretches three miles connecting the north and south ends of the park, as well as an equestrian trail, and a paved all-abilities trail. Hiking and jogging trails are of variable difficulty with moderate elevation change as you head down toward the creek. Trails are slightly muddy in spots in winter and early spring.

How to Get There

BY CAR: Take the SW Terwilliger Boulevard exit off I-5 and head south on SW Terwilliger Boulevard toward Lewis & Clark College. Continue on Terwilliger about one mile past the Northwestern School of Law, heading toward Lake Oswego and following the brown park signs to the park's main entrance. Additional access is from Boones Ferry Road, and south on SW Terwilliger Boulevard, 0.5 miles past the entrance to Iron Mountain Trailhead. PUBLIC TRANSIT: TriMet bus 39 serves the Lewis & Clark College campus at the north end of Tryon Creek State Natural Area but does not reach the park's main entrance and parking area. From the Northwest School of Law there is approximately a mile hike to the Nature Center although this allows direct access to the park's more northern hiking trails.

By David Cohen

More information: Oregon State Parks; Friends of Tryon Creek

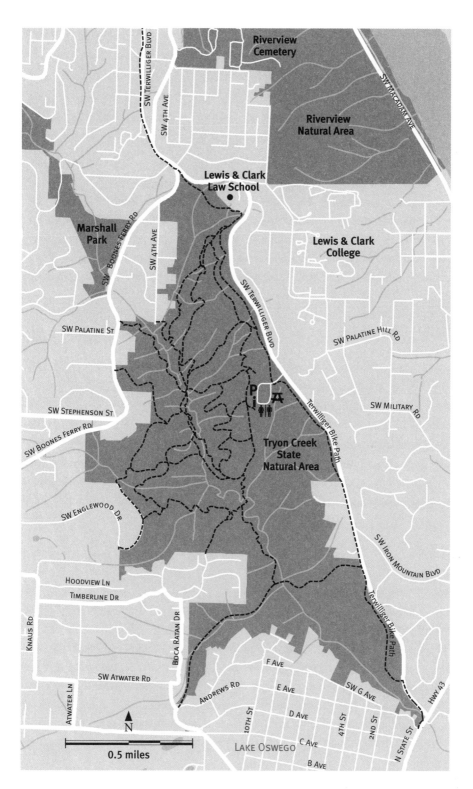

Riverview
Cemetery

SW MACADAM AVE

SW TERWILLIGER BLVD

SW 4TH AVE

Riverview
Natural Area

Lewis & Clark
Law School

Marshall
Park

SW BOONES FERRY RD

SW 4TH AVE

Lewis & Clark
College

SW PALATINE ST

SW TERWILLIGER BLVD

SW PALATINE HILL RD

SW STEPHENSON ST

P

SW MILITARY RD

Terwilliger Bike Path

SW BOONES FERRY RD

Tryon Creek
State
Natural Area

SW ENGLEWOOD DR

SW IRON MOUNTAIN BLVD

HOODVIEW LN

TIMBERLINE DR

Terwilliger Bike Path

KNAUS RD

BOCA RATAN DR

ATWATER LN

SW ATWATER RD

Andrews Rd

F AVE

E AVE

SW G AVE

HWY 43

N

10TH ST

D AVE

4TH ST

2ND ST

N STATE ST

C AVE

LAKE OSWEGO

0.5 miles

B AVE

Lower Willamette River
Oregon City to Portland Harbor

Hogg and Cedar Islands

If you paddle down the Willamette River on its lower twenty-six miles, below Willamette Falls, there are relatively few islands, but there are a couple of interesting ones that are within a mile of one another: Hogg Island and Cedar Island.

Cedar Island is immediately adjacent to Cedar Oak Boat Ramp in West Linn. Just above the island is **Mary S. Young State Park**, which has a seasonal bridge that connects it to the island. The island is ring-shaped today; the shallow lagoon in the center is a legacy of the gravel that was mined in the 1960s. Over the years this lagoon has been utilized heavily for bass fishing. If you paddle a canoe or kayak around the island, you will see some native plants, along with a healthy crop of Himalayan blackberry on the west side. Excavated underneath and among the blackberries are at least two beaver dens. It is common to see beaver at dusk or at night, and you can hear the occasional slap of their tails when they are marking their territory or feel threatened. Cedar Island has a crude walking path that takes you from the bridge to the north, or downstream tip of the island. For most of the year, you can paddle all the way around the island. The back channel becomes progressively smaller as you move upstream, and in the summer months at low tide, you may have to hop out of your boat for a few feet, scoot along, and then jump back in to complete your trip. Given its designation by Clackamas County as surplus property, Cedar Island's future is in limbo, but it has been left relatively unmanaged until recently.

Hogg Island lies about a mile downstream from Cedar Island. Composed of a nearly ten-acre base of basalt, Hogg Island is densely treed with Oregon white oak. There is an abundant understory of snowberry, Oregon grape, and poison oak. This island is mainly ignored by those in powerboats because of its relatively uninviting shoreline (save the small beach on the side channel) and thus has been protected from overuse by river travelers.

If you land on the beach and walk up the bank, a small clearing serves as the main entry point. From the clearing there are occasional game trails that you can follow amid the underbrush, but keep a very wary eye out for the pervasive poison oak.

In the spring you'll see the purple petals of the native camas that has come back in some places on the island's interior thanks to the removal of Scot's broom. This island is owned by Clackamas County and efforts by Willamette Riverkeeper have been

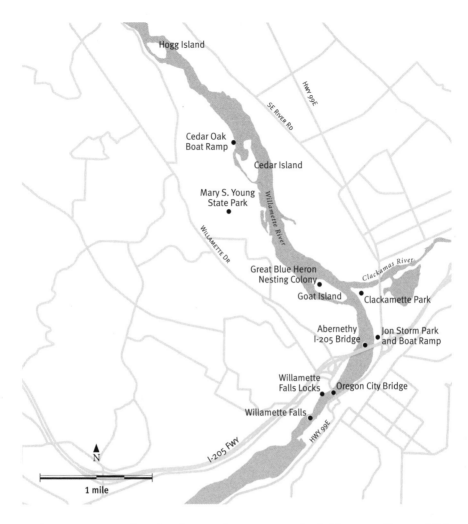

Hogg Island

SE RIVER RD

HWY 99E

Cedar Oak
Boat Ramp

Cedar Island

Willamette River

Mary S. Young
State Park

WILLAMETTE DR

Great Blue Heron
Nesting Colony

Clackamas River

Goat Island

Clackamette Park

Abernethy
I-205 Bridge

Jon Storm Park
and Boat Ramp

Willamette
Falls Locks

Oregon City Bridge

Willamette Falls

I-205 Fwy

HWY 99E

N

1 mile

underway to remove invasive plants and to restore native habitat as well as establish the island as a natural area.

Hogg Island is relatively untrammeled, a bit of a natural oasis in a high-density suburban area, save for the occasional teenage campout in June.

How to Get There

The most convenient put-ins are at Cedar Oak Boat Ramp in West Linn, or at George Rogers Park in Lake Oswego. Access for both parks is from Oregon Highway 43.

Clackamas River to Willamette Falls

Though much has changed over the past 150 years, one can still imagine what the high basalt bluffs must have looked like when native peoples camped there or fished from the rock formations overhanging the chutes of water in the spring.

Navigating the Locks

Built in 1873 as crucial to the flow of goods up and down the Willamette Valley, the Willamette Falls Locks are purported to be the oldest continually operating multi-chamber locks in the United States. The locks are managed by the U.S. Army Corps of Engineers and provide upriver and downriver access for boats of all sizes, including canoes and kayaks. Since 2002, the locks have been subject to federal budget cuts, which have made their operation a yearly issue. A strong push by local individuals, government officials, and others has helped to secure continued funding to the locks to sustain their staffing and upkeep.

Using the Locks

When the locks are open, from upstream or downstream, paddle to a large gate on the west side of the river and look for the calling device to signal the locks office that you would like to pass through. Because the chambers of the locks drain out faster than they fill up, it only takes about thirty-five minutes to go downstream. Typically it takes about forty-five minutes or more to get upstream. Once in the chamber, Corps employees will lower ropes for paddlers and boaters to hang onto as the water level drops or rises depending on your direction of travel.

As you wait for the water to flow out, you can hear the water dropping off the side boards, and glimpse a few bright green ferns growing in the recessed portions of the locks' wood siding. On occasion, people have shared the locks with large sturgeon that are easy to see moving around under your boat when a locks chamber is near empty—and at its shallowest.

It's best to use the locks in summer months when river flows are relatively gentle. A day trip through the locks can take you from Willamette Park in West Linn to Clackamette Park or vice-versa. For multi-day trips, the locks enable you to avoid a tricky portage or car trip past the locks, enabling travel from the Willamette Valley into the Portland area and Columbia estuaries beyond or the reverse.

Be sure to call ahead to the U.S. Army Corps of Engineers Locks office to see if they are operational (503-656-3381). More than one paddler has been left stranded during repairs or other closures!

The best time to do this paddle is in the summer or early fall, when the river level is lower and currents aren't as strong. Winter and spring prove an extreme challenge to make it upstream, with debris and rushing current meeting the confluence of the Clackamas River.

Just upstream of the **Abernethy Interstate 205 Bridge**, you will notice a row of boathouses at Sportcraft Marina and **boat ramp**. In the spring it is common to spot sea lions lounging at the end of the dock. They've made their way from the Pacific—a 130-mile journey—to hunt for salmon at Willamette Falls. Because the salmon have to negotiate fish ladders at the falls, there is a tendency for the fish to get backed up, making it relatively easy for these whiskered mammals to pluck them off and feast. Farther upstream as you pass under the **Oregon City–West Linn Arch Bridge**, the river flows over a basalt trench that is ninety feet deep in places. Here you can paddle up close to the basalt wall that extends upward toward Highway 99E to a height of forty feet or more. Also, as you pass under the Oregon City Bridge, look toward the west side of the river for a view of the historic **Willamette Falls Locks**. The locks are operational, though over the past few years the U.S. Army Corps has sought to close them. There is a small **Locks Museum** operated by the Corps at the site that can be accessed by land.

The sidewalk at the top of the basalt wall in Oregon City was once a popular place for sturgeon fishing. The deep trench in the river is a spawning and rearing place for these large, long-lived fish. Due to decreases in their population, and recognition that this portion of the Willamette River is a key rearing area for sturgeon, the Oregon Department of Fish and Wildlife closed this area to sturgeon fishing in 2010.

Further upstream are two mills: West Linn Paper Company on the west side and the recently closed Blue Heron Paper to the east. Where Blue Heron sits was once a key part of the old town of Oregon City. You can almost imagine what this may have looked like back in the 1840s, with a thriving small town perched at the edge of the basalt cliff, overlooking Willamette Falls. Today, the mills dominate the scene. As you edge close to the falls you can see some large basalt rocks extending toward the river. If you look closely you might notice some circular petroglyphs in the rock. Willamette Falls was once a key fishery, meeting, and trading place of the Kalapuya and Chinook peoples. As you near the falls, keep an eye out for osprey and waterfowl that sometimes reside in the rocks. During the summer months the water will be a deep greenish blue, and there are multiple places to stop for a moment, unaffected by current, and gaze upward at Willamette Falls. If you stay toward the west shore you can typically stay out of the current. What you might notice is that the falls have a uniform horizon line at the top, as opposed to an uneven line of basalt with water flowing over it. This is due to a wall constructed by Portland General Electric to direct water toward their Sullivan Powerhouse at the edge of the falls, on the west side, adjacent to West Linn Paper Company and the locks.

Sullivan Powerhouse has thirteen hydroelectric turbines that harness the Willamette's flow to generate electricity. This facility underwent a Federal Energy Regulatory Commission re-licensing that was completed in 2007, giving it another thirty years at this spot. As part of the re-licensing, PGE was required to improve both upstream and downstream fish passage for native Willamette spring Chinook and other fish.

While the falls have been manipulated for human purposes, the raw power of the river can be seen when flows are high, and a swath of spray and the roar of the falls can be heard some distance away.

As you make your way back downstream, keep an eye out for Canada geese, mergansers, and the occasional breaching sturgeon—these large fish can give any paddler a jolt when they surface for a moment.

How to Get There

Boat access is at Clackamette Park, at the confluence of the wild Clackamas and more urbanized Willamette. Oregon City's **Jon Storm Park dock**, just upstream a quarter mile from Clackamette Park, also provides good access. Both boat ramps provide relatively close access to Willamette Falls.

BY CAR: Clackamette Park: Take SE McLoughlin Boulevard from the north, and just after you cross the Clackamas River, turn right at the signaled intersection at Dunes Drive (across from the Oregon City Shopping Center). Drive west on Dunes Drive, take a right onto Clackamette Drive, and enter the park where Clackamette Drive swings right and becomes Main Street. Drive through the park to the boat ramp, which puts you into the Clackamas River just upstream from its confluence with the Willamette River. **Jon Storm Park:** Follow the same directions, but turn left on Clackamette Drive (the opposite direction from Clackamette Park) and proceed to the parking lot. There is a long ramp down to the boat dock.

Portland Harbor

Paddling a small craft north of downtown in the Portland harbor may strike some as strange, or seemingly unattractive. While it is certainly a highly industrialized area, and there are related hazards to the small boat user, the harbor can be quite interesting, offering an interlude in an environment that illustrates the amazing resiliency of local wildlife.

From the **Cathedral Park Beach**, you can gain good access to the river. The "beach" is a bit crude, but quite useable. As you approach the boat ramp, look for the trail to the left side of the wooden walkway. The beach largely consists of small rocks, interspersed with river sediment and sand, with pilings poking out near shore. There is a gap in a small wooden breakwater that you can paddle through.

Cathedral Park Launching

There are two launch sites at Cathedral Park, on each side of the bridge. The one on the downstream side, at the end of N Baltimore Street, has a large public parking lot. The dock and ramp upstream of the bridge is more informal and is next to the City of Portland's Bureau of Environmental Service's Water Quality Lab, which won several design awards for its stormwater features.

—Mike Houck

Upstream is **Willamette Cove**, a small natural area on the river's east side, just downstream from the railroad bridge. This small Metro-owned greenspace is "natural" with a qualifier, given the fact that this is a riparian area with a gentle rocky beach, covered in part by a blanket of concrete blocks put in place to maintain a cap of soil which covers polluted sediment. The area has been used extensively for industrial purposes, but today it is home to black cottonwoods and Oregon ash in the upland area. Willamette Cove is just downstream from the small superfund site of **McCormick and Baxter** by the railroad tracks. If

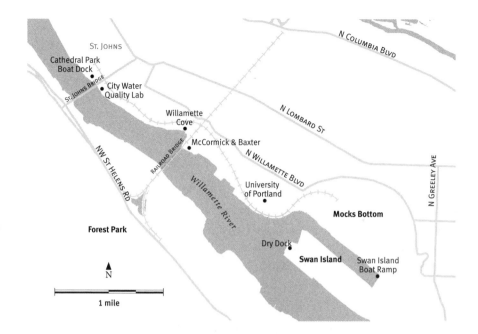

you stay close to shore, you will likely see more wildlife. Interspersed amongst the riprap and terminal bulwarks, you can often find a nice thread of water large enough for a couple of canoes or kayaks.

Downstream of Cathedral Park, you can paddle next to and around piers, pilings, and even ships moored along the river's edge.

As you scan the shoreline, don't be surprised to see spotted sandpipers, Canada geese, and even common mergansers. You may also see bald eagles that hunt the harbor from their nesting sites on Sauvie Island, Ross Island, and beyond. As you travel this stretch of river, try to envision how it once looked, given that most of the extensive historic wetlands have been filled to allow for industrial uses. Because of the once-dense habitat, Lewis and Clark would have missed the Willamette entirely on their 1805–1806 expedition, had it not been for local Native Americans guiding them to the river. Even so, they did not venture upriver very far and did not reach the tremendous falls. Today this reach of the Willamette is dredged to an average depth of forty feet and more in some places.

How to Get There
You can put in at the Swan Island boat ramp or at Cathedral Park underneath the east side of the St. Johns Bridge.

By Travis Williams

Bryant Woods Nature Park

Location: Near the intersection of Childs Road and Canal Road in Lake Oswego, OR **Activities:** Hiking **Facilities:** Parking, Unpaved trails, Interpretive signs **Fees and Regulations:** Pets on leash **Hiking Difficulty:** Easy **Highlights:** A remnant of what was once a large camas meadow in spring; Pileated woodpeckers **Public Transit:** TriMet bus 36

Bryant Woods Nature Park contains a small, wet meadow, a forested upland area, and a stream fed by natural springs. It maintains a connection to the Tualatin River shoreline via adjacent Canal Acres Natural Area. The river greenway and the diversity of habitat types in this seventeen-acre park host a variety of wildlife, particularly birds.

The clean, cold water of Indian Springs is a breeding ground for the northern red-legged frog. Birds to look for include the pileated woodpecker, great blue heron, common yellowthroat, and wood ducks. In the spring, you may also observe the blue flowers of camas (*Camassia quamash*), in a small remnant of what was once a large meadow, ringed by Oregon ash and Oregon white oak. On the eastern edge of the park, Douglas fir and big-leaf maple predominate in a wooded upland area. A warren of short user trails attests to the popularity of this park among neighborhood children.

The main trail at Bryant Woods begins in the parking lot and traces a loop of just over a mile that takes in most of the park, following along the canal, across the northern edge of the park, and back to the parking lot through the wooded upland area on the park's west side. A portion of this trail is formed by the road that once followed along the canal; it is wide and well-graded. This trail would be wheelchair accessible except for a very short section that is unfortunately rocky and uneven. A smaller series of looping trails passes through a wooded seasonal wetland west of the parking lot, where hawthorn predominates. Portions of this trail are flooded during wet weather.

Across Childs Road from Bryant Woods is Canal Acres Natural Area. This thirty-one-acre site, which shares the parking lot for Bryant Woods, is quieter and less visited. The only park development, a wide, linear trail of about a half mile, traces a dry path above a wooded seasonal wetland and ends at the Canal Headgate on the Tualatin River.

Oswego Canal

The camas meadow at Bryant Woods was reduced and the hydrology of the area significantly altered by the construction of the Oswego Canal, which forms the eastern boundary of the park. The canal was hand-dug by Chinese laborers in the 1870s. It was originally constructed to allow Tualatin River steamships to access what was then called Sucker Lake. Now, it controls inflow to that water body, which has been much enlarged and re-christened Oswego Lake.

Access

A loop trail rings the park; a group of short spur trails visit the small, forested wetland in the western leg of the park.

How to Get There

By car: From Oregon Highway 43 in Lake Oswego, turn west (right) on McVey Avenue, and stay straight to continue on SW Stafford Road. Follow Stafford through the traffic circle, then make the next right onto SW Childs Road. Look for the park just past the intersection with Bryant Road, once you pass over the Oswego Canal. **PUBLIC TRANSIT:** TriMet bus 36 stops at SW Pilkington Road and Childs Road, about 0.7 miles away. From the bus stop, walk east on Pilkington to reach the site.

By Jonna Papaefthimiou

More information: City of Lake Oswego Parks & Recreation

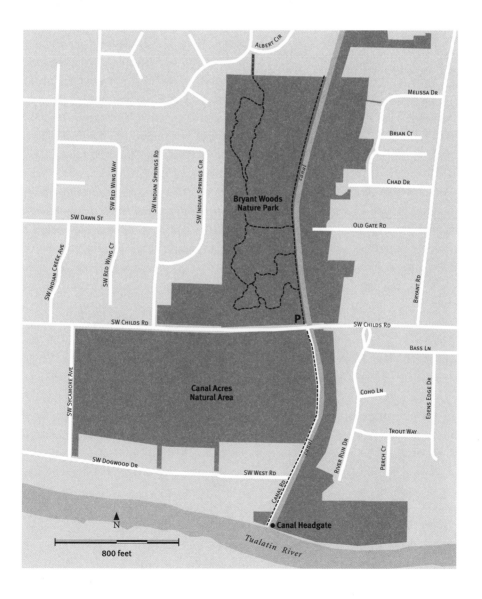

Elk Rock Island

LOCATION: On the east bank of the Willamette River, near SE 19th & SE Sparrow Streets in Milwaukie, OR **ACTIVITIES:** Hiking, Paddling, Boating, Fishing, Birding **FACILITIES:** Spring Park Parking, Paved and unpaved trails, Picnic area, Interpretive signs **FEES AND REGULATIONS:** Hours sunrise to sunset, No pets allowed **HIKING DIFFICULTY:** Moderate **HIGHLIGHTS:** Bald eagles on the banks of the Willamette at Spring Park; The island's grassy landscape of oak woodlands, seasonal pools, and rock gardens are unique in Portland; Elk Rock Natural Area (also known as Peter Kerr Park) includes the inaccessible Elk Rock directly across the river on the west bank, home to a peregrine falcon eyrie and many rare plants; views of Elk Rock Garden at Bishop's Close **PUBLIC TRANSIT:** TriMet bus 33

Elk Rock Island and Elk Rock are are two examples of thin-soiled, rock-outcrop islands and basalt cliffs along the Willamette River between Canby and Portland. The Rock Islands near Canby, The Nature Conservancy's Camassia Natural Area, Hogg or Oak Island near West Linn, and Canemah Bluff near Oregon City are similar landforms. Many of the islands and cliffs in this area, called the Willamette Narrows, have remnant oak and madrone woodlands with openings of prairie grasses and wildflowers. The island's current landscape is thought to have been formed by the Missoula Floods which occurred approximately fifteen thousand years ago. Flood waters from the Columbia River repeatedly inundated the lower Willamette River with over four hundred feet of high-energy water that stripped much of the soil from the underlying basalt bedrock. Since those cataclysmic floods, drought-tolerant oaks and madrone trees, prairie grasses, and wildflowers have colonized the thin, well-drained soils of the island and rock of the surrounding area.

While walking to the island from the trailhead at Spring Park, one can visualize those massive floods, see evidence of their effect on the land and rock formations and, with luck, observe bald eagles. Initially the trail travels downhill and crosses an old Willamette backwater slough channel of willow and cottonwood. Wear boots in the winter as the path is sometimes flooded. As you pass alongside a newer slough channel, stop and listen for an eagle cry or look up and over your right shoulder for their nest in a cottonwood on the slough banks. A short way farther, the path disappears at the edge of a harsh, pockmarked landscape of volcanic rock and isolated pools of water; this is the high-flow channel that seasonally separates the island from the mainland. Check out the rocks as you carefully cross the channel to the island. They are composed of Waverly Heights Basalt, which is thirty to fifty million years old. Its hardness explains why Elk Rock Island exists. After the Waverly Basalt was laid down, subsequent lava flows, called the Columbia River Basalt, topped it. At Elk Rock Island, those later flows were more easily eroded by the high, scouring flows of the Willamette River, leaving the intrusion of the Waverly Heights Basalt exposed in the line of the river, creating the island and the narrows to the west at the foot of Elk Rock.

Once on the island, you can walk the perimeter on graveled trails. Leave the trail at your own risk as poison oak grows everywhere! As you pass through the grassland on the west side of the island, you'll encounter some unusual river-eroded rock basins (filled with rain water in spring) and then a little farther along the trail a stairway leads up to a small woodland of oak, madrone, and wildflowers. The oak woodland area is currently undergoing "oak release"—restoration work that removes encroaching conifers—to ensure the long-term survival of the shade-intolerant Oregon white oak and madrone and their native grass and wildflower associates. See if you can also spot the cinnamon-colored bark of the Pacific yew tree, a small, unusual evergreen that grows in the maple and fir woodlands in the center of the island. As you complete the island loop, at the northwest corner of the island you will find a small inlet and beach. Across the river lies Elk Rock, home to an urban cliff dweller—the peregrine falcon. On another precipice just downriver of the rock is Peter Kerr's former home and garden. Now owned by the Diocese of Oregon, the Elk Rock Garden of the Bishop's Close is open to the public and has wonderful views of the island and river and Mount Hood

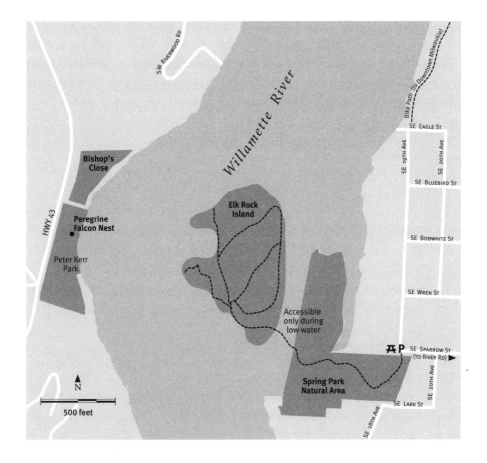

beyond. At the south end of the garden is an extraordinary grove of Pacific madrone and Oregon oak; in the spring, drifts of fawn lilies and false Solomon seal bloom beneath them.

Access

Elk Rock Island can be reached on foot most of the year on a trail through Spring Park and across the high-flow channel that connects the island to the east bank of the Willamette River. However, during times of prolonged heavy rain in winter, and again in late spring and early summer, the island is accessible only by canoe or kayak. The nearest boat ramp is located just downstream in downtown Milwaukie.

How to Get There

BY CAR: From the Ross Island Bridge in Portland, take SE McLoughlin Boulevard (Highway 99E) south four miles to the south end of Milwaukie; veer right onto SE River Road, and after one block turn right (west) on SE Bluebird Street and go approximately one quarter mile. Turn left (south) on SE 19th Street and proceed three blocks to the trailhead at SE 19th Avenue and SE Sparrow Street. The trailhead is on the right. There is limited parking on SE 19th and SE Sparrow. A bike-pedestrian path from SE McLoughlin at the entrance to the water treatment plant takes you to SE Eagle Street and SE 19th Avenue. **PUBLIC TRANSIT:** TriMet bus 33 south to the River Road stops just south of downtown Milwaukie. Walk west to SE 19th Avenue and then south one quarter mile to the Spring Park entrance.

By Mark Griswold Wilson

More information: Elk Rock Island and Elk Rock Natural Areas: Portland Parks & Recreation; Spring Park: North Clackamas Parks & Recreation District; Elk Rock Gardens at the Bishop's Close

Oak Woodlands and Savannahs

THE OREGON WHITE OAK (*Quercus garryana*) figures prominently in the natural and cultural history of the Willamette Valley. Oregon oaks provide food and shelter for a rich diversity of wildlife. Acorns and products from oak-associated plants were harvested and processed for millennia by Native Americans for their sustenance and trade. European explorers marveled at the great expanses of savannah prairie in the maritime Pacific Northwest.

David Douglas, a botanist traveling with a Hudson's Bay Company trapping expedition in 1826, described Oregon's Willamette Valley as a "landscape of undulating grasslands [the] soil rich, light with beautiful solitary oaks and pines interspersed through it ..."

In the early 1850s, about 150,000 acres of oak woodland and oak savannah prairie were recorded in the core of the Portland metropolitan area by land surveyors working

for the U.S. Government Land Office.[1] The woodlands and savannahs the surveyors encountered were not a forested wilderness but rather a landscape that had been shaped originally by the eruptions of Cascade volcanoes and cataclysmic flooding and then later with careful stewardship.

The lava bluffs on the lower Willamette from Cathedral Park in the Portland harbor upriver to Canby have been scoured and exposed by the frequent Columbia River floods that began during the late Pleistocene Epoch (ten thousand years ago). As the sediment-laden floodwater collided with the Tualatin Mountains on its path up the Willamette, cobble and coarse sands were formed into steep escarpments on the east bank of the river upslope of Mocks Bottom and Oaks Bottom. Farther south in the Willamette Narrows near Dunthorpe, Elk Rock, and Canemah, the eroding water carved volcanic basalt into rocky outcrop islands and cliffs. After the floodwaters subsided, drought-tolerant oaks and madrones began to colonize the thin soils on the south- and west-facing slopes of the escarpment and the narrows.

The first peoples of northwest Oregon were active land stewards, regularly re-creating environments in the lower Tualatin and Columbia River Valleys and the upper Willamette to suit their most favored foods. The Kalapuyans, Klikitats, and Chinookans used fire to manage oak woodland and savannah vegetation in order to increase oak, acorn, and camas-bulb production, assist with the gathering of grasshoppers and tarweed, or encircle deer and elk for the hunt. This anthropogenic fire had long-term consequences on our landscape and its flora by ensuring the survival of many shade-intolerant oak woodlands and savannah prairie plants and the wildlife dependent on

Where to Find Oregon Oaks and Madrone

At Waud's Bluff and Mocks Crest in North Portland
> North end of the University of Portland campus overlooking Swan Island—look over the edge of the bluff adjacent to the Lewis and Clark memorial
> Waud's Bluff Trail and the south side of Willamette Boulevard
> Baltimore Woods trail near Cathedral Park

Along the south bluff in the Sellwood and Brooklyn neighborhoods
> SE Sellwood Boulevard at SE 7th Avenue and through Sellwood Park
> Bluff Trail at Oaks Bottom Wildlife Refuge
> Springwater on the Willamette Trail from Oaks Bottom to OMSI

On river terraces, islands, and cliffs
> Willamette Greenway to the Oregon oak grove at Willamette Park in SW Portland
> A madrone woodland at the Elk Rock Garden at Bishop's Close, Dunthorpe
> Elk Rock Island Natural Area in Milwaukie
> Oak Island Trail and in the fields of Bybee Howell Park, Sauvie Island
> A steep, short trail to a unique oak patch on Access Trail #15 in Forest Park

those habitats. It dramatically changed when pioneers arrived in the Oregon Territory; they quickly learned of the fertility of the rich soils and valued the oak for fuel, tools, and lumber. Fires were eliminated and farmers' plows, cows, and invasive species forever changed the valley's "undulating grasslands ... with beautiful solitary oaks and pines...." Many of the Native American elders, who had learned the traditional ecological knowledge of oak woodland and savannah management from their ancestors, passed on too.

Despite this great change, Oregon oaks and the plant and wildlife communities associated with them survive in small places. Recently it was discovered that some oak woodlands in our urban landscape contain intact remnant populations of locally rare and regionally significant plant communities. Over two hundred species of amphibians, reptiles, mammals, and birds are known to use the tree within its range in western Oregon and Washington.[2] Big, old, and isolated Oregon white oaks may have great value for biodiversity by providing stepping-stone connections between fragmented habitats. With the onset of climate change, the habitat connections these legacy trees provide may be an important way to help some wildlife migrate to new, more suitable places to live.[3]

We now realize that in order to ensure the long-term survival of the oak-plant community and the many wildlife species dependent on oak habitats, active ecological restoration work is needed. Recently both small- and large-scale habitat restoration projects have been initiated in the Portland-metro area. Slowly we are learning how to restore and manage oak habitat and developing ecological knowledge that is akin to the traditional knowledge of the Native Americans, who cared for the once-vast oak woodland and savannahs.

By Mark Griswold Wilson, illustration by Allison Bollman

1. The core of the Portland-metro area was recently defined by Christy, Kimpo, et al as the area within a fifteen-mile radius of downtown Portland. This area encompasses approximately seven hundred square miles and includes portions of Clark County in Washington, Multnomah, Clackamas, and Washington Counties in Oregon. For additional information about the historic and existing oak woodlands and savannahs in Portland see: Christy, John A., Angela Kimpo, Vernon Marttala, Philip K. Gaddis, and Nancy L. Christy. 2009. Native Plant Society of Oregon Occasional Paper 3: 1-319.

2. Johnson, David H., Thomas A. O'Neil, T.A. 2001. *Wildlife Habitat Relationships in Oregon and Washington*. Corvallis: Oregon State University Press.

3. Rojas-Burke, Joe. "Large oak trees play a crucial role in the Willamette Valley ecosystem." *The Oregonian*: April 10, 2009.

Aliens Among Us

REMEMBER THE MOVIE *ALIEN*? I do: all scrunched down in my seat, palms sweating, and eyes barely peeking over the seat in front of me. Why the tension? Ridley Scott's a great director, but my angst had much more to do with my introductory parasitology class at Iowa State University, which put the fear of God into me of creatures that take up residence in their human host, or any host for that matter. When it comes to parasites, ignorance is bliss. Knowledge gained in Parisitology 101 tipped me off to the infinite number of beings, mostly microscopic—whether horrid hookworms, pernicious pinworms, or disgusting flukes—that wreak havoc on the human body. I have no doubt that Sigourney Weaver's nemesis is out there ... watching, waiting.

My fascination and fear of parasites may be overblown given that, to my knowledge, I've had only one personal encounter. A few years ago, I was infected with two botfly larvae that were deposited by a sneaky Costa Rican mosquito, whose whining buzz was cunningly muffled to the extent that I was unaware that she was delivering her dipteran package while sucking blood from my arm. The mosquito and botfly have an ecologically elegant relationship. The fly, too noisy and clumsy to deliver its own eggs to a warm-blooded mammal, catches a mosquito, deposits its eggs on the mosquito's belly, and releases it to do its bidding unwittingly. While the mosquito sucks your blood, the eggs erupt, Alien-like, in response to body heat. A creepy but ingenious delivery system.

If you share my fascination with the concept of one life form inhabiting the body of another, but prefer that other isn't you, there are fortunately plenty of opportunities to study parasites from a safe distance. As it turns out, there are myriad examples of similar host-parasite relationships in the plant kingdom. My earliest experience with plant parasites came during a spring break backpack trip down the John Day River in the early 1970s. My inexperience with local flora was revealed when I brought a leafy, pineapple-like "cone" to the morning campfire for show and tell and was informed that what I had taken for a western juniper cone was, in fact, an insect gall. I sliced the dark green "cone" in half with my Swiss Army knife, revealing a tiny parasitic wasp, curled up inside a womb-like cavity. It bore an eerie resemblance to what later I'd see as the Alien.

There are thousands of plant galls, which are abnormal growths caused by a host of organisms including viruses, bacteria, fungi, and insects. When an insect deposits its young into an oak tree, for example, its saliva causes the tree to create a mass of cells that walls off the invading young insect while creating a safe, moist environment

for the insect to mature through the larval and pupal stages. It eventually gnaws its way out of the gall when it reaches maturity. Apparently, the gall-inducing insect even controls the gall's morphology, not the plant. It's also been speculated that the tannin-rich environment supplied by the plant's response confers protection to the larva from fungal invasion.

In the Pacific Northwest, some of the most abundant and largest galls occur on our native Oregon white oak (*Quercus garryana*). In fact, more than 80 percent of galls in North America are on various species of oak trees. When I moved into an apartment in Southwest Portland, back in the mid-1970s and shortly after my John Day back-packing trip, I was attracted by the number of huge, apple-like growths on the oak tree in our front yard. This time I knew that the bulbous, dun-colored growths were not associated with oak reproduction. I also noticed much smaller, reddish, freckled growths on the underside of the oak's leaves.

Sure enough, slicing the gall open with my Swiss Army knife revealed a white, spongy, watery mass of cells, in the middle of which was a hard capsule that when cut apart revealed numerous chambers, each with a creature similar in appearance to the wasp I found in the juniper gall—an amber-colored cynipid wasp. On other occasions I've opened samples of what is the largest gall in the Northwest, the "bullet" or "green apple" gall, and found that the chambers were full of smaller, black wasps, which had parasitized the larger cynipid wasp. While a gall provides a safe environment for a wasp to transition from egg to larva to pupa, eventually eating its way out as a winged adult, the gall is not always impervious to attack by what are known as hyperparasites—parasites that attack another parasite. As the saying goes, "Big fleas have little fleas upon their backs to bite 'em and little fleas have lesser fleas, and so ad infinitum...."

Where the Galls Are

The second most obvious oak gall in the metro region is the smaller, perfectly round, speckled gall. As you walk the Oaks to Wetlands Trail at Ridgefield National Wildlife Refuge, along the paths of Graham Oaks Nature Park in Wilsonville, through the dwarf oak woodland at Camassia Natural Area in West Linn, or along the Terwilliger Boulevard bicycle-pedestrian path near OHSU, look at the fallen oak leaves. It's impossible to miss the speckled galls, which are invariably attached, several to the leaf, usually to the mid-vein or one of the larger secondary leaf veins. These galls, which are formed by another cynipid species (*Besbicus mirabilis*) are specific to Oregon white oaks and occur from northern California to British Columbia. As with the larger "green apple" gall, some trees are infested with huge numbers of galls while adjacent trees are gall free. What starts out as a solid structure in late spring gradually hollows out into the summer months until the once-hard central capsule is supported by a mass of tiny hairs projecting outward from the capsule and attached to the gall's inner wall. Unlike the green apple gall, the single-chambered capsule harbors but a single larva. Interestingly, the larva excretes no waste into its home, waiting until it pupates and emerges as an adult to relieve itself. Very few of the wasps actually make it to adulthood, as they are frequently attacked by another parasitic wasp. Moth caterpillars also invade the speckled gall, eating everything in their path, including the original cynipid gall former.

One of the most amazing things about the speckled gall is that the cynipid wasp that causes it exhibits "alternation of generations." Only asexual females emerge from the speckled galls after which they lay eggs on the buds of oak leaves. The eggs hatch, and the resulting larvae stimulate the buds to produce unspectacular, minuscule galls, from which both males and females emerge in late spring. These sexual males and females then mate; a female lays eggs on the underside of the leaf and *voila!* Another speckled gall is formed.

If I had to choose but one species of native tree to plant with the goal of attracting the greatest diversity of native wildlife it would be Oregon white oak. Not only do oaks attract a unique suite of birds, but they are also tremendous invertebrate magnets, including a host of gall-inducing insects. In addition to green apple and speckled galls, Oregon white oak plays host to twig galls, jumping galls, spherical stem galls—at least thirteen galls—which, with the exception of oak leaf erinea (mites) and oak pit scale (scale insect), are all caused by wasps. While you are exploring the region for galls, you should also look on willows, black cottonwood, roses, thimbleberry, hawthorn, serviceberry, snowberry, poison oak, filberts, ash, and Douglas fir, all of which have their own complement of galls.

By Mike Houck, illustration by Elayne Barclay

Springwater on the Willamette Trail
Rose Quarter to Oaks Bottom Wildlife Refuge

If you're looking for a ten-mile roundtrip ride from the intensely urban to a wilder landscape, with several side-trip possibilities, this is a must-do bike ride. It's eminently walkable as well. I like to start at the **Rose Quarter** transit mall, although there are innumerable places to join or leave the route. My preference is to ride from the Rose Quarter to the **Peace Memorial Park** entrance and take the ramp down to the Vera Katz Eastbank Esplanade. The 1.5-mile esplanade extends from the Steel Bridge south to the Hawthorne Bridge, from where you continue south to Oaks Bottom Wildlife Refuge along the Springwater on the Willamette bicycle-pedestrian trail.

Ride south along the esplanade, which was designed by Mayer/Reed landscape architects and dedicated in the spring of 2001. Make frequent stops to check out the twenty-two interpretive panels depicting historical and natural history highlights along the Willamette. While cyclists seem to love jetting down the ramps that access the 1,200-foot **floating walkway** (the nation's longest) use care riding over the expansion plates. They were designed to allow the walkway to rise and fall up to thirty feet with the tides and river level, and therefore are both noisy and prone to catch a bicycle wheel. Given the sometimes-large mix of walkers, strollers, and runners, it's wise to slow down while cycling the esplanade anyway.

Even though the thin strip of willow and spirea is sparse along the esplanade, it still has many birds. Soon after construction I was amazed to see a sock-like, pendulous bushtit nest hanging not two feet from the trail, the mousy-gray mom flying in and out to feed her young. Hundreds of walkers and cyclists passed by without giving a hint that they saw the nest. Nearby, a diminutive downy woodpecker pecked at the stem of another willow, gleaning insects; a flock of American goldfinches were snatching downy thistle seeds; and a song sparrow male was marking his territory from atop a yellow wooly mullein. Farther down the trail I watched as a Cooper's hawk plucked and ate a plump rock pigeon from its perch in a western redcedar under the Hawthorne Bridge. It's even possible to see the occasional sea lion from the esplanade.

The riverbank has been reshaped here and there to allow for shallow-water habitat, and bioengineered with native plants that pre-treat Interstate 5 runoff before it enters the river. More than 280 trees and 43,695 shrubs, mostly Oregon natives, have been planted along the esplanade to provide a small amount of wildlife habitat.

Under the **Hawthorne Bridge**, I usually stop at the Portland Fire Station to use the port-a-potties or get a drink at the water fountain by the inlay representing the Willamette River and its tributaries and next to the large blocks of Columbia River basalt. I find if I stand on one of the basalt blocks I can see the entire inlaid piece of the river's course from its confluence with the Columbia to its headwaters east of Eugene. A nearby overlook juts out over the Willamette and provides access to the boat ramp.

The **Portland Boat House** is home to numerous rowing clubs, crews, and a coffee shop, and is also headquarters for Willamette Riverkeeper and Alder Creek Kayak and Canoe. Should you want to rent a kayak or canoe on a return trip, you can launch for a paddle upstream to Ross Island from the nearby **boat dock** that was built to accommodate human-powered watercraft. At **OMSI** I like to check out the two overlooks with **interpretive signs**.

Peregrine Falcons, Art, and Eagles

More often than not, especially during nesting season, if I scan the Marquam Bridge from the overlooks adjacent to OMSI I can catch a view of the peregrine falcons, chasing down or chowing down on a rock pigeon—feathers wafting in the breeze as the falcon plucks its prey clean. Amazingly, 6 percent of all peregrines in Oregon nest on Portland-area bridges, the Fremont nest being the most productive in the state. From the OMSI overlooks there are also great views across the Willamette and the first view of the downstream tip of Ross Island as well as the South Waterfront towers on the river's west bank.

Heading south past OMSI and approaching the Opera House there's a large map that orients you to the rest of your ride. Once through the arched entrance to the Springwater on the Willamette, adjacent to the Ross Island Sand and Gravel batch plant, the rest of the ride is off-street.

Along the way keep an eye out for picnic benches and pieces of sculpture that were installed as part of Portland's Percent for Art program, which secures a percentage of construction costs for the installation of art along public transportation projects.

By now I'm ready for a stop at the grassy slope that's full of weedy wildflowers and shrubs, Oregon white oak, and big-leaf maple, along with several picnic benches for my first look at the **Holgate Channel** and **Ross Island**. This is a great place for a snack, birding, or just relaxing and enjoying scenic river views.

Keep an eye out for bald eagles, which nest on Ross Island, and for osprey, which have several nests along the route. In the spring, before the cottonwoods have leafed, I get out my binoculars or spotting scope to check out the great blue herons busily rebuilding their flimsy condominium-like communal nests that stand out in the tall black cottonwoods near the downstream tip of Ross Island. Their colonial nesting behavior provides safety in numbers, although bald eagles have been seen taking young herons from the nests on occasion. It will be interesting to see if the herons continue to nest on Ross Island, given that they've already been displaced once by the eagles, which set up housekeeping in the Ross Island Lagoon.

Ross Island Lagoon

I always scan across the Ross Island Lagoon to the large stand of black cottonwoods jutting out from the west side. Before the cottonwood leaves appear you can just make out the eagles' bulky stick nest. Oftentimes I see Ross Island Sand and Gravel barges entering and leaving the lagoon, either bringing in raw materials from the Columbia Gorge to be processed in huge crushers and conveyors on Hardtack Island, or taking the finished products to market.

Riding south, paralleling the Holgate Channel, you'll reach the northern end of the 160-acre **Oaks Bottom Wildlife Refuge** (see page 76). The forest along the channel is Oregon white ash, black cottonwood, and western redcedar, with a blue and red elderberry, stinging nettle, creek dogwood, and fern understory. I sometimes park my bike and take the pedestrian-only dirt path that winds from a small wooden stile through the riparian forest for about a mile. It is a nice alternative to the busy Springwater trail, and on hot summer days a cool, shady retreat for hikers. The forest is frequently alive with brown creepers, black-capped chickadees, ruby-crowned and golden-crowned kinglets, spotted towhees, Swainson's thrushes, and Bewick's wrens. In the fall look for brilliantly hued yellow slime molds covering the abundant downed willows.

If I'm riding, however, I usually press on south to the entrance to Oaks Bottom Wildlife Refuge's north meadow, which is immediately across from a wooden stile where the pedestrian path emerges. Beyond the stile there is an overlook that provides views of Holgate Channel, East Island, and Hardtack Island. During winter especially, I expect to see the striking white-bodied, green-headed common merganser, which also sports a blood-red bill. River otter play along the banks here as well. Each time I look at the interpretive sign, which depicts changes to Ross and her sister islands from 1852 surveyor's maps to the modern-day configuration of the archipelago, I'm amazed at how much the islands and the course of the Willamette have changed in the intervening 160 years.

Farther south I keep my binoculars handy as I approach the expansive views of the Oaks Bottom Wildlife Refuge wetlands to the east and sweeping vistas of the

Willamette River to the west. For years osprey and Canada geese have set up house on the artificial nesting structures perched atop the erector set–like power poles that border the rail line. One of the most productive stops is at the culvert where the **Willamette River connects with the bottom** ❶, filling the wetlands when the river level is high and draining them during low-water periods. From this vantage during the summer and early fall, I look upstream to the **Oregon Yacht Club's houseboat row** ❷, scanning for purple martins that nest in the large white gourds that hang off a pole from the farthest downstream houseboat. This is also a favorite haunt of the increasingly large population of river otter, which sometimes haul themselves out onto the boom logs or houseboat decks to dine on fish they've caught in the Holgate Channel. Across the river is Willamette Park, a favorite launching point for a Ross Island paddle (see page 85).

A bit farther on I usually dismount, and if I have a scope with me I scan the open water pond ❸ and check out the spectacular 55,000-square-foot wetland mural on the Portland Memorial Mausoleum and Crematorium ❹. In wintertime the pond is full of wintering waterfowl, including hooded and common mergansers, bufflehead, northern shoveler, ring-necked ducks, lesser scaup, green-winged teal, gadwall, pied-billed grebes, and Canada geese, along with the occasional great egret. If the waterfowl take to the skies in a frenzied mass, either a bald eagle or peregrine falcon is likely nearby looking for an easy meal. The pond is also a prime hangout for as many as one hundred great blue heron that feed here year-round.

Another decision point on the trip comes at the **Oaks Amusement Park** ❺, where a ramp provides access to the park's entry road and to the railroad underpass that leads to the Oaks Bottom Wildlife Refuge pedestrian-only **loop trail** ❻. There's also a great **interpretive sign** ❼ that describes the old inter-urban rail system that is rapidly being converted to a regional bicycle and pedestrian trail network.

Again, if I'm on my bike, I continue south another quarter mile to SE Spokane Street and the Springwater trailhead. If I'm in a hurry I'll simply turn around and head back to the Rose Quarter. For a longer ride I'll continue south and east along the **Springwater Corridor** ❽ to Gresham and Boring and the Cazadero Trail (see page 223). I generally like loops, so more often than not I'll cross over the Willamette on the Sellwood Bridge and head back to the Rose Quarter via the **Willamette River Greenway** ❾ through Willamette Park, South Waterfront, and Tom McCall Waterfront Park to the Steel Bridge.

By Mike Houck

Oaks Bottom Overlook

If you want a fabulous overview of Oaks Bottom Wildlife Refuge, take the Springwater on the Willamette esplanade to SE Spokane Street, and then take a left on SE 7th Avenue. Follow SE 7th past Sellwood Park's swimming pool to SE Sellwood Boulevard, which curves to the east, providing a panorama of Oaks Bottom, the Willamette River, and the downtown skyline. For access to a host of restaurants, pubs, coffee shops, and other local services continue to SE 13th Avenue, which curves into SE Bybee Boulevard, and head to downtown Sellwood at SE Milwaukie Avenue.

North Meadow Side Trip

Turn left and uphill, under the railroad bridge, and the paved path takes you across Oaks Bottom's north meadow and wetlands. The path also provides you with the option of either continuing on to the north parking area or to the entrance of the Oaks Bottom Wildlife Refuge loop, a pedestrian-only unpaved path.

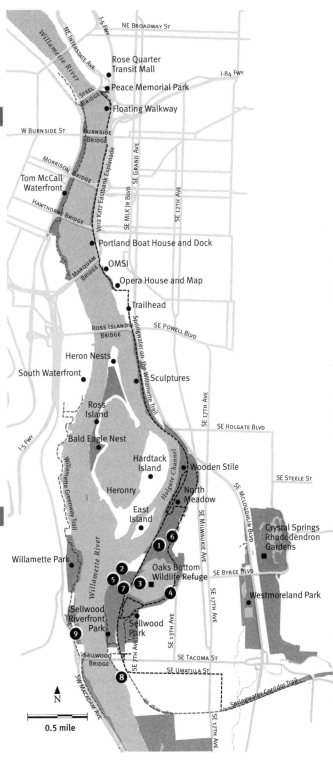

Oaks Bottom Wildlife Refuge

LOCATION: SE Sellwood Boulevard and SE 7th Avenue, Portland **ACTIVITIES:** Hiking, Biking, Wildlife viewing **FACILITIES:** Restrooms, Parking, Paved and unpaved trails, Interpretive signs **FEES AND REGULATIONS:** Pets on leash **HIKING DIFFICULTY:** Easy, Moderate **HIGHLIGHTS:** Great birding year round; Wonderful close-in, two-mile easy walk; Views of the Willamette River **PUBLIC TRANSIT:** TriMet buses 19, 33

In the late 1960s, Oaks Pioneer Park was well on its way to conversion to industrial development and a site for a children's museum, locomotive museum, and a variety of other development scenarios. As early as 1963 the Audubon Society of Portland, Sierra Club, and The Nature Conservancy advocated for Oaks Pioneer Park to be established as Wapato Marsh Wildlife Refuge. In the early 1970s, the Sellwood-Moreland Improvement League argued for the creation of Oaks Bottom as a city natural area, largely to combat the spread of noisy motorcycles. As improbable as it seems today, Portland Parks had recommended that a ten-acre motorcycle facility be carved out of the bottoms, a proposal that was quickly rescinded under a flood of neighborhood-generated letters lambasting the idea.

In 1972, Portland State University urban studies students embarked on a project to develop four scenarios for Oaks Bottom, including a recommendation that the city lease Oaks Bottom to the Audubon Society of Portland, which would manage the wetlands and riparian areas, but that the north and south fills be opened to other recreational uses. Audubon countered that the entire Bottoms should be a wildlife refuge. In 1988, Portland City Council adopted the Oaks Bottom Wildlife Refuge Management Plan, which was developed by Portland park staff, Audubon Society of Portland, a wetland ecologist from the Environmental Protection Agency, Cleveland High School, and the Soil and Water Conservation District. That action established Oaks Bottom as the city's first official urban wildlife refuge. Today, the City Nature Division of Portland Parks & Recreation is the steward of the 160-acre wetland, which was designated by the Audubon Society as a nationally significant Important Bird Area.

Birding the Bottoms

A casual saunter around the wetlands takes two to three hours, depending on how often you stop to watch herons, eagles, and waterfowl. I like to hang out in the Sellwood Park parking lot, where for several years a male Anna's hummingbird has been busy in the treetops, tenaciously guarding his territory. Anna's are year-round residents, so if you see a hummer during mid-winter it's more than likely an Anna's. White-breasted nuthatches also frequent the Oregon white oaks at the north end of the parking lot.

Before starting the two-mile loop, take a short walk to one of the benches located on the grassy strip along SE Sellwood Boulevard. The bluff overlook offers spectacular views of Oaks Bottom, Ross Island, and the Willamette River. The wetlands spread out into the distance, creating a dramatic greensward between the Sellwood neighborhood and Ross Island, the high-rise condos at South Waterfront, and the downtown skyline, which contrasts starkly with the green foreground. This is also a good vantage point to view the 55,000-square-foot wetland mural on the Portland Memorial Mausoleum that overlooks Oaks Bottom to the east. The mural, depicting resident and migratory wetland species common to Oaks Bottom, was a project of the Urban Greenspaces Institute and ArtFX Murals. Completed in fall 2010, it is the nation's largest hand-painted building mural.

To begin the loop trail, return to the parking lot and continue past the parking area to the map and interpretive sign that marks the trailhead. The trail down the bluff can be muddy if it's been raining. You've got a choice of walking clockwise or counterclockwise around the bottoms. To go clockwise, continue straight ahead, downhill to the south meadow. Once at the south meadow continue north on the dirt path paralleling the Springwater on the Willamette trail. In the 1960s and into the early 1970s, what is now a grassy, open meadow was a smoldering, festering landfill. In the early 1980s, ring-necked pheasant and California quail were common sights here. Unfortunately, illegal off-leash dogs have put an end to ground-nesting birds.

Park ecologists have worked with the fire bureau to ensure that the grassland habitat of the south meadow remains free of woody vegetation by using controlled burns to kill off encroaching shrubs and trees. Scan the shrubby habitat for golden-crowned sparrows, spotted towhees, western scrub-jays, and the occasional fox sparrow. Anna's hummingbirds are common as well. In summer, violet-green, cliff, and barn swallows work the large, open, grassy field. Continue walking north until you reach the open pond at the south end of the wetlands. Take a left and pass under the Springwater trail and railroad tracks, and head up the ramp.

Once on the Springwater head north, being aware that cyclists speed along the flat, arrow-straight, paved path. Caution is especially important if you are accompanying children. Keeping to the right as you walk north, scan the pond, which is normally full of waterfowl in winter. Great blue heron are a common sight year-round as are bald eagles. Commonly seen waterfowl include the northern shoveler, green-winged

Portland Memorial Mural

In the winter of 1991 I asked ArtFX Murals owner Mark Bennett if he would paint a giant great blue heron on the west-facing wall of the Portland Memorial Mausoleum overlooking Oaks Bottom Wildlife Refuge. Mark installed a seventy-foot by fifty-foot heron, designed by Portland artist Lynn Kitagawa, which was dedicated on May 18 of that year.

Seventeen years later, Mark asked when we were going to "finish the job," meaning painting the remaining blank walls of the mausoleum. A week later, we met on site to review the eight west- and south-facing walls overlooking Oaks Bottom.

Soon after, the ArtFX team went to work creating the largest hand-painted building mural in North America—a 55,000-square-foot homage to wildlife common to Oaks Bottom.

teal, American wigeon, gadwall, ruddy duck, bufflehead, mallard, ring-necked duck, and the occasional lesser scaup. Common mergansers and pied-billed grebes also frequent the open pond. By early summer, the waterfowl have departed for their nesting grounds and have been supplanted by osprey, which are harassed by eagles seeking to steal a carp or two from the migratory "fish hawks."

Proceeding north along the Springwater trail, be aware of the riparian forest to the left and wetlands to the right. You'll hear, and perhaps see, cedar waxwings, black-capped chickadees, Anna's hummingbirds, song sparrows, black-headed grosbeaks, and Bewick's wrens. Farther along is an expansive view of the Willamette River. Keeping an eye out for cyclists, cross over to the riverside and scope out the Willamette for river otter and mergansers. After mid-May, look upstream to the left, where large, white gourds hang from poles at the downstream end of the Oregon Yacht Club. Those are purple martins nests

Another half mile north the trail takes a steep dip. Cyclists get up a good head of steam here too, so look carefully both ways before crossing to the left where there is an interpretive sign depicting the contrast between the Ross Island archipelago of 1852 and today's Ross Island complex. Continue through the stile and walk a short distance for a scenic overview of the Holgate Channel, East Island, and Hardtack Island. Near the overlook there is an unpaved path that runs north through the riparian forest. If you plan to continue your walk north to downtown Portland and want a respite from the paved path, this dirt path is the ticket: it runs north through the forest for about a mile and then rejoins the Springwater trail.

However, if you want to continue a loop walk, retrace your steps to the interpretive sign and cross the Springwater trail, (again, looking both ways for cyclists), and walk east through the underpass. You are now walking across rubble deposited from construction of the Interstate 405 freeway in the late 1960s and early 1970s. Fortunately for us, civic leader John Gray and another philanthropist negotiated with Drake Construction Company, which had plans to develop the north fill into an industrial park, and persuaded the company to sell it to them. The land was held until the city was able to purchase it, at cost. Today, after removal of invasive, non-native vegetation and planting of native shrubs and trees by Portland Parks & Recreation and the Bureau of Environmental Services, what was an unsightly fill is now a wildlife-friendly meadow and wetlands.

The paved path, which curves east, passes a shallow pond and interpretive signs on the left. The pond was constructed to provide breeding habitat for frogs and salamanders and as an environmental educational site. Birds common to the north meadow include lesser goldfinches, northern flicker, and in the spring and summer, warbling vireos, Wilson's warblers, and yellow-rumped warblers.

Continue on the paved path that traverses the forested wetland until it curves sharply to the left. On the right is a stile that leads to the pedestrian-only unpaved path

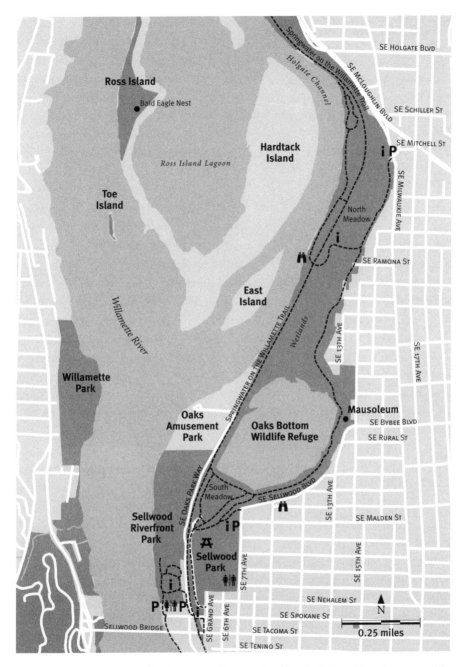

that continues the loop walk. If you take the paved trail to the left you'll end your ramble at the parking lot on SE Milwaukie Avenue. To continue the loop, take the unpaved path along the eastern edge of the wetlands. When you reach the wooden bridge you descend off the north meadow to a forested wetland. The slope on the left has benefited from massive restoration efforts that have removed invasive English ivy and Himalayan

Amphibians—frogs, salamanders, and toads—are in trouble. Loss of habitat, competition from foreign invaders, and diseases have taken a toll on amphibians, locally and globally. The Tadpole Pond at Oaks Bottom was dug with heavy, earthmoving equipment in 2005 and planted with native vegetation by elementary school students in 2007 to provide Pacific chorus frogs, long-toed salamanders, red-legged frogs, and Oregon salamanders a place to breed in safety. This amphibian haven is located next to the paved path on the bottom's north meadow and wetlands.

blackberry. Following removal of the non-native plants, grasses have been planted to stabilize the steep, slide-prone slopes.

Look for subtle vegetation changes along the path. The combination of a more southerly exposure and apparently well-drained soil yields a slightly drier plant community that includes Oregon white oak and a scattering of Pacific madrone. This area is being managed to maintain an open oak-savannah habitat that is distinctly different from the big-leaf maple–dominated habitat near Sellwood Park. Continue walking along the path to the Portland Memorial Mausoleum. Here you can get great close-up views of the huge mural. The portrait of a man peering out of one of the lower windows is of Al Miller, an early refuge proponent.

This part of the walk provides excellent views of the emergent marsh and open water. Take your time and glass the shallow water along the trail's edge for green heron, green-winged teal, red-winged blackbirds, and wood ducks. The trail arcs around the open water and heads west until you arrive, once again, at the south meadow. Turn left and proceed up the switchbacks to the trailhead at Sellwood Park, the end of your two-mile ramble.

Access

Three locations: A parking lot and trailhead on SE Milwaukie Avenue just past the off-ramp from SE McLoughlin; a parking lot at the north end of Sellwood Park at SE 7th Avenue and SE Sellwood Boulevard; the Springwater on the Willamette trail.

How to Get There

BY CAR: From the west side of the Willamette River take the Sellwood Bridge and turn left (north) onto SE 7th Avenue. Park in the parking lot at the north end of Sellwood Park (where SE 7th curves east as SE Sellwood Boulevard). A few feet from the parking lot is a trailhead that winds down the bluff (keep right) to the bottoms. From the east or north take the SE Milwaukie exit off SE McLoughlin Boulevard and turn immediately right into the parking lot that overlooks Oaks Bottom's north meadow. If you prefer a longer walk or bicycle ride you can also access from the Springwater on the Willamette trail. **PUBLIC TRANSIT:** There is a TriMet bus stop at the north parking lot on SE Milwaukie Avenue. TriMet also stops on SE 13th Avenue, a short walk from the trailhead at Sellwood Park. TriMet buses 19, 33

By Mike Houck

Ancient Futures

SQUEALS, SHOUTS, AND LAUGHTER fill the air as the first and second graders from Portland Public Schools Indian Education program's summer school step off the number 19 TriMet bus at Oaks Bottom Wildlife Refuge. Their excitement and anticipation of adventure is contagious. We all laugh—you'd think we were outside for the first time in our lives. But it's not the first time, and the parent chaperones begin to remember their own childhoods spent near rivers, under the trees. It's a warm day, and we head for shade down the paved road that marks the north trailhead of Oaks Bottom.

Since the beginning of time, people have gathered at the confluence of the Columbia and Willamette Rivers to trade, to fish, to sing, to dig, to play and visit, to share stories and food, to exchange ideas and information. As is the custom, tribal communities planned, acted, and lived in consideration of future generations, guided by values that recognize and respect the relationships between humans, plants, animals, water, and earth.

It's cooler beneath the young Douglas firs and western redcedars. Solomon runs over to a cedar and touches the trunk, "The Tree of Life!" His dad helped him make a hat from the inner bark of a redcedar last year, and he wore it one day to summer school for a celebration. The other children join him, patting the branches, squeezing the soft fronds and sniffing. "Ahhhh, smells good!" They crowd together inside the green skirt of sweeping tree arms that touch the earth. The parents stand close by, breathe deep, and remember.

Our next stop is the meadow to watch for deer and *anything* moving. We've talked about how the women burned fields to keep sun-loving plants like camas from being shaded out by too many evergreen trees, and to keep the land open for game like deer and elk to nibble fresh shoots. Tashina reminds everyone that we're making too much noise, and we're scaring the deer away. We have forgotten to use only our eyes, ears, and noses ... too much talking. She also reminds us that we've missed the camas; we're too late. She's right. The beautiful, blue-purple wildflowers bloom in May, and it's late July.

Known by indigenous people as *Nich'wana*, the Big River, the Columbia River watershed and foodshed have offered an abundance of salmon, sturgeon and eels, deer and elk, roots and tubers like camas and wapato, and an unrivaled diversity of berries. Its salmon runs were legend, providing a rich and healthy lifestyle for the People from the Plateau to the ocean. The salmon were running, rivers were flowing, bellies were full, life was good.

We arrive at the tadpole pond, but before we enter we gather near the hedge of native roses. The red jewels, rosehips, we tasted last October are gone and the pink, five-petaled flowers stand just above the children's reach. "Let's smell, let's smell! Let's taste, let's taste!" We offer our Thank You song. I pinch several stems of roses and pass to the children and parents. After lots of sniffing, each person takes one petal and slips it into their mouth. We cluster together, silent, and taste. One parent says she's had rosehips, but didn't know you could eat the flowers. Harry tells her, "We make tea! We make tea with Douglas fir, cedar, Oregon grape, and roses so we don't get sick!" He's off to join his classmates, who are now edging expertly near what little water is left in the pond to watch for red-legged frogs.

Introducing children to the many gifts of the plant world is a multi-sensory, multi-generational experience that introduces them to the gifts each of them carries within. Learning when, what, and how to gather, and knowing the medicinal and nutritional benefits of plants is valuable knowledge, but inherent in that knowledge are the cultural values of reciprocity, respect, and responsibility to the well-being of future generations. In learning a song to sing before gathering branches and leaves for our wintertime tea, the children become aware of relationships that exist and must be cultivated with other life forms beyond the human scale. Expressions of gratitude and respect—vibrations of energy—change the chemistry in their bodies, in the bodies of the plants, the water, and the very air that carries the sound waves of their song. The tea made from plants gathered in such a way is doubly healing and contains the power to nurture and nourish whoever drinks from the pot.

Beautiful but Deadly

Purple loosestrife (*Lythrum salicaria*), a non-native, invasive plant, has largely taken over the wetlands at Oaks Bottom Wildlife Refuge. Its native range is Eurasia, Europe, Russia, Japan, and parts of China and India. It's as beautiful as it is disruptive to native wetland ecosystems. As its name implies, the flowers are a deep purple and when it blooms in Oaks Bottom it can take your breath away. Unfortunately, it also takes wildlife habitat away as it outcompetes and replaces native grasses, sedges, and other flowering plants that provide a higher quality source of nutrition for wildlife. It forms dense, homogeneous mats that exclude native vegetation.

As with many invasive plants, it was introduced into the U.S., in this case in the nineteenth century, as an ornamental plant and for medicinal purposes. It flowers from June to September, although recently the Oaks Bottom loosestrife seems to bloom later in the summer, likely due to varying water levels. So far, the introduction of three insect species for natural biological control of the loosestrife does not seem to be greatly affecting Oaks Bottom's scourge. It is hoped that the biological control will be effective in the long term to avoid the use of herbicides in the wetlands—a tricky endeavor.

—Mike Houck

No frogs are visible, but when Nisa rises from the pond, a traveler has attached himself to her shirt. I watch her face instantly recover from an initial reaction of horror to thrill as she stares eye to eye with a three-inch praying mantis. She steps carefully over sticks and rocks, head back, chest protruding, to proudly show off her new friend. The other children are exhilarated and crowd around her. Some of the chaperones have covered their mouths to hide their gasps. One parent takes Nisa's hand and slowly guides her through the throngs, like royalty, to a mossy hazelnut tree where she leans in so the praying mantis can disembark. Everyone's excited—Nisa proclaims she is now part of the Oaks Bottom habitat—one of our new words.

We still have the river and the wetland to see, so we hurry as fast as thirteen children and five adults can when they're stopping for every butterfly, centipede, and possible deer sighting. We look both ways for bikes before getting on the Springwater on the Willamette trail and heading south toward the "really big pond." Several boys say they can't wait to get a big bike and go fast! The air is filled with "summer snow," the fluff of cottonwood buds riding the wind with their sweet balsam aroma released by the heat of the afternoon. Our group stays to the far right of the trail, little hands reaching for the red-osier dogwood branches, Oregon grapes, and elderberry leaves nearby. The whistle of osprey causes us to stop and look up. We've seen their nest atop the metal tower before and watched for babies. Now, there are three of them soaring overhead. "They're hunting!" Albert says. We move on in anticipation of more birds ahead.

We're here! We can see the big, blue mural of birds across the wetlands and several children start naming them. We scan the water and count six, maybe seven, great blue herons standing in the water. "They're fishing!" We continue to watch and give a collective shudder of excitement as a lone bald eagle lands on a ragged tree stump very close to a heron. One of the parents opens a small pouch and offers tobacco to the sky at the sight of the eagle. We watch quietly. The herons imperceptibly shift their weight and suddenly all take off together, flying to the north through the forest of red alders and Oregon ash, leaving the eagle alone. Shaya looks down and begins scooping up little fists of cottonwood fluff and stuffing it into her pockets. Treasure! The other children follow her lead, stowing away "cotton" to show family at home . . . proof of today's adventures.

Last stop is the river trail. It's a short walk through cranesbill geranium to the river. We look out from the bluff, over the Willamette River, to Ross Island. "There!" We have finally found deer. "There's three deer on the island!" "How did they get over there?" "They musta swam!" "How could they swim that far?" "How can we get over there?" "Let's go over there!" "We need a canoe!" One of the parents is a fisherwoman, Nez Perce, and we watch the river. "I don't fish the Willamette . . . raw sewage, you know." Yes, I know. "Do you think the river recognizes us?" We're quiet now, listening, remembering. We offer a beauty song of thanks to the river.

The term "ancient futures" embodies the wisdom and knowledge that we must bring into the present to create a vibrant and healthy future, honing our skills to listen as the ancestors knew to do, picking up the wisdom on the wind, rustling in the trees, and rushing through the waters. The elders say nothing is lost, only forgotten, and it can be reclaimed.

Harry takes my hand and asks for a "cedar ceremony." Children crave the transformation that ceremony offers them and are hungry for the experience. I'm not sure how he even heard about doing this, and I've never referred to anything as a "cedar ceremony," but the children are defining the world on their terms, creating or listening for a language that captures their hearts and perhaps speaks to their destiny as the inheritors of what earlier generations have left for them to heal. The land remembers us in an enduring embrace.

By Judy BlueHorse Skelton

Ross Island

Exploring the Ross Island Archipelago

The first reference to Ross Island as potential public land was John Charles Olmsted's 1903 report to the Portland Parks Board. Olmsted recommended that the islands be purchased by the city as a riverine playground. Since then, most Portlanders have assumed that the four-island archipelago of Ross, Hardtack, East, and Toe islands would one day be part of the Portland park system.

That prospect became more of a reality when, in 2005, Ross Island Sand and Gravel announced that it would cease dredging Ross Island and the lagoon between Ross and Hardtack Islands. That impetus came from an Endangered Species Act listing of Chinook salmon and steelhead trout as threatened. The operating times for dredging allowed by the federal agencies became so narrow that they decided it would be more advantageous to obtain raw materials from Columbia River Gorge upland sites and barge the materials to their processing plant on Hardtack Island.

As part of renegotiating state and federal permits in 2007, Ross Island Sand and Gravel owner Dr. Robert Pamplin Jr. committed to donating all of Ross Island and most of Hardtack Island (that portion not taken up with their processing plant) to the city. Unfortunately, the donation as envisioned fell through. It was only after a frenetic series of meetings between Dr. Pamplin and the Audubon Society of Portland, Willamette Riverkeeper, and Urban Greenspaces Institute that a greatly modified agreement was struck between Dr. Pamplin and the city, resulting in a donation of forty-five acres on Ross Island that are now managed by Portland Parks & Recreation. The donated portion of Ross Island includes the large black cottonwood grove, where bald eagles have nested for several years, to downstream near the northern tip of the island. The Port of Portland still owns Ross Island's downstream tip, although it is hoped that it too will come into city ownership sooner rather than later. Ross Island, upstream of the eagle nest, and all of Hardtack and East Islands are still in private ownership.

Exploring the Islands

I have found that there is no better way to appreciate the islands and Holgate Channel than from the water, preferably by canoe or kayak. A circumnavigation of the islands is about three miles, which at a leisurely pace takes two and a half to three hours. I normally set out in my kayak early on Sunday mornings when boat and jet ski traffic is low and the Hardtack Island processing plant is shut down. Paddling Ross Island anytime of year is rewarding, but in early spring, beginning around mid-February, both great blue herons and bald eagles resume nesting activity. It's between then and the herons' egg-laying in early April, before the black cottonwoods leaf out, that one can view the herons' fantastic courtship behavior and the refurbishing of their loose-knit stick nests.

There are several good put-in points for a Ross Island paddle: the relatively new dock just upstream of the Hawthorne Bridge; Sellwood Riverfront Park; and **Willamette Park boat ramp**, which I prefer. I also favor the floating boat dock, although during fishing season or later in the day on weekends jockeying with powerboats and finding a parking spot is a pain.

From Willamette Park, it's best to get across the river as quickly as possible, heading across the upstream end of the **Oregon Yacht Club houseboats ❶** near Oaks Pioneer Park. If you let your kayak float quietly downstream by the houseboats you'll sometimes see river otters haul themselves out to munch on a fish. By mid-May, purple martins have returned from the south to nest in the large white gourds that houseboat residents have hung from two poles in the floating community.

As you approach the upstream end of Ross and Hardtack Islands, you'll see a low, obviously **artificial berm ❷** that connects the two islands. It was put in place in 1926 by the U.S. Army Corps of Engineers to divert the Willamette west of the islands in order to facilitate scouring a deeper channel for river traffic. The berm also created a quiet lagoon that benefited Ross Island Sand and Gravel's aggregate extraction. If the river is running high, you can paddle downstream through the narrow, **shallow channel ❸** between **East and Hardtack Islands**. This channel is generally avoided by water skiers and is more likely to offer a tranquil paddle than the main Holgate Channel. The upper portion of the Holgate Channel and Ross Island Lagoon are off limits to wake-producing, high-speed, motorized traffic. A restricted, five-miles-per-hour "slow, no wake zone" is being sought for the entire channel.

When the river is running low, the channel to the west of East Island is impassable, even in a kayak. I've had to drag my kayak through this channel on more than one occasion when I decided to chance it at low water. Then, the Holgate Channel is the only option. As you paddle downstream, you'll see joggers, cyclists, and walkers on the Springwater on the Willamette trail (see page 71) at the top of the old railroad berm.

I prefer to hug the eastern shore of Hardtack Island en route to the Ross Island Lagoon to avoid getting in the path of rowing crews that generally use the middle of the channel. As a matter of courtesy, it's best to give way to single or team crews, given that their workouts entail going in a straight line. Hugging the shore it's also more likely you'll come across a great blue heron skulking along the bank, or if you're really lucky, the more secretive, tiny green heron. During winter you also stand a good chance of seeing large flotillas of common mergansers that hang out on the Willamette all winter and nest in tree cavities on the Sandy and Clackamas Rivers in summer. Look

Heron Watching

The best time to view great blue herons is mid-February into mid-April, before the black cottonwoods leaf out. You can see their nests on Ross Island from the Willamette Greenway Trail at the end of SW Curry Street at South Waterfront. If you stand on the greenway trail and train your scope or binoculars on the island, you cannot miss the bulky stick nests. The nests are more difficult to see from the river's east side. It is equally difficult from a kayak, although you can get much closer to the heronry and watch for the adults flying into and out of the nests. If you observe the heronry in mid to late June, after the young have reached near-adult size, you will see them vigorously flapping their wings, preparing for their first forays out of the nest.

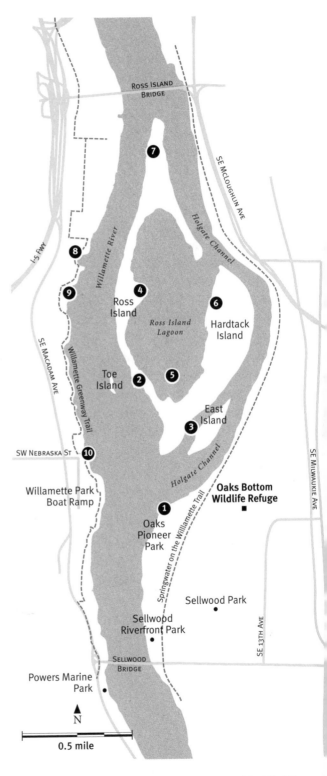

for beaver-chewed branches that have been stripped of their bark. River otters have become more abundant around Ross Island as well.

Across the Holgate Channel, look for the large, older power pole with a messy stick nest on a platform. Most likely, from June to well into July, there will be osprey in the nest. Some years Canada geese beat the osprey to the punch and take over the nest. I've also observed osprey setting up house after the young goslings have fled. Other years they simply find another nesting platform or snag. Recently, osprey have proliferated along the lower Willamette. On your circumnavigation you are likely to see at least four of their nests.

About a half mile downstream, the entrance to the Ross Island Lagoon opens up to the left. As soon as I paddle into the lagoon, I look directly across it to the large grove of black cottonwoods jutting out over the water. There I often see bald eagles and their nest ❹. This huge stick nest is easily seen, even after the cottonwoods have leafed out. For more than thirty years, there was a heron colony here with fifty or sixty nests. In 2000, the bald eagles moved in and the herons relocated downstream near the tip of Ross Island. The buoys anchored in the lagoon several hundred feet out from the eagle nest warn boaters to stay away. That applies to paddlers as well, to avoid harassing the eagles during nesting season. If you're close enough to read the signs, you're probably too close and should back off and observe them with binoculars from a distance of at least four to five hundred feet.

A paddle to the **southern end of the lagoon** ❺ provides a good look at the results of restoration that Ross Island Sand and Gravel has undertaken as a condition of their 2007 permit, which requires the creation of about thirty-five acres of shallow water, emergent wetland, and upland habitat. Once these habitats have been established, there'll be excellent birding opportunities in this section of the lagoon.

On my way back to Holgate Channel, I enjoy a slow paddle past the processing plant ❻, especially if it's in operation. It's fascinating to watch the rock crushers, barges, and conveyor belts as they process sand and gravel. Be careful to avoid any direct interaction with working barges though.

Once back in the Holgate Channel head downstream. Another quarter to half mile downstream the installed utility pole at the northern tip of Ross Island is a good marker to start looking for **great blue heron nests** ❼. Just upstream of the pole, I've counted twelve to fifteen nests, tucked in the tops of the cottonwoods that are midway across the island. If the nests are obscured by leaves in late May or early June, when the young are big enough to see, I sit quietly in my kayak and wait for a parent returning from foraging for food, most likely winging in from the direction of Oaks Bottom. Following their path into the trees you're more likely to locate a nest from the water. If not, you'll surely hear the loud cacophony of the young as they vie for their share of the piscine booty their parents regurgitate into the nest.

Once you've rounded the downstream tip of Ross Island, continue upstream, hugging the shore. The South Waterfront condos rise dramatically on the west bank of the Willamette. While paddling close to Ross Island, keep a sharp eye out for cavities in the bank, some of which are beaver dens. Smaller holes might be the telltale sign of a belted kingfisher nest. Two parallel grooves on the bottom rim of the hole are a sure sign it's a kingfisher nest.

If you choose to explore the Willamette's west bank, head across from here and paddle upstream, again hugging the shore to avoid wakes. You'll parallel the Willamette Greenway Trail and pass two small remnant wetland areas, **Cottonwood Bay** ❽, which is owned by Portland Parks & Recreation, and **Heron Pointe Wetlands** ❾, which is privately owned and has been restored with native plantings and improved with swales to treat stormwater before it enters the Willamette from the nearby condominiums and parking lots.

When leading a group paddle, I head toward little Toe Island, which is frequently crowded, and set a course back to Willamette Park. Good beacons to shoot for are the bright, white tips on the park's dock. I generally paddle diagonally from the upstream tip of Toe Island and point my kayak toward the Willamette Sailing Club on the river's west bank, just downstream of Willamette Park. That allows me to paddle close to the newly created shallow water and mud flats ❿ between the sailing club and Willamette Park that attract hordes of gulls, shorebirds, and waterfowl.

By Mike Houck, illustration by Evelyn Hicks

Portland's Icon:
The Great Blue Heron

DURING A 1986 SPEECH that mayor Bud Clark gave at the downtown Hilton ballroom, he described seeing great blue herons gliding by skyscrapers on his canoe outings. Afterward, I approached him about declaring the heron Portland's official city bird. Bud shouted a couple of his signature "whoop, whoops," and two weeks later he issued a proclamation before city council—the great blue heron became the city's official bird.

While adopting an official city bird may sound frivolous, the process led to the annual Great Blue Heron Week, when Friends groups and government agencies pay tribute to the heron. Ever since, Portland's mayor has read, and the city council has approved, a new proclamation with numerous clauses establishing why Portland cares that herons live in our midst. The annual proclamation ends with city commitments to undertake habitat acquisition, restoration, and management during the coming year to protect and improve heron habitat and, by extension, fish and wildlife habitat generally throughout the city. More recently, Metro has followed Portland's lead, proclaiming what will be done at the regional scale to improve conditions for herons and all of the species that share their habitat along the region's rivers, wetlands, and streams.

Soon after Clark's initial proclamation, Bridgeport Brewpub created Blue Heron Ale, ArtFX Murals installed a seventy-foot-high great blue heron mural on the west-facing wall of the Portland Memorial Mausoleum, and Oregon's poet laureate, William Stafford, uniquely captured the philosophy that nature belongs in the city with his poem "Spirit of Place."

Great blue herons are one of our most charismatic megafauna. They're the largest heron in North America and impossible to miss, standing over three feet tall, with a wingspan over six feet. No animal, save perhaps the salmon, is so iconographic a representation of nature in the Pacific Northwest as the great blue heron. Its image is everywhere: blue heron ale, blue heron cheese, blue heron condominiums, blue heron streets, even blue heron music festivals.

Ardea herodias, also known as "big cranky" or "shite poke," may be statuesque and beautifully adorned, but it is no melodic songster. Its call, especially when startled, is at best, a raspy harsh croak that it shouts as it flies off, neck tucked into a loose S-shape.

The great blue's feathers are slaty-blue, with reddish "shoulder patches," its breast streaked with black and white vertical stripes. The heron's head is light colored with two black plumes coming off its crown and draping across its back. Long white plumes also extend down the neck. During breeding season the bill changes color from a dull

Out of their loneliness for each other
two reeds, or maybe two shadows, lurch
forward and become suddenly a life
lifted from dawn or the rain. It is
the wilderness come back again, a lagoon
with our city reflected in its eye.
We live by faith in such presences.

It is a test for us, that thin
but real, undulating figure that promises,
"If you keep faith I will exist
at the edge, where your vision joins
the sunlight and the rain: heads in the light,
feet that go down in the mud where the truth is."
—WILLIAM STAFFORD, 1987

yellow to a brighter yellow-orange, and additional white nuptial plumes flow down its back.

Great blue herons are found from Alaska to South America, and across the United States. While herons migrate from colder climes in the Midwest and Northeast, they live year-round in the Pacific Northwest. In our region herons can be found virtually anywhere there is water, from the smallest tributary to the Willamette and Columbia Rivers.

Herons are the ultimate eating machines, trying anything they can stab or snap up with their long, killer bill. There's an account of a heron piercing a two-inch-thick canoe paddle with its dagger-like bill. While they primarily eat fish, it's not uncommon to see herons stalking small rodents in grasslands around Portland International Airport or farm fields on Sauvie Island. I've watched great blues spear huge carp in the open pond at Oaks Bottom Wildlife Refuge and then take a half hour positioning the fish so that the fins won't lodge in their throats. The herons then perform a neat flip, taking the carp head first into their gullets, but it takes a long time for the fish to make it down their throats.

Spotting the Great Blue

Herons nest in colonies throughout the metro area, the largest ones being along the Columbia Slough near the St. Johns Landfill, Jackson Bottom Wetlands, Heron Lakes Golf Course, and Goat Island near West Linn. Numerous smaller colonies can be seen on Ross Island, Koll Center Marsh in Beaverton, and along Rock Creek off NW Evergreen Parkway in Hillsboro. New nests are rickety-looking stick platforms, usually in black cottonwood or sometimes in Douglas fir. In older colonies the nests look more substantial, although even these look incapable of holding the three or four young that will eventually fledge at adult size.

If you arrive at an active colony in mid February, you'll have the opportunity to watch mated pairs bonding with one another through ritualistic neck stretches, bill snapping, and tugging over nesting materials, which are usually small branches gathered from the ground by the male and presented to the female. While herons reuse the previous year's nests, they do not necessarily return to the same nest in the colony.

Great blues are serially monogamous, choosing a new mate annually. In our region they lay three to five light blue eggs in mid to late April, after which both female and male incubate—females at night and males during the day, for about one month. It takes six weeks or so before the young approach adult size and start beating their wings, preparing to fledge. Before fully fledging, they become "branchers," venturing in forays to nearby limbs where they flap their wings vigorously, building up strength for their first flight, which comes at about eight weeks. If you want to see young herons at their most raucous—they are incredibly boisterous as parents return to the nest with food and each young bird vies to get as much food as it can gobble down—visit a heronry late May to mid-June. (They sometimes fledge as late as early July, but more often by mid to late June.)

Once fledged, the young will sometimes continue to fly back to the nest, where they are fed by the adults. Eventually, they leave the colony and can be seen around the region hunting for fish and rodents on their own. They are easily distinguished from the adults by the lack of plumes and their dull, gray bill.

By Mike Houck, illustration by Lynn Kitagawa

The Willamette Greenway

Rose Quarter to Powers Marine Park

This ramble has multiple options, from a twelve-mile out-and-back trip along the Willamette's west bank; a six-mile and return outing on a TriMet bus or Portland Streetcar; or a twelve-mile loop, taking in the west side Willamette Greenway trail and returning along the Springwater on the Willamette trail past Oaks Bottom Wildlife Refuge.

Whatever the option, start at the **Rose Quarter Transit Center** and head to the River Walk, a cantilevered bike-ped path across the Willamette River to Tom McCall Waterfront Park. The path, added to the Steel Bridge through complex negotiations with the Union Pacific Railroad Company, was installed in spring 2001 as part of the **Vera Katz Eastbank Esplanade** project.

From the path, or at the seawall, I am always on the lookout for glaucous-winged and herring gulls or Canada geese that might be hanging out around the downstream grain elevators or the bridge abutments. Double-crested cormorants, with their bright-yellow gular pouch, are abundant during winter—perched on nearby pilings, their wings hung out to dry in the weak winter sun, or diving for fish around the seawall. You can also see a multitude of rock pigeons along with the occasional peregrine falcon that swoops from nearby perches atop the Fremont Bridge. Being a moss fancier, I also check out the moss-covered seawall for *Grimmia pulvinata*, one of my favorite Portland-area mosses, and one which is just as content to grow on the calcium-rich concrete walls as on its native rocky substrate. *Grimmia*'s white, hairy "leaf" tips allow it to exist on the xeric substrate by reflecting sunlight during the hot, dry summer months.

As you turn south, riding past the giant sculptures, don't miss the one at the **Friendship Circle**, which resembles a huge, vertical glass cutter, commemorating thirty years of sister-city status between Portland and Sapporo, Japan. If it's a sunny weekend day, I watch out for strollers, cyclists, and joggers, all of whom own a piece of the waterfront trail. In spring this section of Waterfront Park is awash in pink cherry blossoms. The cherry tree trunks are covered with lichens—the gray, leafy *Parmelia* and bright-orange, crusty *Xanthoria*. Near the trunk base where water collects, there's a profusion of the more mesic-loving mosses. Take a closer look and you'll see reddish-brown, puffy, lenticular-shaped blotches on the trunks. The tree actually "breathes" through these horizontal lenticels, which function as pores through which the tree exchanges gases with the surrounding atmosphere. A lenticel's shape can be used taxonomically to identify the tree. It's not unusual to see bushtits, ruby-crowned kinglets, and black-capped chickadees gleaning insects off the cherry trees.

Next stop is the beautifully designed **Japanese American Historical Plaza** and Bill of Rights Memorial at NW Davis Street. The memorial commemorates the large pre–World War II Japanese-American community, *Nihonmachi* ("Japantown"), that was located nearby in historic Old Town. It tells the poignant story of Japanese Americans' internment in Pacific Coast camps during World War II. Numerous haikus evoking the internees' sentiments are inscribed on the memorial's stonework along with a copy of the Bill of Rights.

Farther south, across from the fire station at Naito Parkway and SW Ash Street, is the new Saturday Market pavilion, a sewage treatment station, and Portland Loo, one of Portland's newest additions to the urban landscape and one of a very few public restroom stops on this ramble. A plaque in the path describes "the clearing"—the deforested spot to plat the city—and reminds us that Native Americans lived here first. Another plaque points out that the Willamette River's west bank used to be 150 feet west of the seawall at SW Stark Street and Naito Parkway. This is also the former site of the Stark Street Ferry, which took traffic across the Willamette before the Morrison Bridge—Portland's first bridge at the original town site—was built in 1887. It's also the first clear view of Ross Island, a couple of miles upstream.

As the paved path curves, just past the restrooms under the Hawthorne Bridge, you have the option to walk or cycle straight across the grassy bowl or to continue right on the paved path and semi-circle around to the **RiverPlace Hotel** and marina. The grassy bowl is a favorite hangout for grazing Canada geese and gulls, so watch your step! This is the first opportunity to get close enough to actually touch the river by climbing down the rocky bank. From the hotel, you can choose to head south down SW Harbor Way and turn left at the end of the block on SW Montgomery Street or dismount in front of the hotel to walk through the privately owned waterfront portion of the **Willamette Greenway Trail**. The colorful waterfront route will take you along shops and restaurants (Happy Hours Here!)

Old Skunkhead

Sometimes referred to as "old skunkhead" by early ornithologists, owing to its black and white striped head, the white-crowned sparrow is a species of many regional dialects. In an old PBS NOVA science episode "Why Do Birds Sing?" researchers identified seven unique dialects in the San Francisco Bay Area alone. There is a distinctive difference in the songs from the birds of Portland compared to the birds where I grew up in Estacada. Listen carefully and you'll hear some white-crowneds clip the end of their song, which contrasts with the much more drawn-out song heard elsewhere in the region. It's not uncommon to hear them singing in the middle of the city. I almost always hear them before I see them; the male perched on the edge of a building or on landscaping. I hear their melodious song most often along the Willamette River and I've even seen them on downtown ecoroofs singing their hearts out. Look and listen for them around manicured, grassy areas at South Waterfront, Hoyt Arboretum, and Washington Park.

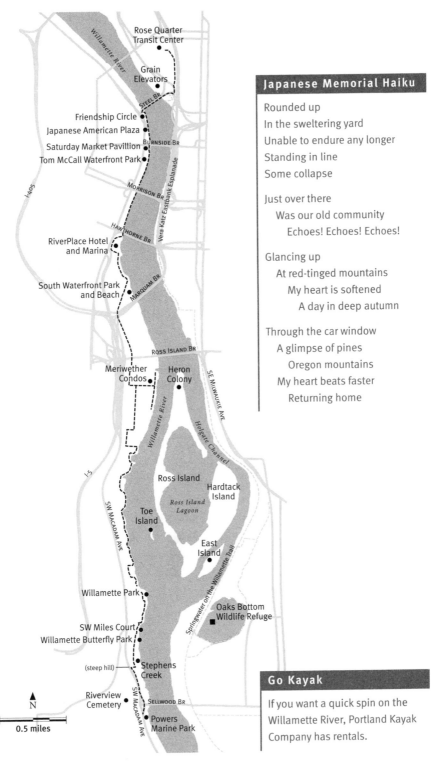

Japanese Memorial Haiku

Rounded up
In the sweltering yard
Unable to endure any longer
Standing in line
Some collapse

Just over there
    Was our old community
        Echoes! Echoes! Echoes!

Glancing up
    At red-tinged mountains
        My heart is softened
            A day in deep autumn

Through the car window
    A glimpse of pines
        Oregon mountains
            My heart beats faster
                Returning home

Go Kayak

If you want a quick spin on the
Willamette River, Portland Kayak
Company has rentals.

overlooking the marina on a sidewalk full of oar-wielding paddlers, baby-stroller-pushing parents, and other pedestrians. Either route will get you to **South Waterfront Park**, which in summer is ablaze with wildflowers. But even in winter the native plantings and grasses are beautiful. Continuing on the pedestrian way the trail ends abruptly under the Marquam Bridge. Here there are two paths down to the river. At low water this is the only sandy beach on this reach of the Willamette River.

From here, the way to South Waterfront is along SW Moody Avenue, pending completion of the Willamette Greenway Trail from its current terminus at the River Forum building to the south. The next opportunity to access the temporary Greenway path is to take a left at SW Curry Street and proceed to the end at South Waterfront, riverward of the **Meriwether Condominium** tower.

The ramble from South Waterfront to **Willamette Park** at SW Nebraska Street is fully described on page 98. We'll pick up the route in Willamette Park.

Stephens Creek

Stephens Creek is one of the few streams in Southwest Portland that still flows freely to the Willamette River. The lower reach runs through Riverview Cemetery, the largest tract of open space in the watershed. Near its confluence with the Willamette, it meanders through a three-acre Pacific willow–forested wetland behind the Macadam Bay Club moorage, adjacent to the Willamette Greenway trail. The wetlands here provide critical rearing and refuge habitat for native, endangered Chinook and coho salmon, steelhead, rainbow and cutthroat trout, and Pacific and brook lamprey. The city removed an abandoned combined sewer overflow pipe, resloped the banks, revegetated the area, and installed large pieces of wood to increase shelter for fish. The site was replanted with native vegetation to increase habitat complexity and provide shade and overhanging vegetative cover.

—Dawn Uchiyama

From Willamette Park continue south on the Willamette Greenway Trail. It skirts along the eastern edge of the park and dumps you onto SW Miles Court for a short distance before picking up again at the old **Willamette Butterfly Park**, which is slated for relocation into Willamette Park. Portland Parks & Recreation plans to put in a major wildlife habitat restoration program at this site, while ensuring that one of the most scenic Willamette overlooks remains. Back on the Greenway path it's a steep downhill to the confluence of **Stephens Creek** and the Willamette River, offering excellent views of the city-owned wetland where Portland Parks and the city's Bureau of Environmental Services have undertaken a massive fish habitat enhancement effort.

If you're on your bike be sure to gear way down, as the uphill to SW Macadam is extremely steep.

The next stretch is my least favorite portion of the ramble. There is a very narrow paved path between barricades to the right and a Himalayan blackberry patch on the left. This path parallels SW Macadam Avenue, then dumps you onto a wide parking area. Go through the parking area, heading to the left down to the entrance of Powers Marine Park, a city-owned slice of narrow riparian habitat, with by far the most accessible river access in Portland. Named after Powers Furniture Company owner Ira Powers, the fourteen-acre parcel was donated to the city for a park during the Great Depression. When the Willamette runs low there's almost a mile of exposed beach here. The willow and cottonwood forest provides excellent birding.

From **Powers Marine Park** you have three options: return to downtown the same way you came along the Willamette Greenway; catch a TriMet bus 35 nearby on SW Macadam Avenue; or continue your ramble across the Sellwood Bridge and take the Springwater on the Willamette trail past Oaks Bottom Wildlife Refuge (see page 76) back to the Steel Bridge and Rose Quarter.

By Mike Houck

Future Impacts

This area is slated for major changes with the rebuilding of the Sellwood Bridge and potential installation of the Portland to Lake Oswego streetcar. Both projects will affect trail alignments and will have physical impacts on Powers Marine Park and its means of access. There are, however, plans to extend the Willamette Greenway trail to Lake Oswego as well, although combining the streetcar and trail projects through the narrow Elk Rock area will be a challenge.

A Cheapskate's Ramble
South Waterfront to OHSU and back

This five-mile ramble is for the frugal walker who wants to avoid paying for the scenic tram ride between Oregon Health and Science University (OHSU) and South Waterfront. And, while it's infinitely more circuitous and time consuming than simply paying for the round-trip from South Waterfront, a walk along the Willamette, up the rustic trail to George Himes Park and down scenic Terwilliger Boulevard is so much more rewarding. And the trip back on the tram is free! I guarantee this ramble is a great workout!

South Waterfront Greenway
After disembarking from the **Portland Streetcar** ❶ at South Waterfront, I start my trek in front of the Meriwether condos at the end of **SW Curry Street** ❷. A walk along the temporary Willamette Greenway ❸ provides views of the Ross Island great blue heron colony ❹ and a variety of songbirds. At this point the trail is much wider than the greenway trail to the south, thanks to a deal struck with the developers that allowed the buildings to be higher than would otherwise have been permitted, in exchange for widening the greenway. The entire riverbank here is slated to be improved for fish and wildlife habitat in the next few years.

As you stand on the greenway trail, look directly across to Ross Island to see the flimsy-looking heron nests—looking something like condos—high atop the black cottonwoods. The herons return to their communal nest site in mid-February and are clearly visible until the cottonwoods leaf out. South Waterfront residents have observed bald eagles taking young herons out of their nests recently, so it remains to be seen how long the heronry will remain. The herons abandoned their colony on the Ross Island Lagoon several years ago when the eagles moved in.

As you make your way back between the John Ross and the Meriwether condos, be sure to check out the swales that treat stormwater runoff. While you cannot see the more than three acres of ecoroofs above you, they are also designed to retain and treat stormwater before it's sent to the large bioswale at the north end of the greenway.

> ## Willamette River Overlook
>
> A short walk down SW Nebraska Street from George Himes Park to SW Parkhill Way affords fabulous views of the Ross Island Lagoon, and sweeping views of the Willamette River, Mount Tabor, Mount Talbert, and Mount Scott, with Mount Hood in the distance. You can also see the entire mural on the Portland Memorial Mausoleum at Oaks Bottom Wildlife Refuge.

Unfortunately, there is a gap between the greenway trail at South Waterfront and where the trail picks up again at the River Forum building a half mile or so south, so you need to thread your way south along neighborhood streets to pick up the greenway trail again at **SW Bancroft and SW Moody Streets** ❺. The trail takes an abrupt left turn at the red brick **River Forum building** ❻, and you're back on the greenway trail ❼ near **Cottonwood Bay** ❽, next to the Avalon Hotel.

Heron Pointe Wetlands

Check out the interpretive sign at Heron Pointe Wetlands ❾ for information about this postage-stamp-sized wetland. This small but significant spot is an important amenity to the Heron Pointe Condominium Home Owners Association, which helped remove invasive, non-native vegetation, and replant native spirea, creek dogwood, and willows. I've seen pileated woodpeckers, beaver, and an array of songbirds, including lesser goldfinches, violet-green swallows, song sparrows, and Anna's hummingbirds here. Heron Pointe is a classic example of "small is beautiful" when it comes to urban wetlands. Yes, it pales in comparison to Ross Island in scale, but it is no less important as a tiny remnant wetland on the west bank of the Willamette.

Willamette Park warrants a quick stop before heading up the hill to George Himes Park. I like to walk the **narrow path** ❿ hugging the Willamette to scope out the mud-flats ⓫, which used to be covered by water but over the last few years have gradually silted in, resulting in excellent habitat that attracts western sandpipers, least sandpipers, killdeer, and other shorebirds during fall and spring migration. During the winter, hordes of gulls gather on the exposed mudflats, along with American wigeon, green-winged teal, and other waterfowl.

Next, I check out the **newly planted wetland swales** ⓬ that are designed to treat some of the runoff from Willamette Park's extensive parking lot before allowing it to flow into the river. Plantings include cascara, western redcedar, snowberry, spirea, lodge-pole pine, red alder, and Oregon white oak. It's worth a short walk out onto the **floating dock at the boat ramp** ⓭ to scope out Ross Island and the river for osprey, bald eagles, and the occasional peregrine falcon. Last pubic restroom until Terwilliger Parkway!

Willamette Park to George Himes Park

Time to head to George Himes Park via SW Nebraska Street and SW Corbett Avenue to the dead end at **SW Iowa Street and SW Viewpoint Terrace** ⓮. This is the trailhead to George Himes Park. The trailhead is marked with a SW Trails marker. Take the wooden

Trail Diversions

The trail from SW Iowa Street to George Himes Park will be closed due to repair work on the Interstate 5 bridge under which the trail passes. For an alternative route, walk south along SW Corbett Avenue to SW Custer Way, taking a set of steps following Custer Way along I-5 and under the freeway onramp up to SW Terwilliger Boulevard on the south end of the bridge. Then travel north to George Himes at SW Nebraska Street.

More information: ODOT I-5 Viaduct Project, 503-731-8246

steps and continue uphill, passing under Interstate 5 and SW Macadam Avenue bridged high overhead. It's an often-muddy uphill trek through a mixed big-leaf maple and Douglas fir forest. Bear left, up several switchbacks, and you emerge into **George Himes Park 15** at SW Nebraska Street and SW Terwilliger Boulevard.

As you walk back uphill to SW Terwilliger, take the bicycle and pedestrian path north to SW Capitol Highway, cross over at the signal, and continue north on Terwilliger to the **Chart House Restaurant 16**, where you can stop for a libation and a view to the east. Unfortunately, the view is somewhat restricted by the restaurant itself and by vegetation that has grown up over the years. While it would undoubtedly be controversial, this is one of a handful of examples where some very limited pruning might be in order to open up a fabulous vista.

The rest of the ramble is a mostly downhill stroll along the Terwilliger path to **SW Campus Drive 17** and OHSU. Getting to the Tram is a bit tricky, however. Walk up the hill on Campus Drive past the Casey Eye Clinic and take an immediate right into the garage. As you enter the garage you'll see the Tram icon. Walk through the parking garage to the OHSU School of Dentistry elevator. Take the elevator to Tram BR (Bridge to School of Dentistry). Exit the elevator and go through the door with the Tram logo. Walk past the door to the stairs—unless, of course, you'd like to walk up eight flights—and turn to the left where an elevator will take you to the 9th floor, Kohler Pavilion, and entrance to the Tram. Wait in line for the Tram and, *voila*, you'll return to the OHSU Tram stop at South Waterfront, gratis!

By Mike Houck

Side Trip!

Keep your eyes peeled for the 40-Mile Loop Trailhead on the left as you walk down SW Terwilliger. The trail offers a great side trip to Marquam Nature Park.

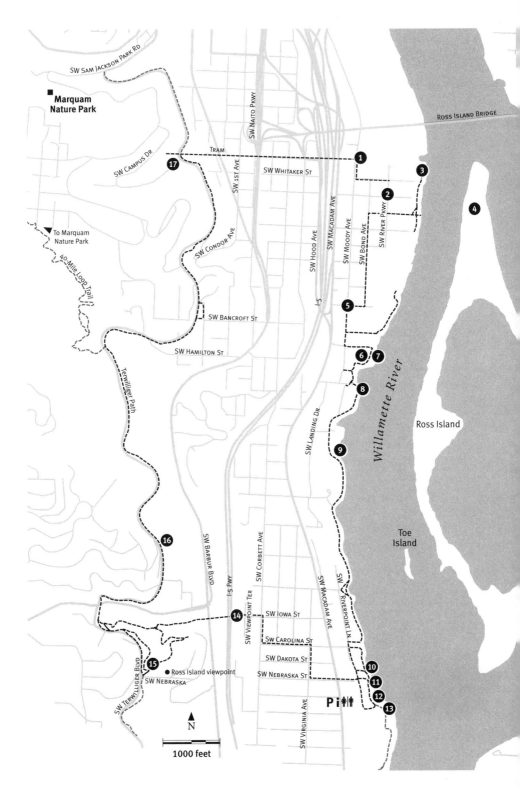

SW SAM JACKSON PARK RD

■ Marquam
Nature Park

SW NAITO PKWY

ROSS ISLAND BRIDGE

TRAM

SW CAMPUS DR

17

1

SW WHITAKER ST

SW 1ST AVE

SW RIVER PKWY

2

3

▼ To Marquam
Nature Park

SW CONDOR AVE

SW HOOD AVE

SW MACADAM AVE

SW MOODY AVE

SW BOND AVE

4

40-MILE LOOP TRAIL

I-5

5

SW BANCROFT ST

SW HAMILTON ST

6

7

Willamette River

Terwilliger Path

8

SW LANDING DR

Ross Island

9

16

SW BARBUR BLVD

SW CORBETT AVE

SW VIEWPOINT TER

SW MACADAM AVE

SW RIVERPOINT LN

Toe
Island

I-5 FWY

14

SW IOWA ST

SW CAROLINA ST

15

SW DAKOTA ST

10

Ross Island viewpoint

SW NEBRASKA ST

11

SW NEBRASKA

12

SW TERWILLIGER BLVD

SW VIRGINIA AVE

P i ♀♂

13

▲
N

1000 feet

Peregrine Falcons

TODAY IT IS NOT UNCOMMON to look up and see the sickle-shaped silhouette of a peregrine falcon slicing through the clouds above our city. The peregrine haunts our urban landscape just as it has passed gracefully above medieval cathedrals, and castle ramparts for centuries. This wildest of creatures—the fastest living thing on earth—has made Portland its home.

A mere generation ago, the peregrine (*Falco peregrinus anatum*) was absent from our skies. Widespread use of the pesticide DDT from the 1940s to the 1960s caused peregrines and other top predators, such as bald eagles and osprey, to lay eggs with thin eggshells. Peregrine eggs broke during incubation, leading the bird's population to crash. By 1970, the American peregrine falcon was almost extirpated from the continental United States. There were no known nest sites east of the Mississippi River and only a handful in the western United States—no peregrine falcons were known to be nesting anywhere in Oregon.

The banning of DDT in 1972 and the listing of the American peregrine falcon under the Federal Endangered Species Act in 1973 were the first steps on the long road to recovery. Natural reestablishment of populations was augmented by an intensive captive rearing and release program, the largest effort of its kind ever undertaken. Captive-raised peregrines were released on Mount Hood and at several locations in the Columbia River Gorge. In 1980, the restoration efforts began to pay off: peregrines were discovered nesting at Crater Lake.

Urban Peregrines

Records of peregrine falcons nesting on human-made structures date back to the Middle Ages, when they were discovered nesting on castles and cathedrals. While it may seem surprising that this fiercest and fastest of predators has a habit of occupying human structures, in fact, bridges and skyscrapers have many of the specific attributes sought by peregrines when selecting nest sites.

Peregrine falcons do not build stick nests. Instead they nest on high, inaccessible cliff ledges, hollowing out an area of sand and gravel known as a scrape. The nest is called an eyrie. Peregrines prey primarily on other birds. Although they are not large birds (females are about the size of a raven, and males are crow-sized), they have been documented taking species ranging in size from hummingbirds to cackling geese. Even though they are not fast fliers off the mark, their primary hunting strategy is to climb

high in the sky and then drop in dives known as stoops at over two hundred miles an hour. Prey is often killed on contact.

Urban bridges and skyscrapers with their high, inaccessible ledges and abundant populations of rock pigeons and starlings meet many of the peregrine's nesting needs. Since peregrine recovery began, peregrines have established nest sites in cities across the United States.

Fremont Bridge

In the spring of 1993, birders noted a pair of falcons frequenting Portland's Fremont Bridge. In April of 1994, biologists finally observed the moment that they had been awaiting: a pair was observed entering and departing a platform under the lower deck on the east end of the bridge, a clear indication that they were incubating eggs! A month later Portland's first peregrine falcon eyas (nestling) hatched in a scrape hollowed out from a bed of pigeon poop.

While the community greeted the falcons with great excitement, biologists greeted them with trepidation. Although by 1994 the peregrine falcon had been listed as an endangered species for more than two decades, the Fremont Bridge was only the twenty-sixth peregrine nest site discovered in Oregon since the peregrine recovery program was initiated. Oregon was averaging only a little over one new nest site per year.

Peregrines are sensitive to nest disturbance and urban nest sites come with hazards not associated with cliff sites. News helicopters, bridge maintenance activities, construction projects, and other human activities near the nest site can cause nest failure. Bridges are particularly hazardous for nesting peregrines because young falcons sometimes fledge prior to being able to fly. The air currents associated with cliffs tend to rise in updrafts that keep young falcons on the nest ledge as they flap their wings and build up strength for their first flights. Conversely, bridges have downdrafts and small, isolated ledges that allow young falcons only a minimum of movement. When they do fall, the first step can be a fatal plunge to the ground or water below.

Biologists weighed the options. On the one hand, the new urban eyrie would give people a chance to see these amazing birds flying and nesting overhead. On the other, there was concern that the hazards associated with the urban landscape would preclude the nest from being productive and contributing to the population. There was even discussion in those early years of climbing into the nest and removing the nestlings so that they could be relocated to "safer" peregrine nests on Mount Hood.

In the end, it was decided that the birds would be left to their own devices ... almost. Audubon committed to establishing a program to monitor, protect, and raise awareness of the falcons, and in 1995, with strong support from peregrine specialist Joel "Jeep" Pagel of the U.S. Forest Service, Peregrine Watch was born. Over the first decade of Peregrine Watch, more than 50 percent of the young from the Fremont Bridge would be rescued by Peregrine Watch volunteers as the birds fledged into the river, onto Naito Parkway traffic, in front of trains, or crashed into windows. In a particularly Portland-flavored incident, a young peregrine was even run over by a bike. Disturbance factors ranging from bongo-playing hippies to Hollywood movie crews to Portland bomb squad training exercises to Bill Clinton's motorcade were managed successfully. Peregrine Watch volunteers even prevented a suicide attempt, calling in a bridge jumper who suddenly appeared near the nest during a monitoring session. During the early years, Peregrine Watch monitoring equipment was stored behind the bar at Bridgeport Brewpub—volunteers were instructed to indulge only after their monitoring sessions were complete.

Over the years Peregrine Watch has expanded to include not only monitoring and outreach but also scientific research, captive rearing and release programs, banding, and nest augmentation. The Oregon Department of Transportation has developed a management plan specifically for falcons nesting on bridges.

An Expanding Urban Peregrine Population

In 1998, a second pair of peregrines began nesting on the St. Johns Bridge, and in 2001 additional pairs established themselves on the Interstate 205 Abernethy Bridge in Oregon City and Interstate 5 Interstate Bridge spanning the Columbia River. The male falcons (known as tiercels) on both the St. Johns and Abernethy Bridges were birds that originally fledged from the Fremont Bridge. Local populations were further augmented by peregrines that were captive-reared and released by Portland Audubon. Peregrine falcons were removed from the federal endangered species list in 1999 and the Oregon endangered species list in 2007.

By 2010, there were more than 160 sites across Oregon where peregrines have nested at least once since the start of recovery. Ten of those sites, more than 6 percent, are located within the Portland-Vancouver metropolitan region. The Fremont Bridge, the site that biologists once considered removing nestlings from for their own protection, has become Oregon's most prolific known nest site, having fledged fifty young over seventeen years! All Portland-area peregrine nest sites combined have fledged more than 140 young. Their annual average productivity of 2.4 young per nest exceeds both statewide and nationwide averages for peregrines. More than 150 volunteers and a multitude of agencies and organizations have participated in Peregrine Watch, helping ensure that Portland does its part in aiding the recovery of this amazing species.

By Bob Sallinger, illustration by Lei Kotynski

Peregrine Spotting

Peregrines show great fidelity to their nest sites, and although they may move from ledge to ledge, they will typically use the same cliff or structure year after year. They are fiercely territorial, so if you see more than two adults at a site, the resident pair will most likely be attacking the interloper. Although "peregrine" means "wanderer," and many peregrines do engage in long migrations, our local climate is mild enough that our peregrines tend to remain year-round—many additional peregrines migrate in from the north to pass the winter.

During the late fall and winter months, watch for peregrines at any of our local wetlands such as Smith and Bybee Lakes and Oaks Bottom. Peregrine breeding season begins just after the winter solstice.

> January through July they can be found nesting on many of the larger Willamette River Bridges.

> February, March, and April bring spectacular aerial courtship displays. During May they display prolific hunting activity as they feed their young in the nest.

> June and July are ideal for watching the young learn to hunt and fly. Great viewing of the nesting cycle can be had at Cathedral Park beneath the St. Johns Bridge, from the West Bank of the Willamette River beneath the Fremont Bridge, on the Springwater on the Willamette trail behind OMSI near the Marquam Bridge, and from Elk Rock Island looking west across the Willamette to the cliffs on the opposite bank.

Eagles and Ospreys

Bald eagle and osprey populations, along with peregrine falcons, have rebounded from tremendous declines caused by DDT.

Ospreys, once known as fish hawks for their exclusively fish-based diet, were dangerously close to disappearing, although they never were listed under the Endangered Species Act. Their numbers have increased from a low of thirteen pairs along the Willamette River between Eugene and Portland in 1976 to more than three hundred pairs in 2010, according to Chuck Henny and U.S. Geological Survey studies. Their large stick nests, which are reused year after year and can weigh up to several hundred pounds, can be seen today on channel markers, utility poles, electrical towers, and in snags bordering the lower Willamette and Columbia Rivers and at local wetlands. A truly migratory species, ospreys leave the metro region by late September for wintering grounds in Mexico and Central America and return like clockwork in late March. Nesting ospreys are tolerant of other nesting pairs and there are many places along the lower Willamette where several nests are visible from a single vantage point.

Bald eagles were slower to recover than ospreys and remained on the federal endangered species list until 2007. As recently as 1990, there were only a few nesting pairs in the entire Portland-Vancouver metro region. However, over the past twenty years local populations have exploded and they can now be found at wetlands and natural areas throughout the region. Key viewing locations for nesting eagles include Jackson Bottom, Ross Island, Smith and Bybee Lakes, and Sauvie Island. Many eagles pass the winter in Oregon, and local wintering populations far exceed local breeding populations. Sauvie Island Wildlife Area provides an ideal location to see wintering bald eagles. For the intrepid eagle watch, drive to Sauvie Island before dawn and follow Sauvie Island Road to the Columbia County line—there you are likely to see as many as thirty bald eagles flying across the Multnomah Channel from their winter roost in Forest Park to spend the day foraging in the island's wetlands.

Oblivious to Distraction

ARCHIE CLARK, A TWENTY-FIVE-YEAR-OLD YAKAMA NATION LOGGER when I met him in the summer of 1994, picked his way across a rickety ribbon of narrow plywood scaffolding, ignoring the mist dripping from his nose and eyebrows, hearing only the voices of his ancestors above the roar of Willamette Falls.

"If you fall in, we'll pick you up downriver," shouted Sergeant Ted Lame Bull, an Inter-Tribal Fisheries Enforcement officer, adding with a smile: "Somewhere . . ."

Clark smiled grimly, barely breaking cadence as he swept his traditional dip net into the river's confused current. Heavy, wet air swept in waves over glistening charcoal-colored boulders. Floodlights, installed for nighttime tourists crowding the railings on highway pullouts above the falls, glowed in artificial rainbows through the scrambled froth.

Clark ignored the relentless invasion of mist, mesmerizing his audience with his even dipping. Drop, sweep, lift, drop, sweep, lift . . .

For ten thousand years Clark's ancestors have visited the falls to collect the bounties of their mother earth—salmon and steelhead, such as this night; lamprey eels that somehow grasp and flip relentless paths up vertical and treacherously slippery basalt walls; the eggs of nesting geese, gulls, and ducks, and, later, flightless goslings gathered in nursery flocks.

Early eastern settlers viewed Willamette Falls as an interruption, an end point for the Oregon Trail, something to circumvent with locks and to cross with bridges so commerce could connect their communities.

The tribes, however, recognized the tumbling waters as a source of life; and today we're learning much the same lesson.

Huge sturgeon spawn each spring and summer in the heavy current downriver. Introduced shad by the tens of thousands do the same, and salmon and steelhead draw enormous sea lions from as far away as California and Alaska to feast on the milling schools.

Within several hundred yards downriver of the falls, pools up to one hundred feet deep tame the rapids and the Willamette recovers its placid path to sea.

Fishermen in aluminum boats join others casting on the river's banks. Watercraft of all kinds launch recreational dreams in warm summer weather, and all eyes are automatically drawn to the river from a dozen crossings down to its mouth.

The Willamette is our anchor, a sense of place, a faithful presence.

Once near, on or around the water we, like Archie Clark, are immersed in its current ... oblivious to distraction.

Rhythms

It was spring and we launched the boat in Milwaukie to troll for Chinook salmon, paying only passing attention to an osprey struggling toward us, barely above the river's surface.

Gripped in its talons was a large wriggling carp. The bird strained to control the fish as it drew nearer and nearer before circling to gain enough altitude to coast to its riverside nest. Suddenly, the osprey dropped the fortunate fish, which flopped twice on the surface and disappeared to soothe its wounds. The osprey flew into a tree and resumed its watch.

Overhead, a bald eagle we hadn't seen (but the osprey probably had and decided to cut its losses given the large size of its package) swooped over the ripples where the carp had vanished. Eagles, sometimes viewed as bullies, often let ospreys do the work.

Neither won in this attempted pilferage.

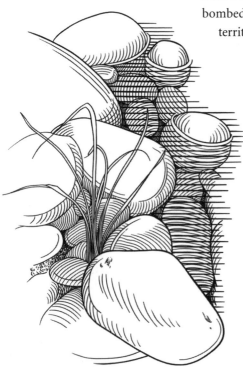

Out of nowhere, a red-tailed hawk fearlessly dive-bombed the eagle, defending a nearby nest or territory of its own, no doubt.

The eagle, unfazed, soared slowly off, but as the hawk returned, two crows erupted from a riverside neighborhood and took up the attack. They, too, must have been spurred by the same motive that drove the hawk into the air against the eagle.

As the hawk moved off, three or four blackbirds in turn went after the crows and the entire feathered dogfight disappeared around the bend.

Stunned by the sequence, we easily imagined a similar drama constantly occurring in the river beneath the boat.

Big fish chasing little fish, little fish chasing insects, insects chasing whatever insects chase.

And the city around us hummed on ... oblivious to distraction.

Risks

From the shoreline of the quiet bay protecting the boat launch at Meldrum Bar Park in Gladstone, a mallard hen leads her just-hatched brood of ducklings at dusk into the water for their first swim across to a large gravel peninsula.

They hang close, then separate in the minefield of gravel and stones as the hen waddles toward the safety of the river.

From among a crowd of picnickers, a pit bull spots the brood and bursts toward the hen. She spots the danger and, quacking loudly, darts in front of the brood, but still angling toward the water.

Confused, the ducklings scatter in a fan as the dog grabs one, shakes and tosses it aside and then gets another, barely inches from the safety of the lapping current. It returns briefly to each tiny carcass, sniffs, then trots back to the bonfire.

Out in the water, the hen collects the survivors and heads downriver.

At the turn of the millennium, *The Oregonian* ran a series of articles called "River of Risk," detailing environmental insults to the Portland Harbor section of the Willamette River. We found decades-old contamination bubbling from shorelines and watched as pipe-cutters with blow torches dropped sparks and slag into the water at terminals.

With the help of the Oregon Bass and Panfish Club, we caught smallmouth bass and crappie and had them tested for PCBs by Oregon State University. Our findings were adopted by state and local agencies, happy for updated information about the city's infamous Superfund site.

On one outing, Inara Verzemnieks, a reporter who speaks Russian and Ukranian, went along to help interview an immigrant crowd fishing near the river's mouth for carp and other scrap fish.

I was reminded of a magazine piece long ago in which a river rat living beneath a bridge near Three Mile Island in Pennsylvania was checked for radiation after the near-meltdown of the nuclear power plant in 1979.

The memorable phrase, as I recalled to Inara, went something like: "How do you explain a roentgen to Ralph, the river rat?"

Inara thought for a moment, then turned to her ethnic subjects to ask whether they knew the danger of making soup from the heads of contaminated fish. There was a flurry of strange words, then a final short sentence delivered by a man who appeared to be their leader.

Inara turned to me: "They're not very worried. He said it could be worse. He said this river is clean compared with where they came from."

And so we press on in our own forefathers' tradition.

We plan new bridges and debate who has to clean up what.

We argue over slowing our boats down to preserve serenity.

We want to shoot sea lions, stop geese from pooping in our parks, tell the neighbor to stop feeding raccoons, keep coyotes from eating our cats but won't keep our bird-eating cats indoors.

We are oblivious to distraction.

Release

I finish an evening of crappie fishing in the Swan Island Lagoon under the glow of Coleman lanterns. We've tossed a few small fish to raccoons on the shoreline. They're a living oxymoron to the lagoon's moored ships, industry, and rotting piers.

At midnight, the jet sled skims easily from the lagoon out onto the darkened glassy waters of the Willamette River. The sled's wake ripples apart reflections of shoreside lights, and I revel in the cool breeze created by the powerful outboard's momentum through the warm summer evening.

Wind in my face is invigorating. I'm not nearly my sixty-five years; I'm a teenager again.

A lone beaver looms ahead from the reflected water, and I turn the helm slightly to avoid it.

The animal swims resolutely through the swell and into the gloom as we pass, and I again face the wind.

… Oblivious to distraction.

By Bill Monroe, illustration by Lynn Kitagawa

Tanner Springs Park

Location: Pearl District, between NW 10th and 11th and NW Marshall and Northrup Streets, Portland **Activities:** Walking, People watching, Picnicking, Urban wildlife and bird viewing, Photography, Environmental education **Facilities:** Parking, Paved and unpaved trails, Interpretive signs, Picnic area, Boardwalk, Floating pontoon, Rain Pavilion, Seat walls **Fees and Regulations:** Pets on leash **Hiking Difficulty:** Easy **Highlights:** An urban wetland park in a dense downtown neighborhood; Artwall; Ospreys diving after fish in the pond **Public Transit:** Portland Streetcar and numerous TriMet buses

Tanner Spring Park is an urban wetland park unique to both Portland and city parks across the country. Its creation was framed by the unprecedented concept of becoming a wetland oasis within a newly created, dense, downtown neighborhood. Tanner Springs was conceived in a 1993 City of Portland study that reviewed the possibilities of "daylighting" Tanner Creek. Daylighting refers to the process of unearthing streams, bringing them back to the surface from buried pipes, and restoring at least a portion of their ecological function. Tanner Creek historically flowed from the Oregon Zoo in the West Hills through Jeld-Wen Field, eventually joining the Willamette River at Centennial Mills. It was buried in underground pipes in the late 1800s. Its natural wetlands were developed into a railroad yard.

The overall goal of Tanner Springs Park was to create a contemplative environment in a new urban neighborhood that would be a complement to two other Pearl District parks—an interactive water park (Jamison Square) two blocks south and an active recreation park (The Fields Park) two blocks north. Tanner Springs was also designed to pay homage to both the natural history and the industrial railroad history of its setting.

Risky Reflections

As many as one billion birds die each year in the United States due to collisions with windows. Window strikes are increasingly recognized as second only to habitat loss and fragmentation of habitat as primary causes for bird population declines. Simply put, birds do not recognize glass as a barrier. During the day they see reflections in the glass as a continuation of habitat and fly full-speed into it. Male robins are notorious for repeatedly attacking their own reflection in windows, mistakenly believing their image is a competitor. In addition, many bird species migrate at night and are actually drawn to illuminated windows on tall buildings, especially under foggy weather conditions. They can either crash directly into the windows or circle until they fall from the sky, exhausted.

Many cities including Portland have Lights Out campaigns that promote dimming of lights on tall buildings during migratory periods. Portland is developing Bird Friendly Building Guidelines with building design strategies that reduce collision risks. At home you can reduce window collisions by creating visual markers on windows to break up reflections. Place birdfeeders less than three feet or more than thirty feet from windows.

—Mary Coolidge and Bob Sallinger

Tanner Springs has a variety of features that exemplify Portland's commitment to promoting sustainable design and connecting people with nature. Its features include: a wetland and pond with a pontoon walkway; a rain pavilion at the northwest corner; and an art wall constructed of railroad rails embedded with glass panels incorporating "insect art." A boardwalk along NW 10th Avenue will eventually tie Jamison, Tanner, and the Fields Park together. Tanner Springs was planted with trees, grasses, and wetland plants native to the Willamette Valley. The final park design also included naturalistic stream features, interpretive signage, and tiered seating areas.

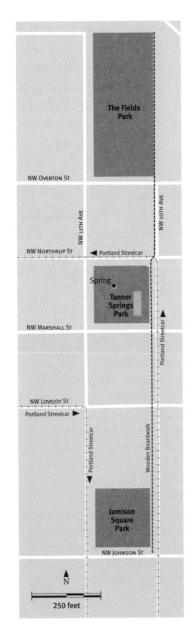

I visit this park when I want to connect to a naturalistic environment in an urban setting without a lot of commotion. Typically, I only have to share the park with another ten to twenty people, when just two blocks south at Jameson Square there will often be over a hundred visitors, or if an event is being held, as many as a thousand. By contrast, at Tanner Springs I see couples on the benches having intimate conversations, a few people hanging out at the wetland pond boardwalk, others practicing yoga on the lawn, photographers, and one or two park strollers. A white-crowned sparrow might be singing from a nearby perch, and if you are lucky, you might see an osprey harvesting fish from the pond. Early morning and dusk are the best times to visit the park, when the natural light creates terrific photographic opportunities of native grasses in contrast with the urban setting.

Access

Entrances from surrounding streets. Given the park's size, this is a stroll not a hike.

How to Get There

PUBLIC TRANSIT: Portland Streetcar provides immediate access to the park along NW 10th Avenue and NW Northrup Street. Many TriMet buses also stop nearby.

By Mike Faha

More information: Portland Parks & Recreation

September Is for Swifts

SWIFT WATCH IS THE QUINTESSENTIAL Portland outdoor activity. Each fall, Vaux's swifts gather at the Chapman Elementary School chimney and for a month or so, put on an unbelievable aerial sunset show.

Vaux's swifts (*Chaetura vauxi*) arrive in Portland from their southern wintering grounds in late April and nest throughout the area. During the summer months, you will see and hear them in neighborhoods, flying high in little bands of six birds or so, eating insects. In late August, they start gathering at Chapman Elementary School in Northwest Portland's Wallace Park to roost in the school's large chimney. Ever greater numbers of swifts gather over the next month and each night treat delighted onlookers to aerial vortices and antics with a climactic downward "pouring" of birds into the chimney—an avian tornado—as the sky darkens. Since 1993, Audubon Society of Portland volunteer naturalists have hosted Swift Watch to invite the community to the event and interpret the phenomenon.

Because Swift Watching during high season from mid to late September has become a bit crowded, I like to go a few times during the season. In late August or early September there are not many swifts or people, but you can see and really hear the birds as they chase each other around with their polite let-me-in "please, please, please, please, please" chirps. The weather is gorgeous, and since sunset is still late, there is plenty of time to get there after work.

By mid-September, the flock of swifts and swift watchers has grown exponentially. The swifts, by the tens of thousands, put on their extraordinary show as they collect, swirl, change direction, chase, and twitter throughout the evening. Just when you think they have all arrived, another hundred come flying in from the east ... and look! More from the northwest.

The drama has increased in recent years as a neighborhood Cooper's hawk has homed in on this fine source of an evening meal. Though Coops normally chase their bird prey through dense foliage, this particular bird merely sits out in the open. On the chimney. Waiting. At some point, the swifts need to begin their evening descent into the chimney, and one unlucky bird gets nabbed. The Cooper's hawk will often fly to a western redcedar tree near the school to enjoy the easy meal.

Also watch for a peregrine falcon that flies quickly through the swirl of swifts. The swifts will turn and give chase, and I have rarely seen a peregrine prevail. When the falcon gets tired and turns tail, the crowd gives a raucous cheer for the underdogs!

It's not only the swifts that provide quite a spectacle: kids sliding down the hill on cardboard, picnickers with gourmet spreads, a fascinating array of hairstyles and tattoos, dogs (on leash please!), young, old, smart, goofy, Portlanders and out-of-towners alike. Many birding enthusiasts arrange trips specifically to be in Portland for this early fall spectacle.

By late September, the crowds of watchers have increased, but the numbers of swifts have noticeably declined. As the weather changes and our Northwest insects lay their eggs and die, the swifts need to head to Southern California and Mexico with the other migratory aerial insect eaters. The swifts leave a few thousand at a time, until one very cold, wet day in late September or early October, the last hearty souls move on.

By Jennifer Devlin, illustration by Lynn Kitagawa

More information: Audubon Society of Portland

Did You Know?

The Vaux's swift, named after William S. Vaux (pronounced "vawks"), is the smallest swift in North America. Large groups are collectively known as a box, flock, screaming frenzy, or swoop of swifts.

—Mike Houck

What About That Chimney?!

Since most of old-growth snags have been removed from our forests, Vaux's swifts now use chimneys as nesting sites. In 1993, people noticed swifts collecting in the Chapman School chimney and rather than fire up the furnace, students and teachers piled on sweaters and coats. The school was committed to protecting the swifts and in 2000 the school and the Audubon Society of Portland helped raise funds to replace the heating system. The swifts are now provided with a permanent fall roost site in the decommissioned chimney.

Marquam Nature Park

LOCATION: SW Marquam Street and Sam Jackson Park Road, Portland **ACTIVITIES:** Hiking, Wildlife viewing, Photography **FACILITIES:** Parking, Paved and unpaved trails, Interpretive signs/shelter, Drinking water **FEES AND REGULATIONS:** Open 5 am to midnight, Pets on leash **HIKING DIFFICULTY:** Moderate **HIGHLIGHTS:** Part of the 40-Mile Loop trail and the 4-T Trail, which begins at the Oregon Zoo and offers round-trip connections by trail, tram, trolley, and train; Panoramic views of the city and the Cascade peaks at Council Crest Park **PUBLIC TRANSIT:** OHSU Tram; MAX Red and Blue Lines; TriMet buses 8, 51, 61, 64, 65, 66, 68

Nature heals. How appropriate, then, that adjacent to Oregon Health Sciences University, the state's preeminent medical facility, you will find Marquam Nature Park. It's a quiet green corridor that takes you into forest thick with sword fern, big-leaf maple, and Douglas fir. Here sterile halls give way to birdsong and the crunch of gravel beneath your feet (watch out for the not-so-crunchy banana slugs). Greenways like Marquam are vital to urban wildlife as well as a welcome respite for city dwellers.

The park is comprised of 176 acres, the bulk of which was saved from development in the 1960s by a group that became the Friends of Marquam Nature Park. The Friends offer guided hikes and help organize restoration efforts vital to returning the park to its natural splendor.

The Marquam Trail runs 3.2 miles from Terwilliger Boulevard up to Council Crest, then another 1.8 miles on to Washington Park. Like the nature park, the trail bears the name of prominent Portland pioneer Philip A. Marquam, a judge and state legislator. The Marquam Trail is well marked with spur trails leading to the park shelter, which features interpretive signs and drinking water.

You need to be in good shape to tackle the hilly terrain in this park, but your efforts will be rewarded when you break from the shady forest into sunlight and green grass atop Council Crest, the highest point in Portland. Here, violet-green and barn swallows dive and swoop on a summer's day. No matter the season, the views from Council Crest will impress upon you a sense of history and of place—there being none quite like Portland.

Access

The trail is accessible from OHSU, Washington Park, or Council Crest Park. Trails are hilly and mostly unpaved, rising in elevation from 300 feet at the Marquam Park shelter to 1040 feet at Council Crest Park. The Marquam Trail crosses several residential streets with limited parking. Trail intersections are well marked with maps available at major street crossings.

How to Get There

BY CAR: Marquam Street off Sam Jackson Park Road, near Duniway Park. Also enter from Terwilliger Boulevard, Broadway Drive, Fairmount Boulevard, Sherwood,

Marquam Hill, or Greenway Roads. **PUBLIC TRANSIT:** The downtown trolley links with the OHSU Tram, which accesses the Marquam Trail via the 4-T Trail. MAX Red or Blue Line to the Oregon Zoo. TriMet buses 8 (Jackson Park), 61, 64, 65, 66, and 68 (Marquam Hill) or 51 (Vista/Council Crest).

By Connie Levesque

More information: Friends of Marquam Nature Park and Portland Parks & Recreation

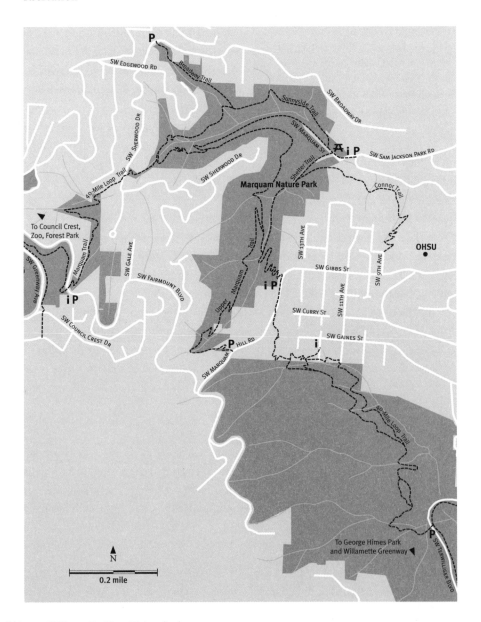

Wildwood Trail and the 40-Mile Loop

THE WILDWOOD TRAIL runs the spine of Forest Park, connecting to a maze of trails and fire lanes, and provides access to some of Portland's most iconic parks and natural areas, including Washington Park, Hoyt Arboretum, Pittock Mansion, and the Audubon Sanctuaries.

At thirty miles, it's also the longest unbroken segment of the 40-Mile Loop trail system. The Loop, now covering more than 140 miles around Portland and much of Multnomah County, was inspired by John Charles Olmsted's 1903 report to the Portland Park Board. Escorted by Portland Park Board member Colonel L. L. Hawkins, Olmsted recommended that Portland develop a forty-mile series of parkways and boulevards that would connect Portland's most important parks, including what became Washington Park and the "forested reserve" we know today as Forest Park.

The Wildwood Trail starts behind the World Forestry Center and climbs five hundred feet through Hoyt Arboretum and another three hundred feet to Pittock Mansion. From there the trail descends into Balch Creek canyon near the Audubon Society of Portland's sanctuaries, where it joins Lower Macleay Trail and parallels Balch Creek for a distance. At the "stone house," the Wildwood splits off from Lower Macleay and heads back uphill and north for twenty-five undulating and twisting miles through Forest Park until it terminates at NW Newberry Road.

If you're up for the entire 140 miles of the Loop, it's possible to wind your way down to the Willamette River on a spur trail off the Wildwood, cross the St. Johns Bridge, and head out to Smith and Bybee Wetlands Natural Area. From there you can cycle seventeen miles east along the Marine Drive bicycle path all the way to Fairview and Gresham. In Gresham, you can walk or cycle six miles back to the Springwater Corridor at the Main City Park, and from there it's another twelve miles back to the Willamette River. Once you cross the Willamette, the Loop climbs six miles back up the East face of the West Hills to Terwilliger Boulevard—the one Olmsted parkway that was actually built—and continues up to Council Crest and another two miles back to the World Forestry Center.

By Mike Houck

Hoyt Arboretum

Location: 4000 SW Fairview Boulevard, Portland **Activities:** Hiking, Nature study, Wildlife viewing **Facilities:** Restrooms, Parking, Paved and unpaved trails, Visitor Center, Bill deWeese Classroom, Stevens Pavilion Picnic Shelter, Wedding Meadow, and Redwood Deck are available as rental facilities **Fees and Regulations:** Hours 5 am to 10 pm, No biking, Pets on leash **Hiking Difficulty:** Easy, Moderate **Highlights:** Over 6,000 labeled trees with interpretive and wayfinding signs; Vietnam Veterans of Oregon Memorial; Hoyt Arboretum Visitor Center for trail maps and information about the plant collections **Public Transit:** MAX Red and Blue Lines; TriMet bus 63

Hoyt Arboretum's habitat is truly unique in Portland. Its 187 acres include natural areas, groves, exotic conifer species, mixed-age exotic deciduous trees and shrubs—all sharing space with generous patches of grassland. Add to this a major dose of topography and you've got the most varied upland habitat on Portland's west side. Owned and managed by Portland Parks & Recreation, the arboretum straddles the SW Fairview Boulevard ridge above the Oregon Zoo and the Japanese Garden. Its highest point on the ridge is 900 feet. Its lowest point of 650 feet is along W Burnside Road below the Wildwood Trail crossing. Intermittent water is found in several ravines, the most significant of which is Johnson Creek running through the conifers toward Burnside (not to be confused with the eastside Johnson Creek).

The arboretum's trail system is legendary. Ten miles of pedestrian trails provide great access to the arboretum's plant collections of over six thousand specimens. Walkers and joggers get the added bonus of a great cardio workout in beautiful surroundings. And if that's not enough, the arboretum is well connected to other parks via the 40-Mile Loop's Wildwood Trail, which begins here and passes through other areas in Washington Park before turning north to Pittock Mansion and Forest Park. The Marquam Trail connects the arboretum to Council Crest, Marquam Nature Park, and Terwilliger Parkway to the south.

With its altitude and varied forest cover, the arboretum is a great spot to view migratory songbirds, especially in the spring. The grasslands and woodlands are home to an array of small mammals, amphibians, and reptiles. Of course, where there are small mammals, there are raptors and other predators such as coyotes.

Larger mammals also make appearances. The arboretum's forested connection to Forest Park and beyond means that deer are frequently spotted, but on an irregular basis. Elk and bobcat are also reported, but rarely. As in other natural areas in Portland, black bear and mountain lion are only remote possibilities.

Access

There are twelve miles of trails throughout the arboretum, most having gravel surface and including elevation gain and loss with grades easy to moderate. The half mile

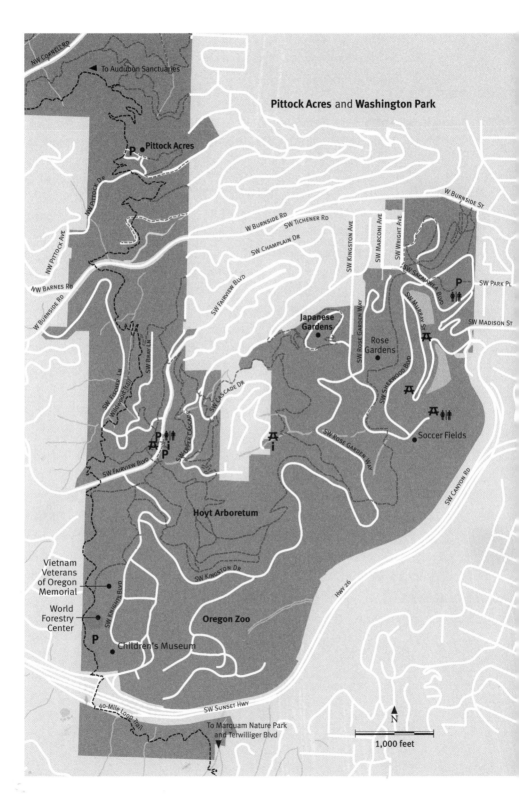

Pittock Acres and Washington Park

To Audubon Sanctuaries

NW CORNELL RD

Pittock Acres

NW PITTOCK DR

NW PITTOCK AVE

W BURNSIDE RD

NW BARNES RD

W BURNSIDE RD

W BURNSIDE RD

W BURNSIDE ST

SW TICHENER RD

SW CHAMPLAIN DR

SW FAIRVIEW BLVD

SW KINGSTON AVE

SW MARCONI AVE

SW WRIGHT AVE

SW SACAJAWEA BLVD

W BURNSIDE ST

SW PARK PL

SW MADISON ST

Japanese Gardens

SW ROSE GARDEN WAY

Rose Gardens

SW SHERWOOD BLVD

SW MURRAY ST

SW FISCHER LN

SW BRAY LN

Wildwood Trail

SW CASCADE DR

Maple Cascade

SW ROSE GARDEN WAY

SW ROSE GARDEN WAY

Soccer Fields

SW FAIRVIEW BLVD

Hoyt Arboretum

SW CANYON RD

SW KINGSTON DR

Vietnam
Veterans
of Oregon
Memorial

World
Forestry
Center

SW KNIGHTS BLVD

Oregon Zoo

Hwy 26

Children's Museum

40-Mile Loop Trail

SW SUNSET HWY

To Marquam Nature Park
and Terwilliger Blvd

N

1,000 feet

Overlook Trail from the Washington Park Light Rail Station is paved and has a 5 percent grade. The Bristlecone Pine Trail is an accessible trail with ADA parking located on Fischer Lane, not far from the visitor center. The arboretum's visitor center is fully accessible.

How to Get There

BY CAR: U.S. Highway 26 (Sunset Highway) west to Oregon Zoo exit; north through the Zoo parking lot to Knights Boulevard; uphill to the stop sign at Fairview Boulevard. Turn right (northeast) onto Fairview. The arboretum's visitor center is located 150 yards on your right with two small parking lots. **BY BIKE:** Kingston Boulevard or Fairview Boulevard up from Washington Park, or take Fairview down from Skyline Boulevard. The bicycle-friendly TriMet bus 63 also goes directly to the Hoyt Arboretum Visitor Center. Otherwise, take the bicycle-friendly MAX to the Washington Park MAX Station and bicycle up Knights Boulevard to Fairview Boulevard (see above public transportation and car instructions). A bike rack is available at the visitor center. Bicycles are not allowed on arboretum trails. **PUBLIC TRANSIT:** TriMet bus 63 weekdays only from SW 18th Avenue and Morrison Street to the Hoyt Arboretum Visitor Center. Also, daily MAX Red and Blue Lines Light Rail service to the Washington Park MAX Station. From the MAX Station, head west and cross the street toward the World Forestry Center, then go right and take the Overlook Trail for a half-mile walk uphill to the visitor center.

By Jim Sjulin, Mat Sinclair, and Sue Thomas

More information: Hoyt Arboretum Friends; Portland Parks & Recreation

Washington Park

LOCATION: Washington Park and its associated attractions, including the Zoo and Hoyt Arboretum, are bordered by US Hwy 26 south and east, Burnside Road north, Vista Ave east, Portland ACTIVITIES: Hiking, Biking, Tennis, Plant and wildlife viewing FACILITIES: Restrooms, Parking, Paved and unpaved trails, Visitor center, Picnic area/shelter, Interpretive signs/info, Tennis courts, Archery range, Playing fields, Children's playground, Rose garden, Small-gauge railroad, Gift shop, Snack shack, Reservable spaces, Japanese Garden FEES AND REGULATIONS: No fee for Rose Gardens or public park, Separate entrance fees for Zoo, Japanese Gardens, World Forestry Center, and Children's Museum, Pets on leash HIKING DIFFICULTY: Easy, Moderate HIGHLIGHTS: The International Rose Test Garden gives Portland its famous nickname, The City of Roses; Zoo; Hoyt Arboretum; Japanese Gardens; Natural areas of the park resemble the wilderness of nearby Forest Park; MAX Washington Park Station is the deepest transit stop in North America, with a fantastic core-sample geologic time-line display PUBLIC TRANSIT: MAX Red or Blue lines; TriMet buses 63, 20; Washington Park Shuttle (summer only)

The City of Portland acquired the first forty-one acres of Washington Park in 1871. At that time, cougar and bobcat stalked through these Tualatin Mountains, which were thickly forested and scarcely accessible to Portland's mere eight thousand residents. Logging, landscaping, and a cable car civilized the park in the decades after 1871 and the Oregon Zoo was relocated farther up the hill from Washington Park. But portions of the park are still a likely place to look for other, less ferocious native wildlife, including dozens of bird species, several types of squirrel, and even the occasional deer.

Land was eventually added to Washington Park, along with new attractions: first the Zoo; then the World Forestry Center; and in 1917, the International Rose Test Garden. In 1922, the park grew to its current size through the addition of the County Poor Farm, most of which became the Hoyt Arboretum. Later came the Zoo Railway, the Portland Japanese Gardens, and finally, the Portland Children's Museum, which replaced the old OMSI site. The Japanese Gardens, Children's Museum, Zoo and Zoo Railway, and World Forestry Center are all now managed independently. When these attractions are included, the park's total area is more than three hundred acres. But Portland Parks & Recreation manages just the 130 acres of the park proper, including the rose garden, arboretum, and public amenities: lawns, trails, picnic areas, an archery range, sports field, tennis courts, an accessible children's playground, memorials, and statuary.

The steep ravine along the south side of Washington Park is accessible to visitors only via the Zoo Railway's Washington Park excursion train, which runs Memorial Day to Labor Day. If the presence of other excited riders, both young and old, is not too distracting, the train offers new views of Washington Park natural areas. Two of the railway's trains are also wheelchair accessible when boarding at the Zoo.

Wildwood Trail

While the International Rose Test Gardens and the Oregon Zoo often steal the show, Washington Park also contains the first three miles of Portland's thirty-mile-long Wildwood Trail, which is a Portland icon in its own right. Most of the natural areas in Washington Park can be viewed from the Wildwood, which begins near the Vietnam Veteran's Memorial and Washington Park MAX Station. This trailhead can also be reached via the 40-Mile Loop Trail that comes over Council Crest to the Sunset Highway canyon. The Wildwood Trail is then an extension of the 40-Mile Loop through Washington Park and to the far reaches of Forest Park, terminating at NW Newberry Road.

From its beginning in the south portion of the park, the Wildwood Trail makes its way up to a summit with excellent views of the city and the Cascade peaks beyond. From there, it continues north and down through the Hoyt Arboretum, past the archery field and into Washington Park proper. A spur trail, "Mac," continues down past the Children's Park, Rose Gardens, and the picnic areas and lawns around the main pedestrian entrance on Park Place. The Wildwood makes a sharp U-turn at the Mac trail turnoff and heads back north and up, past the Japanese Gardens and through more of the arboretum, to cross Burnside and reach Pittock Acres and then Forest Park. On its way, the Wildwood passes through uncultivated portions of the park, which, outside the arboretum, are mixed second-growth forest with Douglas fir predominating.

The Washington Park segment of the Wildwood Trail doesn't have the sense of silent, interior habitat that exists along some other portions of the trail. However, it still has much to recommend it. It is easily accessible by MAX, well graded, and well traveled. The views are memorable, and the topography often challenging. It is an excellent place to begin or end an ambitious long hike on the Wildwood, and its location also provides an opportunity to enjoy native plants, wildlife,

Japanese Gardens

In 1958, Portland became a sister city to Sapporo, Japan, and soon thereafter business leaders and the mayor decided it would be wonderful for Portland to have a traditional Japanese garden. On June 4, 1962, the city council created a commission to establish the garden on the site of the former Washington Park Zoo. The Japanese Garden Society of Oregon was formed in 1963. Takuma Tono, a Tokyo Agricultural University professor and internationally recognized authority on Japanese landscape design, was commissioned to design and supervise the development of the garden, and he began landscaping that year. In the summer of 1967, the Portland Japanese Garden formally opened to the public. The 5.5-acre Japanese garden is composed of five separate gardens: Strolling Pond Garden, Tea Garden, Natural Garden, Flat Garden, and Sand and Stone Garden. Through the careful use of plants, stones, and water, areas of serene and quiet beauty emerge. The land is now leased from the City of Portland. The gardens present urban naturalists and garden enthusiasts alike a place for quiet contemplation.

—Mike Houck

and real hiking in the city—an experience as authentically Portland as Voodoo Doughnut or a trip to Powell's City of Books.

Even those Rose City residents who prefer to hike the wilder sections of Forest Park or beyond should probably stop and smell the roses at the International Test Gardens once a year. Those who don't care for summer crowds might brave the weather on Valentine's Day, or try it New Years Day to see the first bloom of the year—there's always one hardy, or confused, bush in flower.

Access

Narrow, curvy parkways make for a scenic drive and a challenging bike tour. Pedestrians are better off on the Wildwood and smaller Washington Park trails, which tour the park and pass by the major attractions. One segment of steep ravines is visible only via the Washington Zoo Railway, which boards at the zoo and, in summer, near the International Rose Test Gardens.

How to Get There

BY CAR: U.S. Highway 26 west to exit #72 to enter at the Zoo; or follow Burnside west from downtown Portland, take a hairpin left onto Tichener Road, then follow the signs to the Rose Garden; or take Park Place west to the historic main entrance above PGE Park. **PUBLIC TRANSIT:** MAX Red or Blue Line to Washington Park Station; TriMet bus 63 runs hourly from near Jeld-Wen Field through Washington Park, from the Park Place entrance to the Zoo and back (does not run on weekends). The Washington Park Shuttle (summer only) circles through the park every twenty-five minutes. TriMet bus 20 travels up Burnside from downtown; exit at NW Hermosa Boulevard and walk a short distance west along Burnside to the Wildwood Trail crossing; follow it south down through Hoyt Arboretum.

By Jonna Papaefthimiou

More information: Portland Parks & Recreation

› **Refer to map on page 119**

Pittock Acres Park

Location: 3229 NW Pittock Dr, Portland West Hills **Activities:** Hiking, Historic Pittock Mansion tours **Facilities:** Restrooms, Parking, Paved and unpaved trails, Visitor Center, Picnic area/shelter, Interpretive signs/info, Historic home, Gift shop **Fees and Regulations:** Grounds free, Entrance fees to mansion, Parking lot gated at 9 pm, No pets allowed inside, Pets on leash outside **Hiking Difficulty:** Easy, Moderate **Highlights:** Views of Portland skyline and Cascade peaks; Gardens; Historic Pittock Mansion; Birding, especially spring songbird migration **Public Transit:** TriMet bus 20

Pittock Acres Park encompasses fifty-four acres of land surrounding Pittock Mansion, the landmark estate of prominent turn-of-the-twentieth-century Portlanders Henry and Georgina Pittock. The twenty-two-room mansion was built in 1914, and Portland City Parks acquired the house and grounds in 1964.

Henry Pittock established *The Oregonian* as a daily paper and leveraged his success in the newspaper business with investments that reflected a faith in the limitless natural resources of the West—railroads, steamboats, ranching, mining, and pulp and paper. Fittingly, his home's lavish interiors are rivaled by equally extravagant views of nature. From the rear garden, visitors can see the wooded hills below, the city skyline, the Willamette and Columbia Rivers, and the Cascade Range beyond. The formal gardens around the home reflect Georgina Pittock's passion for flower gardening—she established the Portland Rose Festival. The well-tended collection of ornamentals is now labeled with genus and species. The formal gardens have a paved path that is wheelchair accessible.

Most of the acres in the park are made up by the rocky promontory between Hoyt Arboretum and Forest Park, which are connected by the Wildwood Trail. The summit is just over one thousand feet above sea level, compared to an average elevation of just 173 feet across the city. This, of course, means the trails through the park are steep. Fortunately, city sounds drop away with the topography, so birdsong and chipmunk chatter are most noticeable on the trails, and visitors have a sense of wildness just a short distance from the trailheads.

The elevation of the park results in great views, and the steep slopes also make the park a natural stopping place for migrating spring songbirds. At other times, visitors may be treated to sights of swifts, swallows, and raptors. The variety of habitats, from scattered trees and lawn to a second-growth Douglas fir forest, enhance this landscape's avian appeal. Birders have a good chance to spot morning doves and band-pigeons, warbling and Cassin's vireo, pine siskin, red crossbills, black-headed grosbeaks, purple finches, and over one hundred other species.

There is a fee to tour the house, but it is free to use the park and gardens, restrooms, and drinking fountains. These amenities and ample parking make this a good place to access the Wildwood Trail.

Access

The mansion and landscaped areas are accessible via a paved walkway from the parking lot; the house and garden are wheelchair accessible. Other portions of the park are accessible via the Wildwood Trail, which is steep but well maintained.

How to Get There

BY CAR: Follow W Burnside Road west; turn right on Barnes Road (sign for Pittock Mansion here), turn right on Pittock Drive. **PUBLIC TRANSIT:** TriMet bus 20 travels up Burnside from downtown; exit at NW Hermosa Boulevard and walk a short distance west along Burnside to the Wildwood Trail crossing; follow it north to the mansion.

By Jonna Papaefthimiou

More information: Portland Parks & Recreation; Pittock Mansion

> **Refer to map on page 119**

Swift or Swallow?

Standing on the bluff overlooking the city in summer, especially in early morning, one is often bombarded by a flight of darting small birds that could be swallows. Or are they swifts? The only swift around here is a Vaux's, the same one that inhabits the chimney at Chapman Elementary School just prior to fall migration. The trick in distinguishing swifts from swallows is their flight pattern and wing shape. Swifts have swept-back, jet-fighter-like wings and a seemingly alternating wing beat that make them appear somewhat bat-like in flight. Swallows clearly flap their wings together and their wings appear much straighter in profile. If you have good light, identification is much less problematic given the swift's brown or gray color, contrasted with the white rump, face, and belly of violet-green swallows, the blue back and stark white belly of tree swallows, the blue back and rust bellies of barn swallows, and the orange or buff rump patch and "headlight" of cliff swallows.

—Mike Houck

Forest Park

FOREST PARK IS AN UNPARALLELED RESOURCE, a rarity even among the world's urban parks. Blanketing a steep slope rising northwest of downtown and situated fully within Portland's city limits, the park spans more than five thousand acres of native forest. Equally as important, however, is the fact that Forest Park has retained connectivity to the larger and wilder forests of Oregon's Coast Range. This wildlife corridor provides a means for larger mammals to include the park in their seasonal wanderings. As a result, deer and elk are not an uncommon sight in the northern reaches of the park. Although elusive, bobcat and coyote thrive, and the occasional black bear and spotted owl sightings serve to reinforce the park's wild character. In spite of development pressures and the encroachment of non-native invasive species, Forest Park still features an impressive biodiversity of native flora and fauna for an urban park—one hundred species of birds and more than fifty species of mammals. In fact, the vast majority of the species spotted in the area when Captain William Clark ventured up the Willamette River in 1806 are still found here today.

It has been said that Forest Park was a good idea that just wouldn't go away. Its origins can be traced back to the creation of the Portland Municipal Parks Commission in 1900. The commission hired the Olmsted Brothers to conduct a park planning study, and brought John Charles Olmsted to Portland in 1903. Alluding to the forested hills commonly known as the Tualatin Mountains, Olmsted declared that "no use to which the land could be put would begin to be as sensible or as profitable to the city as that of making it a public park. . . ." Nevertheless, several earnest attempts to realize this vision failed in the decades to come. The land became the target of real estate development schemes, multiple logging efforts, and at least one failed attempt at oil drilling. In spite of all this, the efforts of the City Club of Portland, the Committee of Fifty, and other dedicated citizens eventually led to the establishment of Forest Park's original 4,200 acres in 1948. Over the next six decades, land acquisition efforts by various entities have added more than eight hundred acres to the park's original core, and these efforts continue today. Clearly, the region owes a great debt to the vision and persistence of these early advocates.

Today, Forest Park is a popular destination for hikers, trail runners, dog walkers, mountain bikers, and even equestrians, attracting locals and out-of-town visitors alike. The park offers roughly 70 miles of trail to the recreational user, including the 30.2 miles of the Wildwood Trail. A short walk in from any of the park's forty or so trailheads will quickly induce a sense of remoteness that is remarkable for an urban setting.

The sights and sounds of a deep forest habitat define the experience, although the steady hum of the city and occasional clamor from the industrial area below may also be heard at times. The song of the Pacific wren permeates the forest year-round, and the wild cackles of the pileated woodpecker and northern flicker are a less common delight. Recent research has confirmed that the park holds a thriving population of northern pygmy-owl, who are just one of the dozens of native birds actively nesting in Forest Park. In recent years, bald eagles have returned to nest in the northern section of the park. Two of the larger watersheds in the park, Balch and Miller Creeks, feature vibrant populations of native cutthroat trout and coastal giant salamanders. Significant portions of Forest Park are dominated by big-leaf maple and red alder; these deciduous trees are a legacy of the recent history of human and natural disturbance, primarily logging and wildfire. In other areas of the park, a mix of conifers prevails—Douglas fir, western hemlock, and western redcedar being the most common. Throughout Forest Park, native ferns and evergreen shrubs such as Oregon grape and salal dominate the forest floor. In early spring, wildflowers begin to emerge and for several weeks entire hillsides are covered in trillium. As the weather dries out in late spring, the trails begin to see heavy use that lasts well into autumn. Winter is an ideal time of year to find solitude, as incoming Pacific storms convert nameless ephemeral streams to raging torrents, and mud is more plentiful.

While Forest Park's native flora continues to provide habitat for a broad array of wildlife, growing recreational use and the spread of non-native invasive species increasingly pose a threat to the park's ecological health. In the years to come, Forest Park's managers and stewards will need to find a way to accommodate growing numbers of recreational users without unduly compromising the ecological health and biodiversity of this remarkable asset. The Forest Park Conservancy, a nonprofit organization that has evolved from the original Committee of Fifty, works in close partnership with Portland Parks & Recreation to protect and restore Forest Park. The conservancy employs a year-round field crew to work on trail maintenance and habitat restoration projects, and has attracted a growing corps of dedicated volunteers. In 2009, more than 1,500 volunteers joined the conservancy for regular work parties. For those who cherish this unique treasure that we have been fortunate enough to inherit, it is a means of reinforcing the ongoing legacy of stewardship, and helping to hand off a healthy and intact Forest Park to the generations to come.

By Stephen Hatfield, illustration by Allison Bollman

More information: Portland Parks & Recreation; Forest Park Conservancy; Marcy Houle's book, *Forest Park: One City's Wilderness.*

Northern Pygmy-Owls

SHAKESPEARE MADE NO SPECIES DISTINCTION when he regularly referred to the most identifiable creature of the night: "The owl, night's herald, shrieks, 'tis very late; / The sheep are gone to fold, birds to their nest." For most of us the owl is a bird of mystery, seldom glimpsed but most often imagined as large, fierce, and nocturnal. Owls have voices that rightly hush our lips, tingle our skin, and bring us quickly to our senses, and to our sense of wilderness. In Portland's Forest Park five species of owl are breeding residents, and though all maintain their secrecy and are wild predatory birds, one of them is neither large nor nocturnal.

The northern pygmy-owl is a contrarian. At merely two ounces and about six inches long, it eschews the perceived benefits of large size and is able to nest in tree cavities with entrances less than two inches wide. Instead of conducting itself like the western screech-owl and securing a few tens of acres for its territory, the Napoleonic pygmy-owl defends hundreds. And rather than hunting by night, it hunts and is active by day, but remains inconspicuous all the same.

On calm mornings males start their activity precisely at dawn by flying up to the tip-top of the tallest available tree and calling with a mighty "toot"—the monotonous, whistled note repeated every two or three seconds. The call carries far and wide above and below the forest canopy, but no one's spine is made to shiver by this vocalization, except perhaps that of the chickadee, deer mouse, or nuthatch. In March and April some males call almost continuously for hours at a time, but will cease at dusk. Thus spring is the season when pygmy-owls are most easily found, but only by the attentive observer who first hears and localizes the call, and then makes the necessary maneuvers on the forest floor that allow scrutiny of the many treetops that must be checked to find such a prized reward. But this hard-won sighting will most often represent only the smaller half of a breeding pair. Unlike other owl species of which both sexes may call and duet, a vocalizing pygmy-owl is almost certainly a male.

The female northern pygmy-owl is perhaps the most mysterious of all North American owls. Though often 20 percent larger than her mate, she seldom vocalizes loudly, except for a few brief courtship exchanges immediately prior to egg laying. To remain undetected near the nest, the female restricts her breeding season vocal communication to a barely audible contact call that is reminiscent of a soft "chitter" sound sometimes made by Douglas squirrels. Contact calls are often exchanged when the female receives prey that her mate has brought to the nest, where she remains vigilant during most of the breeding period. But make no mistake; the female pygmy-owl is

not a kept woman. She is a capable and efficient hunter as well as a devoted parent. Once her owlet nestlings—which may number as many as eight and are sometimes reared in an abandoned hairy woodpecker nest—can thermoregulate on their own, she will exhaust much of her day capturing mice, voles, and small birds whose misfortune it was to stray within her domain. After the mother leaves the nest her young owlets will then be provided for by both parents for about two months before they are left to fend for themselves. The adult female pygmy-owl then fades back into the forest like an apparition, only to be coaxed back into form by the voice of her mate the following spring.

The northern pygmy-owl is among the least studied owls in North America and remains a species of concern in some western states and provinces, mainly due to a lack of information about its population dynamics, movements, and capacity for breeding success. From 2007 to 2011 an investigation was undertaken to understand the breeding biology and habitat preferences of pygmy-owls, and this most comprehensive study to date was undertaken in Forest Park, right here in the city of Portland. An examination of forty-six nest attempts has made clear that pygmy-owls have an obvious preference for nesting in mature forest, interior stands that contain large, tall coniferous trees and that are far from an abrupt forest edge. Furthermore, pygmy-owls that nested at sites containing the greatest structural complexity (ground cover, shrubs, large trees, abundant snags, steep slopes and streams) successfully raised the most owlets. This was an unexpected result for a bird that has often been labeled a forest-edge species.

To be clear, however, pygmy-owls do not shun humans or their structures. Pygmy-owls will occupy territories and readily nest near noisy, heavily traveled commuter routes such as NW Cornell and Germantown Roads. They will visit backyard birdbaths for a dip, and may also frequent bird feeders—but to capture and eat songbirds, not seeds. They will even nest close to homes and businesses as long as large tracts of mature, complex forest engulf these structures and include features that allow a diversity of plants, fungi, microbes, and creatures, particularly woodpeckers, to flourish. In our region, pygmy-owls could almost certainly be seen outside a kitchen window, above a garage, below a bridge, or next to a business if we choose to integrate manmade structures into a multifaceted habitat that mimics the healthiest portions of Oregon's mature, montane forests.

By John Deshler illustration by Elayne Barclay

Audubon Society of Portland Sanctuaries

LOCATION: 5151 NW Cornell Road, Portland
ACTIVITIES: Hiking, Wildlife viewing, Birding
FACILITIES: Restrooms, Parking, Unpaved trails, Visitor center, Wildlife viewing structures, Interpretive signs/info **FEES AND REGULATIONS:** Hours dawn to dusk, No pets
HIKING DIFFICULTY: Easy, Moderate **HIGHLIGHTS:** Incredible birding and nature/ecology study opportunities; Miles of forested trails; natural history programs; Classes and tours on site; Interpretive center; nature bookstore; Wildlife Care Center; Volunteer naturalists roam the trails, often with live education birds of prey perched on their arms **PUBLIC TRANSIT:** TriMet buses 18, 15

Established in 1902, Audubon Society of Portland was one of Oregon's first conservation organizations. The society has long been at the epicenter of many of Oregon's most important conservation achievements, from helping to establish the first wildlife refuges in the West to protecting spotted owls and old-growth ecosystems to pioneering efforts to protect urban greenspaces. Audubon has had a sanctuary above Balch Creek next to Forest Park since 1931, when it secured twelve acres of a mostly deforested dairy farm. Today, the Audubon campus includes three sanctuaries totaling 150 acres. Visitors can explore more than four miles of trails through a lush second-growth forest, see native birds and other wildlife, and discover the region's natural and cultural history through interactive displays. The society offers seasonal presentations and opportunities to interact with live, native birds and animals being rehabilitated at the Wildlife Care Center.

Visitors are frequently greeted in the parking lot by volunteer naturalists with injured, non-releasable birds such as spotted owl, peregrine falcon, red-tailed hawk, or raven. These birds can't be released back into the wild due to injury or imprinting.

The interpretive center provides a wealth of information about the flora and fauna of the site. Birdfeeders offer opportunities to see a variety of northwest bird species including band-tailed pigeons, evening grosbeaks, red-breasted nuthatches, spotted towhees, rufous hummingbirds, and downy woodpeckers. Keep an eye out for Cooper's hawks that prowl the area looking for an easy meal. In the evening, watch for raccoons and northern flying squirrels that sometimes attempt to raid the feeders. The staff and volunteers offer expert natural history information; and the nature store is well stocked with books and other items.

The Sanctuaries

The three wildlife sanctuaries—Collins, Uhtoff, and Pittock—comprise 150 acres of forested habitat accessible by trailheads on both sides of NW Cornell Road.

The Collins Sanctuary, the youngest of the three, is dominated by big-leaf maple and alder trees that allow dappled light and glimpses of sky. Eventually, conifers will replace these deciduous trees. In a new agreement with Metro and a partnership with Friends of Trees, the society will plant ten thousand native trees and shrubs over the

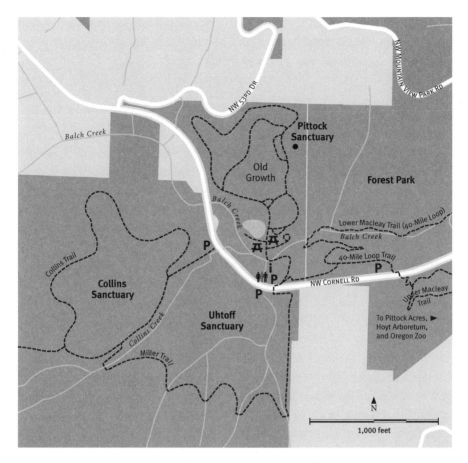

next decade. Today, there are a few places along the Collins loop where hemlocks, Douglas firs, and western redcedars stand tall. A small cluster of sizable Douglas firs can be seen along the north Collins Trail that is closest to Cornell Road. It is advisable to wear long pants and long-sleeved shirts on the Collins Trail in the spring and summer due to stinging nettles.

From the south Collins Trail, a sign directs hikers to the Miller Trail, named in honor of Al Miller, one of Audubon's early environmental activists from the 1960s. This trail traverses through the Uhtoff Wildlife Sanctuary, dedicated to Portland Audubon's first executive director, Mike Uhtoff. This section of trail climbs quickly. At the first bridge two massive snags stand in a low canopy and are framed by one big cedar and a hemlock. The second bridge is another good spot to stop and take in an open forest view before gradually descending and walking over and along one of five ravines that cut through this sanctuary. The hike back to the campus passes by the native plant nursery and to the Uhtoff Sanctuary trailhead and parking lot.

The Pittock Sanctuary, located directly behind Audubon's main building, offers places for reflection and respite but requires a fairly steep descent along a narrow trail to the bridge crossing over Balch Creek. The Pittock Wildlife Sanctuary is the most heavily used of the three and has a number of interpretive signs that showcase components of a forest ecosystem within an urban watershed. Balch Creek is home to coastal giant salamanders and remnant landlocked populations of cutthroat trout. Sightings of the trout populations have become rare in recent years, and the fish may be on their way to disappearing altogether.

The Pittock Sanctuary features a boardwalk alongside a small pond. Look here in the spring for mallards with ducklings hiding among the yellow pond lilies. Rough-skinned newts lurk just below the surface. You can find tracks from raccoons, weasels, skunks, fox, coyote, and even black bear in the mud surrounding the pond. A pavilion at the pond's edge offers shaded rest and a great spot to sit and enjoy the serenity. A series of interconnected loop trails extend outward from the pond area. Be sure to check out the grove of Douglas fir trees estimated to be between 350 and 450 years old on the Old Growth Loop. The giant trees, high, closed canopy, and cool temperatures here are emblematic of what our Pacific Northwest forests must have been like before logging changed the landscape. Along the Woodpecker Trail look for prolific signs of woodpeckers, such as the large, square holes drilled by the Pacific Northwest's largest woodpecker, the pileated.

One of my most memorable bird sightings occurred several years ago here. Dear friends were visiting from the Netherlands, along with their six-year-old son. The four of us turned off on the second spur of the Woodpecker Trail and began hiking slightly uphill. It was early afternoon in late July, and I didn't expect any bird or animal activity. More often than not, I hear a pileated woodpecker in the woods but rarely see it. In this case, I heard it as we rounded the trail, and a steady stream of sawdust flying down the snag provoked me to look up. There it was, this magnificent bird madly pounding on a dead tree. It kept us joyfully entertained for several minutes.

Wildlife Care Center

No trip would be complete without a stop at the Wildlife Care Center, which cares for nearly three thousand wild birds and animals each year. Several cages housing non-releasable birds are located around the Care Center and at the start of the Pittock Trail. Observation windows in the Care Center courtyard allow visitors to observe wildlife surgeries. Staff and volunteers welcome questions about wildlife issues and are eager to share ideas about how people and wildlife can live together harmoniously in urban environments.

Access

The Audubon complex at Cornell Road consists of three interconnected sanctuaries: Pittock, Uhtoff, and Collins. Pittock Trail starts from the main parking lot and Uhtoff Trail begins on the other side of NW Cornell Road from the Nature Store. The Collins Trail starts a few hundred yards west on Cornell, where there is also a small parking lot. Car traffic can be heavy at times, and it's a frequent route for bicyclists, so walking in single file is a good idea. Trails may be slippery, and there are many bridges to cross and stairs to climb.

How to Get There

By car: From NW Portland follow Lovejoy Street past NW 25th Avenue. Lovejoy winds up the hill and turns into Cornell Road after the "right turn without stopping" stop sign. Head west on NW Cornell Road, passing through two tunnels. The Audubon campus is on the right, one quarter mile past the second tunnel near the bottom of the hill (a nearly blind entrance). From the east side of the Willamette River, take Interstate 5 south and take the Highway 30 exit across the Fremont Bridge. Stay right, then merge left to Vaughn Street, heading west, to NW 25th Avenue and turn left. Head south on 25th to NW Lovejoy Street and turn right, following directions above.

Public transit: No direct service. The closest bus is TriMet 18, which stops at the corner of Cornell and Westover, about a mile short of the sanctuary (runs only during rush hour). From there, it's an uphill walk to the sanctuary, with a trail that provides a route around the two tunnels. The next closest bus is 15 on the corner of NW Lovejoy Street and 23rd Avenue (a long uphill hike). It runs frequently during the day.

By Meryl Redisch

More information: Audubon Society of Portland

Mount Tabor Park

Location: Southeast Portland, between Belmont and Division on the north and south, and 60th and 71st Avenues on the east and west **Activities:** Hiking, Biking, Birding **Facilities:** Restrooms, Parking, Paved and unpaved trails, Picnic areas **Fees and Regulations:** Hours 5 am to midnight, Pets on leash (an off-leash area on the south side of the park) **Hiking Difficulty:** Moderate **Highlights:** A Tertiary-era volcano at the end of Portland's bustling Hawthorne district; One of the finest vistas on the east side; The best place in east Portland to view migrant songbirds in April, May, and early June **Public Transit:** TriMet buses 4, 15, 71

When the Olmsted Brothers, America's foremost landscape architectural firm, reviewed Portland's parks and greenspaces in 1903, Mount Tabor—a Tertiary Period volcanic butte about four miles east of downtown Portland—was one of the areas they chose to single out. By then, the first of several reservoirs for Portland's celebrated Bull Run water supply had been constructed on the south side—reservoirs that still store upwards of 140 million gallons of water, although a 2010 EPA decision puts the continued use of these historic landmarks as reservoirs in doubt.

In 1903, Mount Tabor was still well removed from the city, semi-rural, and covered with orchards. Nonetheless the Olmsteds, visualizing Portland's eastward expansion, urged the city to protect the hill, and following their recommendation, the park bureau began its acquisition in 1909. We can all be grateful for the Olmsteds' planning as, nearly a century after it was envisioned, Mount Tabor Park is an eastside highlight of The Intertwine parks and trails network as it knits country and city together better than almost any place in Portland.

At the time of its acquisition, there was no suspicion that Mount Tabor was an extinct volcano. But in 1913, its origins were revealed when a road-building crew discovered traces of volcanic cinders in the northwest corner of the park. Subsequent excavations exposed the throat of the three-million-year-old volcano, which can now be viewed from the edge of the North ("Volcano") Parking Lot.

But this 190-acre park can be appreciated for more than its geologic history. From the west side of the grassy knoll at its 643-foot summit, visitors can experience the best view of Portland on the city's east side, while Mount Hood and the Cascades can be glimpsed through the trees on the summit's western edge.

The park is also a hotspot for resident and migrant birds, and an unofficial checklist contains upwards of 150 species (including a rather impressive list of rare migrants—"one-day wonders"—that have shown up over the years). Because it contains such a diversity of habitats—parkland dotted with tall firs and big-leaf maples, thickets and hedgerows, and a remnant coniferous forest near the summit—Mount Tabor is a good birding spot year-round. But it is especially spectacular between late March and mid-June, when this green atoll becomes a magnet for the migrating songbirds that are pouring through Portland. During that period, a short stroll around the

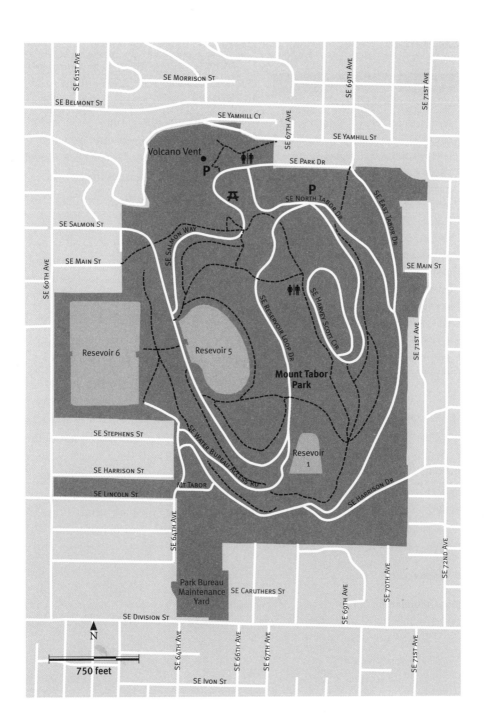

SE 61ST AVE
SE MORRISON ST
SE BELMONT ST
SE YAMHILL CT
SE 67TH AVE
SE 69TH AVE
SE 71ST AVE
SE YAMHILL ST
Volcano Vent
P
SE PARK DR
P
SE NORTH TABOR DR
SE EAST TABOR DR
SE SALMON ST
SE SALMON WAY
SE MAIN ST
SE MAIN ST
SE 60TH AVE
SE RESERVOIR LOOP DR
SE HARVEY SCOTT CIR
Resevoir 6
Resevoir 5
SE 71ST AVE
Mount Tabor
Park
SE STEPHENS ST
Resevoir
1
SE WATER BUREAU ACCESS RD
SE HARRISON ST
SE LINCOLN ST
MT TABOR
SE HARRISON DR
SE 64TH AVE
SE 72ND AVE
Park Bureau
Maintenance
Yard
SE CARUTHERS ST
SE 69TH AVE
SE 70TH AVE
SE DIVISION ST
N
SE 64TH AVE
SE 66TH AVE
SE 67TH AVE
SE 71ST AVE
750 feet
SE IVON ST

butte can easily turn up thirty to forty species. Because of Mount Tabor's rich spring-time birding opportunities, the Audubon Society of Portland regularly schedules bird song walks in the park during April and May.

Sounds of Spring

Winter's crawl into spring is punctuated by a number of bright spots, but one of the finest signs of spring is the return of birdsong. The gradual swelling of the avian chorus stretches from late January (when year-round residents tentatively begin to sing) into June (when the last of the neotropical migrants straggle in). No place in Portland offers a richer array of singing birds than Mount Tabor, especially at the peak of migration in late spring. To acquaint, or reacquaint yourself with these songs, Audubon Society of Portland sponsors Bird Song Walks at Mount Tabor and other locations throughout the spring.

Mount Tabor is so close to downtown that gorgeous summer afternoons invariably find the park extremely crowded; but come in the early morning—especially on a car-free Wednesday—and you will find yourself in nearly sole possession of a rolling, wooded 190-acre estate in the heart of the city.

Access

The entire park is crisscrossed with paths more conducive to strolling than hiking. All are well maintained and some are paved, but the climb to the summit involves a 370-foot elevation gain. The park's summit is always closed to vehicular traffic; the entire park is closed to cars on Wednesdays.

How to Get There

BY CAR: From the west the easiest approach is along SE 60th Avenue, from which several streets enter the park. From the north, follow SE Belmont to 69th Avenue; turn south on 69th, then right on Yamhill Street, which enters the park. On the south side of the park, Lincoln (western approach) and Harrison (eastern approach) Streets connect to form a through route. **PUBLIC TRANSIT:** TriMet bus 4 Division (exit at 66th Avenue and Division Street and proceed north on 66th into the park); 15 Belmont (exit at 69th Avenue and Yamhill Street and follow Yamhill into the park); and 71 (exit at 60th Avenue and Hawthorne Street and follow the sidewalk past the reservoirs and into the park).

By Bob Wilson

More information: Portland Parks & Recreation

138 | Lower Willamette River Watershed

Exploring North Portland
Rose Quarter to Smith and Bybee Lakes and back

My favorite way to explore the North Portland Peninsula is by bike. A convenient starting point is the **Rose Quarter Transit Center** if you're coming from outside the downtown core. Head north on N Interstate to the first greenspace overlooking the rail yards near **Overlook Park.** The only real hill en route is on N Interstate up to Kaiser Permanente and N Overlook Boulevard.

At the dead end on N Skidmore Place is **a little greenspace gem ❶** tucked away on the bluff overlooking rail yards and the industrial district. There are a few scattered orchard trees, with one particularly large apple tree, and a couple of benches and great views of the West Hills, Willamette River, and north to the Swan Island shipyard, Waud Bluff, and the University of Portland. A narrow dirt path runs through the park, so it's best to walk your bike. This small neighborhood greenspace was purchased by Metro with 1995 bond measure funds.

After walking through the park, ride east on N Skidmore Court to N Concord Avenue to the overpass that spirals up and over Going Street. I'm always sure to gear way down to get up the steep corkscrew path over Going and down to the neighborhood's quirky **Pittman Addition Hydropark ❷** at the bottom of the ramp. Here, there's a tiny wayside with a bench and marker declaring that Simon G. Stanich Park is "of the people, by the people, and for the people." It's worth a short stop at the hydropark to look at the tile mosaics on picnic benches, bicycle sculptures, and a small, colorful sign that admonishes park users to "be nice or leave!" A short barkdust trail runs the length of the park providing access to two picnic tables and three canopied wooden chairs. The hydropark is owned by the Portland Water Bureau.

From here, it's a pleasant ride through North Portland neighborhoods along Concord and Alberta, with a brief detour to take in the architecturally interesting **Adidas campus ❸**—a redevelopment of the old Bess Kaiser Hospital—and its huge shoe sculptures. Riding north on N Delaware Avenue, take a left onto N Willamette Boulevard where signs announce you are now in the Columbia Slough watershed. For safety's sake, especially if I'm leading a group, I'll deviate one block north to N Killingsworth Street to catch the traffic light, especially if traffic is heavy on N Greeley Avenue. And, depending on what time of day I started and how hungry or thirsty I am, I may make a quick stop at the myriad **food carts at Killingsworth ❹**. There's plenty to choose from—barbecue, bakery items, ice cream, coffee—and an ATM.

Continue riding west on Killingsworth to N Willamette Boulevard, and then head north on N Willamette Boulevard to N Rosa Parks Way, where there's a left turn for bicycles only onto Willamette Boulevard. Ride north on the now much wider Willamette Boulevard and follow the spacious on-street bike path north along Mock's Crest to the University of Portland, which is visible in the distance atop Waud Bluff.

As you ride along Willamette Boulevard, look down into Mocks Bottom below and note the dramatic contrast with what once was a similar river feature—Oaks Bottom Wildlife Refuge. While Oaks Bottom was protected as Portland's first official urban wildlife refuge, Mocks Bottom's wetlands were filled for industrial development and shipyards. And the plant communities along the bluffs are also strikingly different. The Mocks Crest and Waud Bluff community consists of substantial native ponderosa pine, Oregon white oak, and Pacific madrone, with an understory dominated by poison oak. The bluff overlooking Oaks Bottom by contrast is primarily big-leaf maple, black cottonwood, and Douglas fir, with a few scattered oaks. This contrast is due to a combination of factors, including a more southerly exposure and more well-drained soils along Mocks Crest, whereas the bluff at Oaks Bottom is more northerly facing.

On the left, just before the University of Portland campus, is the hard-to-see **Waud Bluff Trail ❺**, a rocky access trail that leads down to Swan Island and the railroad tracks. Years ago, I took middle school students down this path to birdwatch in the few extant wetlands that have long since been filled. Still, it's a nice stroll through an oak and pine forest (and the poison oak that always accompanies oak and pine in our region). Lock up your bike and take a short walk down the rocky trail that turns into a dirt path after a few hundred feet. The informal trail will eventually be a great connector to the long-hoped-for North Portland Greenway (npGREENWAY), a Willamette Greenway trail extension from Swan Island north through Metro's **Willamette Cove** natural area, Portland's Water Quality lab and Cathedral Park.

Back on the bike, the next stop is the scenic overview at the **Captain William Clark Monument Sculpture ❻** on the University of Portland campus. As tempting as it may look, I never ride straight onto the campus mid-curve off Willamette Boulevard. It's too dangerous, given the volume of traffic. Instead, I ride to the formal entrance and take the access road past the soccer fields, past the Pilot House student center (a handy stop with real restrooms, bookstore, ATM, email access, and The Cove cafeteria) to the end of the parking lot and take a left and ride past the Buckley Center.

The monument marks what some argue is the upstream extent to which Captain William Clark paddled six miles up the Willamette with his Native American guides. The Corps of Discovery missed the mouth of the Willamette twice on their voyage down and back up the Columbia and had to be guided back from the Sandy River to explore this far up the Willamette. There are spectacular views of the working harbor, West Hills, and an oak, madrone, and ponderosa pine forest.

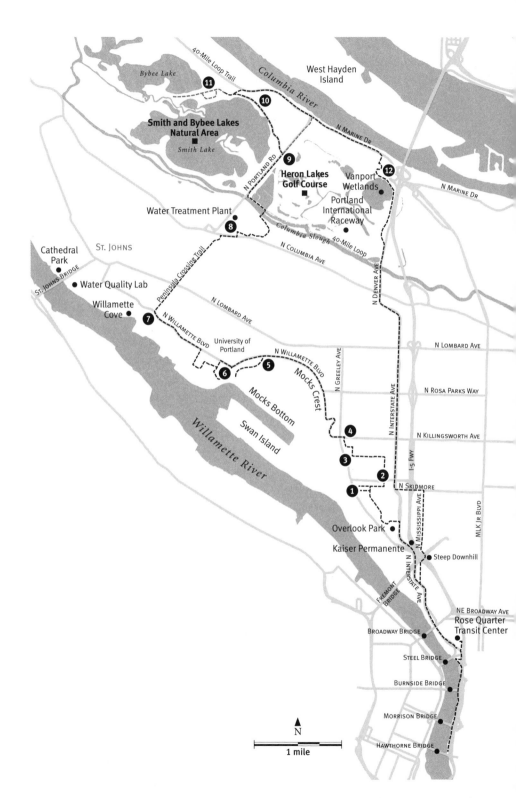

On to the Wild Side

After riding through campus past the Clive Charles soccer complex and the large-domed Chiles Center, continue north on Willamette Boulevard to N Carey Boulevard and the **Peninsula Crossing Trailhead at N Princeton Street** ❼. The Peninsula Crossing Trail—the first off-street part of the trip—was constructed on an abandoned city right-of-way by Portland Parks & Recreation and Metro with funds from the 1995 regional greenspaces bond measure. Along the way, there are several street crossings that warrant caution. There are sculptures and basalt blocks lining the entire route to N Columbia Boulevard.

At N Columbia, rather than riding on the busy street, I opt to ride the sidewalk east to the first traffic signal, crossing carefully down the short hill on N Columbia Court to the **trailhead markers** ❽ across from the entrance of the Columbia Boulevard Water Treatment Plant. Unfortunately, the plant is not open to the general public so don't count on a restroom stop here; the next one is at Smith and Bybee Lakes. Ride on past the plant to the left of the railroad tracks. This is where the "wild" part of the ride starts.

The trail splits in two shortly beyond the railroad crossing. Take the left path heading up a very short, steep hill that provides a great overlook. At the top of the left path there's a sculpture with a hole drilled through it. Look through and see if a raptor is roosting on the distant snag. Continue down the hill past a small shed with an ecoroof. There is a canoe launch with steps down to the Columbia Slough just before you come to the bicycle-pedestrian bridge that crosses the slough. A stop in the middle of the bridge gives you great views. Look for great blue herons, green herons, waterfowl, and red-tailed hawks.

On the north side of the slough there are two options. If Smith and Bybee is not my destination and I'm short on time, I take the shortcut back to the Rose Quarter by taking a right and riding to N Denver Avenue. If, however, I want to complete the entire loop, I ride to the left and catch N Portland Road and ride north to the off-street **entrance across N Portland Road** ❾ to the Smith and Bybee Wetlands Natural Area.

Smith and Bybee Wetlands Natural Area

Smith and Bybee Lakes are part of Metro's two-thousand-acre natural wetland area (see page 300). It is the largest wetland in Portland and home to threatened western pond turtles and western painted turtles as well as hundreds of bird species. On the left is a canoe launch, which is worth checking out for views of Smith Lake. Look for interpretive signs and restrooms ❿ on the right as you pedal down the bicycle-pedestrian path. After a quick restroom stop and perhaps a bite to eat under the covered picnic area, get back on the bike-ped trail and ride to the entrance to a paved path that runs between **Smith Lake and Bybee Lakes** ⓫. It may seem counterintuitive, but bikes are not allowed on the paved path. I was quite embarrassingly reprimanded by the Metro naturalist for guiding a group ride into the lakes area. So, take my word for it, either walk your bike or lock it up at the trailhead!

The walk through Smith and Bybee alone is worth the entire ride. On warm spring and summer days western pond turtles bask in large numbers on the partially submerged logs in the blind slough just a few hundred feet along the trail. Hooded mergansers, wood ducks, American wigeon, gadwall, and both great blue and green herons also frequent this quiet backwater. During the summer the trail is covered in a soft, velvety layer of black cottonwood seeds. Common songbirds include Bewick's, Pacific and house wrens, spotted towhees, black-capped chickadees, ruby-crowned and golden-crowned kinglets. In summer the flute-like songs of Swainson's thrushes echo throughout the dense cottonwood forest.

A path on the left takes you on a short loop walk to a blind overlooking Smith Lake. I've seen as many as four hundred common egrets and flocks of white pelicans from the blind as well as bald eagles, osprey, and thousands of waterfowl during the winter. After completing the loop and getting back on the main trail, I always take the out-and-back, dead-end trail for an overview of Bybee Lake. In the open, reed canarygrass fields you'll find common yellowthroats, American goldfinches, cedar waxwings, and northern flickers. Scanning Bybee Lake usually turns up lesser scaup, bufflehead, northern shovelers, and pied-billed grebes, depending on the time of year.

Horses to the Barn

The route back to the Rose Garden takes you along N Marine Drive and provides great views of the Columbia River, with equally impressive views of Mount Hood in the distance. After riding on the bicycle-pedestrian portion of the 40-Mile Loop trail along Marine Drive, I always cut through the parking lot at TriMet's Expo MAX Station, crossing Marine Drive at the signaled stop just opposite the transit center **12**. Then I make a quick stop to scan the ninety-acre Vanport Wetlands, a mitigation site purchased by the Port of Portland to compensate for wetland losses on port property. The goal of the port's mitigation plan was to remove invasive reed canarygrass and plant a native-dominated wetland and vegetative buffer. There is an open water habitat in the winter and spring. Formerly owned by King Broadcasting of Seattle, the wetland was renamed in 2001 to commemorate Vanport City and the flood that wiped it out in 1948.

The Port reports that the wetlands have attracted over one hundred species of birds, including yellow-headed blackbirds, which have successfully nested and fledged young. That makes Vanport Wetlands one of the few locations for yellow-headed blackbirds in the region.

The rest of the ride is very urban along N Denver Avenue (from where it's possible to head back west along the Columbia Slough to the Columbia Boulevard Water Treatment Plan if you're looking to get back to North Portland peninsula). Or to complete the full circuit, continue on Denver to N Interstate Avenue for a gentle, but longish uphill ride. The striped on-road bike lane disappears and reappears for the first mile or so of Interstate. From here you can either take the MAX or ride directly back to the Rose Quarter on N Interstate. At this point, especially on a hot spring or summer day, I'm usually hankering for a cold liquid refresher and a burger. The best route for that is to cut over to N Mississippi Avenue via N Skidmore Street and head south on Mississippi, which has a plethora of eateries, a great brewpub, and a bike shop in the event of a mechanical breakdown. From there a monster downhill stretch takes you to N Russell Street and N Interstate Avenue, and back to the Rose Quarter starting place. If you happen to live in Northwest Portland, you can exit N Interstate to the Broadway Bridge.

By Mike Houck

GREEN INFRASTRUCTURE

STANDING NEXT TO PORTLAND's NE Sandy Boulevard, cars whizzing by, it's quite a stretch of the imagination to consider that under all the concrete there's a direct connection to the Columbia Slough or the Willamette River. It's pretty much out of sight, out of mind. We have, as virtually all cities have, engineered water out of our daily lives. Every street is lined with mile after mile of mini-dams—curbs—which channel every drop of rainwater into the nearest storm drain. From the storm drain it's a long, circuitous, piped journey to the nearest stream or river.

In winter this cumulative deluge of water, which otherwise would have found its way into the groundwater, overwhelms the region's wetlands, streams, and rivers. In hot summer months, cool groundwater that would have replenished streams and rivers, instead flows into the Pacific Ocean.

We know there are better ways to manage water in a city. In Portland and elsewhere in the region, what used to be called sewage agencies are now environmental service and watershed protection agencies. Portland's Bureau of Environmental Services and the Tualatin Basin's Clean Water Services (formerly Unified Sewerage Agency) are combining their grey, piped infrastructure with green infrastructure to improve watershed health.

Green roofs, green streets, disconnected downspouts, bioswales, raingardens, and an expanded urban forest canopy are slowly complementing, and in some instances replacing, highly engineered, expensive grey infrastructure with cheaper, greener, smarter ways of dealing with urban stormwater. Formerly treated as a nuisance, stormwater is now viewed as a precious natural resource. In Portland's Pearl District and elsewhere in the city, water has become an art form. The following essays describe greening the city's infrastructure, an effort that not only improves the water quality and ecological health of our rivers and streams but also addresses climate change and brings more wild into the city.

By Mike Houck

Who'll Catch the Rain?

Friend, it is time to turn the corner and find where you began.
Begin again with all you lost but never forgot.
Remember when you tasted rain?
Rise up where one-way thinking intersects surprise.

—KIM STAFFORD

BEFORE THERE WERE CITIES, rain fell onto ancient forests, grasslands, and wetlands. Rainwater slowly worked its way through the soil. Some of it lingered in the branches and leaves of dense tree groves. Wetlands held onto seasonal floodwaters. The rivers were clean and full of salmon. The natural system was catching the rain just fine.

As early American settlements grew into modern cities, we treated rain as a nuisance to be disposed of as quickly as possible into our streams and rivers. In Portland, the Columbia Slough and Willamette River became open sewers despoiled by torrents of rainwater, sewage, and trash. It didn't take long for this muddy, stinky mess to threaten the health of residents who came into contact with the water or of salmon on their way home from the sea. Catching the rain in pipes turned out not to be the best solution.

In time, we built separate sewer systems and sewage treatment plants. While these improvements had immediate and significant beneficial impacts on our streams and rivers, they did not address damage caused by rain running off roofs, parking lots, streets, and construction sites. Only in recent years have we begun to develop new and creative ways to slow the rain down, keep it out of the pipes, use it to irrigate plants, and release it to the groundwater and eventually to rivers and streams. We have come to embrace natural rain-capturing methods of earlier times.

By Jennifer Devlin, illustration by Nathan Kappan

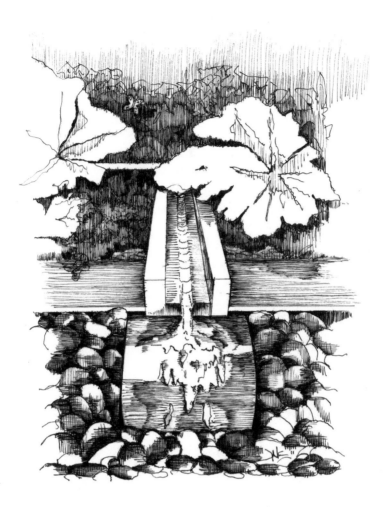

The Art of Rain Catchin'

There are plenty of creative ideas to catch rain. Artists and landscape architects are lending their ideas: downspouts that are splashy waterwheels, plazas where we can linger among wetland plants and splashing sounds, and streetscapes that are a breath of fresh air with blooms and fragrances. Ecoroofs are now good for spiders and nesting birds as well as catching rain. Rain gardens feature works of art and double as frog ponds. Some folks are trying to figure out how to incorporate solar and wind energy into these projects. Many Portlanders have de-paved parking lots, added yard trees, and put ecoroofs atop their garden sheds. Developers are part of the act too, building green streets and tree-lined boulevards and daylighting creeks out of pipes.

Everywhere you go, notice where the rain goes. Listen to it plunk on roofs and glug along the downspouts. Watch it pool and shimmy. See it disappear into street drains along with motor oil and candy wrappers. Wonder about rain. Get inspired! Try your own ideas.

—Jennifer Devlin

Storming Downtown Portland

Stormwater tour of downtown Portland

The Pacific Northwest is considered a hot spot in the nation for green infrastructure implementation. Where we used to pave, pipe, and channel, we are now reclaiming permeability, planting trees, and restoring natural functions lost long ago to our urbanizing environments. We are creating spaces and places that are healthier, safer, and more livable for people. What's more, in the process we are providing habitat for wildlife, birds, pollinators, and amphibians.

So where are all these integrated spaces that are so good for our communities? The following walking tour will give you a variety of examples of these green treasures in a place you might least expect to find them: the heart of Portland's downtown.

And Off We Go ...

Start at the south end of downtown at the western edge of Portland State University's campus at SW 12th Avenue and SW Montgomery Street.

Green Street—Planters ❶

SW 12th Avenue between Montgomery and Mill Streets

When it rains, street runoff that isn't properly managed carries dirt, oil, chemicals, and other pollutants into rivers and streams. Four infiltration planters on SW 12th show a more natural stormwater management approach. Stormwater flows along the curbs into the planters where vegetation and soil slow down and filter pollutants before the stormwater soaks into the ground. In the past, stormwater was directed into pipes and, during heavy rainfall, contributed to sewage-laden overflows in the Willamette River. Constructed in summer 2005, this project manages eight thousand square feet of impervious area. Look for the interpretive sign that provides a diagram of how it functions. The design allows space for on-street parking.

Walk south along 12th Avenue, take a left at Montgomery, and go to the courtyard on the east side of PSU's Epler Hall.

Creative Downspout Disconnect, Stormwater Planter, and Reuse ❷

Stephen E. Epler Hall, SW 12th Avenue and Montgomery Street

The plaza outside Stephen Epler Hall demonstrates an artful and interesting stormwater treatment. Roof runoff from the building flows to river-rock splash boxes, then into granite-block-lined channels, or runnels, conveying stormwater to a system of vegetated stormwater planters. Instead of being piped underground and out of sight, the water is visible and celebrated. The runnels also collect runoff from surrounding pavement. Downspouts from the **King Albert Hall** ❸ roof also drain to planters. The soil and plants in the planters filter stormwater before it collects in an underground storage vault. After additional sand and UV filtering, the water is pumped into the sanitary system for toilet flushing on the first floor of Stephen Epler Hall. Some of the water irrigates the landscape around the building. The system saves over one hundred thousand gallons of potable water each year. See the interpretive sign for plant species and a system diagram.

Next, simply turn around at the interpretive sign to see an ecoroof on PSU's bike garage.

Ecoroof Bike Garage ❹
West of SW 12th Avenue on Montgomery Street

My mother used to tell me to quit looking at my feet. Look up! It's an ecoroof—a great way to reclaim a patch of impervious area, in this case the roof of a bike shelter. Bikes never had it so good. This ecoroof keeps stormwater from a 1,120-square-foot surface from ending up in sewer pipes. Overflow from the ecoroof trickles into the planter by the streetlamp. Overflow from the planter goes into the storm drain.

Now, walk east for half a block and take a right (south) at SW 11th Avenue, a pedestrian-only street. Go half a block and take a left through the **Walk of the Heroines** ❺, one block south of Montgomery Street. Continue one more block to the South Park Blocks.

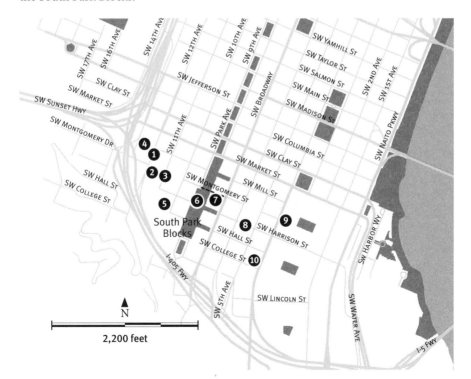

Mature Canopy Trees ⑥
PSU Park Blocks

Portland's Park Blocks are the city's oldest parks. Landowner and tanner Daniel H. Lownsdale donated the land for public use in 1852. The city began landscaping in 1877 by planting 104 Lombardy poplars and European and American elms. There are now over three hundred trees in the South Park Blocks. In 2004, PSU students estimated that South Park Block trees contribute $3.4 million in aesthetic and environmental value to the city. Other researchers have found that a mature tree, such as one of the large elms in the Park Blocks, can absorb up to 550 gallons of stormwater a year. The Park Blocks show how visionary ideas can make significant impacts in the future.

Next, walk left, diagonally back to SW Montgomery Street.

Montgomery Green Street ⑦
PSU North Plaza between SW Park Avenue and Broadway Street

The Montgomery Green Street project is an example of one of Portland's first Green Street connectors. These are streets that connect people to places they want to go—to schools, commercial areas for shopping and work, entertainment areas, and parks. Green streets provide facilities for stormwater management as well as safe and pleasant routes to encourage people to walk and bike whenever possible. As of 2010, two blocks have been transformed with hopes that over time Montgomery Green Street will stretch from the West Hills through the PSU campus to the Willamette River.

The first block was completed in 2009, and serves as an east-west connection for pedestrians and bicyclists. The site is graded so that water flows into the landscaped planters to be filtered and managed. The vegetation and trees provide a respite from the hard surrounding pavement and invite the passerby to stop and rest awhile. Notice the scuppers about a foot off the ground that bring water from the sky bridge.

Now cross SW Broadway, continue walking east on SW Montgomery under the sky bridge, and cross SW 6th Avenue to Montgomery Plaza.

Stormwater Fountain Planters ⑧
Urban Center Plaza between SW 6th and 5th Avenues

The Urban Plaza block was a retrofit of an existing plaza. The fountains were in need of repair, and so the opportunity was seized to cut away some of the existing impervious bricked area, inserting the green infiltrating facilities. The facilities manage runoff from portions of the plaza. This is an excellent example of being able to capitalize on redevelopment opportunities to integrate a green element. It is said that a city redevelops every forty years. Bit by bit, we can reclaim our urban spaces to realize greater benefits for people and the environment. Find the grates in the walkway to see the path that rainwater takes to get to the planter. The two planters below receive sheet flow from the plaza.

Continue east on SW Montgomery, then cross 4th Avenue and note the green streets facilities here. Continue along a pedestrian way to the west side of the Cyan Building.

Private Stormwater Management **9**
Cyan Apartments, Montgomery between SW 4th and 3rd Avenues

This building features an ecoroof and water harvesting for irrigation. Water leaves the ecoroof, flows through open runnels in the courtyard, then cascades into large above-ground planters on the east side of the building bordering the Lawrence Halprin–designed Pettygrove Park. The attractive design celebrates water as both a visual and functional resource. Pray for rain so you can see this in action.

Now, walk back around to SW 4th Avenue and turn left (south) on 4th. Walk three blocks to SW College Street.

Green Street—Curb Extension **10**
SW 4th Avenue and College Street

Although operating much like the 12th Street planters (using soil and plants to filter and infiltrate stormwater), this facility has one important difference. Instead of being located behind the curb, it extends into the street, replacing street pavement. Considered the workhorse of green street designs, vegetated curb extensions are often coupled with efforts by the city's bureau of transportation to slow traffic and create safer pedestrian and bicycle experiences. Search for where the water enters and exits the curb extension. Remember that water flows downhill.

By Linda Dobson

More information: Portland's Bureau of Environmental Services

What's That Din?

Beginning about mid to late April, as you walk along any street with a decent urban forest canopy or through the South Park Blocks, just after the elms and maples have leafed out, you'll hear a loud din emanating from high in the deciduous treetops. The cacophony is the chorus of wintering as well as migratory birds—fresh back from their several-thousand-mile journeys from warmer climes—as they glean insects on the newly emerged leaves and buds. While some of the birds in the treetops are early neotropical migrants, such as warblers, the majority are overwintering pine siskins. They're the ones making that pervasive "zzzst, zzzst, zzzst" buzzing.

Crane your neck upward and you might get a glimpse of the small, heavily streaked, finch-like siskins with pale to brightly yellowed wingbars and slightly forked tails. You've got them most winters at your bird feeder, along with American goldfinches and bushtits. Siskins are an irruptive species, appearing in great numbers one year or season and then disappearing the next. They nest in the mountains but can be seen throughout the metro region most winters and into early spring.

—Mike Houck

Storming East Portland

Stormwater tour of North, Northeast, and Southeast Portland

On an appropriately rainy fall afternoon Linda Dobson, who directs Portland Bureau of Environmental Services' Sustainable Stormwater Division, and I rambled about North, Northeast and Southeast Portland to take a look at the rapidly expanding system of swales, planters, and ecoroofs that—while distant from any stream or river— are contributing to the health of the Willamette River.

In 2008 Portland embarked on an ambitious Grey to Green initiative for improving watershed health by taking some of the pressure off the city's aging grey infrastructure and integrating green infrastructure. Portland's thirty-seven-inch annual rainfall generates about ten billion gallons of stormwater. Having invested over $1 billion in the "big pipe" project that will have the capacity to reduce combined sewer overflows into the Willamette River and Columbia Slough, the city now wants to protect this investment by keeping stormwater out of this piped system to allow for additional volume as the population grows over the next couple of decades.

Green Infrastructure

Green infrastructure includes expanding the urban forest canopy, creating bioswales that infiltrate rainwater into the groundwater, and installing ecoroofs that take the "peak" off rain events before the water can reach storm drains. The focus of Portland's

Greening the Grey

Traditional "grey" infrastructure refers to roads, sewers, and other utilities. Green infrastructure, by contrast, is infrastructure that utilizes or mimics the natural environment in a way that solves issues like urban stormwater management. An example of green infrastructure is the use of floodplains to store floodwaters rather than relying on "grey" dams and levees. "Going green" results in multiple benefits for each dollar spent. For instance, by protecting or restoring floodplains, in addition to addressing flooding, there is more wildlife habitat and open space, improved water quality, and additional park land.

Portland's Grey to Green initiative emphasizes the use of green infrastructure to manage urban stormwater and improve watershed health throughout the city. Removing invasive plant species, protecting sensitive natural areas, improving fish habitat, planting trees, and creating green streets, and protecting and restoring sensitive fish and wildlife habitat yields multiple benefits. Portland's Grey to Green initiative will install over forty acres of ecoroofs, plant over 80,000 trees, add four hundred acres of important wildlife habitat to the park system, restore over one thousand acres of degraded natural area, and green up neighborhood streets.

sustainable stormwater program is to treat stormwater as a valuable natural resource. The key to innovative green stormwater management is to integrate it into the built and natural environments, as opposed to the traditional engineered, or grey, approach in which stormwater is simply directed into pipes that carry it to the nearest stream, river, or wetland—out of sight, out of mind.

Sustainable stormwater management relies on vegetation, either in created or natural systems, to slow and filter water and, wherever possible, allow it to infiltrate into the ground as it would in a natural landscape. Using these techniques can reduce stormwater runoff in residential developments by as much as 65 percent and can also remove up to 80 percent of sediments and heavy metals, and 70 percent of nutrients—all of which pollute urban waterways. Perhaps you'll see some examples on this ramble that you can bring to your own neighborhood.

NORTH PORTLAND
Mississippi to the Albina Triangle
North Mississippi Avenue is not only one of Portland's newest, hippest neighborhoods—home to pubs, coffee joints, and a plethora of food carts—it's also a hotbed of innovative stormwater projects.

The ReBuilding Center **1**
3625 N Mississippi Avenue
Our United Villages, the nonprofit organization out of which the ReBuilding Center operates, was founded in 1998. The ReBuilding Center, which moved from NW 23rd Avenue to N Mississippi Avenue in 2000, carries the region's largest volume of used building and remodeling materials. Its goal is to promote the reuse of salvaged and reclaimed materials. Given that philosophical bent, it's appropriately also one of the early demonstration sites for Portland Bureau of Environmental Services' new stormwater design efforts. Over 2,000 square feet of planters, 35,000 square feet of rooftop, and 3,800 square feet of parking lot have been retrofitted to address on-site stormwater management at this Portland icon of recycling. The stormwater features include flow-through planters next to the center's fancifully designed entrance on Mississippi; infiltration planters, where water is directed back into the ground; and pervious paving in the parking lot.

Mississippi Commons **2**
3727 N Mississippi Avenue
Another great place to combine a stormwater ramble with food, coffee, or a beer is Mississippi Commons, a collection of buildings that were converted from light industry to mixed-use artist space, offices, and retail. Part of the project involves providing complete on-site stormwater management. Two downspouts were disconnected from the roof and directed to a two-level, steel-lined basin. The basin empties into a

grate-covered trench in the ground, which in turn flows into an infiltration planter. Vegetation, soil, and material in the planter slow and filter the stormwater before it soaks into the ground.

The infiltration planter sits in the center of a public courtyard. A third downspout was piped under the concrete and bubbles into the planter. More than a half million gallons of stormwater are infiltrated and treated on site each year instead of entering the combined sewer system. During large storm events, an overflow pipe directs the water underground to a drywell. Additional overflow spills onto an adjacent pervious paved courtyard through an opening in the planter wall.

The stormwater features were designed as amenities that contribute to the property's public space and add landscaping to the surrounding built environment. This project, constructed in 2004, cost about $40,000 with a little over half coming from EPA grants. If you look between the chiropractic center and the yellow Jet building you'll see a beautiful downspout that directs stormwater from the roof to the central bioswale.

Across the street ❸ the formerly impervious surface has been replaced with pervious pavers that allow water to seep between the cracks. There are numerous box planters adjacent to the Tupelo Alley apartments ❹. While they are not connected to a bioswale, they do have the ability to retain small rain events. This is a nicely designed infill development that addresses some stormwater issues.

Pistils Nursery Ecoroof ❺

3811 N Mississippi Avenue

In addition to providing the neighborhood with roaming roosters and hens, Pistils Nursery has an inviting ecoroof, which from spring through early autumn is a pleasant place to enjoy the verdant nursery fare and perhaps sip a beverage. The ecoroof is open to the public.

Albina Triangle ❻

Corner of N Prescott and N Mississippi Avenues

This is another neighborhood-inspired project that takes stormwater from the surrounding ten thousand square feet and directs it into a densely vegetated strip along N Mississippi. What was once an ugly, uninviting paved area has been converted to an attractive public plaza. A variety of birds, mammals, and insects are depicted on the curved wall that separates the plaza from the grassy knoll to the south. City Repair and the Portland Development Commission worked with the neighborhood on the project. Portland Bureau of Environmental Services helped catalyze the final design with funding from its Green Streets program.

The second leg of our stormwater ramble samples curb extensions, bioswales, rain gardens, and parking strip planters.

Voodoo Doughnut **7**

501 NE Davis Street

A great way to start this stormwater ramble is to pick a rainy weekend morning. Why on a rainy day? To appreciate innovative stormwater treatment in action you've got to get wet! And what better way to start a wet stormwater ramble than with a fresh, hot, glazed donut and a cup of java? (There are also some way cool pinball machines at Voodoo, increasingly a rarity in Portland.) After you've secured your doughnut and coffee, look across the street to the intersection of NE Davis Street and NE Sandy Boulevard. **8**

Immediately in front of two huge advertising signs, what used to be an unusable paved space (and public right of way) is now a small, green oasis, thanks to a collaborative effort by the Portland Bureau of Transportation and Oregon Department of Transportation. Note the curb cuts that direct water from both the street and the sidewalks, bypassing traditional pipes, into a nicely vegetated triangle. Believe it or not, public rights of way occupy over 40 percent of the urban landscape in Portland. This is a classic example of how an ugly public right of way can be beautified, increasing adjacent property values and helping to manage stormwater all at the same time.

NE 22nd Avenue and NE Sandy Boulevard **9**

This stop is a two-fer. The first feature is on the southeast corner where NE 22nd Avenue intersects Sandy Boulevard. Here, asphalt has been replaced with a bioswale, possessing quite the artistic flair. It's been planted with sedges, rushes, and Oregon grape. There is only one inlet at the west end. Water flows over the weirs. Can you find the outlet? It's in plain sight in the middle of the circular bioswale. If it rains so much that the water overwhelms the vegetation the stormwater goes into the overflow so the sidewalk is not inundated. Most of the facilities you see on this ramble have overflows in the event of a large rain event. Rain in Portland, however, usually comes in a small, steady drizzle that can be captured quite easily in these bioswales.

Just across the street, at the corner of NE 21st Avenue and NE Sandy Boulevard **10** and in front of the KATU TV news station, is another beautifully designed bioswale. The design is similar but with two inlets, and is densely planted with rushes, Oregon grape, and low-growing shrubs. Note this facility also has a round overflow in the center. If you didn't start your ramble with a Voodoo doughnut—or if you did but are still hungry—and want to support a local social service agency, you might make a quick stop at Albertina's Restaurant and Shops at NE 22nd. The restaurant is run by the Albertina Kerr Centers, which assist developmentally disabled citizens.

NE Cesar Chavez and NE Sandy Boulevard ⑪

On the north side of Sandy Boulevard, in front of Poor Richard's and adjacent to Starbucks and the TriMet bus stop, is another de-paving example. Here, pavement has been replaced with a rain garden filled with dense plantings of wetland vegetation and shrubs.

Hollywood District's Harold P. Kelley Plaza, NE 42nd Avenue and NE Sandy Boulevard ⑫

We continue our food-themed stormwater ramble at Harold Kelley Plaza, adjacent to the Hollywood Burger Bar, which proudly announces it serves tap water. A narrow bioswale has been inserted along a row of stately redwood trees and behind benches, complementing the adjacent small public plaza. If you time your visit well, there is a farmers market across the street on NE Hancock Street, between 44th and 45th Avenues, open Saturdays, May through October.

SOUTHEAST PORTLAND

SE 55th Avenue and SE Belmont Street ⑬

Neighborhood activists initiated the rain garden and curb extension across the street from Mt. Tabor Presbyterian Church as a traffic calming feature. Their original request was to install speed bumps that would slow traffic coming down the hill off SE Belmont Street. After Portland's Bureau of Environmental Services brought some stormwater money to the table this dangerous intersection with poor sight lines was improved with the dual objectives of better managing stormwater that flows down SE Belmont and slowing down traffic. The water flows into what might best be described as a "super curb extension." It's also safer to wait for the TriMet bus with the large curb extension in place. Stop in for a cup of coffee or tea at the nonprofit TaborSpace Coffee House across the street in the church (5441 SE Belmont).

Tabor to the River—SE 59th Avenue ⑭

SE Hawthorne Boulevard to SE Lincoln Street

Six curb extensions are scattered along SE 59th, all of which are intended to help reduce basement flooding and are part of Portland's Bureau of Environmental Services' Tabor to the River project, which extends from the Willamette River to Mount Tabor between SE Hawthorne and SE Powell Boulevards, and covers about 2.3 square miles.

Around the corner at 58th Avenue and SE Lincoln Street ⑮—a low automobile traffic "bike boulevard"—there are stormwater planters in the parking strip. Notice how the street slopes toward the planters and curb cuts, allowing water to flow into the planters.

By Mike Houck

More information: Portland's Bureau of Environmental Services

› **Refer to map on page 159**

A Wild in the City **Ramble**

A Bird's Eye View
Portland Ecoroof Tour

When I ride my bike from St. Johns to my office downtown, I ride along Willamette Bluff in North Portland. On a sunny day, I can see all of Forest Park, the silhouette of buildings downtown, and Mount Hood in the distance. Stopping off along the bluff, I stand high above the North Reach of the Willamette River, and gaze over thousands of square feet of rooftops that stretch across Mocks Bottom and Swan Island between the river and me. It's one of the few panoramic views in Portland—one of the best places to see buildings and their roofs and to get a sense of the watershed perspective.

Over the last few decades we've adapted how we develop so that sensitive watershed areas and functions are better protected and restored. Where forests were removed, we're planting street and yard trees to enhance the urban canopy. Where streams were buried, we're daylighting them, bringing them from their underground pipes and culverts, and planting riparian, streamside vegetation. Where roads were paved to divert stormwater runoff to sewers, we're designing green streets to slow and filter rain where it falls.

Portland's rooftops have begun to change shape as well. Once designed to convey and remove stormwater from the building, they now present acres of opportunity. Ecoroofs, lightweight vegetative roof systems, transform a sea of hot, black tar into a living, breathing resource. With more ecoroofs being built in Portland over the last decade, each rooftop now has the potential to play a role in watershed protection, each roof potentially acting as a sponge that soaks up rain, a filter that cleans and cools the air, and a treasure trove for foraging birds and pollinating insects.

Looking down at Mocks Bottom, I imagine the roofs covered with wildflowers, sedum, and grasses. I think about the possibility of residents along Willamette Bluff enjoying their new "front yards." Is it possible that an industrial area could be designed to enhance our rivers and streams? Across Portland it's beginning to happen, roof by roof. While they're often difficult to see and even harder to access, there are a few locations in town where you can visit an ecoroof.

South Waterfront **1**
SW Gibbs Street and SW Moody Avenue
For a distant view, take the Portland Streetcar to South Waterfront. Exit the streetcar at the SW Gibbs stop, cross the street to the terminal for the Portland Aerial Tram, and board the Tram to OHSU. At the top of the Tram, walk to the edge of the viewing platform. Look south toward the river to the South Waterfront development. You'll notice

that several of the South Waterfront buildings have ecoroofs that vary in shape, design, and texture. With the Willamette River, Ross Island, and Oaks Bottom Wildlife Refuge as the backdrop, it's easy to see the connection between these building roof areas and the sensitive surrounding natural area.

Multnomah County Building 2
501 SE Hawthorne Boulevard
From downtown, take the TriMet #14 bus across the Hawthorne Bridge, and look for the large brick building up ahead. Get off at SE Hawthorne Boulevard and 6th Avenue, cross the street, and enter the large, red brick building. Sign in at the security desk and take the elevator to the 5th floor. Exit the elevator toward the windows and find the exit to the terrace. Visit this outdoor room anytime from early summer to late fall to see blooming Oregon wildflowers. Ecoroofs like this one help clean the air and keep temperatures cooler, which is particularly valuable in areas like the Central Eastside Industrial District, with lots of large, flat roofs and an intersecting interstate highway.

Jean Vollum Natural Capital Center 3
721 NW 9th Avenue
Take the Portland Streetcar to the Pearl District, and get off at NW 10th Avenue and Irving Street. During the week, you can access the Jean Vollum Natural Capital Center's roof by taking the inside elevator to the third floor or walking up the exterior stairs to access the terrace. The center's ecoroof is visible from the surrounding apartment buildings, offering a natural alternative to typical rooftop environs.

Cathedral Park Place 4
6635 N Baltimore Avenue
From downtown St. Johns, travel west on N Philadelphia Avenue to the St. Johns Bridge, and start to climb the bridge along the north sidewalk. About halfway to the top of the bridge, look north toward the river and you can see the ecoroof on the large, orange industrial building adjacent to the railroad tracks at Cathedral Park Place.

This innovative ecoroof was built on an existing warehouse and uses recycled carpeting to help drain runoff and retain soil. An ecoroof like this one helps create opportunities for enhancing biodiversity and habitat, especially considering the proximity to the river and migratory corridors.

By Matt Burlin

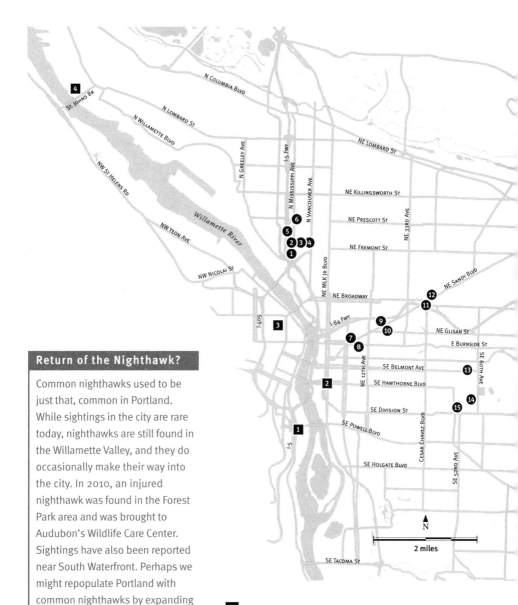

Return of the Nighthawk?

Common nighthawks used to be just that, common in Portland. While sightings in the city are rare today, nighthawks are still found in the Willamette Valley, and they do occasionally make their way into the city. In 2010, an injured nighthawk was found in the Forest Park area and was brought to Audubon's Wildlife Care Center. Sightings have also been reported near South Waterfront. Perhaps we might repopulate Portland with common nighthawks by expanding ecoroofs to include appropriate nesting habitat on some of the huge roofs in the industrial district of Northwest Portland. It would be nice to hear the high-pitched "yank" calls and the sensational "booming" displays of courting male nighthawks again.

—Mike Houck

1 BIRD'S EYE VIEW ECOROOF TOUR

1 STORMING EAST PORTLAND TOUR

Gimme Shelter:
In Praise of Portland's Urban Canopy

*... every tree near our house had a name of its own and a special identity.
This was the beginning of my love for natural things, for earth and sky,
for roads and fields and woods, for trees and grass and flowers; a love
which has been second only to my sense of enduring kinship with birds
and animals, and all inarticulate creatures.*

—Ellen Glasgow (1874–1945)

TRAINED AS AN ENVIRONMENTAL ENGINEER and having had a very bad experience
in high school biology, I have lived my life in avoidance of the biological sciences.
It has always seemed to be lots of memorization. I don't deny the importance of
the field or the joyful rewards of its study (my wife is a biologist). It's just not for me.
For years, on neighborhood walks, my wife pointed out beautiful trees, their names
and their unique qualities, all of which I have since forgotten. Yet in the last two years,
I've developed a strong love and passion for my neighborhood trees and Portland's
urban tree canopy.

As I ride my bicycle down SE 20th Avenue in the spring, summer, and fall, I marvel
at the canopy that shades and cools me. It's so expansive that it sometimes completely
covers the street. To me, a city watershed manager, this always seems analogous to
the canopy cover we strive to achieve for our urban streams. The tree canopy cools the
stream, stabilizes the bank, and feeds our fish.

Heroes of Green Infrastructure

Portland's urban forest covers 26 percent
of the city and removes eighty-eight thousand tons of carbon dioxide per year.
Mature trees also increase property values up to 25 percent and a tree with a
thirty-foot crown "drinks" up to seven
hundred gallons of rainfall annually.

On mornings of moderate rainfall, I
love how I can go on a long walk with my
dog without an umbrella and be kept dry
by the trees that intercept the rain before it
hits the ground. And each year in July,
when somehow our block party lands on
the hottest and sunniest day of the summer, I appreciate how one particularly
dense stand of trees provides the spot we
all gravitate to for hanging out, the spot that's shady and cool. Clearly you don't have
to be an evangelical biologist to "get" trees.

But besides the visceral and enhanced quality of life that trees provide, they are
living and productive superheroes of green infrastructure—better than any human-
made device.

A friend and colleague told me that when she sees neighborhood trees on her walks, she asks herself, "Who planted this tree, a decade or maybe over a hundred years ago?" Was it planted knowing that it would connect its planter to generations far into the future? Did they know they'd be planting a tree for their neighborhood descendants?

So I look at trees differently now. And I still can't remember most of their names or whether they are deciduous or evergreen, but I do often think of and worry for their future and our future without them. What of the neighborhoods where planting strips are empty because we haven't yet figured out how to engage those communities in the wonder of trees? Is our strategy for replacing trees effective, so that as this living infrastructure ages and dies a tree at a time, a new, younger, and just-as-productive tree will replace it? How can we engineer our urban environment to have the capacity for bigger and more beautiful trees at the same time that we seek to move more people into the same space—seemingly reducing the room available for trees? Clearly this is the next level of enlightenment for bureaucrats: how will we steadily and effectively increase and maintain this wonderful living resource?

By Mike Rosen, illustration by Nathan Kappan

Grey to Green

WHEN WERE "HUMAN" AND "NATURE" DIVIDED? When did the city become a place for people, but not wildlife?

In Portland it can be different. Portland is a place where "grey" and "green" are not just colors, but interwoven parts of our urban fabric—elements of the city's essential infrastructure. Urban habitat is the life support system that sustains us.

All around, quietly, without our noticing, trees cool and clean the air, soak up stormwater, filter out pollution, hold the slopes our homes rest on. A stream delights us when we stop to look or listen while it carries away runoff from our yards and driveways. What if we treated our urban habitat as if it were precious, as if our lives and livelihood depended on it?

In noticing, we'd see the lines blur. We might notice a killdeer nesting on an ecoroof, a heron snatching fish from a backyard pond, forests being planted along the freeway, cemeteries as ecosystems, and rain gardens downtown.

When the lines between human and nature are blurred, perhaps we can find new ways to live in the city, to design and plan for buildings, streets, sidewalks, parks, and playgrounds in ways that connect people, wildlife, and water. Perhaps we would look for ways to weave a tighter, more complex and interesting urban fabric, where many shades of green create intriguing textures when woven with the grey—steel, concrete, stone, and wood.

New possibilities emerge. Pavement is torn up from behind a church to plant a rain garden. A single parking space becomes a micro-park. Streets are no longer just places to drive, but places to be, to enjoy, places that connect us to nature and to each other.

We should imagine and ask for more. A tree is not an ornament. It's an investment and an act of hope. We should know that forests in the West Hills and East Buttes protect native fish and frogs and prevent landslides and flooding downstream. The pieces should fit together—for a swale to be a classroom, a bikeway to lead to the park. Even the flowers we plant for hummingbirds should be part of a bigger plan, a broader intention to create a healthier habitat for all of us, a network connecting Powell Butte to the Columbia River, Rocky Butte to the Willamette Bluffs.

With thought and imagination we can interweave grey with green.

By Marie Johnson

TUALATIN RIVER WATERSHED

THE TUALATIN RIVER WATERSHED drains 712 square miles between the Coast Range and the Tualatin Mountains (Portland's West Hills). The valley's clay soils were deposited by the backwaters of the Missoula Floods at the end of the last ice age, approximately fifteen thousand years ago, and are some of the richest agricultural soils in the state of Oregon. From west to east, dominant land uses in the basin are forestry, agriculture, and urban development. Much of the original, rich swampland has been drained for agriculture and urbanization, but important restoration efforts have been undertaken, particularly in rural areas.

Half a million people live in the basin and significant efforts to mitigate the impacts of urbanization include developing a model sewage treatment system, establishing riparian buffer protections, and the public acquisition and restoration of natural areas and refuge lands. Stormwater runoff remains the biggest impact on urban streams, including the Tualatin River, and efforts to reduce runoff and diminish impervious areas are slowly beginning to emerge.

The Tualatin River itself is eighty miles long, originating in the Coast Range in the Tillamook State Forest. Entering the valley floor at Cherry Grove, the river changes quickly from a fast-flowing mountain stream to a slow, meandering river. Near Gaston the river passes Wapato Lake—a traditional food-gathering ground of the Atfalati band of the Kalapuyans—which will soon be a unit of the Tualatin River National Wildlife Refuge. From Wapato Lake, and west of Metro's newly acquired Chehalem Ridge Natural Area, the river runs north through farmland and future refuge lands.

Scoggins Creek, with a constant supply of cold water from Henry Hagg Reservoir, enters the river near Dilley. Washington County's Joint Water Commission drinking water plant withdraws water from the river to supply four hundred thousand customers in the valley. Gales Creek, known for its remnant run of steelhead trout, enters the river just south of Forest Grove's Fernhill Wetland, one of the birding hotspots in Washington County. From here the river takes a turn to the east and runs south of Cornelius through farmlands until it hits Jackson Bottom Wetlands Preserve south of Hillsboro.

The river then meanders through farmlands and suburbs for the rest of its run until it enters the Willamette River at historic old West Linn, upstream of Willamette Falls. A paddlers' water trail runs from Rood Bridge Park in Hillsboro, through the Tualatin River National Wildlife Refuge to Stafford. Public access is abundant in the Tigard and Tualatin areas and future facilities are planned for Farmington, Scholls, Sherwood, and Stafford. Wildlife watchers will find numerous sites providing great access to nature in the basin. Between Gaston and Forest Grove, flooded farm fields along Oregon Highway 47 provide great opportunities for seeing tundra swans and other waterfowl in the winter. Metro and the U.S. Fish and Wildlife Service are acquiring lowlands in the area from willing sellers for future wildlife refuge expansions.

By Brian Wegener

On the Bluebird Trail

MY ALARM RINGS AT 6:30 AM on Tuesday, the day I monitor my bluebird nest box route in Sherwood. (Bluebirds no longer commonly nest within the city of Portland.) I dress for variable weather this early May, as there may be rain, cold, sun, and wind. Then I assemble the basics of bluebird route monitoring: a small mirror to look inside the wooden nest boxes; mealworms to provide a supplement, since bluebirds depend on sufficient insects to feed themselves and their young; my annotations from last week; a field notebook (preferably waterproof!) and pencil to record my weekly observations; a list of my nest box locations and landowner names/addresses; the telephone number of the volunteer bander who provides my field training and mentoring; and my dashboard Prescott Bluebird Recovery Project Volunteer plaque.

As I travel from my home in Southwest Portland to Sherwood, I watch for traffic delays, hazards, and birds. I pass Tigard, Tualatin, and the Tualatin River National Wildlife Refuge, and turn off on Highway 99W to climb to the hills outside Sherwood

and onto Parrett Mountain. If I am fortunate, I have been able to catch a glimpse of both the bald eagles on the refuge, and the black-capped chickadees, spotted towhees, and red-breasted nuthatches at home near Tryon Creek State Natural Area.

The hills outside Sherwood are wrapped in mist. It will be another cool day on the Bluebird Trail. At the first nest box, mounted on a power pole on Parrett Mountain Road, a female bluebird exits as I park about thirty yards away. I am excited because she might be laying eggs or perhaps incubating a completed clutch of four to six eggs. Using my mirror, I peek inside the nest box and see that there are five beautiful blue eggs in a soft cup formed of dry grasses. Recording the date and my finding, I hear soft, non-musical notes and turn to see both the drab female and the bright blue male bluebird watching from the power lines above. I leave a feeding of ten or so mealworms in the dish next to the box. A mile down the road, I turn into a long, private-property driveway where the landowners have partnered with our project to put up nest boxes. They have enough acreage for two nest boxes—both of which might be occupied by the territorial bluebirds. The first nest box contains the beginnings of a nest and a pair of bluebirds is perched nearby. The second nest box, three hundred yards away, not only has a nest but in it are six bluebird eggs being incubated by the female. The male is close by, waiting to bring a caterpillar which he has gleaned to feed her. I have calculated that these eggs should hatch in six days (normal incubation is fourteen days from the date the last egg is laid). I will report to my bander so that the nestlings will be banded ten to fourteen days after they've hatched. Twenty-one days after hatching, the young fledge from the nest cavity and do not return.

At the next stop on my route, I find that violet-green swallows (*Tachycineta thalassina*), also secondary cavity nesters, have built a beautiful grass nest cup lined with soft white feathers collected from local chicken coops. There are five tiny white eggs in the nest. I will continue to watch this nest, although swallows are not banded by our project.

Bluebirds

There are three species of bluebirds: eastern, western, and mountain. All are insectivores (sustaining themselves over the winter on insects plus berries). They are secondary cavity nesters, depending on other species with stouter bills, like northern flickers, to create cavities in tree snags and wooden fence posts. The only bluebird in the northern Willamette Valley is the western bluebird (*Sialia mexicana*). These birds prefer open, mowed fields with interspersed low trees and shrubs where they can perch to watch for insect prey and defend their nest sites. They require about one hundred yards of space between nesting sites with other bluebirds and are most commonly found in orchards, vineyards, old burns, and mowed farmlands. In good nesting seasons and habitats with abundant food, second and sometimes third broods are attempted in a nesting season. The birds flock during the winter at lower elevations, commonly returning to the foothills to nest in the spring.

The next two nest boxes I visit are empty with no evidence of nest building.

Later, on another private property, I find that bluebird eggs I have been monitoring have just hatched. The tiny (as small as my little fingernail) hatchlings must have emerged within the last twenty-four hours. They are pink and totally without feathers. Their eyes will not open for at least five days. The female broods them to maintain their body temperature and ensure their survival, incubating them for about five days, while the male provides food for all.

The day has begun to brighten and the sun appears. Birds, including raptors and songbirds, go about their morning activities. Fields begin to show movement as livestock, horses, llamas, alpacas, sheep, and goats stir. Crops and vineyards are tended. Residents walk their dogs, ride their horses, and stroll on the country roads. Many stop to talk and inquire about the bluebirds and their success in nesting.

Thriving on the camaraderie of the neighbors and the activity of the birds, I complete my route in a leisurely two hours, not including my travel time. It is rewarding and enjoyable, and I am already looking forward to next week. If the spring weather is cold and wet, there are few insects available for the birds' foraging and feeding, so I might return again this week to provide additional mealworms, especially considering the new nestlings to be fed.

By Nancy Fraser, illustration by Robin M. Jensen

Cooper Mountain Nature Park

LOCATION: 18892 SW Kemmer Road, Beaverton, OR **ACTIVITIES:** Hiking, Wildlife viewing **FACILITIES:** Restrooms, Parking (extremely limited; do not park on residential streets), Unpaved trails, Interpretive signs/info **FEES AND REGULATIONS:** Restricted hours, No pets **HIKING DIFFICULTY:** Easy, Moderate, Difficult **HIGHLIGHTS:** Trails meander through conifer forests, prairie, oak woodlands; Grand views of Chehalem Mountains; Close-up looks at rare white rock larkspur, northern red-legged frogs; A small prairie that has been relatively undisturbed for hundreds of years **PUBLIC TRANSIT:** No direct service

Overlooking the Tualatin Valley, perched atop ancient lava flows that have been uplifted several hundred feet, sits Cooper Mountain Nature Park. This destination offers rare prairie habitat, abundant Oregon white oak woodlands, and amazing vistas of the surrounding Tualatin Valley, including stunning views of the Chehalem Mountains to the south and Mount Jefferson to the southeast. The park features 3.5 miles of gravel trails (with varying degrees of difficulty), a nature playground, and an education classroom.

One of the most unusual habitats of Cooper Mountain is the upland prairie. Less than 1 percent of the Willamette Valley's original upland prairies still exist, so visitors to Cooper Mountain are lucky to find one in such close proximity to Portland. Among the wildflower highlights is the endangered white rock larkspur (*Delphinim leucophaeum*). In fact, the largest population in the world of this particular flower is believed to exist at this site.

Impressive Oregon white oak woodlands, from shrubby oak savannah to large mature trees, can be found throughout the park. It is thought that Native Americans burned Cooper Mountain historically, as they did throughout the Willamette Valley, to improve habitat for game and to renew camas-growing areas. Since the mid-1800s, settlers eliminated the use of fire, allowing fast-growing conifers to outgrow and shade the oaks, which support diverse flora and fauna.

Since Metro purchased the park in 1995, extensive restoration has been underway to restore the oak savannah habitat at Cooper Mountain. One of the methods of restoring oaks involves removing large conifer trees and burning the understory to reduce competition of faster-growing vegetation. Burning has also been used as a management tool for removing non-native vegetation and accumulating thatch in the prairies at the park.

Hiking trails reveal something new to see each season. In the early spring, you can find early bloomers such as the Pacific hound's-tongue (*Cynoglossum grande*) and the small-flowered blue-eyed Mary (*Collinsia parviflora*). In later spring, there are vast fields of beautiful nodding flowers of white fawn lilies. As spring progresses and summer is waxing, wildflowers throughout the park become even more spectacular. Watch for the rare larkspur and meadow checker-mallow (*Sidalcea campestris*). Birds become a main attraction at the park in spring and summer. The first glimpse of the western bluebird whets one's appetite to return daily to find out what birds are returning for the season.

The Cooper Mountain Loop trail will take you down to the lower end of the park, where you may spot the northern red-legged frog that frequents an abandoned quarry pond. These frogs are considered a sensitive species in Oregon. As summer progresses, the pond dries up and the frogs will migrate to the surrounding forest. During the hotter days in the summer, Cooper Mountain can feel rather warm due to its southern exposure. This exposure and its higher temperatures support plant communities associated with the upland prairie habitats that are tolerant of dry conditions.

Hotter days up on the slopes of Cooper Mountain play an important role for certain wildlife communities, but might be a challenge to us humans so bring plenty of sunscreen and

Treetop Acrobats

The squirrels you are most likely to see around our urban and suburban neighborhoods are fox squirrels and eastern gray squirrels, which were introduced from the eastern United States. Alas, the beautiful western gray squirrel does not adapt well to human development, and there are few places now that it can be found within the metropolitan region. Keep a lookout for this large, pale, gray tree squirrel with its huge, bushy tail in large, intact habits closer to the urban growth boundary. Noted naturalist Dick Forbes once described these "treetop acrobats" as seeming to flow rather than run.

—Bob Sallinger

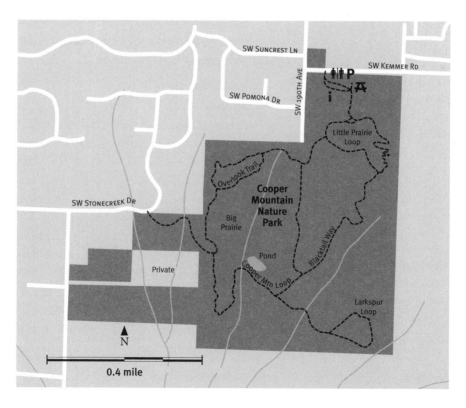

a wide-brimmed hat for protection from the sun. The Little Prairie Loop, located on the east side of the park, is one of the most popular hikes during the heat of the day. This trail will take you through the coniferous forest where you can enjoy a variety of woodland wildlife such as Douglas squirrels and Cooper's hawks.

Once fall arrives, the brightly colored reds and yellows of the leaves will highlight your walk. One of the showiest of the leaves is poison oak, which can be safely observed from the trails. Fall ushers in a flurry of activity from the Columbia blacktail deer. Large male deer with antlers can often be seen feeding in the early mornings. Antler rubbings on some of the moderately sized shrubs and small trees mark the mating season. The rubbings indicate a buck's territory and are also a result of antler polishing.

Merlins and Kestrels

Peregrines may be our back-from-the-brink, bird-of-prey rock stars, but they aren't our only falcons. Our most common is the diminutive American kestrel. At seven or eight inches long, these plump, rust-and-steel-colored raptors are less than a third the size of peregrines, and feed on equally diminutive prey—as small as grasshoppers and as large as mice (or sparrows, as suggested by their earlier name, sparrowhawk). They can be found in both urban and suburban areas around the region, and are commonly seen perched on wires or hovering over fields, highway median strips, and other open spaces that ring the city.

The region's other falcon—the understated merlin—is slightly larger than the kestrel and preys on smaller birds. Merlins (formerly known as pigeon hawks) aren't year-round residents, but slip into town in small numbers in the fall and winter, when they fly largely under the radar. They also fly with the pointed, swept-back wings which are common to all falcons, and which make this formidable family of predators among the fastest of all birds.

—Bob Wilson

When winter sets in, one is hard-pressed to find a more peaceful site in the metropolitan area. On occasion, the park will be lightly blanketed with a dusting of snow, even when the surrounding lower elevations are just wet. Like elsewhere, life slows down during the winter on Cooper Mountain. The season offers rare glimpses of wildlife in the park, such as coyotes hunting for food in the prairies during the middle of the day. Another common winter sight is the red-tailed hawk, soaring effortlessly in the persistent winter winds near the park's summit.

How to Get There

BY CAR: From SW Farmington Road in Beaverton turn south at SW 170th Avenue and drive for 1.4 miles. Turn right at SW Rigert Road for 0.2 miles. Turn left at SW 175th Avenue for 0.8 miles. Turn right at SW Kemmer Road for 0.8 miles. From downtown Portland: Interstate 5 south to Highway 217. From Highway 217 take the Scholls Ferry Road exit and head west on Scholls Ferry past Murray Boulevard. At SW 175th Avenue, turn right and go north 1.8 miles. Turn left on Kemmer Road. The park entrance is 0.8 miles on the south side of Kemmer Road. **PUBLIC TRANSIT:** No direct service

By Scott Hinderman

Jenkins Estate

LOCATION: 8005 SW Grabhorn Road, Beaverton, OR **ACTIVITIES:** Hiking, Biking, Horseback riding, Wildlife viewing **FACILITIES:** Restrooms, Parking, Paved and unpaved trails, Visitor Center, Picnic area/shelter, Wildlife viewing structure, Interpretive signs/info **FEES AND REGULATIONS:** Restricted hours, Pets on leash **HIKING DIFFICULTY:** Moderate **HIGHLIGHTS:** Historic home with ornamental gardens; Upland forest; Great views into the Tualatin Valley from higher elevations; Plants and animals of note include Pacific madrone, Oregon white oak, fairy slipper orchid, western gray squirrel **PUBLIC TRANSIT:** TriMet bus 52

Tucked into the foothills of Cooper Mountain, the historic Jenkins Estate is a forty-five-acre park featuring beautifully manicured gardens and natural areas. Named after Ralph and Belle Ainsworth Jenkins, the estate was completed in 1915. The Tualatin Hills Park & Recreation District purchased the property in 1974.

The upland forests of Jenkins Estate are entrancing. A number of older Pacific madrones curve gracefully to the sky in search of light. An occasional Oregon white oak stands out among the Douglas fir, bigleaf maple, and western redcedar canopy. Watch for poison oak throughout the site. You can often spy western gray squirrels scurrying through the brush and up into the trees. Two small seasonal streams cut through the park, including the headwaters of a tributary to Butternut Creek. The understory has undergone a major restoration. While there is still the occasional ivy or blackberry vine, the resurgent native vegetation is quite diverse with thimbleberry, fringecup, wood violet, Solomon's seal, woodland strawberry, piggyback plant, miner's lettuce, and Hooker's fairybells. If you are lucky, you might even catch a glimpse of fairy slipper orchids during their brief spring foray.

This park provides a variety of options for hikers. Walk an easy loop around the top of the hill or get a workout on a larger loop that traverses the slope down to Farmington Road. For a little extra variety, pass through the rhododendron gardens on your way back up the hill where you will likely see a hummingbird or two. Continuing up the hill, just behind the main house is a stand of Douglas firs where a pair of great horned owls has been known to nest each winter. This location offers a great vantage point for both the nesting owls and colorful flowers, as the understory is open and carpeted with wildflowers in the spring.

How to Get There

BY CAR: From Beaverton-Hillsdale Highway/Farmington Road go south on SW Grabhorn Road. The Jenkins Estate has two entrances. The first is at the top of the hill, which leads to the historical buildings, ornamental gardens, the paved trails, and a number of soft-surface trails that head into the natural areas. If you round the corner and head farther up Grabhorn, you will come to the second entrance, which leads to Camp Rivendale, a summer day camp on the back side of the estate. The camp features multiple picnic shelters, a play structure designed for people with special needs, and a number of soft-surface trails leading into the natural areas. **PUBLIC TRANSIT:** TriMet bus 52 on Farmington Road comes within approximately one mile of the park.

By Melissa Marcum

More information: Tualatin Hills Park & Recreation District

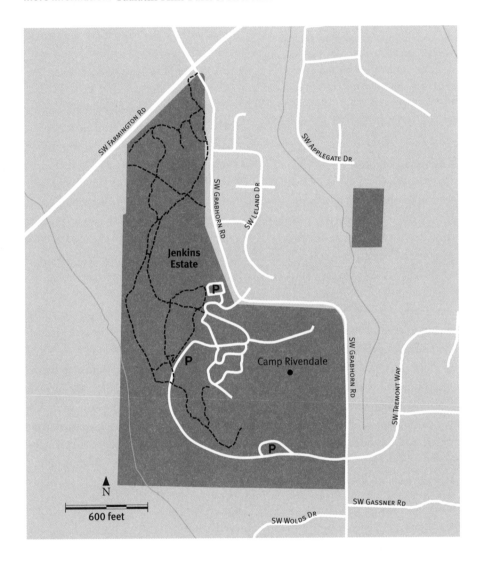

Tualatin River National Wildlife Refuge

LOCATION: 19255 SW Pacific Highway, Sherwood, OR **ACTIVITIES:** Hiking, Wildlife viewing **FACILITIES:** Restrooms, Parking, Paved and unpaved trails, Visitor Center, Wildlife viewing structure, Photography blind, Interpretive signs/info **FEES AND REGULATIONS:** No jogging, No biking, No pets, Restricted hours (closed Mondays), Possible future entrance fees **HIKING DIFFICULTY:** Easy **HIGHLIGHTS:** Rich and diverse habitats; Home to nearly 200 species of birds, over 50 species of mammals, 25 species of reptiles and amphibians, and a wide variety of insects, fish, and plants **PUBLIC TRANSIT:** TriMet bus 12

The refuge, managed by the U.S. Fish and Wildlife Service, is one of a handful of urban refuges in the United States whose mission is to connect people with nature and foster understanding and stewardship of the natural world. From dawn to dusk, people have access to the Atfalati Unit located at 19255 SW Pacific Highway between King City and Sherwood. Refuge staff, volunteers, Friends of the Refuge, and interns all participate in providing programs that bring nature and people together.

The Wildlife Center is the hub of activity including botany and bird programs, early morning and night walks, and special presentations focused on the natural and cultural history of the refuge. Visitors can explore an exhibit about the history and development of the refuge and how it is managed to accommodate wildlife. Nature's Overlook, a sales outlet operated by the Friends of the Refuge, has a quality selection of books and gifts—all profits supporting refuge needs. Volunteers are on hand to provide information about the refuge, and a spotting scope is always trained on something of interest to be seen from the large viewing window in the center. Discovery Packs, filled with loaner binoculars, field guides, and activity suggestions are available to aid in refuge exploration.

The refuge is a place where human activities focus on the passive and sensory—observing, listening, feeling—in order to wind down, contemplate our connections, and blend into the natural world for a brief time. Because it is "Wildlife First" on the refuge, many activities—biking, jogging, and dog walking—are not allowed.

The one-mile, year-round trail leads from the Wildlife Center out to the Wetland Observation Deck. This easy trail, complete with a surface suitable for wheelchairs and strollers, winds through a variety of habitats and features including ponds, oak savannah, creeks, the Tualatin River, and riparian forest—all culminating with a view of the seasonal wetlands. In the winter, it's a watery wonderland filled with jostling, honking waterfowl. In the spring, most of the waterfowl leave for their breeding grounds farther north and the shorebirds come through and visit the receding shorelines. Spring also brings songbirds that build their nests and raise young. Successions of wildflowers come into bloom and trees leaf out. In the summer, early morning or evening is best to spot wildlife—maybe you will see a deer and fawn, river otters frolicking in the waterways, or busy songbird parents tending their nests. In fall, the leaves of deciduous trees turn to golds and reds; the songbirds have raised their young and migrated to warmer places; and the wetlands fill with water for waterfowl coming back through to rest and refuel on their journey south or to spend the winter. Nature's cycle is ever-changing.

A three-mile seasonal loop trail is open during summer offering access to other parts of the Atfalati Unit. However, this trail is closed from October to May to give sanctuary to the migrating and breeding waterfowl traveling along the Pacific Flyway.

A photo blind is available for photographers by reservation and is accessible throughout the year. Both expert and novice nature photographers may also be interested in the Friends of the Refuge Photo Club that meets monthly.

Other units of the refuge, closed to public access, are located along stretches of the Tualatin River. These areas are being restored and preserved for the benefit of wildlife. By visiting the Atfalati Unit throughout the year, you can learn about how the closed sanctuary areas are managed by the refuge for native habitats.

So come and explore the refuge when the day is fresh and the wildlife is more apt to be active and visible. Stop every so often, take a deep breath, and look around. Listen to the sounds. Rain or shine, in all seasons or times of the day, the landscape offers continually changing vistas and experiences. You might see waterfowl skidding in on the winter ponds, a bald eagle perched in the oak tree by the Wildlife Center, dragonflies skimming across a vernal pool, deer out in the fields, or an owl in the riparian forest.

Access

Refuge visitor facilities are all Americans with Disabilities Act–accessible, and easily managed by wheelchairs, strollers, and families with young children. Visit the refuge website to learn about current program offerings and schedules.

How to Get There

BY CAR: From the north drive southbound on Highway 99W and continue through the town of King City. Approximately 0.7 miles beyond the Cipole Road traffic light, turn right into the refuge. Look for brown highway guide signs. From the south drive northbound on Highway 99W, approximately one mile north of Tualatin-Sherwood Road. Look for brown highway guide signs directing you to make a U-turn in order to enter the refuge. **PUBLIC TRANSIT:** TriMet bus 12 (Barbur)

By Carolyn Uyemura

More information: Tualatin River National Wildlife Refuge; Friends of Tualatin River Refuge

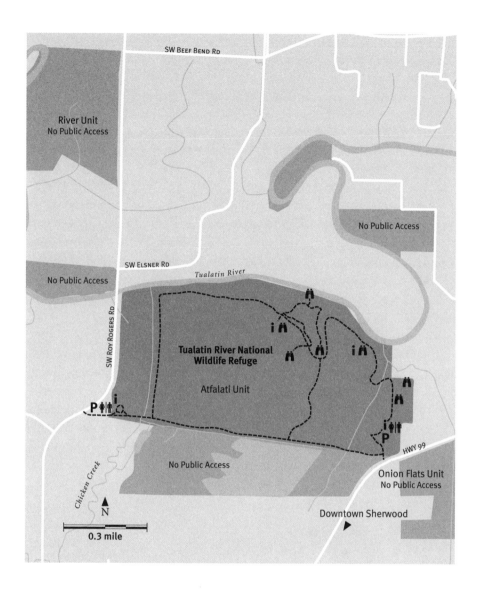

River Unit
No Public Access

No Public Access

No Public Access

SW BEEF BEND RD

SW ELSNER RD

Tualatin River

SW ROY ROGERS RD

Tualatin River National Wildlife Refuge

Atfalati Unit

No Public Access

Chicken Creek

N

0.3 mile

HWY 99

Onion Flats Unit
No Public Access

Downtown Sherwood

Crows

If Men had wings and bore black feathers, few of them
would be clever enough to be crows.

—The Reverend Henry Ward Beecher

AS I PASS BY THE CROWS cawing and squawking and leaping about on the corner by Burger King, I imagine them engaged in some sort of illicit swap meet. One would shriek, leap in the air, and then float back down onto the curb. Another would cock its head and follow suit.

"I will trade you three French fries for a patch of fur from a golden retriever's tail . . ."

"Throw in a shiny hairpin and a nickel, and you have a deal."

Eventually they complete their business and light off together, rolling and tumbling with the wind, traveling past power lines and warehouses, still cawing back and forth until they reach the limits of my hearing.

American crows (*Corvus brachyrhynchos*) are virtually ubiquitous on the urban landscape, and it is easy to pass them by as "just another bunch of crows." However, if you stop to watch a group (known as a "murder") for a few minutes you will find that they invariably are up to something interesting.

Birds of a Feather Flock Together . . . and with Us as Well

As scavengers, crows have enjoyed a long and highly successful (at least on their end of the bargain) association with humans dating back to time immemorial. The crow's close proximity to humans through the ages has made it a central character in the mythologies and fables of many societies throughout the world. The corvid family, of which crows are members, enjoyed special protection in England during the fifteenth and sixteenth centuries due to the role they played cleansing medieval cities of putrid meat and other undesirable refuse that accumulated on city streets. Whereas many bird species have experienced stark declines in the face of urban and suburban growth, crows have realized their highest population densities in these landscapes where they are able to exploit our waste stream and prey upon other species made vulnerable by habitat fragmentation.

Crows are the ultimate social birds. Adults mate for life, and young from the prior nesting season will often remain with their parents though the first year of life to assist with raising the following year's clutch. The extended period that young crows spend with their parents is vital to learning many of the behaviors and social skills they will need to survive. In fact, of any bird found in the metropolitan landscape, crows typically spend the longest period of time with their parents after leaving the nest. Their cognitive ability has been compared with non-human primates and parrots, and they are one of the few animals that have demonstrated tool-making capabilities.

It is not uncommon for people to come across young crows shortly after they leave the nest and assume that they are in need of "rescuing." They are nearly full size when they fledge but often take several days to become fully airborne. Their large size and the active presence of their extended family make young crows highly conspicuous. In fact, many people mistake the loud and chaotic approaches and departures of a young crow's relatives for aggressive behavior, when in reality what is happening is that the extended family is providing the vulnerable youngster with

guidance and care. A sure sign of a young crow is light blue rather than black eyes. If you see young crows hopping about during the springtime with other crows flying about, enjoy them from a distance but please leave them alone.

In fall and winter, crows form massive communal roosts that can range in size from hundreds to thousands of birds. These flocks provide crows with protection from predators and also are believed to play a significant role in helping spread information about food sources. It can be a truly disconcerting, but amazing spectacle to suddenly see hundreds of crows descending upon an urban neighborhood as the sun is setting.

Mobbing

Crows often provide the first indication that a bird of prey is in the area. They will aggressively mob hawks and owls to drive them away. Listen for the sound of raucous cawing and watch for crows looping madly about a tree or telephone pole or building—you will frequently find a disheartened red-tailed hawk or great horned owl perched in their midst looking for its chance to escape the din. At Audubon's Wildlife Care Center, we always warn people who come out to watch rehabilitated birds of prey being released not to be surprised if crows seem to magically appear within seconds of the hawk's taking to the sky. I can recall many a quiet, peaceful morning when we gently released a raptor only to hear a distant "caw" followed quickly by several more "caws" as dozens of crows seemed to materialize out of thin air to give chase.

Interestingly, many people worry about the well-being of birds of prey when they observe crow-mobbing behavior. The fact is that the crows may present an annoyance, but they pose no real threat to the predators. However, turnabout is fair play. Urban conservationist Don Francis tells a great story about a crow harassing a red-tailed hawk sitting on a light post. The hawk eventually abandoned its perch and circled lazily upward with the crow following suit and cawing as it rose. Eventually both birds disappeared into the clouds. Several minutes later the crow drifted back down to the light post alone. Thinking the show was over, Don prepared to leave when suddenly the red-tail came screaming out of the sky and slammed into the crow without warning and proceeded to pluck and eat him on the spot.

Havoc

Perhaps Portland's most famous crow is a bird appropriately dubbed Havoc. Havoc was discovered in downtown Portland, where he spent his days drinking out of the Benson bubblers, dodging traffic, and barking at blonde women. He apparently had been illegally raised as a pet and then set free. Eventually his antics resulted in his capture and delivery to Audubon's Wildlife Care Center, where he immediately released himself from the confines of the pet carrier in which he found himself imprisoned, flew to the nearest sink, turned on the faucet, and had himself a nice, long, cool drink. Once satiated, he turned to the assembled staff and volunteers, gave three high-pitched barks—"whoop, whoop, whoop"—and bowed.

Havoc lived at Audubon's Care Center for a year, during which he served as an education bird, teaching kids about the importance of keeping wild animals wild. With a penchant for blondes, baths, mice, and mealworms, he quickly became a favorite of the general public. However, he hated captivity. He would greet us each morning by springing up and down in his cage like some manic, feathered pogo stick. Failure to satiate his ever-changing desires quickly resulted in what only can be described as a vindictive temper tantrum, a full-fledged squawking, shrieking, food flying, ankle pecking, crow freak-out. His tastes were expensive too—one day I turned to find him removing the prism from a five hundred dollar ophthalmoscope.

He was sent for a short time to live at Oregon State University, where he participated in a study of captive crows. The professor in charge arranged for a cohort of blonde coeds to visit Havoc on a daily basis to keep him reasonably entertained. Eventually Havoc was set free on a property at the edge of the urban growth boundary, where the neighbors were apprised and accepting of a somewhat odd bird. He spent many months in the vicinity perfecting the art of pushing azalea pots off porches and showing up uninvited at local barbecues.

One day Havoc was sighted keeping company with other crows. However when the flock left to roost, Havoc was left behind, apparently absorbed in watching a man fly his model airplane in the field below. As time wore on, his interactions with the flock increased. The last known Havoc sighting was at a local school. A man working in the school basement turned to find Havoc barking at him from the window well. That was just around sunset. The next morning the flock had moved on and Havoc was nowhere to be found.

Egg Sucking Crow and Gator Gull

Nowhere is the crow's ability to exploit the urban landscape better exemplified than on the rusty, creaky ramparts of the Interstate Bridge. I came to know the Egg-Sucking Crow and his aquatic counterpart, Gator Gull, when I was monitoring

---

Ravens

People often confuse crows and ravens. While American crows are common in the Portland-Vancouver Region and across western Oregon, common ravens tend to be found at higher elevations toward the Coast Range and the Cascades. However, the occasional raven does make its way through the metro region, so sightings are possible. Ravens are significantly larger than crows. Their call is typically a much lower, guttural, croaking "quork" as opposed to the crow's more nasal "caw." The raven's tail is wedge-shaped while the crow's is fanned. Up close the raven's beak is huge relative to its head and curves downward while the crow's beak is more dainty and pointed. Crows and ravens are both members of the corvid family. Other members of this family found in Portland include western scrub-jays, which are common throughout our urban neighborhoods, and Steller's jays which frequent heavily forested areas such as Forest Park.

peregrines that nest high atop the bridge. The bridge is actually home to a motley assortment of creatures that eke out an existence in the shadow of the falcons, death from above. The dominant denizens of the bridge are rock pigeons that nest in the nooks and crannies and hundreds of thousands of starlings that roost in virtually every spot not occupied by a pigeon. The first time I monitored at this site, I was suddenly surprised by an early evening rain shower, only to subsequently realize that in fact the bridge was actually awash in bird excrement from the massive clouds of birds undulating overhead. Peregrines ripped through the flocks picking off prey at will.

Two particular birds, however, for years have managed to survive on the bridge without presenting themselves as peregrine prey. Gator Gull is actually a glaucous-winged gull that earned his name by abandoning traditional gull food fare for squab. He sits low in the water beneath the bridge and casually approaches the unsuspecting pigeons that come to the edge of the cement footings to drink from the river. In a flash he grabs them by their necks and drags them into the water. The struggle ends quickly, and he plucks and consumes his prey as he floats safely on the water. He rarely is seen taking to the air.

High above, a crow also appears to have developed some interesting and perhaps unique survival skills. Sit still for an extended period on the bridge and there is a very good chance Egg-Sucking Crow will hobble by. I have never seen him fly. Instead he wanders about the erector set–like bridge structure on foot, robbing eggs from pigeon nests. He pops quickly in and out of holes in the steel bridge framework. Sometimes he comes out empty-handed. Other times he is preceded by a flush of pigeons. Invariably he eventually emerges with an egg in his beak. I have watching him carry an egg around with him in his beak for extended periods of time, occasionally appearing to swallow it, only to pop it back up, like a little kid pretending to eat his vegetables. I know it is anthropomorphizing, but he always looks guilty, up to something. I imagine Egg-Sucking Crow and Gator Gull as elderly birds chuckling over the ways they tricked Peregrine.

Sunset

Take some time at sunset, as the landscape grows quiet to listen for crows. In the springtime listen for the gurgling "gug, gug, gug" sound of young being fed, and see if you can figure out where they are nesting. Then you can observe the complex interactions of the extended family caring for this year's brood. In the fall, look for black silhouettes crossing the sky, cawing as they converge on a communal roost. Common creatures, yes, but also incredibly complex and fascinating.

By Bob Sallinger, illustration by Virginia Church

Jackson Bottom Wetlands Preserve

LOCATION: 2600 SW Hillsboro Highway, Hillsboro, OR **ACTIVITIES:** Hiking, Wildlife viewing, Education Center **FACILITIES:** Restrooms, Parking, Unpaved Trails, Wildlife viewing structure, Interpretive signs/info **FEES AND REGULATIONS:** Suggested $2 donation when visiting Exhibit Hall; Education Center Hours 10 am to 4 pm Monday through Sunday; Trails open dawn to dusk (some seasonal trail closures); No pets, No bikes **HIKING DIFFICULTY:** Easy **HIGHLIGHTS:** Excellent bird and wildlife spotting; Active bald eagle nest; Great wetland views from observation deck and throughout the preserve; Interactive exhibits and interpretive displays (including the only bald eagle nest on exhibit in North America) in Education Center; Small nature store **PUBLIC TRANSIT:** No direct service

Jackson Bottom Wetlands Preserve is a 725-acre wildlife refuge located in the floodplain of the Tualatin River. The preserve is part of a vast mosaic of open space reaching from Fernhill Wetlands in Forest Grove to the Tualatin River National Wildlife Refuge in Sherwood.

The 4.5 miles of hiking trails provide opportunities for birdwatching, photography, contemplation, and exploring nature with children. One of the truly wonderful things about Jackson Bottom Wetlands Preserve is the diversity of wildlife that can be seen throughout the year. Over two hundred species of birds have been recorded on the preserve. Sightings of deer, coyote, river otter, short-tailed weasel, beaver, and mink are reported. Seldom seen, but present, is the resident bobcat. In spring, it is a wonderful place for tracking, and winter brings large flocks of migrating waterfowl, including tundra swans.

A new series of interpretive plant signs gives visitors information on identification, cultural use, wildlife attracted to the plant, and other interesting facts. A series of interpretive bird signs helps the viewer identify species. Exhibits in the education center change with the seasons and focus on not only Jackson Bottom Wetlands Preserve but also the Tualatin River Watershed.

Many visitors come just to walk and enjoy the solitude of the trails and wetland, taking a break from the constant activity of life in a large metropolitan area. For children, Jackson Bottom Wetlands Preserve is the place to come to see garter snakes, frogs, and insects of all kinds, and to enjoy the magic of a natural setting.

Access

There are two access points. The northern site, about a half mile south of downtown Hillsboro, has a covered ADA-accessible observation shelter and paved parking lot, but no trails. A half mile farther south on Oregon Highway 219, you'll find the Wetlands Education Center and approximately 4.5 miles of trails. The entire bottomland can be flooded from November through March, and so all the trails there are closed during these months. The trails in the upland area are open all year.

How to Get There

BY CAR: Jackson Bottom Wetlands Preserve is located just over a mile from downtown Hillsboro. From Highway 219 heading south the site is clearly marked. You will reach the north view site in approximately half a mile, and the south entrance and Wetlands Education Center in about a mile. **PUBLIC TRANSIT:** No direct service

By Sarah Pinnock

More information: Jackson Bottom Wetlands Preserve

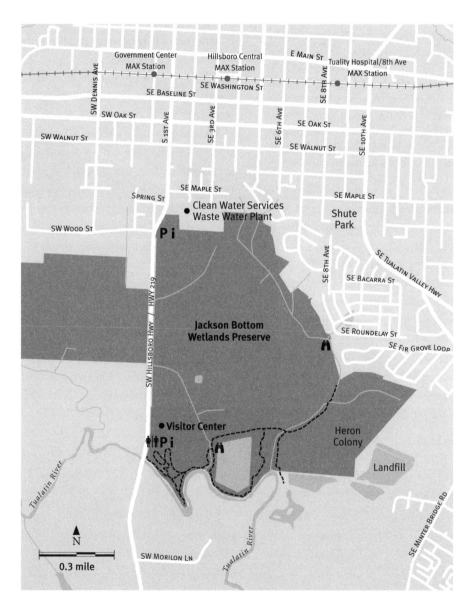

Fernhill Wetlands

Location: 1399 SW Fern Hill Road, Forest Grove, OR **Activities:** Hiking, Wildlife viewing, Birding **Facilities:** Parking, Unpaved trails, Wildlife viewing structure, Interpretive signs/info **Fees and Regulations:** Hours, dawn to dusk; No pets **Hiking Difficulty:** Easy **Highlights:** Fantastic waterfowl watching; Resident bald eagles; Northern Willamette Valley, Coast Range, and Mount Hood views **Public Transit:** MAX Blue Line; TriMet bus 57

One of the great things about Fernhill Wetlands is the way its primary trail loops along the shoreline dike of Fernhill Lake, reaching deep into the heart of the wetland where for long stretches water surrounds and wildlife abounds. At just over a mile, the loop alone can take no more than twenty minutes or no less than two hours, depending on one's purpose. And that, it seems, makes all the difference to many among the growing number of locals who've discovered this inconspicuous treasure right on the edge of town.

This is not to say that Forest Grove's backyard wetland has become crowded, but its "personality" certainly has changed in recent years. Ardent birders from far and near continue to appreciate Fernhill for its diversity of species and seasonal rarities. Yet Fernhill also has become a destination for people of all ages who come here mainly for casual exercise in a setting of intrinsic wonder. By themselves or with family or friends, they arrive by car, bicycle, foot, and even high-tech stroller to walk or jog among the lakes, ponds, and marshes that make up the wetlands. No bird books or binoculars for most of these folks: just legs that need moving, lungs that need filling, and bodies and minds that find rejuvenation at Fernhill for reasons they may not, nor need not, necessarily know. The effect, either way, is the same.

The surroundings—immediate and more distant—are also key to the attraction and impact of Fernhill Wetlands. To the west, across the Gales Creek floodplain, rise the first, sharp, carpeted ridges of the rain-snagging Pacific Coast Range—reminders of why the erstwhile sleepy Tualatin River sometimes surges far beyond its banks. To the south rests a narrow valley through which the Upper Tualatin runs with relative haste from Scoggins Reservoir to Fernhill and beyond. And to the east stands Mount Hood—all of it—which is why I like to begin my walks in that direction, preferably on a bright autumn day in mid-afternoon's warming golden glow.

On days so precious as these, I head for the snow-mantled mountain and toward the tangled, tangibly frenetic metropolis that creeps ever closer. But here, for now, the latter remains far enough away, and when I duck off the dike at Dabbler's Marsh Trail then quickly down a path that slopes to its shore, all the world beyond is swept aside by a breeze that rustles great cottonwood trees. They form a soothing hollow before the marsh's watery mirror, a sanctuary that is among my favorite stops. A single hooded merganser glides effortlessly into view while a nearby beaver plies the water with eerily silent power. Its home, their dam—which spans the marsh near its widest point—has withstood so many seasons it's a veritable land bridge, thick and deep with vegetation.

Eventually though, peaceful ponderings give way to the sound of bickering that breaks out between mallards that, just moments before, were happy to share the same small island. Soon it seems there's not a duck dry or afloat without something to say. So it's back to the Dabbler's Marsh Trail where I continue on its course toward a sturdy platform that looks downstream, beyond my last stop and into the waters beyond. Swallows slice the sky around and above me; a Cooper's hawk, meanwhile, perches in marsh-side deadwood, preening, preoccupied. I'd love to stay, but evening comes quickly this time of year and with it my anticipation, so I breathe it all in, then head back to the dike and turn again toward majestic Mount Hood in the far distance.

A pale orange sun peers through a veil of thin high clouds streaming forth from the Pacific, casting the mountain in a ruddy alpenglow. Soon, the entire wetland will be aglow, all open water reflecting ever more colorful cloud cover. Such sunsets make for special evenings at Fernhill, yet as the trail turns southward and deeper into the heart of the wetlands, I know that color is but the opening act, that the primary actors in the main event are only now homing in on center stage.

All day, in the valley to the south, geese have been feasting since early morning. Mostly, they glean from harvested crops what's left behind and whatever else they find. Then, just in time to arrive at Fernhill as dusk begins its descent, the geese come streaming: horizontal row after row after row after row ... times two, three, four, sometimes more. It begins while it is still quite light, though it is only because I'm on the lookout that I witness the first row materialize on the horizon. And it is a row, a straight line of geese—wing to wing to wing to wing—stretching, it appears, the width of the valley. Add a few more geese and the ones on either end would have to swerve to avoid outcroppings. Up the valley they flow an easy thousand per row until, upon nearing Fernhill they descend—noisily, cautiously circling around and around, until as more arrive, a chaotic and asymmetrical funnel forms over the wetland. Like planes enduring delays, they wait for their predecessors to make room. But their complaints are loud.

As I have before, I watch with complete strangers who were beginning to head home before becoming caught up by the sight. And as before, I hear repeated through the cacophony roughly the same incredulous words: "Is that *another* row?"

It's a question I can bear hearing again and again, for the awe shared with absolute strangers reminds me that, like "nature" as "other" or "enemy," "stranger" too is but a human construct. And as I make my way home by flashlight shared between new friends, I find myself reminded of Thoreau, who said, "In wildness is the preservation of the world."

Preserving wild places, our precious greenspaces, never felt more imperative.

Access

The primary one-mile loop trail around Fernhill Lake, begins and ends at the parking lot and provides access to most of the habitat types found here. This trail is wide and level but composed of packed gravel and dirt, so when it's wet, things can get muddy. Side trails along Cattail and Eagle's Perch Ponds can be flooded. Dabbler's Marsh Trail is uneven though fairly level and leads to a viewing platform and a smooth gravel road/trail, which runs along the backside of Fernhill where solitude can be found on even the busiest of days. Wheelchair users: as a testament from a wheelchair user, *do* visit Fernhill, but bring a friend so you can manage the primary loop without concern.

How to Get There

By car: From Portland take U.S. Highway 26 (Sunset Highway) west to Exit 57 (NW Glencoe Road) and follow signs south on NW Glencoe Road to NW Zion Church Road, then NW Cornelius Schefflin Road, to NW Martin Road, and then south on Highway 47 past Forest Grove. Do not turn into Forest Grove, but continue south on Highway 47. Cross Highway 8 and in one half mile turn left (third left) onto SW Fern Hill Road. The parking lot is on the left. **Public transit:** No direct service

By Eric L. Brattain

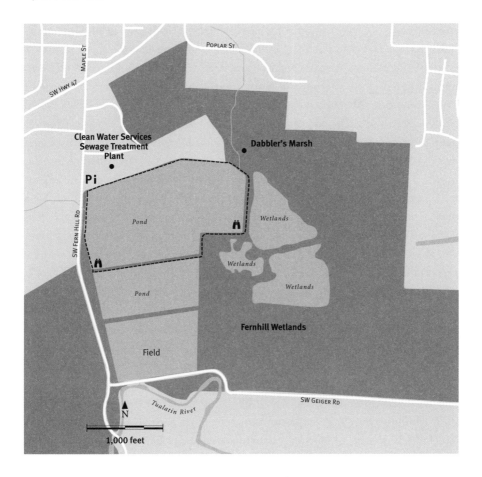

Crossing the Ki-a-Kuts
Cook Park to Hedges Creek Marsh

One of my favorite walking rambles is an early evening stroll between Cook Park and Tualatin's Hedges Creek Marsh. I always start this 3.3 mile walk by perusing the **Cook Park wetlands** ❶, which parallel the soccer fields—on both sides of SW 92nd Avenue. The wetlands are remnants of what was once a much larger marsh system prior to construction of the sports fields. Still, they are home to birds and mammals you'd expect to see in the area—red-winged blackbirds, common yellowthroats, marsh wrens, great blue and green herons, and the occasional Virginia rail. Waterfowl common in winter include American wigeon, wood ducks, mallards, gadwall, and northern shoveler.

Cook Park is chock full of recreational facilities, along with convenient parking and restrooms. I start my walks at the east of the **Nicoli Fields parking lot** ❷. The trail splits near the shelter just before you enter the **butterfly meadow** ❸. If you take a left you'll pass by a native prairie restoration and wetland habitat area ❹ that is off limits to humans and dogs. This path takes you to a cul-de-sac parking area at the end of SW 85th Avenue ❺. But to get to downtown Tualatin I take a right past the covered shelter number four ❻ and proceed through the butterfly garden. Signage is prominent, directing you along the Fanno Creek Trail heading toward Durham Park, and the Ki-a-Kuts bicycle-pedestrian bridge that will take you over the Tualatin River and into Tualatin Community Park and downtown Tualatin. But first, there's the beautifully landscaped Tupling Butterfly Garden just past the picnic shelter that has been planted in ceanothus, spirea, salal, Oregon grape, and other shrubs. The garden is dedicated to Kristen Ann Tupling, local naturalist and financial supporter of the garden.

Shortly past the butterfly garden, nice views of the Tualatin River are just to the right of the paved path as it curves to the left. I like to sit for a bit on the single bench, listening for the unique rattle of belted kingfishers, which I've seen on many occasions darting in and out of their nest cavity located high on the steep muddy banks across from the **Cook Park boat ramp** ❼. I also keep an eye out for the elusive green herons that love the Tualatin's brushy riparian shrubs.

Continuing to the east on the paved path, the route skirts the south side of the prairie restoration habitat, and dips under the BNSF railroad tracks. Just before the railroad tracks there's an excellent map ❽ that gives an overview of Cook Park and the surrounding terrain. After passing under the tracks a left takes you to **Durham City Park** but take a right, up the ramp onto **Ki-a-Kuts Bridge** ❾ over the Tualatin River. According to interpretive signs on the bridge, Ki-a-Kuts was a spokesman for the

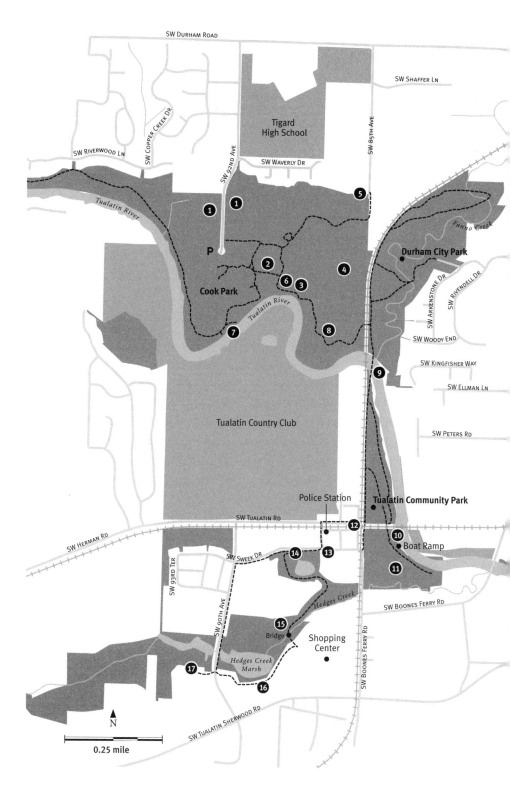

SW DURHAM ROAD

SW SHAFFER LN

SW COPPER CREEK DR

SW RIVERWOOD LN

SW 92ND AVE

SW 85TH AVE

Tigard High School

SW WAVERLY DR

Tualatin River

5

Fanno Creek

1 **1**

P

Durham City Park

2

SW ARKENSTONE DR

SW RIVENDELL DR

6 **3**

4

Cook Park

Tualatin River

SW WOODY END

7

8

SW KINGFISHER WAY

SW ELLMAN LN

9

SW PETERS RD

Tualatin Country Club

Police Station

Tualatin Community Park

SW TUALATIN RD

12

SW HERMAN RD

10 Boat Ramp

14 **13**

SW SWEEK DR

SW 93RD TER

SW 90TH AVE

11

Hedges Creek

SW BOONES FERRY RD

SW BOONES FERRY RD

15

Bridge

Shopping Center

17

Hedges Creek Marsh

16

SW TUALATIN SHERWOOD RD

N

0.25 mile

Atfalati band of the Kalapuya during the early settlement days. The bridge, connecting Tualatin and Tigard, was dedicated in 2007 as a "bridge builder" not only between the two communities but also between two cultures. There are spectacular views of the Tualatin River from the bridge. You'll also see the WES (Westside Express Service) commuter train running parallel to the trail that connects Wilsonville to downtown Beaverton. It'll be noisy during morning and evening rush hours. Just across the bridge, I find the unpaved paths that parallel the Tualatin a nice alternative to the busier paved path. It also provides some good birding opportunities through the heavily forested riparian zone.

Once inside **Tualatin Community Park** there are several options to explore. First, on the left, just past the old, rusty-looking railroad bridge that spans the Tualatin River from east to west, is a large map, a "Paddler's Access Guide to the Tualatin River." The sign is located at the top of a steep ramp that provides access to the Tualatin for canoes and kayaks. The sign, installed by the Tualatin Riverkeepers **10**, is at river mile 25.3, meaning you are twenty-five miles from the confluence of the Tualatin and Willamette Rivers at old West Linn's Willamette Park. The map provides information on paddling times to various points both upstream and downstream from Tualatin Community Park.

Just past the children's play area, which has a cute river otter sculpture in the sandbox, is another interpretive sign **11** that provides information for self-guided walking tours to art, culture, and natural history of the city of Tualatin.

My favorite side loop, before returning to Cook Park, is the mile-and-a-half wetland and natural history walk to Sweek Pond, Hedges Creek Marsh, and the Kaiser Permanente gardens on SW 92nd Avenue. From Tualatin Community Park I walk south to where SW Tualatin Road curves to the west **12**, and then I head west on the sidewalk to the pedestrian crossing in front of the City of Tualatin Police Department, where I cross over to the **Tualatin Heritage Center 13**. If you walk behind the heritage center you'll see a gravel path that will take you on a loop around the **Sweek Pond Natural Area 14**. The gravel path doesn't show up on the official city interpretive signs, but it's the only way to get views of Sweek Pond.

Years ago this was all part of the Hedges Creek Marsh natural area, which has since been fragmented by development. Nonetheless, the pond is a nice postage stamp–sized wetland that's worth exploring on the Hedges Creek walk. I like to sit adjacent to the small interpretive sign and viewing area at the eastern end of the pond to check the pond for waterfowl, beaver, and songbirds in the riparian forest that rings the pond.

After completing the loop, I head south on the sidewalk to the paved path that starts the Hedges Creek Wetland loop. At the end of the large apartment complex an arched wooden bridge **15** crosses Hedges Creek. The bridge is high enough that you get sweeping upstream and downstream views of the creek and its associated wetlands. Downstream, look for an old beaver dam.

Just across the scenic arched, wooden bridge is a large shopping center, complete with the omnipresent Starbucks, which can be pretty inviting on a bitterly cold winter day. After you stop for a hot hazelnut steamer, it's a less than aesthetic but direct route to the wetlands through the parking lot at the back of the shopping center. Walk up the short berm for excellent views of **Hedges Creek Marsh** ⑯. During winter you'll see lots of waterfowl including ring-necked ducks, northern shovelers, gadwall, bufflehead, hooded and common mergansers, and lesser scaup.

My next stop is the Kaiser Permanente Art and Sculpture Garden, just across SW 90th Avenue. As you enter the parking area, the stormwater wetland, though small and scrappy, is a good place to look for a great blue heron or green heron skulking about. In addition to the art display, Kaiser has a wonderful little sculpture garden ⑰ with birds, other animals, and plants common to Hedges Creek Marsh. There are also views of the marsh from behind Kaiser's offices. Be sure to scan the wetland along SW 90th for herons.

Head back north on SW 90th Avenue. There are fabulous views of Hedges Creek Marsh on either side of the street. It's a short distance back to the Tualatin Heritage Center along SW Sweek Drive. From there I retrace my route back through Tualatin Community Park and the Ki-a-Kuts Bridge.

Durham City Park

For an out-and-back option, continue north on the paved path to where it dead-ends near the Clean Water Services water treatment plant rather than returning directly to Cook Park. If you take the paved path across the large, grassy, dogs-off-leash meadow, you'll cross over Fanno Creek and come out into the adjacent neighborhood at the park entrance, off SW Arkenstone Drive. From there it's a short walk to SW Rivendell Drive and SW Upper Boones Ferry Road. If you choose this option, however, you've got a long walk to the nearest TriMet stop at SW Durham Road or SW Lower Boones Ferry Road.

How to Get There

BY CAR OR BIKE: Take SW Durham Road to SW 92nd Avenue, just past Tigard High School and take SW 92nd, which dead ends in Cook Park. **PUBLIC TRANSIT:** TriMet bus 76 takes you near Cook Park at SW Hall Boulevard and SW Durham Road. You can also take the WES commuter rail from the north or south, which stops in downtown Tualatin and is a short walk back to Tualatin Community Park.

By Mike Houck

Urban Vermin

IF YOU BUILD IT, THEY WILL COME. Not the ghosts of baseball legends, but vermin—those annoying creatures that crawl, creep, slither, or slink their way into our homes. We've all swatted the occasional fly as it jittered at the window, swept a spider from the corner with too short a broom, or dodged the moth drawn to our porch light as we fumbled for the keys, praying the neighbors didn't witness our demented dance—or maybe that's just me. Thankfully, this essay isn't about moths or other lone marauders; it's about the social vermin that barge in and invite their kin: carpenter ants, roaches, and rats—oh my.

If I Were a Carpenter

There's nothing like a home crawling with ants to dampen your enthusiasm for a species, no matter its positive press. Edward O. Wilson, the father of sociobiology, did his best to elevate the ant to a place of esteem in the animal kingdom. Ants are, after all, among the most numerous creatures on earth, with over twelve thousand species accounting for 15 to 25 percent of the animal biomass. Perhaps Dr. Wilson should have taken a page from Paris Hilton's book (who knew she could write?), as her PR campaign for Chihuahuas proved curiously successful.

In all fairness, carpenter ants (*Camponotus* spp.) don't actually eat wood, as do termites. Rather, they seek out sites in which to excavate a nest, choosing both wood softened by rot and structurally sound timbers, as well as insulation, paper, and other materials that will yield to their strong jaws. On quiet summer nights, the sound of carpenter ants rustling in your rafters may be the first clue that you've got company. Watch, too, for their telltale piles of sawdust, or frass, which sometimes collects in spider webs.

Carpenter ants, themselves, are unmistakable, being relatively large compared to other ants. Those in the worker caste can be up to half an inch long—not easily confused with the so-called sugar ant, those teeny creatures, the size of a lowercase *i*, that may be drawn to your bowl of overripe fruit. Carpenter ants also like sweets and feed primarily on the "honeydew" they collect from aphids, or on tree sap. To a lesser extent, carpenter ants also eat insects, including crickets, daddy longlegs, crane flies, and moth larvae.

Although you may only spot a few ants scouting out your home, rest assured, there are more where they came from—colonies can be two to three thousand ants strong. Satellite colonies, often built in homes and other structures, contain mature larvae, pupae, and worker ants. The parent colony, usually located some distance from a home in a dead tree, stump, or buried wood, contains the reproductive queen and her entourage of worker ants. Homes built in or adjacent to wooded areas are particularly susceptible to ant invasions.

Short of chemical interventions, preferably aimed at the parent colony, the best way to deal with carpenter ants is to prevent them from entering your home in the first place. Trim back shrubs, trees, and other vegetation that brush against your house, and balance the aesthetics of wood in your landscape with its potential to harbor these tenacious vermin.

The Indestructible Roach

It's been postulated that if humans ever destroyed themselves through collective folly, the one creature certain to survive would be the cockroach. Screenwriters for the animated film *WALL-E* applied this concept to charming effect when they gave their robotic hero a cockroach sidekick.

Rarely are cockroaches so charming in the flesh, which includes a characteristically flattened body, sometimes winged, sometimes not, and long antennae. The world's largest species, the Madagascar hissing cockroach, can reach five inches in length. Thankfully, cockroaches in Oregon are small creatures, which, if seen at all, are usually scrabbling for cover when you flick on the lights. Their scurrying gait drew the attention of Oregon State University researcher John Schmitt, whose work in robotics sought to mimic the roach's kinetic mastery. "They can run fast, turn on a dime," said Schmitt, "and react to perturbations faster than a nerve impulse can travel."

Of the five roach species found in Oregon, only the wood roach is native, and this species generally does not invade homes. Of the others—the American, oriental, German, and brown-banded roach—the German cockroach (*Blattella germanica*) is most common in Oregon homes.

The success of roaches is due in part to their reproductive strategy. Roaches produce capsules, called "ootheca," which, in the German cockroach, can contain thirty to fifty eggs that develop into nymphs before hatching. Over the course of a one-year life span, a female German cockroach can produce four to eight such capsules.

Unlike carpenter ants, roaches do not have a nest per se, but congregate in protective harborage sites—cracks and crevices from which they emerge to feed on our crumbs. It would be impossible to eliminate all potential harborage sites from your home. The best you can do, short of chemical traps and repellants, is to remember that when it comes to roaches, cleanliness is next to buglessness.

You Dirty Rat

The reputation of the rat was spoiled long before James Cagney uttered his famous line in the 1931 film *Blonde Crazy*. Our distaste for this adaptive mammal can be traced to the plague, which ravaged fourteenth-century Europe, although the rat's long, naked tail has probably made humans leap on the nearest chair as far back as there were chairs.

Rats did not content themselves to wreak havoc in Europe. They stowed aboard ships bound for the New World and have been staking out our bird feeders ever since. The Norwegian rat (*Rattus norvegicus*) is the most common species you'll encounter skulking among the spotted towhees. It is distinguished from the smaller black rat (*Rattus rattus*) of plague fame by its gray-brown fur and tail, which, unlike that of the black rat, is shorter than its head and body combined.

In addition to feasting on birdseed, rats will raid the compost pile, fruit tree, garbage can, and given sufficient access, any food it can sink its ever-growing teeth into. Its varied diet is but one of the factors behind its success, another being its prodigious reproductive rate. Like any rodent, rats bear multiple young, up to twenty-two in a litter. The young are sexually mature within three months. In the Northwest, the Norway rat tends to breed primarily in spring and summer, although its presence may be most noticeable in winter when it seeks out the warmth of our homes.

An Evolving Threat

Carpenter ants, roaches, rats, and their ilk have spawned a lucrative pest control industry. In the Portland metro area alone, there are more than seventy-five companies prepared to do battle with urban vermin. Whether you seek professional help or try one of the do-it-yourself treatments that abound on the internet, be sure to use chemicals with appropriate caution. As our defenses against animal pests evolve, so too will the animals themselves. Our society and theirs are likely to rub shoulders or antennae for years to come. Just be thankful you don't live in Madagascar.

By Connie Levesque, illustration by Virginia Church

Hyland Forest Park

LOCATION: 8000 SW 142nd Avenue, Beaverton, OR **ACTIVITIES:** Hiking, Wildlife viewing **FACILITIES:** Unpaved trails **FEES AND REGULATIONS:** Pets on leash **HIKING DIFFICULTY:** Easy **HIGHLIGHTS:** A 30-acre woodland with wetland and upland habitat; Second-growth Douglas fir grove provides an island sanctuary for woodland birds as well as red-legged frog breeding habitat; Unique 1.5-acre off-trail nature play area in the southeast section **PUBLIC TRANSIT:** TriMet buses 62, 88

When you step off the neighborhood street into Hyland Forest Park, you can't help but be more aware to what's around you as your senses change, adjusting from the surrounding suburban development. Stop for a moment and relish this shift. Let your ears attune to the symphony of the urban forest. The sounds of the city are reduced to a dull purr, becoming the bass-line to the more subtle melody of the natural area, created by the disparate songs of the many species of birds who populate the park, the intermittent percussion of a downy or pileated woodpecker or northern flicker, or the soft hum of a solitary bee in search of flowers to pollinate. Squint a bit and take in the various layers, shapes, and colors of the diverse vegetation: from the elegant trillium and humble wood violet on the forest floor, to the charming elderberry and vine maple in the mid-story, to the familiar deep-furrowed bark of the Douglas firs that make up the majority of the park's large trees. Take a deep breath of the rich air, feel the ground beneath your feet, and walk.

The mile and a half of trails that wind through the site will lead you through the various park landscapes. Elderberry and hazelnut overhang the trail in the southern section, while the center of the park has sparse mid-story, a lingering effect of the presence of the invasive species that dominated the site for decades before concerted restoration efforts began in 2001. The light and color change in the Oregon ash–dominated wetland in the northeast corner, which drains into a man-made pond that

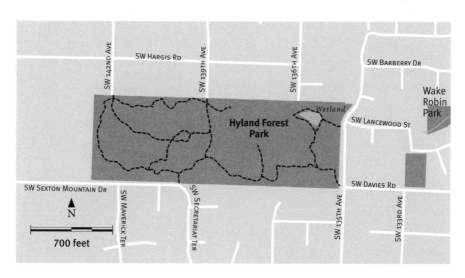

is a breeding site for northern red-legged frogs in the winter months. On the side of the trail at the western end of the wetland resides a peculiarity, often referred to as the Goddess Tree—a contorted big-leaf maple that has grown elegantly around various injuries. Its hollow trunk and disproportionate branches lend a unique, mysteriously anthropomorphic quality that is simultaneously eerie and enchanting.

These features, and the forested beauty that defines this park, make it a lovely destination for an easy hike, run, dog walk (on leash, of course), or birdwatching excursion. Hyland is also a great place to bring your kids. It is the home of the first official off-trail play area in the metropolitan area, a 1.5 acre section of forest where kids are not only allowed, but encouraged to build forts, climb trees, get dirty, and have fun in nature!

How to Get There

By car: From Tualatin Valley Highway, go south on SW Murray Boulevard to SW Sexton Mountain Drive and turn left. Look for the Tualatin Hills Park & Recreation District sign for Hyland Forest Park on the left. **Public transit:** TriMet bus 62 (Murray Boulevard) to the corner of SW Murray and SW Sexton Mountain Drive. Walk 0.1 miles east on Sexton Mountain Drive to the park. TriMet 88 (Hart/198th) stops at the corner of SW Hart and SW Murray Boulevard, about 0.4 miles south of Hyland Forest.

By Jo Linden

More information: Tualatin Hills Park & Recreation District

Lowami Hart Woods

LOCATION: Lowami Hart Woods: SW Hart Road, just east of 152nd Avenue; Brookhaven Park: SW Barcelona Way, just east of 152nd Avenue, Beaverton, OR **ACTIVITIES:** Hiking, Biking, Wildlife viewing **FACILITIES:** Restrooms, Parking, Paved and unpaved trails, Picnic area/shelter, Interpretive signs/info **FEES AND REGULATIONS:** Restricted hours, Pets on leash **HIKING DIFFICULTY:** Moderate **HIGHLIGHTS:** Lowami Hart Woods: upland forest with Pacific madrone, occasional Oregon white oak, and patches of giant fawn lily, Oregon iris, camas, and western wahoo; Brookhaven Park: open wetland meadows and scrubby stream corridors **PUBLIC TRANSIT:** TriMet buses 88, 62

As you enter Lowami Hart Woods Park, all paths lead you downhill toward the soft lull of Johnson Creek. The constant flow of the stream pouring past rocks and large logs masks the sound of nearby suburban traffic. Vegetation is lush throughout the park, with a spectrum of native trees, shrubs, and herbs that have survived attempts by introduced species to conquer the landscape. As you walk along the trail, you will likely flush a number of birds from thick patches of thimbleberry, salal, trumpet honeysuckle, and western wahoo. The ground is carpeted with inside-out flower, western starflower, and enchanter's nightshade. Giant fawn lily, tiger lily, Oregon iris, and common camas can also be found in smaller, more elusive patches throughout the park.

Head northeast on the trail, and you will come to the site center with a bridge that crosses to the north side of the park. This area is a remnant of the park's former days as a Camp Fire USA campground and has been converted to an educational site for visitors, complete with interpretive signage. If you prefer to learn directly from nature, just take a look around. The stream is wide and shallow as it gently meanders around the area with lots of large logs and rocks scattered throughout. Some of these were added as part of a stream enhancement project by Clean Water Services in 2006. Tilt your head toward the surrounding canopy, and you will see a number of Oregon white oaks peeking out from the edges of the surrounding upland tree line and expanding their crowns into the light of the stream corridor.

Once you cross over the stream into the northern portions of Lowami Hart Woods, you can go either direction along a loop path through more upland forests. In the northeast corner of the park, you will come across a connection to the adjacent natural areas of Brookhaven Park. These areas afford great views down into the wetland meadows surrounding Johnson Creek as the stream flows north through the park.

If you prefer a paved route, enter Brookhaven Park from the northern end of Barcelona Way. This trail is brief and begins in an upland forest. From there, you will turn a bend in the path and enter an open, scrubby stream corridor thick with redtwig dogwood, Pacific ninebark, twinberry, and a variety of willows. This area offers a great vantage point for a diversity of wildlife along both the stream corridor and the edge of the forest. The stream winds through thickets of vegetation surrounded by a wide swath of reed canarygrass clumps and is ideal for viewing signs of beaver.

How to Get There

By car: Lowami Hart Woods Park: From Tualatin Valley Highway, go south on Murray Boulevard. Turn right onto SW Hart Road; the park is on the north side of Hart Road, adjacent to SW 149th Avenue. Brookhaven Park: From Tualatin Valley Highway, go south on Murray Boulevard. Take a right onto SW Davis Road and left onto 152nd Avenue. Turn left onto Barcelona Way, which loops back around to 152nd Avenue. On the north end of Barcelona Way, you can access the paved trails of Brookhaven Park; while at the south end of Barcelona, you can access soft-surface trails that lead into both parks. **Public transit:** TriMet bus 88 runs along SW Hart Road, giving access to Lowami Hart Woods Park from the south. TriMet bus 62 runs along Murray Boulevard, which is a short walk west to both Brookhaven Park and Lowami Hart Woods Park.

By Melissa Marcum

More information: Tualatin Hills Park & Recreation District

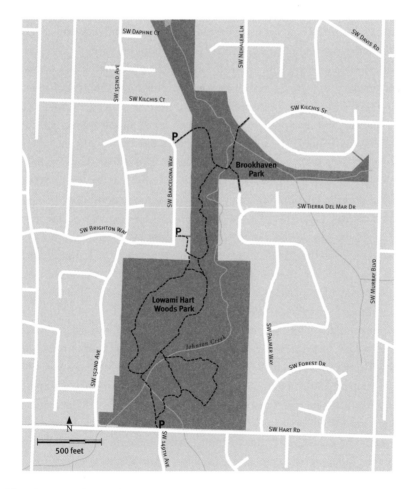

Commonwealth Lake Park

LOCATION: 13000 SW Foothill Drive, Beaverton, OR **ACTIVITIES:** Hiking, Fishing, Birdwatching **FACILITIES:** Restrooms, Paved trails, Picnic area/shelter, Dock, Interpretive signs/info **FEES AND REGULATIONS:** Hours dawn to dusk; Pets on leash **HIKING DIFFICULTY:** Easy **HIGHLIGHTS:** Paved loop trail around lake; open areas and docks for fishing and bird/waterfowl observation; Eurasian wigeon present in winter **PUBLIC TRANSIT:** MAX Blue Line; TriMet buses 59, 20

The twenty-acre park offers a surprisingly peaceful refuge. This is a great site to visit at any time of the year, but the best time to walk the 0.8-mile paved trail around the six-acre lake is on a nice day in mid-spring, when the rose bushes on the north side of the lake are in bloom and scent the air with their delicate aroma. This is a great family-oriented walk, especially for little ones on a small bike or tricycle, or toddling along with mom, dad, and big brother or sister. Spring is also a good time to see mother ducks with their brood of fluffy brown-and-yellow ducklings cruising the lake for nibbles. Please do not feed them. Mallard ducks are so habituated to trail walkers that they hardly move as you pass, sometimes within a foot or two. Canada geese use the lake as a handy stopover on their migrations north and south. Several great blue herons visit the lake every day, sometimes sitting regally upon the rails of one of the fishing docks, sometimes hidden against the branches of the spring-fed pond on the east side of the lake. Mergansers, both hooded and common, are frequently seen, and coots are regular

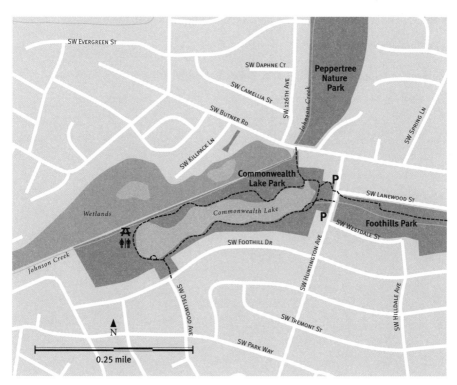

visitors too. American and Eurasion wigeon are often around in large numbers, and their cute whistles can be heard as you approach. Beaver, mink, and even otters have been seen in the lake, although more often these infrequent visitors keep to the cooler, flowing waters of north Johnson Creek that runs along the northerly edge of the park.

It is especially fun to watch the lake through the seasons. The lush, green beauty and heat of summer fades to the orange and red of autumn as the cool rains begin. A winter snow totally changes the view, creating steamy clouds while blanketing noise. Come spring, even the resident ducks seem to rejoice in the sun as the wet, bare branches of trees and shrubs sprout little ears of green. Getting to know a site by visiting through yearly changes is a kind of experience usually neglected, but it is a worthwhile commitment.

Immediately north of Commonwealth Lake is Peppertree Nature Park, a natural shrub-scrub wetland, with limited access. To the east is Foothills Park, a nice meadow and forested park with an unpaved footpath.

How to Get There

BY CAR: Oregon Highway 26 to Cedar Hills Boulevard south, right on Foothill Drive, right on Huntington Avenue. Park near Westdale Street or Lanewood Street. **PUBLIC TRANSIT:** MAX Blue Line to Sunset TC MAX station. Transfer to TriMet bus 59; get off at SW Park Way and Dellwood Avenue. Park access is 0.1 miles northwest. Or TriMet bus 20 (Burnside/Stark) from the Sunset TC MAX Station to SW Cedar Hills Boulevard and SW Foothill Drive and walk west 0.75 miles to the park.

By Julie Reilly

More information: Tualatin Hills Park & Recreation District

Jordan Park

Location: North end of NW 107th Avenue, north of NW Cornell Road, Cedar Mill (Beaverton), OR **Activities:** Hiking, Wildlife viewing **Facilities:** Parking, Paved and unpaved trails, Picnic area/shelter, Interpretive signs/info **Fees and Regulations:** Pets on leash **Hiking Difficulty:** Easy **Highlights:** A small, hidden canyon of green tucked away from obvious view **Public Transit:** TriMet buses 50, 89

Tucked away in Cedar Mills, just east of the more developed Jackie Husen Park, the forested Jordan Park has a delightfully hidden feeling. When you enter the mixed hardwood forest on the edge of a small canyon, you'll sense the cool and calm that is felt from being someplace much farther away. Cedar Mill Creek pours down the center of a wooded valley with a 1,500-foot-long paved trail clinging to the hillside above. The trail winds through groves of alder, big-leaf maple, Douglas fir, and western redcedar, and leads to an overlook of the confluence of Cedar Mill and Kitchen Creeks.

The best views are during the winter when the trees are bare, but the walk is enjoyable any time of year. A short, soft-surface trail winds down to Cedar Mill Creek and several pocket wetlands filled with skunk cabbage and jewelweeds. There is a healthy understory of native herbs and ferns throughout the site, making for a small but continuous show of wildflowers in the spring. A number of seeps and springs along the

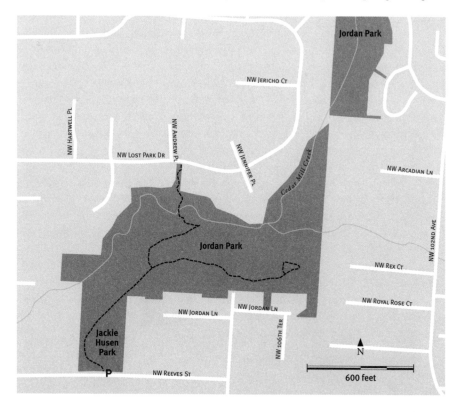

hillsides provide particularly lush pockets of ferns. Keep your eyes peeled for banana slugs as well as the uncommon, chestnut-sized, native forest snails. Small mammals, deer, woodpeckers, and songbirds are also commonly seen.

How to Get There

BY CAR: From U.S. Highway 26 west, take Cedar Hills Boulevard north (which becomes NW 113th Avenue) to NW Reeves Street. Go east on Reeves approximately one third mile and park at the Jackie Husen parking lot on the north side of the street. The trailhead is on the north side of the park. **PUBLIC TRANSIT:** TriMet bus 50 or 89 to Cornell Road and walk north on NW 113th or NW 107th Avenue to NW Reeves Street.

By Bruce Barbarasch

More information: Tualatin Hills Park & Recreation District

Die My Lovely

Invasive species are those plants and animals that have been relocated outside of their natural range, primarily through human activity, to locations where they are able to thrive in a new environment. Invasive plants were either intentionally relocated, largely for their ornamental or culinary desirability, or unintentionally transported as "hitchhikers" on the fur of animals, in freight, or as seed in crops. Simply put, invasive plants are plants out of place.

Many invasives are able to flourish outside of local growing seasons, prolifically reproduce, and thrive in a wide range of habitat types. Fundamentally, these plants disrupt the complex balance of ecosystems. Some species, like garlic mustard (*Alliaria petiolata*), even alter soil chemistry to create conditions that inhibit the growth of other plants. These combined characteristics result in plants with the ability to outcompete native species and dominate the landscape, such as English ivy (*Hedera helix*), Himalayan blackberry (*Rubus armeniacus*), purple loosestrife (*Lythrum salicaria*), giant hogweed (*Heracleum mantegazzianum*), and Japanese knotweed (*Polygonum cuspidatum*).

The National Wildlife Federation estimates that approximately 42 percent of threatened and endangered species are at risk, primarily due to invasive species and their impact on habitat. Portland Parks & Recreation works with volunteers, contractors, and city staff to administer invasive species removal programs, such as The No Ivy League, to address the control of invasive species threatening the health of our native ecosystems. The City of Portland's Early Detection Rapid Response Program aims to detect invasive populations when they are small and limited in distribution in order to reduce costs and improve control success. Metro, the Tualatin Basin's Clean Water Services, and other local park providers all have aggressive invasive removal programs. Given that climate change is likely to bring new invaders to the Pacific Northwest, there will be no quick-fix invasive-plant project. Portland's bureaus and their volunteers are in it for the long haul.

—Kendra Petersen-Morgan

Rock Creek Trail

The sun rises east over the lower reaches of the Tualatin Mountains. From the same direction, water mingles and meanders on its course. Bikes zip by as dogs and their owners meet. As the sun makes its way west, buds of trees burst open and insects rise from the earth. A raptor soars overhead as squirrels cache their harvest. Fishermen's lures plop into the water as walkers pass and children play. Birds settle in for the night as the sun drops of out of view beyond the Coast Range—a signal to the stars, coyotes, and owls that it is now their turn.

The Rock Creek Trail passes through **Kaiser Woods**, **Bethany Lake Park**, **Allenbach Acres,** and has something to offer everyone. It is a great location for wildlife viewing, hiking, biking, and fishing. A favorite play area, known as the Pirate Playground for its ship-like climbing structures and sandy digging pit, can be found just west of Kaiser Road. The relatively flat, paved trail runs four miles one-way along a powerline

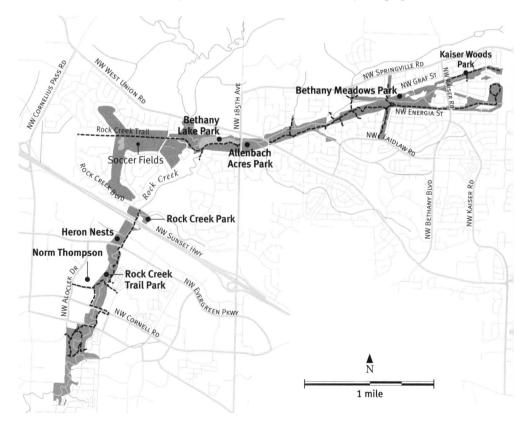

corridor, beginning at Rock Creek Boulevard from the west and ending just east of Kaiser Road, with numerous entrances from adjacent neighborhoods. The trail follows Springville Creek, which meanders west before entering the main stem of Rock Creek, just west of Bethany Lake.

Early morning is the perfect time to see songbirds, especially as spring migration begins. Riparian species can be found in streamside vegetation throughout the corridor, while woodland species are best found in Kaiser Woods. Waterfowl numbers peak mid-winter at Bethany Lake, while raptors are best observed mid-day as heated air rises. Red-tailed hawks and American kestrels can be seen hunting the open areas throughout the trail, while osprey exhibit their fishing skills to humans fishing from the shore of Bethany Lake. During summer, mid-day is the perfect time to watch dragonflies and damselflies at Bethany Lake and along the riparian corridor—great places to observe these amazing insects and learn to separate your darners from your spreadwing dragonflies. Kaiser Woods is the place to see spring wildflowers. This wooded area north of the powerline is full of lilies and other native woodland flowers that come in all shapes and colors.

Heron Nesting Colony

To the south of Rock Creek Park, a paved path heads south off of NW Rock Creek Boulevard, passes under U.S. Highway 26, and continues on the east side of Rock Creek to NW Evergreen Parkway. Just before the parkway, look to the west at the Douglas fir grove. Up o fifteen great blue herons have nested near the tops of the firs for many years. You can easily see the nests with the unaided eye, although binoculars—and better yet, a spotting scope—will enhance the view. The best time to view the heronry is late May to early June, when the young are large enough to easily see—and hear—but have not yet fledged. If you are patient and wait for an adult to return to its nest with food, you'll witness the young screeching and flapping their wings, begging to be fed first—a spectacular scene. The commotion can be heard from a half-mile away. If you continue south across NW Evergreen Parkway (watch the traffic!) the trail meanders along and across Rock Creek and NW Cornell Road. There is also a spur trail that dead ends at NW Aloclek Drive and the Norm Thompson headquarters parking lot.

—Mike Houck

How to Get There

BY CAR OR BIKE: The Rock Creek Trail can be accessed from several places including Rock Creek Boulevard on the west; from the trail at Kaiser Woods Park at NW Kaiser Road between NW Twoponds Drive and NW Twinflower Drive; and between Bethany Lake Park and Allenbach Acres Park on NW 185th Avenue, just south of West Union Road. PUBLIC TRANSIT: TriMet buses 52, 67

By Greg Creager

More information: Tualatin Hills Park & Recreation District

Tualatin Hills Nature Park

LOCATION: 15655 SW Millikan Way, Beaverton, OR **ACTIVITIES:** Hiking, Biking, Wildlife viewing **FACILITIES:** Restrooms, Parking, Paved and unpaved trails, Visitor center, Picnic area/shelter, Signs/interpretive info **FEES AND REGULATIONS:** Restricted hours; No pets allowed **HIKING DIFFICULTY:** Easy **HIGHLIGHTS:** Almost every major habitat type found in the Willamette Valley; Big Fir Trail; Big Pond; spring wildflowers and migrating songbirds. **PUBLIC TRANSIT:** MAX Blue Line; TriMet buses 67, 57

In the heart of Beaverton, Cedar Mill Creek spills into the westward-flowing Beaverton Creek. Surrounding this confluence is the Tualatin Hills Nature Park, a remarkably diverse 222-acre refuge with wetlands, forests, and streams that are habitat for all sorts of insects, amphibians, reptiles, birds, and mammals. The nature park is a fascinating place to observe the seasonal changes, such as the migration of the orange-bellied, rough-skinned newts to their breeding ponds, or the various waves of spring wildflowers or breeding birds. For hikers, joggers, birders, and botanists of all ages, the mosaic of habitats within the Tualatin Hills Nature Park invites much to be discovered by curious eyes and ears.

If you are visiting for the first time, be sure to stop by the Nature Park Interpretive Center for information, to check out interpretive exhibits, or visit the library full of local field guides and books for kids. The employees there are also a great resource for trail suggestions. At each park entrance, a kiosk is stocked with park maps and program and park information.

With roughly five miles of trails, including paved and Americans with Disability Act–accessible trails, you can piece together the hike that fits your desires and entertains your senses. The paved Vine Maple Trail cuts through the heart of the park and provides access to several loop options though an oak and pine forest, a fir forest, or a shady cedar grove. You'll know when you're walking amid the pines when the trail becomes coated in long, golden-brown ponderosa needles. The ponderosas that grow here are a Willamette Valley subspecies of the familiar ponderosas that are prolific east of the Cascade crest. For a few years, a Cooper's hawk pair has nested and raised young in the ponderosa forest. A sure sign of a Cooper's activity is small bird feathers on the ground, since their favorite meal is songbirds.

The park district is working to preserve the Oregon white oak woodland—an increasingly rare ecosystem—in this area of the park. Scan the trees here for one of our region's native squirrels, the western gray squirrel, which has a longer silvery tail and is larger in size than the introduced eastern gray squirrel.

The Big Fir Trail is a popular loop for its flowers, birds, and tall canopy. On this trail, you will wander through a cathedral-like evergreen forest where the spirited song of Pacific wrens echoes through the forest, and snags offer cozy cavities for nesting woodpeckers. The understory of the Big Fir Trail (where it connects to the Ponderosa Loop) is thought to have the greatest diversity of spring wildflowers in the park, including tiger lilies, starflowers, Indian pipe, and the secretive Calypso orchid. If you glimpse into the canopy here your eyes will be drawn to the white Pacific dogwood flowers that seem to float amidst the green. Farther along this trail, you may hear a distant rattle of the belted kingfisher, a good clue that you are near a favorite lookout point, the Big Pond. Birders scan the pockets of the pond through the changing seasons to be surprised by the likes of a secretive green heron, a wood duck family, or a pair of hooded mergansers in the winter.

If you enter the park from the MAX station on Merlo Road, you will venture onto the paved Oak Trail, which meanders along the eastern edge of the forested wildlife preserve. Follow this trail to a wetland boardwalk over Cedar Mill Creek, where you can listen for Pacific chorus frogs' rhythmic chorus in the spring or the ethereal call of Swainson's thrushes in early summer spiraling above the wetland. A short jaunt from the boardwalk is the Tadpole Pond, an important breeding area for red-legged frogs, Pacific chorus frogs, and newts.

Explore by Bike

The paved trails also make for a pleasant bike ride under the forest canopy. If you take the Oak Trail, be sure to connect to the Westside Regional Trail at the Tadpole Ponds. This multi-use trail runs parallel to the park and is an excellent open space to watch for hawks circling overhead and reptiles basking in the sun. A springtime treat is the less common trillium species, sessile trillium (*Trillium chloropetalum*), hidden in the grass.

How to Get there

BY CAR: From Portland U.S. Highway 26 west, take the Murray Boulevard exit 67 and drive south on Murray Road. Turn right onto Millikan Way and continue through the SW 154th Avenue traffic light to the park's entrance on the right. **PUBLIC TRANSIT:** MAX Blue Line to Merlo Road/SW 158th Avenue Station provides access to the northwest entrance of the park. TriMet buses 57, 67

By Sarah Skelly

More information: Tualatin Hills Park & Recreation District

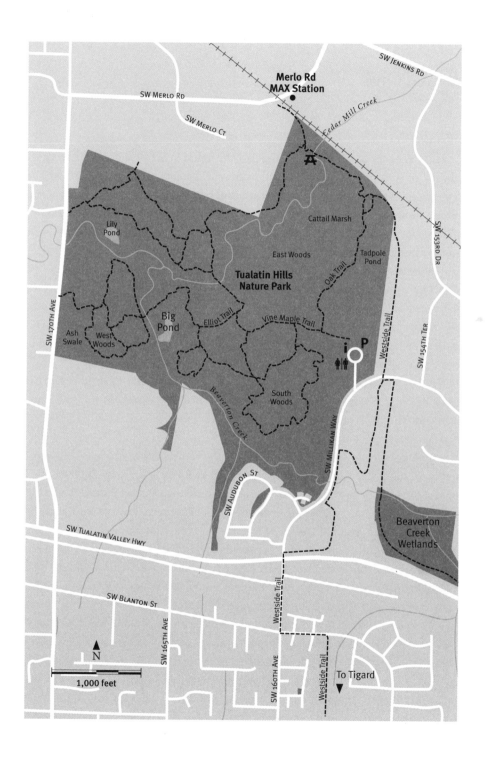

Merlo Rd
MAX Station

SW JENKINS RD

SW MERLO RD

SW MERLO CT

Cedar Mill Creek

SW 153RD DR

Lily
Pond

Cattail Marsh

East Woods

Tadpole
Pond

Tualatin Hills
Nature Park

Oak Trail

SW 170TH AVE

Big
Pond

Elliot Trail

Vine Maple Trail

Westside Trail

SW 154TH TER

Ash
Swale

West
Woods

South
Woods

Beaverton Creek

SW AUDUBON ST

SW MILLIKAN WAY

Beaverton
Creek
Wetlands

SW TUALATIN VALLEY HWY

SW BLANTON ST

SW 165TH AVE

Westside Trail

SW 160TH AVE

Westside Trail

N

1,000 feet

To Tigard

Barred Owls

SEVERAL SPECIES OF OWLS can still regularly be found in our urban landscape. Great horned owls, northern saw-whet and pygmy-owls inhabit our urban forests. The trilling call of the western screech-owl can still be heard in many natural areas and also in some moderately forested developed parks and neighborhoods. The cavity-nesting barn owl raises young on agricultural landscapes and occasionally finds suitable nesting opportunities even on the most developed landscapes under bridges and in the accessible quiet recesses of buildings. The ground-nesting short-eared owl shows up with less and less frequency as our few remaining grasslands are subjected to increased disturbance. Some species, like the old-growth-dependant northern spotted owl, which once could be found in the forested West Hills of Portland, are seen no more. However, the owl that is producing reports with the greatest frequency is a newcomer, and a highly controversial one at that, the barred owl (*Strix varia*).

A large owl with dark eyes, the barred owl is gray-brown in color and has no ear tufts. Its call is a series of loud hoots often described as "who-cooks-for-you, who-cooks-for-you-all." The barred owl is actually a native of the eastern United States but has rapidly spread westward in recent decades.

Biologists hypothesize that tree planting by settlers across the great plains of Canada facilitated its westward expansion. However, it is worth noting that their journey westward might have happened naturally millennia ago, but for the fact that native peoples of North America frequently burned the plains preventing the natural establishment of trees. The full answer will likely never be known; it remains an open question as to whether human activity prevented a natural range expansion or caused a human-related unnatural expansion. Regardless, once the barred owl hit the West Coast, it quickly moved southward establishing itself in the forests of British Columbia and Washington, finally arriving in Oregon in the 1970s.

This adaptable owl now can be found across much of Oregon's landscape, from our old growth forests to our cities. Its proliferation has been nothing short of remarkable. In the early 1990s, the appearance of a barred owl on the urban landscape was something of an anomaly—enough of an oddity that word would quickly spread and nature lovers would gather to gawk. The barred owl had a flair for the dramatic as well. One of the first sightings in Portland occurred when a barred owl chose to perch for several hours outside the downtown branch of the Multnomah County Library. A year later, a barred owl apparently ran out of energy trying to cross the Columbia River,

and the soggy bird had to be pulled from the roiling waters by boaters fishing near Kelley Point Park.

Today, barred owls, along with western screech-owls, are among our most frequently sighted urban owls, and they may well be on their way to becoming our most common urban owl. They can be found in most of our natural areas, less developed recreational parks, and even in our forested neighborhoods. They will typically use tree cavities but will also substitute old hawk, crow, and squirrel nests as well as artificial nest boxes. One pair has raised young in Portland Audubon's sanctuaries on NW Cornell Road for several years. In late spring, visitors to the sanctuary can easily find them teaching their young to hunt by the Audubon pond. Just listen for the frantic alarm calls of robins and song sparrows—the owlets are usually close by. Another pair that has established itself at Tryon Creek Natural Area has developed a habit of occasionally bopping the heads of hikers who venture too close to their young as they learn to fly. Although barred owls are nocturnal, it is not uncommon to observe them at dusk and dawn and during the day, especially when they are courting and raising young.

The arrival of the barred owl in the northwest is not without controversy. Barred owls present a huge threat to one of the Northwest's most imperiled species, the northern spotted owl. The spotted owl is currently listed as threatened under the Endangered Species Act due to the loss of old growth habitat on which it depends. The larger, more aggressive barred owls compete directly with spotted owls for nesting habitat and have been known to kill spotted owls. The rapidly deteriorating status of the spotted owl has biologists considering whether growing barred owl populations need to be controlled in old growth forests. While spotted owls are long gone from the metro region, it will be interesting to see if the barred owl impacts other local wildlife populations. They are generalists, meaning their food preferences are catholic, and will prey upon small mammals, birds, reptiles, amphibians, and invertebrates. The list also includes other owls—how will our pygmy, northern saw-whet, and western screech-owls fare in the presence of this much larger and more aggressive predator?

The debate over what, if anything, to do about barred owls is riddled with ecological and ethical questions. Many species such as house finches, Anna's hummingbirds, western scrub-jays, and green herons are here today as a result of range expansion, and we have come to accept them as part of our ecosystem. For now, barred owls enjoy the full protection of federal law and nobody is proposing any sort of control outside of old growth ecosystems. Urbanites should continue to enjoy this beautiful, charismatic, and highly visible owl. However, as we do so, we should also be reminded of our connection to the broader landscape and renew our commitment of fighting to protect our old growth forests and the barred owl's rapidly disappearing cousin.

By Bob Sallinger and Tammi Miller, illustration by Elayne Barclay

The Westside Trail

The Westside Trail is a regional, multi-use path that will eventually stretch from the Willamette River south to the Tualatin River. The Westside Trail makes a great destination for walking or bicycling, wildlife watching, or just exploring. While some of it is still in the planning stages, most of the trail is complete from the Portland Community College Rock Creek Campus to the city of Tigard. The segment through Beaverton will be completed in sections as funding allows.

If you take the MAX Blue Line to **Merlo Station** it's a nice walk through the **Tualatin Hills Nature Park** to the Westside Trail, which is accessible from the nature park's parking lot. If you drive to the nature park, head south from the parking lot on the Westside Trail through pockets of wetlands and open fields en route to Mount Williams, one of the highest points in the Beaverton area. A quick diversion southwest from the Westside Trail to the paved trail at **Beaverton Creek Wetlands** will yield glimpses of an active beaver colony as well as a variety of dabbling and diving ducks.

Back on the trail heading south, you'll soon reach the base of **Mount Williams,** where the trail sweeps across a steep hillside through second-growth conifers that make a great stopover point for migrating songbirds. On a clear day, there a great vistas of the Tualatin Mountains and surrounding cities. A small, soft-surface trail winds through a Douglas fir forest and into the neighborhoods to the west.

Continuing on the trail south, you'll cross a side trail that passes through the east end of **Summercrest Park.** Beaverton's South Johnson Creek flows through the park and is a great place to look for signs of beaver as well as smaller critters that make the multiple beaver ponds their home.

The trail winds its way through a corridor of shrub-scrub wetlands, then up and down the side of Cooper Mountain. The trail terminates at Barrows Greenway and Progress Lake Park, where the playground and scenic lake make a convenient picnic stop. Future plans for the lake call for the stocking of fish and an accessible fishing dock.

How to Get There

PUBLIC TRANSIT: Max Blue Line to Merlo Road/SW 158th Avenue Station. Turn left on the sidewalk, cross the tracks, turn left onto the asphalt trail, and follow signs to the interpretive center and parking lot where the trailhead can be found.

By Bruce Barbarasch

More information: Tualatin Hills Park & Recreation District

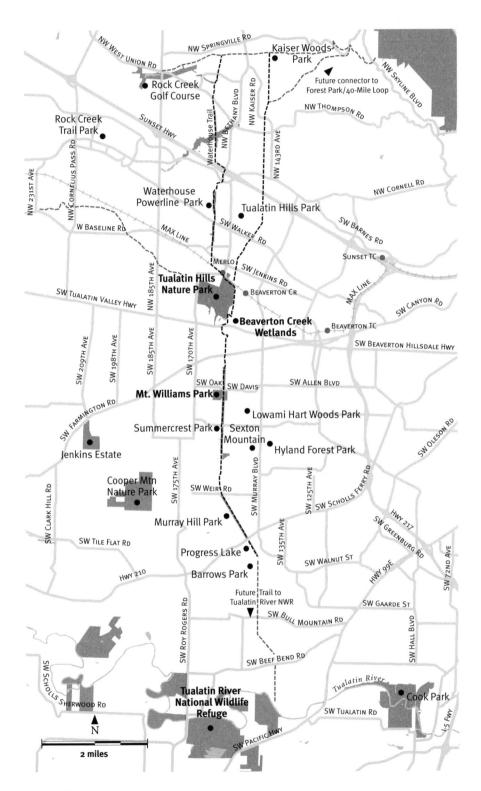

NW WEST UNION RD

NW SPRINGVILLE RD

Kaiser Woods Park

NW SKYLINE BLVD

Rock Creek
Golf Course

Future connector to
Forest Park/40-Mile Loop

NW THOMPSON RD

NW BETHANY BLVD

NW KAISER RD

NW 143RD AVE

NW CORNELL RD

Rock Creek
Trail Park

SUNSET HWY

Waterhouse Trail

NW 231ST AVE

NW CORNELIUS PASS RD

Waterhouse
Powerline Park

Tualatin Hills Park

SW BARNES RD

W BASELINE RD

MAX LINE

SW WALKER RD

SUNSET TC

MERLO

SW JENKINS RD

MAX LINE

SW CANYON RD

Tualatin Hills
Nature Park

BEAVERTON CR

SW TUALATIN VALLEY HWY

NW 185TH AVE

Beaverton Creek
Wetlands

BEAVERTON TC

SW BEAVERTON HILLSDALE HWY

SW 209TH AVE

SW 198TH AVE

SW 185TH AVE

SW 170TH AVE

SW OAK

SW DAVIS

SW ALLEN BLVD

SW OLESON RD

Mt. Williams Park

Lowami Hart Woods Park

SW FARMINGTON RD

Summercrest Park

Sexton
Mountain

Hyland Forest Park

Jenkins Estate

Cooper Mtn
Nature Park

SW 175TH AVE

SW WEIR RD

SW MURRAY BLVD

SW 125TH AVE

SW SCHOLLS FERRY RD

HWY 217

SW GREENBURG RD

SW 72ND AVE

SW CLARK HILL RD

Murray Hill Park

SW 135TH AVE

SW WALNUT ST

HWY 99E

SW HALL BLVD

SW TILE FLAT RD

Progress Lake

HWY 210

Barrows Park

Future Trail to
Tualatin River NWR

SW GAARDE ST

SW ROY ROGERS RD

SW BULL MOUNTAIN RD

SW BEEF BEND RD

SW SCHOLLS SHERWOOD RD

Tualatin River

Tualatin River
National Wildlife
Refuge

Cook Park

SW TUALATIN RD

I-5 FWY

N

SW PACIFIC HWY

2 miles

Fanno Creek Watershed

NAMED FOR ONION FARMER AUGUSTUS FANNO, and flowing through land formerly occupied by the Atfalati (Tualatin) tribe of the Kalapuya, the Fanno Creek watershed includes roughly twenty thousand acres of west Portland, Beaverton, Tigard, and Durham. Tributaries including the Vermont, Woods, Sylvan, Ball, Ash, Summer, Red Rock, and numerous smaller streams join Fanno before its confluence with the Tualatin River near Durham City Park. Despite its dense residential and commercial development, the watershed supports many native plant communities and at least one hundred native birds as well as black-tailed deer, coyote, river otter, beaver, spotted skunk, Douglas squirrel, Townsend's chipmunk, and other mammals. The splash of startled red-legged frogs isn't an uncommon sound along some tributaries. Painted and western pond turtles, both of which are on the state's threatened species list, can be found along these stream corridors. Cutthroat trout remain in breeding populations, and steelhead and coho have been found during fish surveys along with redside shiners, sculpins, dace, lamprey, and crayfish. These native species are challenged by invasive species such as reed canarygrass, Japanese knotweed, nutria, snapping turtles, bullfrogs, and bass. However, many citizen community groups have focused their efforts on the removal of invasive species and restoring natural habitat in many areas of the watershed. These efforts have been very successful and provide the community and visitors with an asset that showcases habitat restoration in an urban setting.

While most of the upper tributaries flow through private lands, many streamside parks—such as Albert Kelly, Gabriel, and Woods Memorial Parks—offer opportunities to explore and view native vegetation such as oak, Douglas fir, cedar, willow, red and blue elderberry, Oregon grape, trillium, and thimbleberry.

Farther downstream, Raleighwood Marsh provides habitat for many native species. However, access is limited, with the next access point at Bauman Park. A soft-surface trail takes you past native trees and shrubs, and immediately downstream the creek emerges into a large wetland and riparian complex bordering the Montclair Elementary and Oregon Episcopal Schools.

The Fanno Creek Trail, which starts at the Garden Home Recreation Center on SW Oleson Road, is bike friendly and paved for just over a mile downstream past the Portland Golf Club and its confluence with Woods Creek and Vista Brook Park. This is a good place to see wood ducks, mallards, and green and great blue herons. The trail ends nearby at SW 92nd Avenue. Largely inaccessible between SW 92nd and Oregon

Highway 217, Fanno flows parallel to Allen Boulevard through mostly forested wetlands largely hidden behind commercial development.

The Fanno Creek Trail resumes downstream from Highway 217 at Denny Road and continues for several miles, offering good birdwatching and botanizing opportunities along the way. The wide asphalt path begins in a mostly open wetland area in Beaverton's Fanno Creek Park. You may see wading birds and non-native bullfrogs just east of the trail in a habitat restoration project from the 1990s aptly nicknamed the duck donut. The park narrows gradually, squeezed between homes and apartments, as you enter dense ash- and hawthorn-dominated riparian forests. The park widens again into a grass-dominated wetland after the pedestrian bridge near Hall Boulevard.

The nearly ninety-acre Greenway Park begins on the west of Hall Boulevard and displays small and medium-sized emergent, shrub-scrub and forested wetlands that support a wide range of species. A short side trip east from the north end of Greenway Park takes you to the historic Fanno Farmhouse and the site of an eighteen-acre restoration project involving the re-meandering of Fanno Creek from its previously straightened channel. This restoration project is now home to native frogs, willows, sedges, rushes, oak, and shrub-scrub wetland communities. During the summer months, it is possible to walk eastward from the main trail to the edge of a marsh area known both as Creekside Marsh and Koll Center Wetlands (See page 214). This wetland is home to cinnamon and green-winged teal, common mergansers, Virginia rail, and common snipe. Great blue herons sometimes roost in the nearby Douglas fir and big-leaf maples. At the center of Greenway Park is a mature, forested wetland with great wildlife viewing opportunities.

Cross under SW Scholls Ferry Road from Greenway and you'll find yourself in Tigard's Englewood Park. Here you can view the results of channel, wetland, and riparian enhancement work completed in 2005. During the summer months, beaver dams create backwater areas along the creek, elevating groundwater levels in support of wetland vegetation. Prior to the project, nearly the entire site was covered in invasive reed canarygrass. On the south side of SW North Dakota Street is another recent enhancement project. The site is dotted by mature Oregon white ash, and while it covers only about five acres, it supports a high diversity of wetland and wet prairie plants. This is an excellent place to study sedges and rushes, and in the summer the small mudflats attract a variety of wading birds.

Almost a mile in length, the reach from SW Bonita to SW Durham Road is privately owned and largely inaccessible. The next public access is at Durham City Park, where a trail begins at the edge of a mixed conifer and broadleaf forest. The trail and pedestrian bridge provide good vantage points to see forest-dwelling birds as well as access under the rail line to the Thomas Dairy wetlands and small oak prairie restoration project. The trail skirts the edge of the field passing through a remnant Douglas fir forest to the south, where it isn't unusual to see pileated woodpeckers and pine siskins. Along the west side of the field, ponds support wintering American wigeon and green-winged teal, hooded mergansers, northern shovelers, and mallards. It is also a place to catch a glimpse of the occasional bald eagle. Off-leash dogs, unofficial trails, and weeds are among the management challenges at the site, where efforts are underway to protect sensitive native plants and ground-nesting birds. Trail connections lead west into Tigard's Cook Park and south across the Tualatin River to Tualatin.

By Peter Guillozet and Bruce Roll, illustration by Elayne Barclay

Koll Center Wetlands

LOCATION: Creekside Corporate Park, Beaverton, OR **ACTIVITIES:** Wildlife viewing **FACILITIES:** Parking, Wildlife viewing structure, Interpretive signs/info **FEES AND REGULATIONS:** No pets **HIGHLIGHTS:** Spectacular views from the knoll at the south end of the pond, next to Creekside VII, just off SW Gemini Drive; Excellent sunsets viewed from the parking lot of Creekside V; Sunrise across the pond from the tennis court/volleyball court area on the north edge of the pond is especially beautiful during the summer months **PUBLIC TRANSIT:** TriMet buses 76, 78

Although it is commonly known by birders in the area as Creekside Marsh, the Tualatin Hills Park & Recreation District calls the thirteen-acre marsh and the shallow, perennial pond Koll Center Wetlands. In the early 1980s, the Koll Construction Company proposed to fill in the marsh for development. Once it was established that the marsh could not be filled, Creekside Corporate Park took form on the upland areas and the marsh was preserved, more or less intact. Unfortunately, saving the marsh's extensive wetland area did not keep it pristine. Much of the lush, forest-green bulrush, sedges, and cattails have been lost to an invasive reed canarygrass mat, the all-too-common result of urban stormwater that has disrupted the hydrology coupled with the unique growth characteristics of this non-native grass. That said, Koll Center Wetlands is still aesthetically pleasing and rich with wildlife.

It's good birding any time of year. During winter, the marsh is full of wintering waterfowl, including the hooded and common merganser, gadwall, American and occasional Eurasian wigeon, wood duck, divers like ring-necked duck and bufflehead as well as the omnipresent mallard. You'll hear belted kingfisher frequently patrolling the marsh margins looking for tiny sculpin or see them sitting patiently in the snags and shrubby trees that ring the pond. In recent years, great blue herons have taken up residence in the forest stand of Oregon white oak, Douglas fir, and Willamette Valley ponderosa pine that line the southeastern edge of the pond. There are excellent views of the nests and the nestlings from the parking lots at Creekside V and Creekside VI. A gazebo behind Creekside VI is an excellent location to look and listen for migratory songbirds, such as white-crowned sparrows and cedar waxwings.

Beaver, otter, and the occasional muskrat can be seen plying the lake at almost any time of year. Along with these natives, the non-native nutria are also commonly seen out in the lake, and the deep "haRUMPH" of bullfrogs can be heard in the shallow-water grasses. The otters are especially fun to watch as they playfully splash about in the middle of the pond.

The marsh is easily viewed from the parking lots on the north and eastern edges, but the corner of the parking lot at Creekside VII provides an elevated vantage from the south end of the lake. It is a very short walk here from Creekside VI, and you have an overview of the entire marsh and pond system from this point. It's common to see

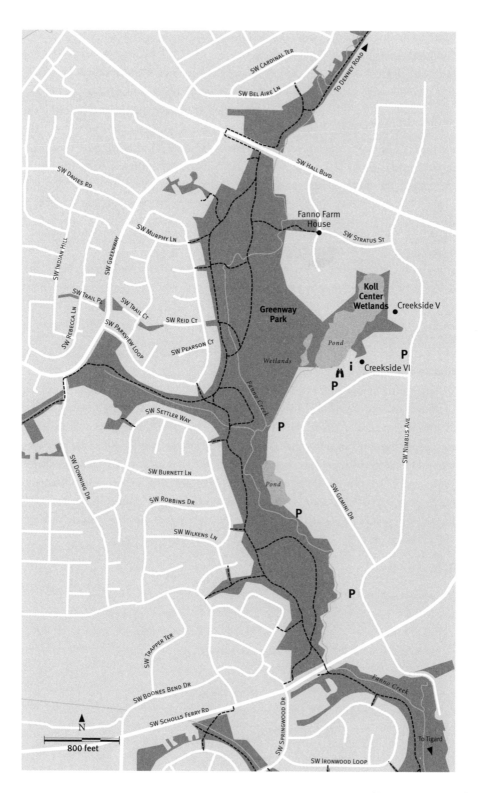

SW CARDINAL TER

SW BEL AIRE LN

To DENNEY ROAD

SW HALL BLVD

SW DAVIES RD

SW MURPHY LN

Fanno Farm
House

SW STRATUS ST

SW INDIAN HILL

SW GREENWAY

Koll
Center
Wetlands

Creekside V

SW TRAIL PL

SW TRAIL CT

SW REID CT

Greenway
Park

SW REBECCA LN

SW PARKVIEW LOOP

SW PEARSON CT

Pond

P

Wetlands

Creekside VI

P

Fanno Creek

P

SW SETTLER WAY

SW NIMBUS AVE

SW DOWNING DR

SW BURNETT LN

Pond

SW ROBBINS DR

P

SW WILKENS LN

SW GEMINI DR

P

SW TRAPPER TER

SW BOONES BEND DR

Fanno Creek

SW SCHOLLS FERRY RD

N

To Tigard

SW SPRINGWOOD DR

800 feet

SW IRONWOOD LOOP

osprey wheeling over the pond, the occasional bald eagle searching for a fat catfish, and great egrets foraging along the pond edges.

Near the tennis court and sandy volleyball court on the north side of the pond, you should be able to see several species of swallows careening across the water in aerobatic displays of agility. Shorebirds, secretive and hard to find, are common in the grasses and muddy edges of the pond, including snipe, dowitcher, sandpipers, and the occasional sora. Red-winged blackbirds provide generally the loudest and most commonly heard calls from the tall grasses and cattails, and they often nest within feet of the parking lots on the eastern and northern pond edges.

Access

By foot or bike from the Fanno Creek Regional Trail in Greenway Park, cross the footbridge just south of SW Hall Boulevard and head through an Oregon white oak grove and past the historic Fanno Farmhouse (owned and operated by Tualatin Hills Park & Recreation District and home to Fans of Fanno Creek). Turn right and go south through the office park to the tennis courts and the sandy volleyball court. The walk around the lake from the north side to the southern, elevated overview takes about fifteen minutes.

How to Get There

BY CAR: From Oregon Highway 217 heading south, take the Progress exit; turn right at the stoplight onto SW Hall Boulevard. Head west on Hall and turn left (south) at the first traffic light after crossing the railroad tracks, onto SW Nimbus Avenue. Drive one block and then turn into the Creekside Corporate Park campus and make your way around to the north side of the pond. To get to the south side of the pond, continue south on SW Nimbus and turn right on SW Gemini Drive. Take the third driveway on your right and make your way to the end of the parking lot next to the pond. All locations provide unique viewscapes and excellent wildlife viewing. **PUBLIC TRANSIT:** TriMet buses 76, 78

By Kyle Spinks

More information: Tualatin Hills Park & Recreation District

Vista Brook Park and the Fanno Creek Trail

LOCATION: SW 88th Avenue off SW Scholls Ferry Road, Beaverton, OR **ACTIVITIES:** Hiking, Wildlife viewing, Tennis **FACILITIES:** Restrooms, Parking, Paved trails, Picnic area, Children's playground, Tennis courts, Interpretive info **FEES AND REGULATIONS:** Pets on leash **HIKING DIFFICULTY:** Easy **HIGHLIGHTS:** Small pond with wood ducks and green heron; Fanno Creek Greenway Trail access **PUBLIC TRANSIT:** TriMet buses 56, 45

Vista Brook Park offers a great place to casually or actively recreate. There are bird-watching opportunities around the pond and all along the regional trail, and a large expanse of lawn for picnicking. You can toss a Frisbee or just lie on the grass. Two tennis courts and a kids' play structure offer active recreation for all ages.

Thick willows that now nearly block the view of the pond along the eastern edge of the park are the best place to look for black-headed grosbeaks, cedar waxwings, western wood-pewees, and warbling vireos during the late spring and early summer. Wood duck boxes along the pond are now regularly occupied by western screech-owls that raise a family almost every year. The brushy trail margins are excellent for over-wintering sparrows the rest of the year. Green herons and great blue herons often are seen at the pond, and red-winged blackbirds are quite vocal all around the marshy stands of cattails.

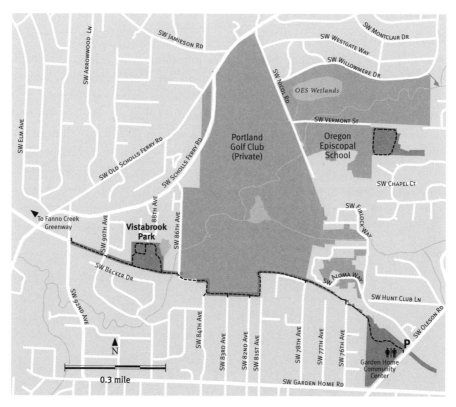

The paved trail that loops around the park provides access to the Fanno Creek Regional Trail that follows the old Oregon Electric Railway route that once extended from the Garden Home area westward into Beaverton. This wide, flat trail winds through established neighborhoods and is lined with mature Douglas fir and cottonwood trees towering over shorter trees and shrubs, all of which provide nesting and foraging habitat for a wide variety of songbirds and squirrels. Bewick's wrens are commonly heard in these shrubby areas, and spotted towhees can be seen and heard almost any time between early spring and late fall. Look for the apple trees that line this old railway route, a living reminder of the days when workers traveling to and from Beaverton would toss apple cores out the train windows.

The park trail and regional trail are fully Americans with Disabilities Act (ADA)–accessible, and the regional trail serves as a critical link in the Willamette-to-Tualatin Fanno Creek Greenway Trail. The trail provides access to the east, across Fanno Creek and south of the Portland Golf Club all the way to Tualatin Hills Park & Recreation District's Garden Home Recreation Center on SW Oleson Road. To the west the trail is complete as far as SW Allen Boulevard. From there, the next publicly accessible section of the trail is south of SW Denney Road to the west of Oregon Highway 217, but the section between Scholls Ferry Road and Denney Road is slated for completion by 2015. This section of the trail will follow the northern edge of Fanno Creek and offer excellent views of bird habitat in this important wildlife corridor.

How to Get There

BY CAR: Go to SW 88th Avenue, about a quarter mile south of SW Scholls Ferry Road. **BY BIKE OR FOOT:** The park may be accessed from the west off SW 92nd Avenue at SW Allen Boulevard, about two blocks east of SW Scholls Ferry Road, or from the east off SW 86th Avenue. Both access points have an ADA-compliant asphalt path. The trail from the east originates at the park district's Garden Home Recreation Center on SW Oleson Road, where there is ample parking, including a recently installed pervious asphalt parking lot. **PUBLIC TRANSIT:** TriMet bus 56 stops on the west side of SW Scholls Ferry Road across from SW 88th Avenue and just south of SW Allen Boulevard. If you want to walk from the Garden Home Recreation Center on SW Oleson Road, you can catch the 45 bus, which stops at the corner of SW Garden Home and Oleson.

By Kyle Spinks

Clackamas River Watershed

That was a day to be remembered ... on the banks of the Clackamas. ... Imagine a stream seventy yards broad divided by a pebbly island, running over seductive riffles, and swirling into deep, quiet pools where the good salmon goes. ... Set such a stream ... surrounded by hills of pine, throw in where you please quiet water ... and a hundred-foot bluff ... and you will get some faint notion of the Clackamas.

—Rudyard Kipling, 1889

THOUGH A BIT CHANGED from the day in 1889 when Kipling waxed poetic about his angling adventure near the present-day town of Carver, the Clackamas River is still renowned for its steelhead and salmon fishing. Even though it no longer teems with the number of fish that the Native Americans knew, the watershed still supports the last substantial run of wild coho salmon in the entire Columbia River Basin. Tributaries of the river such as Clear, Deep, and Eagle Creeks provide key habitat for salmon and steelhead. The watershed today also supports municipalities, industries, and agriculture. The Clackamas basin is the primary source of high-quality drinking water in Clackamas County.

Originating in the Cascade foothills southeast of Portland between Mount Hood and Mount Jefferson, the Clackamas watershed drains an area of about 940 square miles—roughly the size of the Hawaiian islands of Maui and Molokai put together. The upper two thirds of the watershed is public land characterized by steep basalt canyons covered with dense coniferous forests consisting mainly of Douglas fir, hemlock, and western redcedar. This part of the watershed, primarily managed by the U.S. Forest Service as part of the Mount Hood National Forest, is a close-by getaway for Portland metropolitan area recreationists. In the reach above the North Fork Dam and Reservoir upriver from Estacada, Oregon Highway 224 follows the twists and turns of the upper Clackamas River, giving views of quiet, deep, blue-green pools alternating with riffles and frothy whitewater. Forty-seven miles of the upper river are designated as part of the National Wild and Scenic River System, considered to be "outstandingly remarkable" for its fish, wildlife, recreation, historic, and vegetative values. The steep gradient of the upper river creates rapids that attract adrenaline-seeking kayakers and rafters.

Portland General Electric operates three hydroelectric facilities—North Fork, Faraday, and River Mill Dams—and operates five parks in the upper part of the watershed.

From Faraday Dam above Estacada to River Mill Dam below, the Clackamas becomes a slow-moving reservoir lake, the color of deep jade. In the lower third of the watershed below River Mill Dam the river again runs free but slower and quieter than in its wild, whitewater upper reaches. Here, the river winds its way through canyons of remnant forest, past farmland, tree farms and nurseries, rural home sites, and groves of cottonwood, until it enters the urbanized area near Carver. After flowing eighty-three miles west from its headwaters, the Clackamas River merges with the Willamette River in Oregon City.

Stunning views of Mount Hood framed by rolling hills are a hallmark of the lower Clackamas watershed. Once, only a few rural hamlets dotted the farmland between Clackamas Town Center and Estacada. In the last few years, however, the lower watershed has experienced dramatic growth. Housing developments sprout where once there were lush pastures, cows, berries, and barns.

There is a strong constituency of residents, anglers, and recreationists who advocate sustaining this watershed's health with attention to recreation, fish and wildlife, and drinking water. Many residents help keep the watershed healthy by planting streamside vegetation to help cool the water along the tributaries and main stem of the river, and by reducing or eliminating the residential and agricultural use of pesticides and herbicides that can affect fish and drinking water. Barriers to fish passage have been removed, and new developments are encouraged to minimize impervious surfaces to help storm water recharge the groundwater rather than run off into the creeks.

It's amazing, really—considering all the growth in its lower watershed—that if Kipling were to be set down in his spot on the Clackamas today, he'd hardly know the difference.

By Jo Anne Dolan

What Goes Up Must Come Down

EVERY YEAR BEGINNING IN LATE SEPTEMBER, stylish, robin-like birds, each with a black band across its breast and a dashing orange eye stripe, throng Pacific Northwest valleys. These birds—unfamiliar to many non-birders—are varied thrushes (*Ixoreus naevius*). For seven months their shy and skulking presence is a regular feature of the forested lowlands of western Oregon and Washington. Then in April, just after beginning to give voice to the series of eerie, penetrating, drawn-out notes that characterize their territorial song, they abandon the Portland area for their breeding ground in the high altitudes of the Cascades—unlike the majority of our winter visitors that breed in the high latitudes of northern Canada.

In the late nineteenth century, pioneer ecologist C. Hart Merriam made a biological survey of Arizona's San Francisco Peaks. What caught his attention was that his four-thousand-foot climb up Humphreys Peak recapitulated in miniature a four-thousand-mile journey from the Sonoran Desert to the Arctic. His observation that plant and animal communities changed as he gained elevation almost exactly as they would if he were traveling north through North America was an important contribution to emerging theories about "life zones" in the new science of ecology.

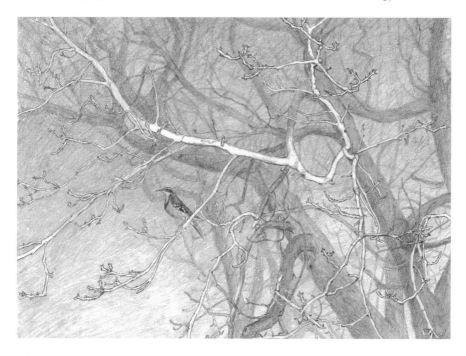

Merriam's theories have been reconsidered over the last century, although that hasn't seemed to make much difference to the birds and many northwest species that continue to take advantage of the "shortcut" micro-migration between the temperate valley floor and the boreal regions of the high Cascades. In the Portland area, several species join varied thrushes in their seasonal migration up and down the Cascades. Chickadees, fox sparrows, ruby-crowned kinglets, and evening grosbeaks all exhibit some altitudinal migration. Perhaps most familiar to Portlanders are the dark-eyed juncos (*Junco hyemalis*) that flock to valley feeders in winter and take off for Portland's hills—and higher up—soon after beginning to sing in April.

Many people imagine that the migratory impulse is inborn in all birds, but while migration is part of the life story of many, perhaps most, species, it is by no means universal. Even in species that are called to migrate, there is considerable variety in how different populations and different individuals answer the call. Some creep a short distance north, or south, or up; others strike out on journeys of hundreds—or thousands—of miles.

Why Migrate?

Modern speculation about the origins of long-distance migration has tended to concentrate around two ideas: that birds began migrating from what is now their winter range in search of adequate breeding habitat; or alternatively, that birds began the seasonal trek from their breeding range in search of adequate winter sustenance. Of course, there may be truth to both of these theories ... and both may miss the mark. In fact, while we tend to think about "The Story of Migration," the fact may be that there are about as many migration stories as there are migrants.

It is believed that long-distance migration began eons ago on a differently configured planet. Short-distance migrations on the other hand, including altitudinal migration, may be more recent, more subject to local conditions, less genetically hardwired, and altogether more comprehensible than the often shocking journeys of the long-distance champions. Still ... why is it that, come April, varied thrushes are moved to abandon balmy northwest valleys and move up thousands of feet and several life zones to rear their young in our montane forests?

When all is said and done, one of the most remarkable things about migration is that, for such a major natural spectacle, there is so much we don't understand. But we can be sure of this: migration is an evolving process as changes wrought by geology and climate (to say nothing of human encroachment) continue to force new responses from birds seeking to feed and breed. And we humans—silent observers of this avian flux—respond in our own way seeking to comprehend what ornithologist Scott Weidensaul suggests may be "the most compelling drama in all of natural history."

By Bob Wilson, illustration by Virginia Church

Deep Creek Canyon and the Cazadero Trail

LOCATION: Northern Clackamas County, OR between Boring and the Clackamas River **ACTIVITIES:** Hiking, Biking, Wildlife viewing **FACILITIES:** Unpaved trails **FEES AND REGULATIONS:** Pets on leash **HIKING DIFFICULTY:** Easy, Moderate **HIGHLIGHTS:** Birding; Tranquility; A pleasant creek in a beautiful forested canyon **PUBLIC TRANSIT:** MAX Blue Line; TriMet buses 84, 31

From the air, the Deep Creek Canyon is a striking natural feature. Its distinctiveness owes to the sharp break in both slope and vegetation where surrounding nursery lands give way to forested ravines. Both Noyer and North Fork Deep Creek descend over five hundred feet from the Clackamas River bluff to Highway 224 and the Clackamas River. The larger North Fork Deep Creek drains roughly three hundred acres, mostly as a dark verdant canyon sweeping almost four miles north and east to Boring and a headwater tributary on Zion Butte.

Someday the Deep Creek Canyon will surely provide a place of discovery and exploration for children seeking wildness beyond the urban neighborhoods planned for the adjacent City of Damascus. For now it mostly marks the natural boundaries of future urbanization and provides the principle wildlife corridor connecting Johnson Creek, Gresham's buttes, and the Clackamas River corridor. The canyon is large and isolated enough topographically to support passage for large mammals such as deer and cougar. The riparian corridor provides habitat for smaller vertebrate species, including a variety of native bird, amphibian, and fish species such as steelhead and cutthroat, coho and Chinook salmon, and lamprey eel. The diversity of habitats in the Deep Creek Canyon include mature mixed riparian and upland forests, cobble talus, and basalt cliffs, the latter known to host nesting peregrine falcon along the Clackamas bluff. For all these reasons, the Deep Creek Canyon is an acquisition target area under the 2006 Metro Regional Natural Areas Bond measure.

But there's more. The North Fork of Deep Creek also promises to be a critical recreational corridor for the region, thanks to the existence of the old Oregon Water Power and Railway Company rail line, built in 1903 and discontinued in 1943. The right-of-way is currently owned almost entirely by Oregon State Parks and is now popularly known as the Cazadero Trail. For over two decades, trail and greenspace advocates have cultivated the dream of walking or biking on a multi-use path from downtown Portland to the Pacific Crest Trail in the Mount Hood National Forest. The twelve-mile Cazadero Trail is a critical link in this increasingly popular regional vision.

Cazadero is Spanish for "a place for the pursuit of game" and was the name given to the first hydroelectric dam built on the Clackamas River in 1903 upstream of Estacada and the terminus of the rail line. Allegedly, a railroad official's wife, who was fond of Spanish culture selected the name.

The Cazadero Trail starts at the end of the Springwater Corridor Trail in Boring, where the first phase of the Boring Station Trailhead Park is scheduled for completion in 2011. The trailhead park project will include the long-awaited paving of the Spring-water Corridor trail from Rugg Road to Boring. By then, state parks will have completed the first three miles of the Cazadero Trail. The trail begins just southwest of the gas station at the intersection of Highway 212 and Richey Road, directly across the street from the planned Boring Station Trailhead Park and continues a little over five miles to Barton Park.

The trail descends gradually along the old rail grade with Deep Creek to the left. You can get a good look at the creek from a culvert crossing where the power lines intersect the trail. Boring's Mountain View Golf Course can be seen southeast of the creek. After about 0.7 miles, the canyon hill slopes of mature Douglas fir and western redcedar close in on either side of the creek and trail. However, because of the power line, the trail itself is not enclosed in canopy. Brushy hazelnut, ocean spray, ninebark, and other shrubby trees grow at the canyon bottom allowing only occasional views of the creek. You'll encounter plenty of jays, robins, and the occasional northern flicker. At about a mile, you will reach some isolated residences. (Please respect private property and stay on the trail.) Metro is acquiring land to protect the forested areas of North Fork Deep Creek for water quality and fish and wildlife habitat, which will also help preserve some of the natural scenic views along the Cazadero Trail.

Continuing south, the signs of civilization become less and you'll feel the canyon's depth when the eastern ridge top comes into view. A few small landslides along the hill slope to the west are indicative of the geomorphic processes that gave form to the Deep Creek Canyon over millions of years. At three miles, the trail meets an abrupt brushy end at the former location of a rail trestle that once spanned North Fork Deep Creek. From this location you are about a half mile from Barton Park and will hear Highway 224 in the distance. It's crucial to respect private property; please stay on the existing trail and do not attempt to continue hiking south. Doing so could jeopardize relationships with adjacent property owners who are critical to completing the trail to Barton Park.

Finishing this final segment to the Clackamas River requires trail crossings at North Fork Deep Creek, Deep Creek farther downstream, and Highway 224. Metro

Aplodontia!

Aplodontia (*Aplodontia rufa*) go by many names that make no sense. They are called "boomers" although they typically make no sounds. They are also called "mountain beavers" although they are not beavers nor necessarily are they mountainous. Aplodontia are the oldest members of the rodent family found on earth. This rodent, somewhat bigger than a softball, builds elaborate burrows in forested and riparian habitats. You probably won't see an aplodontia, but look for their distinct burrow entrances, often distinguishable by a vegetated tent-like structure believed to keep out the rain. Carefully organized piles of drying vegetation also surround the burrows that the aplodonia will eventually drag inside and store for food.

—Bob Sallinger

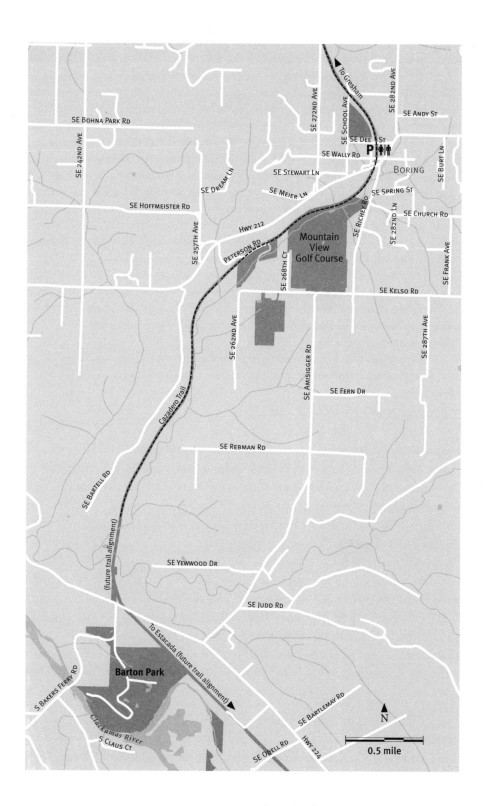

has acquired over three hundred acres of natural area along the Clackamas River near Barton Park, making it a spectacular future destination at the three-mile mark. Barton Park offers trail users camping, picnicking, ball fields, and Clackamas River activities including fishing, swimming, and watercraft launching. From Barton Park, the Cazadero Trail will eventually head nine miles east along the Clackamas River to Timber Park in Estacada. This section is being planned in three phases and will re-use the historic Eagle Creek trestle crossing.

Other proposed routes to the Pacific Crest Trail (PCT) include a trail that would go up the mainstem Deep Creek and connect with the Tickle Creek Trail to Sandy and then the Oregon Trail-Barlow Road (Highway 211). The U.S. Forest Service is planning another route, the Urban Link Trail, from Estacada to a PCT connection in the Ollalie Lakes Scenic Area. These ambitious trail projects are not without their challenges including, most importantly, funding. However, the increased awareness of and enthusiasm for the Cazadero Trail makes it one of the most promising new trail projects in the region.

Access

The Cazadero Trail and Deep Creek Canyon can be accessed south of Boring from Highway 212 just west of the intersection with Richey Road.

How to Get There

BY CAR: From Portland take Highway 212 east or from Gresham take Telford Road and SE 272nd Avenue to downtown Boring. **BY BIKE OR FOOT:** The most enjoyable way to get to Deep Creek Canyon and the Cazadero Trail is to simply bike or walk out the Springwater Corridor trail to Boring. **PUBLIC TRANSIT:** MAX Blue Line to Gresham Transit Center; TriMet bus 84 from Gresham Transit Center to Boring TriMet bus 31 (Estacada) to Barton

By Jim Labbe

More information: Metro

Salamanders

THE PACIFIC NORTHWEST is famous for dampness, and except for a few weeks of drought in the summer, it rarely disappoints. Sun-loving creatures such as *Homo sapiens* are ambivalent about this liquid extravagance, but it suits slugs and snails just fine … and salamanders love it.

Salamanders are herptiles—or, more affectionately, "herps"—a term that naturalists give to reptiles and amphibians as a group. Specifically, salamanders are amphibians so, as the word suggests, most of them spend part of their life on land and part in water. Salamanders are, you could say, the amphibious analog of reptilian lizards. But while lizards like it hot and dry, salamanders prefer cool and wet; as a result, lizards are abundant on the east side of the Cascades, but the west side is salamander country.

Salamanders and lizards look superficially similar—both have long bodies and tails—but a close look will reveal that lizards are covered in dry scales while salamander skin is moist and generally smooth.

The most common salamanders in our area are rough-skinned newts. Their pebbly brown back and vivid orange abdomen make them easy to recognize. In the animal kingdom, bright orange and red usually means "don't eat me," and rough-skinned newts are not kidding. Their poison is the same tetrodotoxin contained in blowfish, and the amount found in a single newt is plenty to kill an adult human if ingested, making handwashing after contact a really good idea. These newts are most frequently seen in late April and May as they emerge from a winter spent hunkered down under logs and debris, and head for water to breed. The Audubon Society of Portland is a great spot for newt-watching on the sanctuary trails and in the pond, where they can generally be viewed through much of the summer.

coastal giant salamander

If rough-skinned newts are our most frequently seen salamanders, coastal giant salamanders (*Dicamptodon tenebrosus*)—formerly Pacific giant salamanders—are perhaps our most arresting. At up to a foot long, they are the largest terrestrial salamanders in North America, and stumbling across one on a forest trail has certainly caused me to take a couple of steps back, especially since—surprisingly for salamanders—they can both "bark" and bite. Okay, their bark may not be much to get excited about, but their bite can draw blood.

Coastal giant salamanders are also well known for exhibiting neoteny, a sort of hiccup in normal salamander development. Along with frogs and toads—their amphibian kin—salamanders are the only vertebrates that go through metamorphosis. Except for a few strictly terrestrial species, salamanders pass through intermediate stages between egg and adulthood, during which they live exclusively in water. Salamander larvae are the functional equivalent of tadpoles—larval frogs—but they are not, in my view, quite as cute. Rather, they look something like more aquatic versions of their adult selves. They are distinguished by the possession of gills and prominent dorsal and ventral fins. As they metamorphose toward a more terrestrial lifestyle, these larval structures are lost. However, in some species—giant salamanders prominent among them—individual salamanders reach sexual maturity without losing these juvenile characteristics. These developmental dead-enders are described as "neotenous" and such individuals go on to spend their entire life in water.

Rough-skinned newts and coastal giant salamanders may be our region's most noticeable salamanders, but the Portland metro area is home to a half dozen more species, including the northwestern salamander, the longtoed salamander, and the ensatina. These and other salamanders are apt to occur wherever there is water,

ensatina

and the region's extensive wetland refuges certainly harbor their share. But Portland-area puddles can also provide adequate habitat, and the moist forests of Portland's West Hills are excellent salamander territory with the Audubon pond, as mentioned, being particularly blessed with rough-skinned newts.

That said, salamanders are generally not so easily seen. They're a secretive tribe, taking refuge under water and under logs, and as a result, herp hunters tend to spend a lot of time on their knees and in the mud. It is also the case that amphibians are not doing well in many places. Of the twenty-odd salamander species in the northwest, nearly half have been listed as "sensitive" in Oregon and Washington. The reasons for this are not perfectly understood, but the usual suspects—habitat loss, environmental toxins, and introduced species—are clearly among the factors.

Happily, Portland-area salamanders seem to be doing relatively well ... at least they aren't conspicuous on federal or state lists so far. Perhaps this should be taken as good news for the moment, both for salamanders and—since amphibians are considered indicators of environmental health—for the region. And along with cautious optimism, perhaps we could draw from this the inspiration to continue treating our place with care. After all, these ancient vertebrates have been around for a long time, and it's nice to think that our children's children's children will have plenty of opportunity to find salamanders lurking under logs in the winter and making their trek to breeding ponds every spring.

By Bob Wilson, illustrations by Allison Bollman

JOHNSON CREEK
WATERSHED

THE JOHNSON CREEK WATERSHED covers fifty-four square miles and includes parts of five cities (Damascus, Gresham, Happy Valley, Milwaukie, and Portland), in two counties (Multnomah and Clackamas). Johnson Creek originates in the foothills of Mount Hood near Boring and flows generally westward for approximately twenty-four miles before entering the Willamette River just south of the Portland-Milwaukie border, 18.5 river miles above the Willamette's confluence with the Columbia River.

Approximately fifteen thousand years ago, the Missoula Floods deposited thick, coarse sedimentary materials in the northern part of the watershed west of Gresham, and in the southern part west of Interstate 205. This relatively flat and permeable portion of the watershed contrasts with the steeper slopes and silty soils of Gresham's volcanic buttes, which are the source of most of Johnson Creek's tributaries, including Veterans, Kelley, Butler, Sunshine, and Badger Creeks. An exception is Crystal Springs Creek, which is fed by groundwater. Kelley and Crystal Springs Creeks contribute most of Johnson Creek's streamflow.

Prior to European settlement, the Johnson Creek Watershed was inhabited and heavily used by Native Americans. Starting in the 1840s, white settlers began clearing land for farming and timber. Johnson Creek is named for one of these settlers, William Johnson, who in 1846 built a water-powered sawmill on the creek. Today, only eight thousand acres of the watershed is forested, much of it on private lands to the east.

Early farmers increased the meandering of the creek, inserting 180-degree bends to expand the floodplain and increase nutrient deposition. By the 1930s, the watershed had substantially urbanized, and flooding came to be viewed as a problem rather than a benefit, a view that continues to this day. In response to flooding concerns, the federal Works Progress Administration widened and straightened much of the lower fifteen miles of Johnson Creek, lining the channel with rocks. The trapezoidal, masonry-lined stream channel is visible throughout the lower watershed. Today it is recognized that historic flood prevention efforts were largely counterproductive, and there has been significant public and private investment to reconnect Johnson Creek to its historic floodplain. In 2008, the City of Portland completed a project just south of the Springwater Corridor trail at Powell Butte, creating one hundred acre-feet of additional floodwater storage and restoring twenty acres of historic channel habitat and five acres of off-channel rearing and refuge habitat for native fish. There are numerous other smaller examples of similar projects throughout the watershed, notably at Tideman Johnson Natural Area, the Errol Creek–Johnson Creek confluence, and Brookside Wetland.

Land use in the upper watershed is predominantly rural-residential and agricultural (largely tree nurseries) with less than 10 percent impervious surface. The lower watershed is heavily urbanized, dominated by residential as well as commercial and industrial areas, with generally greater than 25 percent impervious surface. Johnson Creek experiences seasonal extremes in flow, with summertime flows being lower than minimum standards established by the Oregon Department of Fish and Wildlife for salmonids, and extremely high winter floods that result in erosion as well as property damage.

As of 2006, there were an estimated 175,000 residents in the watershed, making it one of the most densely populated watersheds in Oregon. Almost three-fourths of Johnson Creek Watershed is within the current Urban Growth Boundary, six thousand acres of which have been brought into the region's urban growth boundary within the past decade. More recently, both Clackamas and Multnomah Counties designated additional areas as urban reserves for future urban expansion. There are currently about 4,600 acres of parks and open space in the watershed. This total continues to increase, with nearly nine hundred acres acquired since 1995 with funds from voter-approved bond measures and other sources.

By Matt Clark

The Springwater Corridor
Sellwood Riverfront Park to Gresham

This is a twenty-seven-mile, round-trip bike ride from Portland's Sellwood Riverfront Park to downtown Gresham, with multiple options for extending the trip. If you're not into an out-and-back trip, in Gresham you can jump on the MAX Blue Line back to the Rose Quarter Transit Center in Portland. From there if you need to get back to Sellwood Riverfront Park take the Vera Katz Eastbank Esplanade and head south five miles along the Springwater on the Willamette trail.

Rails to Trails
In 1903, the original Springwater Rail Line (also known as the Cazadero Line) was established as part of Portland's interurban electric rail system hauling passengers and freight between Portland and Cazadero, a few miles upriver from Estacada. Service to Estacada ended in the late 1930s, and passenger service on other segments ceased in 1958, after which the line received limited use to haul lumber from Boring mills until all rail traffic ceased in 1990.

When the Oregon Department of Transportation studied potential improvements at SE McLoughlin Boulevard, the agency determined that it would cost $3 million to replace the old interurban railroad bridge over McLoughlin. Astute trail advocates and park planners pointed out that it would cost roughly half that much to buy the entire rail line from McLoughlin to Boring—eighteen miles of public right-of-way as compared to one hundred–plus feet of bridge repairs—and it would also complete one of the most sought-after legs of the 40-Mile Loop trail system. The agency agreed, and the subsequent acquisition represented the first urban rails-to-trails effort in Oregon. The Springwater Corridor opened as a bicycle path in 1996. The only problems left to solve were the "three bridges gap" (across Johnson Creek, SE McLoughlin, and the Union Pacific railroad tracks) and the "Sellwood gap," an on-street detour through the Sellwood neighborhood.

Closing the Gaps
In 2006, the three bridges were constructed, completing what had been the trail's most significant gap. Now only the Sellwood gap remains, and its completion will result in one continuous off-street bicycle-pedestrian trail from downtown Portland to Boring, a 22.3-mile one-way ramble.

Heading East

It's a short ride on quiet neighborhood streets from **Sellwood Riverfront Park** ❶ to the current trailhead at SE 19th Avenue and SE Linn Street. From there, it's a short distance to the three bridges—the contemplative overview of Johnson Creek, the flashy orange arch over SE McLoughlin Boulevard, and the solid crossing of the railroad tracks—and into Johnson Creek Canyon. After crossing Johnson Creek, you'll see where massive tree root wads and long log sections have been installed to provide in-water habitat for salmon. I sometimes take a side path leading to Eastmoreland Racquet Club and SE Berkeley Place, where I've seen belted kingfishers and great horned owls several times. More often, I ride to the junction of the Springwater Corridor and a short, steep path to the left that connects on the north to SE 37th Avenue and Crystal Springs Boulevard. There's an informative interpretive sign here and a steep downhill ride into **Tideman Johnson Park**. This six-acre park, donated by Mr. Tideman Johnson in 1942, was a favorite stopping-off point for Fourth of July picnics when the old interurban rail line was in business. Today it's a quiet, contemplative natural area that has been under restoration for several years. The wooden walkway winds east along Johnson Creek to an overlook that provides a great panorama of the restored creek, including the downstream high-flow channel that contains the creek at flood stage and provides off-channel resting areas for salmon and steelhead.

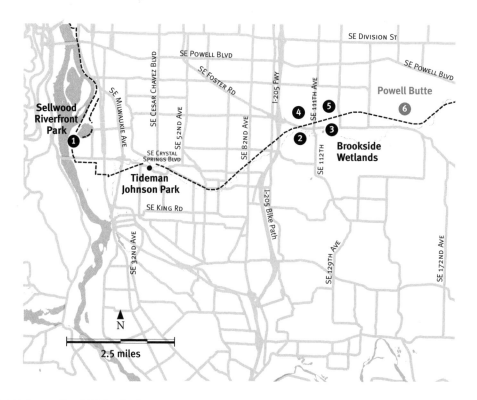

Not much farther east is the old 1930s-era Works Progress Administration (WPA) waterfall, where the creek was divided and a fish ladder installed in one channel to provide upstream passage for fish. This is one example of the many reaches of Johnson Creek that were straightened and riprapped with hand-laid basalt rock by WPA-era workers in an ill-conceived effort to "improve" Johnson Creek. Just a few hundred feet farther is the first major trailhead, at SE 45th Avenue and Johnson Creek Boulevard, 1.5 miles into the ramble. There are restrooms, a parking lot, and a cute watershed-themed mural on a nearby building. There are also numerous services nearby on SE Johnson Creek Boulevard.

From here east it's a relatively uneventful, flat ride toward Gresham. The only tricky spot is at SE Bell Avenue and SE Johnson Creek Boulevard, where the trail continues on a diagonal at the old Bell Station, now Bell Station Market—a former stop on the old Springwater Line.

Around SE 111th Avenue there are several notable stops. The first is Portland Bureau of Environmental Services' (BES) stream and wetland restoration projects ❷ at the East Lents floodplain, a perennially flooded reach of Johnson Creek between SE 106th and SE 110th Avenues, formerly owned by the Schweitzer family.

A second large-scale restoration effort is at **Brookside Wetlands** ❸, just south of SE Foster Road at SE 111th Avenue. This was the first, major BES flood mitigation

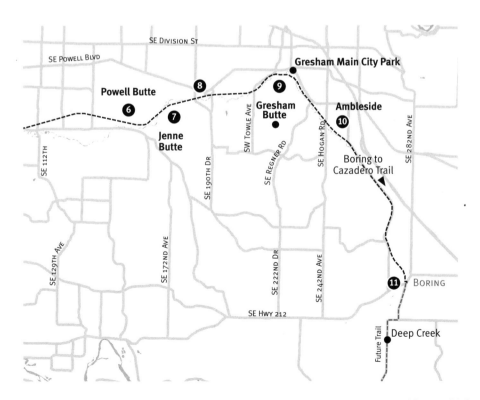

Between mile markers 12 and 13 of the Springwater Corridor, you'll see a welcome pull-out south of the trail. Mosaic art depicts species that use the area, such as northern flicker, Steller's jay, rufous hummingbird, black-capped chickadee, coho salmon, red-side shiner, sculpin, crayfish, lamprey, and dragonflies. Plant species in this area include red alder, black cottonwood, Nootka rose, Oregon grape, salmonberry, and skunk cabbage.

The WPA rechanneled Johnson Creek in the 1930s, which put many folks to work, but the project unfortunately separated Johnson Creek from its floodplain, eliminating flood storage, native fish habitat, and vegetation. Eighty years later, the City of Portland removed over 140,000 cubic yards of fill and reintroduced Johnson Creek to its historic floodplain. From the viewpoint, you can see the sixteen-acre site where the new meander is carving its memory into the landscape. The interpretive sign details the history of the Schweitzer family homestead and how the site has changed over the decades.

—Maggie Skenderian

project on Johnson Creek, covering fourteen acres. Both sites require a short detour south of the Springwater Corridor trail.

The next stops on the Springwater Corridor are **Beggars-Tick Wildlife Refuge** ❹ and Zenger Farm. It's worth the short side trip on SE 111th Avenue to the wetland overlook at Beggars-Tick marsh, named for the native wetland sunflowers, *Bidens frondosa* and *B. cernua*, both of which flower in the late summer and fall. If you walk anywhere near *Bidens*, you'll soon find out how it got its name from the two-pronged black seeds that will adhere to your clothing. Winter waterfowl are the biggest attraction, and during the colder months, bufflehead, ring-necked ducks, hooded mergansers, and northern shovelers are common.

Back on the Springwater Corridor from Beggars-Tick, it's a short ride to the north side of **Zenger Farm wetlands** ❺, where you should keep an eye out for Virginia rails, whose closest local relatives are the sora, sandhill crane, and American coot. Since they're often hidden deep amidst the wetland spirea, sedges, and rushes, you're more likely to hear their high-pitched, tinny "ditick, ditick, dick, dick, dick" than to see them. But I have seen them here several times, walking with their chicken-like gait along the trail or wandering in the shallow wetlands at the trail's edge.

Upslope and to the south is Zenger Farm, a two-acre urban farm devoted to Community Supported Agriculture. BES purchased the historic homestead property in 1994. The nonprofit Friends of Zenger Farm organization leases the farm from BES to promote "sustainable food systems, environmental stewardship, and local economic development through a working urban farm."

Another two miles east is Powell Butte rising to the north of the trail. **Powell Butte Nature Park** ❻ (see page 249), is a 611-acre natural area with numerous pedestrian, mountain bike, and equestrian trails crisscrossing the forest and upland meadows to the butte's 650-foot summit. There are several ways to access the park. If you are riding a thin-tired road bike you can lock your bike and hike up the south end's Black-tailed Deer Trail on the left. Be sure to use this trail and not the one farther along. That area north of the Springwater has been designated as one of Powell Butte's few nature preserves.

If you want to take a shorter, easier ride to the top of the butte, you can reach the parking area and a handicapped-accessible paved trail to the summit by riding east to SE Circle Avenue, then riding north to the Johnson Creek trail, which leads to the Anderegg Trail and the butte's access road. The killer 360-degree view of the Cascade Mountains and nearby volcanic buttes is worth this side trip.

From the south side of Powell Butte, it's another 1.5 miles to Gresham's **Jenne Butte Park** ❼ and a bit farther—just west of SE 190th Avenue near Powell—is the **Linnemann Railway Station** ❽, one of two stations that remain along the old Springwater Line. This replica of the 1903 station (the original burned in the 1990s) will be a museum and major Springwater trailhead in the future. Nearby, historic Cedarville Park, now privately owned, was one among the many recreation and dance hall sites along the interurban rail line that attracted city folk from Portland to then-rural Gresham.

Just beyond the Linnemann Station is **Gresham Butte** ❾ (see page 241), another of the east county volcanic buttes, and beyond that is **Gresham Main City Park**. Johnson Creek runs right through the park, which the city is restoring. If you plan to take the MAX Blue Line back to Portland, this is your jumping-off point. The nearest MAX station from the Main City Park is a half-mile ride north to Gresham Terrace at NE 10th Drive between NE Kelly and NE Hood Avenues.

If you brought a picnic lunch there are picnic shelters and tables at the park. The renovated historic downtown is just a few blocks to the north where there are restaurants, bike shops, coffee bars, shops, brewpubs, and the Center for the Arts Plaza.

Other Options
Return alternatives: You can ride north from Gresham on neighborhood streets and intersect with the east-west leg of the 40-Mile Loop that runs along the north side of N Marine Drive. Head west on Marine Drive to the I-205 bike path, ride south and connect with the Springwater Corridor to continue a loop back to Sellwood Riverfront Park. Or continue west along Marine Drive to the Expo Center MAX station and either take the MAX back to the Rose Quarter Transit Center or ride south on N Interstate and N Mississippi Avenues.

North: Another option is to ride from N Marine Drive north on the I-205 bike path and cross the Glen Jackson Bridge to the Clark County trail system. For more detailed information on these extended routes, consult Metro's *Bike There!* map.

South and East: Continuing east on the Springwater Corridor you'll come to SE Hogan Road and the quiet community of **Ambleside** ❿, which is home to the tall, spire-shaped Hogan Cedars, a variety of native western redcedar unique to Ambleside. Johnson Creek meanders through this turn-of-the-century planned community where well-heeled Portlanders retreated to summer homes in the early 1900s. Ambleside is home to belted kingfishers, wood ducks, and other birds, which feed in the birch-lined wetlands. Today it remains a quiet, shaded glen. Immediately adjacent to the north is another early twentieth-century landmark, the old Columbia Brick Factory. Downstream are Gresham's pioneer cemeteries, with gravesites dating back to the mid-1800s.

For now, the Springwater ends three miles south of the small village of **Boring** **11**. Oregon State Parks is extending the Cazadero Trail from Boring to Deep Creek. The trail will eventually continue to Barton Park and up the Clackamas River to Estacada and the Pacific Crest Trail.

By Mike Houck

Gresham Buttes

LOCATION: Buttes and lava domes south of Johnson Creek in Gresham, OR **ACTIVITIES:** Hiking, Wildlife viewing **FACILITIES:** Unpaved trails **FEES AND REGULATIONS:** Pets on leash **HIKING DIFFICULTY:** Moderate **HIGHLIGHTS:** Pleasant loop hikes from downtown Gresham along Johnson Creek, through surrounding neighborhoods, and over the wooded buttes; Connections to the Springwater Corridor **PUBLIC TRANSIT:** MAX Blue Line; TriMet buses 4, 9, 12

"Gresham: It's a Butte" reads the message on t-shirts produced by the Gresham-based Butte Conservancy. And so it is. Gresham has over a half dozen buttes that are part of the broader Boring Lava Dome complex created from eruptions 100,000 to six million years ago. Most of Gresham's buttes are clustered south of downtown and gently drain to the north by the main stem of Johnson Creek. Ranging from eight hundred to a thousand feet in elevation, they include Gresham Butte (formerly Walters Hill), Gabbert Hill, Towle Butte, Hogan Butte, Butler Butte, and Sunshine Butte. Just to the west, Grant and Jenne Buttes rise to the north and south of Johnson Creek and the Springwater Corridor. All of these forested domes support important headwater tributaries to Johnson Creek and include over 850 acres of protected natural area purchased by the City of Gresham and Metro with bond funds approved by voters in 1990, 1995, and 2006. Combined with hundreds of acres of forested buttes acquired in east Portland and north Clackamas, the Gresham Buttes are part of the emerging network of protected habitat and open space that aspires to be "Forest Park East." The most recent acquisitions in Gresham came with the downturn in the real estate market in 2007 and 2008, when Metro acquired or was gifted 130 acres formerly threatened by controversial hill-slope subdivisions. Ninety-two of those acres were generously donated by the Persimmons Development Group.

The best way to tour the buttes is via the **Gresham Butte Saddle Trail**, which can be explored as a loop from the Springwater Corridor. Begin by hiking south of the Springwater Corridor and Johnson Creek on Towle Avenue. Turn left on SW 19th Street and go to the end of a cul-de-sac to access the west end of the trail. After about half a mile along the undulating path through mixed Douglas fir and big-leaf maple, you'll intersect an unpaved access road that heads south to Gabbert Hill and north to Gresham Butte and SW Blaine Avenue. On a spring morning, you'll see or hear many of the forest bird species found throughout the region: perhaps a scolding Steller's jay, a busy spotted towhee kicking in the underbrush, or even the eerie song of a varied thrush.

Keep hiking east through the saddle and begin to descend along a small ephemeral headwater tributary through a canopy dominated by cottonwood and maple and an understory with young western redcedar. This unusual canopy mix of shade-intolerant deciduous trees over shade tolerant cedar is typical of sites with soils heavily disturbed by past logging and fire. Similar stands are common in Forest Park. Normally shade-intolerant Douglas fir dominates after fire, windthrow, or other natural disturbance; the firs are only rarely replaced by mature cedars and hemlocks if left undisturbed for thousands of years. It will be interesting to see if cedar eventually dominates these historically logged sites, essentially bypassing the Douglas fir stage of northwest forest succession. The young cedars found here may be Hogan Cedars, a unique, narrow columnar form of the western redcedar that grows only in Gresham. Its population is centered about one mile away where Hogan Road meets Johnson Creek.

You'll eventually reach a trail juncture. The trail to the left connects with SE 15th Street. Follow the left trail to Meadow Court and the trailhead at SE 19th Street. Follow SE 19th and then turn left on Regner Road to eventually intersect with the Springwater Corridor. From there you can head east on the Springwater Corridor trail, with stops at Main City Park or Gresham's pioneer cemetery via Walters Road, before reaching your starting point at Towle Avenue.

Plans call for more trails in the buttes, but limited park maintenance funds have delayed these plans indefinitely. A recent habitat enhancement project removed over four acres of non-native holly and clematis on Gresham Butte; the area will be maintained as an upland meadow with native grasses and pockets of native shrubs. There are also plans for the proposed Hogan Butte Nature Park featuring one of the most scenic vistas in the region. However, funding remains the biggest challenge to expanding recreational opportunities in the Gresham Buttes. One can only hope that as more Gresham residents discover these wild public spaces, funding and support for stewardship and improved access will grow too.

Access

The Gresham Buttes have a mix of developed trails, game trails, and old logging roads open to the public. The Gresham Butte Saddle Trail passes between Gresham Butte and Gabbert Hill. It is wide and graveled and accessible from the Springwater Corridor via low-traffic residential streets.

Grant Butte Loop

A 1.1-mile segment of the Gresham to Fairview Trail provides views of Grant Butte and wetlands that border the Johnson and Fairview Creek watersheds. The trail begins at the intersection of the Springwater Corridor and vacated 10th Street and heads north across a pedestrian bridge over Powell Boulevard. The trail, which rises above the wetlands, is a good place to spot a red-tailed hawk or American kestrel. After about one mile, the trail gradually descends back to the wetlands. Here the paved trail veers to the right, aligning with the old railroad grade. If you follow the unpaved two-track road on the railroad grade south through the wetlands, keep an eye and ear out for American bittern, reported to be relatively common here.

If you are looking for a longer trip, continue on the Gresham-Fairview Trail north to NW Halsey Street then via a sidewalk to the Interstate 84 multi-use path. Future extensions of the trail will connect to the Columbia Slough Trail and the Marine Drive multi-use path.

How to Get There

BY CAR OR BIKE: From the west take the Springwater Corridor to Towle Road. Go south to SW 19th Drive. Go left and follow SW 19th to the trailhead at a cul-de-sac. From the east take the Springwater Corridor to SE Regner Road. Go south on SE Regner to SE 19th Street. Take 19th west to the trailhead at Meadow Court. **PUBLIC TRANSIT:** MAX Blue Line or TriMet buses 4, 9, 12 to Gresham Central Transit Center, which is within walking distance to the Springwater Corridor access at Main City Park.

By Jim Labbe

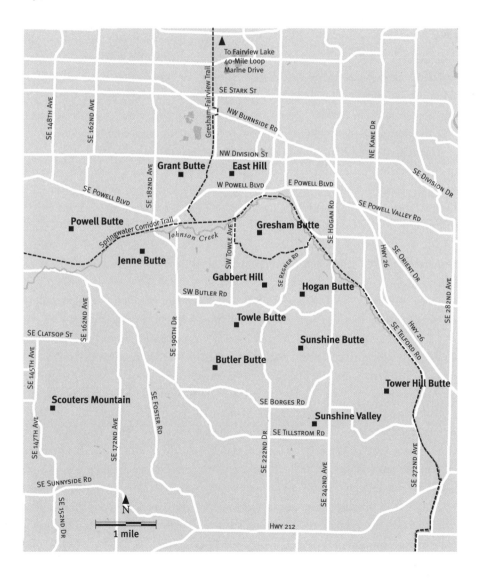

Gresham Woods and Butler Creek Greenway

Location: Mile 14 to mile 15 on the Spring-water Corridor and Johnson Creek in west Gresham, OR **Activities:** Hiking, Biking, Wildlife viewing **Facilities:** Unpaved trails **Fees and Regulations:** Pets on leash **Hiking Difficulty:** Moderate **Highlights:** Views of Johnson Creek and surrounding riparian forest; Johnson Creek Watershed Council's restoration projects **Public Transit:** TriMet bus 9

The forty-acre natural area preserve along Johnson Creek and the Springwater Corridor trail stretches from Linneman Station to Towle Road. Gresham Woods' trails form the northern extension of the Butler Creek Greenway and Trail and encompass over eighty additional linear acres, including land owned by Centennial School District.

If you take one of the two trails south from the Springwater Corridor trail, you will wind through the forested section of Gresham Woods, across an expanse of the Johnson Creek floodplain of willow and cottonwood to a viewpoint of Johnson Creek, near the confluence of Butler Creek and Johnson Creek. The trail then passes through upland forest of Douglas fir and western redcedar, salmonberry, and wildflowers.

Gresham Woods has been the focus of restoration and enhancement efforts over the last decade by the cities of Portland and Gresham, with help from the Johnson Creek Watershed Council, Gresham Kiwanis, AmeriCorps volunteers, Hollydale Elementary students, and others. The cumulative effect has been dramatic, as native plants have replaced ivy and blackberries. Recent bird surveys have found Cooper's hawks, western tanagers, Anna's hummingbirds, and willow flycatchers. On spring evenings you might also hear the breeding calls of Pacific chorus frogs, which use shallow pools and ponds to lay their eggs throughout the site. In the early mornings you may also spot rough-skinned newts, red-legged frogs, and long-toed salamanders crossing the trails to get to their favorite breeding and feeding ponds.

The main north/south trail in Gresham Woods eventually crosses Johnson Creek on a high bridge with excellent views of the creek. If you continue south on the trail past SW 14th Drive, you enter the Butler Creek Greenway. Follow the trail and Butler Creek through a small hollow in the middle of a neighborhood where restoration efforts have replaced blackberries and ivy with native trees and shrubs. Cross over SW Binford Lake Parkway and see if you can spot the native western painted turtles basking on the platforms that Gresham has installed in the middle of Binford Lake. These shy critters will spook if you are too loud, so keep your voices down and your eyes peeled. Continue around the west side of the lake where you'll encounter big trees and snags.

The trail eventually reaches Butler Creek Community Park, a developed park with playgrounds, paved trails, and picnic areas in a developed residential neighborhood. Shorter trails connect to these neighborhoods along Butler Creek's tributaries. Someday, the trail may connect all the way to the Gresham Buttes and perhaps to the envisioned East Buttes Loop Regional Trail.

Access

There are several access points, but the site is best reached from the Springwater Corridor or from the creek crossing at SW 14th Drive. The forested riverside natural area has a series of gravel and natural surface walking trails that connect to the Springwater Corridor, Johnson Creek, and a bridge to SW 14th. The area is closed after dark.

How to Get There

BY CAR OR BIKE: The easiest way to get to Gresham Woods is to bike 0.2 mile east on the Springwater Corridor from the Linneman Station Trailhead just east of SE 182nd Avenue. For cars, parking is available along Powell Loop and also at Linneman Station, which has restrooms. **PUBLIC TRANSIT:** TriMet bus 9 (Powell) from Portland or Gresham Central; get off at the first stop east of 182nd and Powell Boulevard.

By Jim Labbe

More information: City of Gresham; Johnson Creek Watershed Council

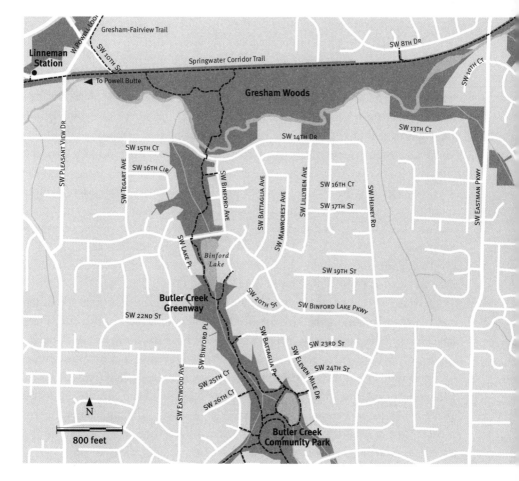

Sharpies and Coops

I STUDIED BIRDS BEFORE I BECAME A BIRDER. Birds were part of my college curriculum, along with plants, rocks, and other things natural. But that's all they were, just birds—a challenge to identify, sometimes a challenge to even find, and something to write about in my journal.

The day I became a birder, I was working on a particular problem in the field. My job was to locate the nest of a pair of spotted towhees, as well as those of seven other species in the California coastal scrub community, and I was totally baffled. The birds were getting the best of me; I couldn't figure them out. The disequilibration in my brain reached a snapping point one evening, and I just sat down at the edge of a little clearing in the coyote brush and gave up. Letting go was the best thing I could've done because the towhees I was watching didn't notice. They just kept on doing what they were doing. Suddenly something clicked, and it all began to make sense to me. I found their nest, and I went on to find the other nests that summer too.

What I noticed was this: there are no random acts, no idle behavior, no just hanging out when you are a bird. Every move you make, every sound uttered has meaning for you, and as often as not, for someone else too. When in flight you are coming from and going to specific places for specific reasons. You choose a perch above all others. There is a reason for everything you do. That's the way it is when you're a bird, and especially if you're a songbird.

The accipiter is one reason for all of these very deliberate actions. Or, to be more specific, sharp-shinned and Cooper's hawks. You see, in the songbird's world there live these red-eyed, steel-taloned, hook-beaked monsters that can appear seemingly out of nowhere and pursue you through thicket and tangle until their eight bony "fingers" reach out to wrap you in a pointy death grip. Then they eat you. With neighbors like that you don't fool around if you want to be around.

Because "sharpies" and "Coops" (as birders call them) rely on stealth, speed, and surprise when they hunt, they are not seen by us humans nearly as often as say, red-tailed hawks. But they are out there, even in Portland. Just you watch, and one day you'll see a flash of gray and black shoot across 82nd Avenue and disappear into a backyard full of trees. It will probably be one of the Mount Tabor Cooper's hawks (*Accipiter cooperii*) out hunting. Accipiters are hawks of forest and edge and the Metro area provides plenty of habitats for them to hunt and nest in. Mount Tabor, with its mix of wild and landscaped forest, has long hosted at least one pair of nesting Coops, and the surrounding neighborhoods provide additional hunting territory.

Sharp-shinned hawks (*Accipiter striatus*) are the smaller cousins of the Cooper's. The two accipiters look so much alike that more than one birding relationship has crashed on the rocks over their identification. There are many fine points to separating the two species in the field, but let's face it: sometimes it just has to go down as a "carp" or a "shoop." Just feel happy and excited to have seen it. Both species nest in Oregon, but the sharp-shinned's nesting range extends all the way to Alaska, whereas the Cooper's hawk does not venture far into Canada. I feel like I see a lot more Coops around town than sharp-shinneds, especially during the summer.

One October I was watching a scrub jay perched on a wire when it suddenly plummeted straight down into the weeds below. A second later a sharp-shinned came dancing along on the wind. Sharpies are not so heavy as Cooper's and a good breeze will cause them to have a bumpy flight pattern. Being a smaller bird, you'd think that size would be the key field mark for separating them from Coops. Besides the usual caveat that size can be difficult to judge in isolation, there is another problem: all three species of accipiter (the northern goshawk is the third and largest of all) exhibit extreme sexual dimorphism, with females being considerably larger than males. So a female sharp-shinned and a male Coop are very difficult to distinguish on size alone. And for that matter, the same is true for a female Coop and a male goshawk.

Watch for other clues that will help you make the call. First of all, it is a good thing to learn the difference between juvenal plumage and adult plumage. A juvenile accipiter, less than a year old, is brown overall, solid colored on the back and with dark streaks on a lighter breast in the front. Adult birds have a black cap, are blue-gray on the back and have orange- or rust-colored barring on the breast. All ages show a distinctly banded tail—brown and black in young birds and gray and black in adults.

Speaking of tails, as a group accipiters are distinguished by their long tails and short, rounded wings. This design aids them in pursuing their avian prey through vegetation. In proportion to the body, the sharpie's tail is shorter than the Coop's. It tends to be square at the end with central and outer tail feathers about equal in length. The Coop's tail is long relative to its body and appears rounded at the end with longer central tail feathers than outer ones. This field mark is not always reliable, though, since in the natural course of events, birds molt old tail feathers and grow in new ones. So you might see Coops with squared-off tails and sharpies with rounded ones.

Block-headedness seems to be strictly a Cooper's thing, however. This field mark is best used when you have a perched bird, and then not always. It works like this: If you see that the back of the head is square you pretty much have a Coop. If it is rounded, then it could be either. The square look comes from the bird raising its hackles, something sharpies don't do.

Another head thing that is very reliable, specific to adult birds, particularly when they're perched: If the nape, or back of the neck is lighter colored than the cap and the back, it's a Coop. If the cap, nape, and back appear seamlessly similar in shade, it's a sharpie.

Now that you know a bit about these two species, here is a tip to help you see them more often around town: let the prey birds find the birds of prey for you. Look for bird behavior that suggests there is imminent danger in the neighborhood, then look for the danger. When I notice pigeons flying in a tight flock and circling above the trees, I look for a Cooper's in the area, and sometimes find one. Or it could be a sudden alarm call and dash to safety by the robin on the lawn that gets me casting about for a furtive, winged assassin. Or watch for odd behavior, such as the scrub jay already mentioned that dropped from the telephone wires like a stone when it saw the sharpie before I did.

Predators like the accipiters aren't the only reason why songbirds are so deliberate in their actions, but they are definitely one of the reasons. They can also make the life of the bird watcher more exciting, so keep your eyes open, and good luck!

By Steve Engel

Clatsop Butte Park and Natural Area

LOCATION: SE 152nd Avenue and SE Belmore Street, Portland **ACTIVITIES:** Hiking, Wildlife viewing **FACILITIES:** Unpaved informal trails **FEES AND REGULATIONS:** Pets on leash **HIGHLIGHTS:** Dramatic views of Mount Hood, downtown Portland, and the Cascade foothills; Beautiful cedar forest on slopes above Foster Boulevard and Johnson Creek **PUBLIC TRANSIT:** No direct service

Clatsop Butte Park and Natural Area in Southeast Portland was once close to being subdivided for large houses but now provides much-needed open space for this rapidly growing part of the region. It forms a key linkage in a series of acquisitions that protect wildlife and natural habitat in the Johnson Creek Watershed. It's a quiet place where you're likely to encounter only neighbors from adjacent homes, but Portland Parks & Recreation's planned improvements will make this park a popular destination.

The park is situated atop one of the Boring Lava domes, and there are dramatic views in all directions. Clatsop Butte is a quieter alternative to Powell Butte for view seekers, especially on a clear winter day. Looking east from the high point is an iconic, virtually unobstructed view of snowcapped Mount Hood. When would-be developers bulldozed the site's soil into two large mounds, they surely did not imagine that these would someday provide viewpoints for park users! To the south, Mount Jefferson's snowy distant summit is visible. Larch Mountain at the western end of the Columbia Gorge can be seen in the northern foreground, with Silver Star Mountain, Mount Adams, and Mount St. Helens appearing on the horizon beyond. Downtown Portland and Forest Park's long ridgeline are visible to the west.

The park's open, grassy field has several scattered oaks and is framed by two small stands of firs. An intermittent stream drains two wetlands directly downhill into Johnson Creek. The Clatsop Butte Natural Area is dominated by alder, big-leaf maple, and western redcedar with small meadows and streams interspersed. Birds observed in both open and forested areas include red-tailed hawk, pileated woodpecker, northern flicker, western scrub-jay, lesser goldfinch, spotted towhee, black-headed grosbeak, and lazuli bunting.

The sixteen-acre park was purchased by Portland Parks & Recreation from a developer in 2000. The adjacent twenty-seven-acre Clatsop Butte Natural Area, managed by Portland parks, was purchased with 2006 Metro Greenspaces bond funds. Portland, Multnomah County, and Metro are assembling other key parcels of upland forest habitat on the south bank of Johnson Creek as, through acquisition and restoration activities, they seek to complete an interconnected wildlife and recreation corridor to protect the watershed. City park planners envision that the broad ridge extending from Clatsop Butte west to Mount Scott could become "Forest Park East."

Clatsop Butte Park future plans may include a recreation area with playfields, a terraced meadow, a performance space, and a series of soft-surface trails encircling the open area with access to the deep forest that lies at the park's edges.

How to Get There

By car: SE Foster Road to SE Barbara Welch Road; proceed south on Barbara Welch to SE 152nd Avenue, then left on 152nd to the park. On-street parking is permitted on SE 152nd Avenue and SE Aston Loop to the west of the park. **Public transit:** No direct service

By Ken Pirie

More information: Portland Parks & Recreation; Johnson Creek Watershed Council

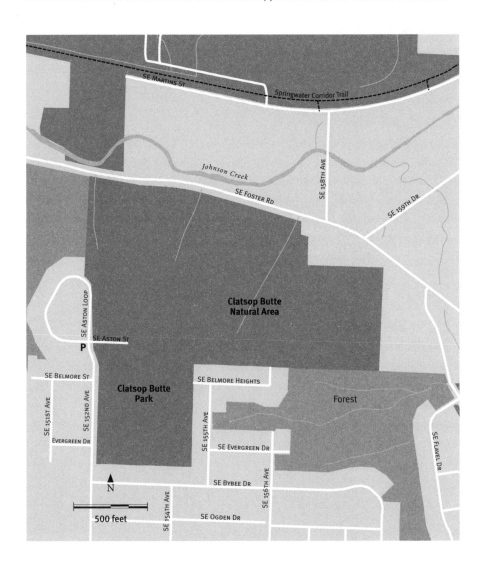

Powell Butte Nature Park

Location: 16160 SE Powell Boulevard, Portland; Entrance on SE 162nd Avenue, south of SE Powell (immediately north of the Springwater Corridor) **Activities:** Hiking, Biking, Wildlife viewing **Facilities:** Restrooms, Parking, Paved and unpaved trails, Visitor Center, Picnic area/shelter, Interpretive signs/info, Mountain finder **Fees and Regulations:** Restricted hours; Pets on leash; A 140-acre wildlife habitat area is only open to the public by permit; Some trails closed during wet season; Plant harvesting prohibited **Hiking Difficulty:** Easy, Moderate, Difficult **Highlights:** Extensive trail system for hikers, bicyclists, and equestrians; Spectacular views of the Cascades and local buttes; Excellent wildlife viewing and raptor watching; Migratory birds during the spring and fall; Satyr anglewing butterfly sightings **Public Transit:** TriMet bus 9

Powell Butte, owned by Portland Water Bureau and cooperatively managed with Portland Parks & Recreation, has approximately ten miles of trails throughout upland meadow and forest habitats that range from fully accessible to high challenge for hikers, mountain bikers, or equestrians. The Springwater Corridor trail passes by the butte's south boundary and connects to the lower end of the Pioneer Orchard and Wild Hawthorne Trails. Picnic tables are located at the parking lot and restroom area on the north slope. A new visitor information center will be located near the parking lot. The multi-use building will feature information on Portland's water supply, park ecology, trails information, and park history. The center also will have meeting space. The Mountain View Trail, which begins at the parking lot, is paved and ADA accessible.

Habitats

There are three distinct habitat types on the butte—open meadow, mature Douglas fir forest, and oak savannah. The six-hundred-acre extinct volcano's diverse habitats support an abundance of wildlife. Over one hundred species of birds as well as a variety of mammals, reptiles, amphibians, and invertebrates, such as the ochre ringlet and red admiral butterflies, occur on the butte. Removal of invasive species by fire and other means and planting native species have allowed the meadow and oak-savannah habitats to reestablish. Although the meadow vegetation will never be completely native, there is now a mix of native and non-native grasses. In the forested areas there are many large Douglas fir trees and a healthy understory of native plants.

Harvesting of nettles, fern heads, and other native plants is strictly prohibited. It is a threat to butterflies and to the health of the butte.

The summit, at 630 feet, is dominated by an open, gently rolling grassy meadow. The meadow supports a wide variety of native and non-native grasses and wildflowers. An old orchard of walnut, apple, and pear trees occupies the highest point of the meadow, which was used for years as forage for cattle. In addition to affording spectacular views of cascade peaks—Mount St. Helens and Mount Adams to the north; Mount

Jefferson to the southeast; and Mount Hood to the east—the butte is a premier area to observe American kestrel and red-tailed hawks "kiting," or hovering into the strong winds from the nearby Columbia River Gorge. At the northeast corner of the orchard is a "mountain finder," which highlights the regional buttes and mountains. Coyote, deer, northern shrike (winter), and northern harrier also forage in the open, grassy habitat and along the meadow's margins. The insect-like song of the savannah sparrow is one of the most common spring and summer sounds of the meadow. The brilliantly marked lazuli bunting can also be seen on occasion near the orchard. Rarer meadow/orchard species include western meadowlark, short-eared owl, eastern kingbird, and northern bobwhite.

The flanks of Powell Butte support mixed forest with some large western redcedar and Douglas fir in isolated pockets. There are basically two types of forests on the butte: The first, predominant Douglas fir with some big-leaf maple, Oregon white ash, and red alder (occurring in wet seeps), is found on the steeper slopes of the north, west, and south sides of the park. The second forest type is dominated by big-leaf maple and is restricted to the flatter area near the summit on the drier south slope. This habitat hosts a wide assemblage of birds, mammals, herps, and invertebrates typical to many forested areas in western Oregon. Most notable include nesting great horned owls, pileated woodpeckers, Swainson's, varied, and hermit thrushes, and several species of warblers (yellow-rumped, Wilson's, orange-crowned, black-throated gray, and Townsend's). Common winter residents include Pacific wren, song and fox sparrows, spotted towhee, American robin, black-capped and chestnut-backed chickadees, dark-eyed junco, and Steller's jay.

History

The butte was first logged in the late 1800s. With subsequent sustained grazing by Meadowland Dairy herds, the upper portions of the butte have remained in open pastureland. The flanks of the butte support regenerated forest. Former city commissioner John Mann is credited with first having seen the butte's water storage, open space, and recreational opportunities. Mann instigated the city's purchase of the butte from George Winston in 1925 for $135,000. Since then, there have been numerous plans for the site. In 1935, airport and federal radio receiver towers were proposed. In 1938, part of the land was leased to Powell Valley Road Water District for their water reservoirs, three of which are presently on the butte's lower northeast corner. A prison farm for alcoholics and drug addicts was proposed in 1946.

The butte saw Mann's original intent begin to materialize in 1977 when the design of reservoirs for Portland's water supply began. Today there are two buried fifty-million-gallon reservoirs on the north side of the butte at its deepest point.

In the early 1980s, the Portland Water Bureau suggested a cooperative management scheme with Portland Parks & Recreation, primarily due to interest in the butte by citizens and Portland parks, management considerations, and other factors. Funds were obtained from the Land and Water Conservation Fund and planning was started with a citizen's advisory committee and public hearings. Ultimately, a management plan was devised, and Powell Butte Nature Park became a reality in July 1990.

Geology

Powell Butte is a cinder cone that is part of the Boring Lava Field, a system of over a hundred small vents, cinder cones, and shield volcanoes created during the Pliocene, one to five million years ago. Mount Sylvania and Larch Mountain are other examples in this region. Cinder cones are not actually uplifted volcanic cones, but are the result of vents, which allowed lava to ooze over the landscape. This hot material interacted with water and surrounding soils to create erosion-resistant landforms that remain after adjacent land has given way to eons of wind and water erosive forces. The result is the number of peaks that dominate east Portland: Rocky Butte, Mount Tabor, Kelly

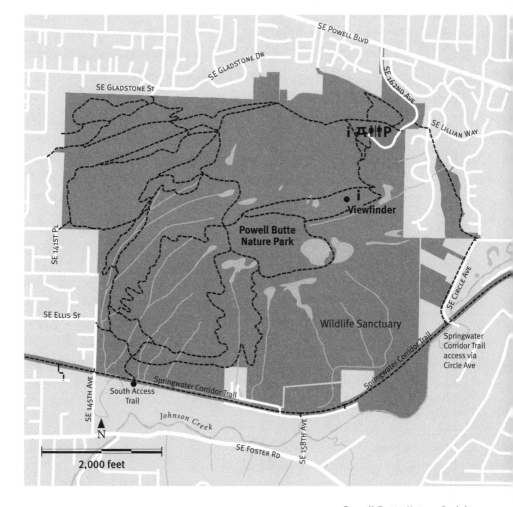

Butte, the Sandy River bluffs, and Powell Butte. Most of the material that can readily be seen on the butte today is the cobbley, sandy Troutdale Formation material. Construction of each water storage reservoir required the excavation of more than 350,000 cubic yards of this formation. The material from the first reservoir was placed in a valley on the south side of the butte. A stroll over this portion of the butte will reveal the characteristic rounded rocks typical of the Troutdale deposits.

Access

The main trail begins at the public parking area and includes a 0.6-mile paved, 5 percent–grade path that ascends to the mountain viewfinder at the top of the butte. Paved or compacted gravel service roads are an integral part of the access on the butte. The majority of the ten miles of trails in the forest are soft surface. Soft-surface trails are closed if muddy to prevent damage and erosion.

How to Get There

BY CAR: Head east on SE Powell Boulevard. Turn right at SE 162nd Avenue and travel south on the main park entrance road to the parking lot about midway up the north side of the butte. BIKE OR HIKE: Access the south entrance to the park along the Springwater Corridor, approximately 0.75 mile east of SE 136th Avenue. Other less formal access points are along the west (SE Ellis Street and SE Holgate Boulevard) and east (SE Circle Avenue) park boundaries. PUBLIC TRANSIT: TriMet bus 9 (Powell Boulevard) stops at SE 162nd Avenue; walk south along the park entrance road approximately half a mile to the parking area and restrooms.

By Emily Roth

More information: Portland Parks & Recreation; Friends of Powell Butte

Spotted Towhees

The nasal call "zhreeeee" of the spotted towhee (*Pipilo maculatus*), formerly known as the rufous-sided towhee, can be heard in virtually every wooded park or greenspace within the city. Although present year-round, towhees lie low until late winter, and then once March arrives they begin to sing their varied but shortened versions of the eastern towhee's song (only the "te-e-e-e-e" portion of the eastern towhee's "drink your te-e-e-e-e-e"). Along with song sparrows (*Melospiza melodia*), towhees are seemingly everywhere in the city's parks in early spring. But unlike sparrows, the towhee is among the showiest of birds. As if its bright rufous flanks and white belly weren't enough, its striking red eyes set off against its rich black hood and back, and white-spotted wing coverts give it a highly distinctive and unforgettable look. Towhees sometimes nest in backyards but are more inclined to retreat to wooded parks with a thick understory to raise their young. Most towhee pairs attempt to raise two broods per year, and the occasional lucky pair may even raise three. Towhees seem to have adapted well to the city and are regular visitors to backyard feeders. If we had a "songbird for the city" designation, no question, it would have to be the spotted towhee.

—Michael Murphy

Anna's Hummingbirds

SOME OREGON BIRDS are named for their physical traits, others after naturalists such as ornithologist Thomas Bewick, German naturalist Georg Wilhelm Steller, or William Clark—not so the Anna's hummingbird. To appreciate this bird's decidedly feminine moniker, imagine yourself in Italy in the nineteenth century. The breeze off the Mediterranean carries the scent of olive trees. The walls of your villa collect the sun's heat, radiating its warmth long into the night. In your garden, lit by moonlight, walks a woman of incomparable beauty—Anna, the Duchess of Rivoli. You would do anything for Anna. You would gift her a winged green jewel with a ruby crown and throat, a caged hummingbird from the New World, as exotic to Italy's shores as corn and potatoes, though, surely, more marvelous.

The Anna's hummingbird (*Calypte anna*), bears the name of this Italian duchess, wife of Prince Victor Massena. The honor was given to her in 1829 by the French naturalist René Primevère Lesson. A year later, Lesson would name the blue-throated hummingbird (*Lampornis clemenciae*) for his own wife, Clemence.

On the Move

Today, Anna's hummingbirds seem to be following the example of their famous seafaring ancestor. Although restricted to North America, the species' range has been expanding. Anna's hummingbirds originally occurred along the coast of California, but can now be found as far north as British Columbia and east into Arizona.

In Oregon, Anna's hummingbirds can be spotted year-round, a gift for any birder with a case of the winter blahs. And it's a gift that keeps on giving—the population of hese mid-sized hummers with green backs and grayish bellies is growing. Each February, the Cornell Laboratory of Ornithology and the Audubon Society sponsor the Back Yard Bird Count. In 2010, Oregonians recorded 559 Anna's hummingbirds, 139 of these in Portland. Counts from 1998 showed just 62 statewide, with only 8 birds in Portland. Admittedly, more people participated in 2010, but when effort is factored in, the increase in Anna's hummingbirds holds.

Discerning Taste

We can thank our green thumbs, in part, for the Anna's expansion. Our gardens extend the blooming season for nectar-rich flowers, augmented by feeders hung from decks and balconies. Given such bounty, who wouldn't choose to live in Oregon instead of California? Native plants remain the best source of nutrients for Anna's, as they do for

other wildlife. Flowering currant, with its pendulous red blooms, is an especially good choice for hummingbirds.

In addition to nectar, Anna's dine on tree sap and are fond of spiders (no one said the birds were perfect). Anna's are thought to be the most carnivorous of the hummingbird clan, plucking spiders from their webs and snapping up insects on the wing. Anna's also use silk from spider webs and insect cocoons to weave cup-shaped nests, which are camouflaged with snippets of lichen.

Courting Our Favor

Males begin defending their territories as early as December and maintain their vigil atop an exposed branch of a tree throughout the nesting season. Once you hear an Anna's announce itself—a buzzing *bizzle-bizzle fit fit fot*—it's easy to spot. Look for a small bird on a bare twig near the top of a tree. The Anna's is about four inches long, the size of a bushtit. Depending on the angle of the light, you may or may not see the iridescent red on the male's crown and throat, a field mark absent or much reduced in females. The long, slender bill, though, is distinctive. The birds resemble tiny narwhals, with their rounded heads scanning back and forth, their long bills angled as though probing the ice.

If you're lucky, you may also observe, or at least hear, the male's courtship display. Sometimes the loud *peek* sound made by the courting male's tail feathers is the first clue that an Anna's is nearby. The male shoots straight up into the air, then plummets, spreading its tail at the bottom of its characteristic J-shaped flight. Until recently, researchers weren't certain if the "peek" was a vocalization or a sound made by feathers. High-speed photography and electronic analysis finally tipped the scale in favor of feathers. Track down the hummingbird episode on PBS's *Nature* for some fascinating footage of the Anna's display.

Wintering Over

While other hummingbirds breed in Oregon, only the Anna's winters here regularly. On those rare December days when the pipes freeze and traffic slides to an icy halt, the phones at the Audubon Society of Portland often ring with callers concerned for the hummingbirds they've been feeding. They needn't worry. Hummingbirds enter a state of torpor during inclement weather, a condition similar to hibernation. Their respiration slows, their heart rate drops, they fluff their feathers and hunker down for the duration. Rarely do our cold snaps last long enough to rattle these well-adapted little birds.

Where to See an Anna's

If you don't have Anna's hummingbirds in your own yard, take a walk through your neighborhood—you're bound to spot a few. A hike along the Willamette River, the Springwater Corridor, or Fanno Creek will also prove fruitful. These pathways will take you through a number of hummingbird territories, and more than likely, your trespass will be announced. Wear something red to elicit the best response from the male hummers. Plan your walk for late winter or early spring when the trees are bare and the birds more visible. If you get too cold, you can always think of Italy.

By Connie Levesque, illustration by Lei Kotynski

Leach Botanical Garden

LOCATION: 6704 SE 122nd Avenue, Portland **ACTIVITIES:** Hiking, Wildlife viewing **FACILITIES:** Restrooms, Parking, Unpaved trails, Visitor Center, Interpretive signs/info **FEES AND REGULATIONS:** Restricted hours, No pets **HIKING DIFFICULTY:** Moderate **HIGHLIGHTS:** Botanical garden with over 2,000 species of exotic and native Pacific Northwest flora; Trails through relatively natural forested riparian habitat adjacent to a beautiful section of Johnson Creek **PUBLIC TRANSIT:** TriMet buses 10, 71

Leach Botanical Garden encompasses sixteen acres along Johnson Creek near SE 122nd Avenue. The nine-acre nursery and garden includes the historic estate of John and Lila Leach. The garden specializes in preserving and showcasing Lila's original garden collection and other Northwest native plants. Over two thousand species, hybrids, and cultivars can be viewed on a self-guided tour surrounding the manor house. Another eight acres of adjacent properties purchased in 1999 and 2009 buffer the garden and provide space for future expansion.

The main entrance leads to the doorstep of the Manor House, the historic home of John and Lila. Today, the Manor House provides office and meeting space. Rooms on the main floor and the adjacent outdoor patio are available to rent for weddings, retreats, and other private events.

Visitors can enjoy the extensive network of trails extending from the nursery to the stone cabin along the banks of Johnson Creek. You'll encounter an interesting mix of native and non-native trees, shrubs, vines, and herbaceous plants. Late summer is a pleasant time to stroll the quiet shaded paths and to take in the tranquility of Johnson Creek at low flow. At that time of year, you might hear the "yank, yank, yank" of a red-breasted nuthatch or the plaintive call of the black-capped chickadee, or spy a foraging brown creeper or downy woodpecker.

Both volunteers and staff maintain Leach Botanical Garden. The administrative office building (6550 SE 122nd Avenue) also houses offices of the Environmental Education Association of Oregon and the Audubon Society of Portland's east Portland satellite office.

Access

The garden is reached via the main entrance at 6704 SE 122nd Avenue and has a network of trails through both the landscaped and the natural areas. The hours are Tuesday through Saturday, 9 am to 4 pm, and Sunday, 1 pm to 4 pm. The garden is closed Mondays and some holidays.

How to Get There

BY CAR: From SE Foster Road go south on SE 122nd Avenue about one quarter mile. The main entrance of Leach Botanical Garden is on the left just before crossing Johnson Creek. A parking area is located just south of Johnson Creek on the right in view of the main entrance. **PUBLIC TRANSIT:** TriMet bus 10 from downtown Portland or Lents Town Center or bus 71 from Lents Town Center and Clackamas Transit Center both stop near SE Foster Road and 122nd Avenue.

By Jim Labbe

More information: Portland Parks & Recreation; Leach Botanical Garden

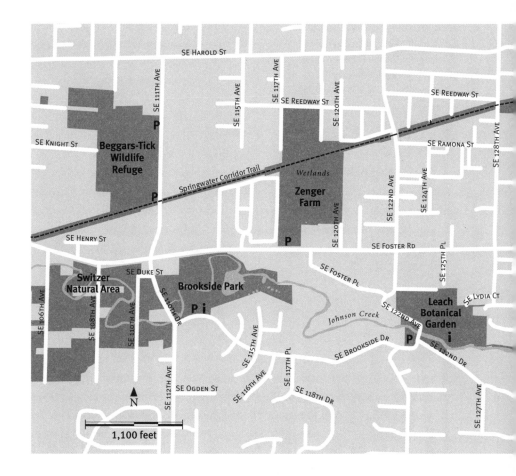

Zenger Farm

LOCATION: 11741 SE Foster Road, Portland ACTIVITIES: Hiking, Biking (Springwater Corridor), Wildlife viewing FACILITIES: Parking, Paved trail on Springwater, Unpaved trail on farm, Interpretive signs/info FEES AND REGULATIONS: Restricted hours, No pets HIKING DIFFICULTY: Easy, Moderate HIGHLIGHTS: Surrounded by industrial and residential development, Zenger Farm is a natural urban oasis with wonderful views of the ten-acre wetland and two-acre sustainable farm; Hands-on farming opportunities; educational tours; Classes and workshops PUBLIC TRANSIT: MAX Green Line; TriMet buses 10, 71

Originally a dairy farm owned by the Zenger Family, the site was purchased in 1994 by the City of Portland's Bureau of Environmental Services to protect the ten-acre wetland. The wetland is fed year-round from an onsite spring and provides habitat for five native amphibian species: the long-toed salamander, northwestern salamander, rough-skinned newt, Pacific chorus frog, and red-legged frog. All five breed in the cool, spring-fed ponds. Many insects, including dragonflies, mayflies, and damselflies also breed in the wetland pools.

Coyotes have been known to eat plums from the row of orchard trees at the transition from wetland to upland farm. Deer beds can be found throughout the tall grass and bats forage for insects during the summer evenings. Red-winged blackbirds, mallards, and Canada geese nest in the wetland. Violet-green, tree, and barn swallows can be seen darting above the grass in the wetland and on the hillside catching insects. Occasionally the pellets from great horned owls can be found under the old western redcedar tree by the pond. Red-tailed hawks soar above the farm and perch in the big-leaf maple trees that line the property to the east. Western scrub-jays are a common sight and sometimes a Steller's jay can be heard imitating a red-tailed hawk close to the Douglas fir trees. Killdeer can be seen and heard running in the farm fields during the spring months. Ring-necked pheasants often make their loud alarm in the morning, and very rarely, an American bittern can be heard from somewhere in the tall wetland grasses. A green heron sometimes forages in the wetland during the day, flying in from the south, staying for a few hours, and then flying back to the south.

Uphill from the wetland is a very unique, educational urban farm. The two-acre farming operation includes a chicken tractor which houses laying hens, a flock of heritage breed turkeys, honeybees, an orchard, a red wiggler worm compost bin, and two acres of vegetable fields. Sustainable farming practices are used, and the produce is sold and eaten locally. The land is farmed year-round and crops are rotated through the fields. During the rotation cycle some of the fields are planted with non-food cover crops (like clover or buckwheat), which add nutrients and organic matter to the soil and protect against erosion. Flowers are planted between the vegetable crops, adding color and beauty to the farm and helping to attract beneficial insects. This site serves as a model for integrating healthy farming practices and wetland stewardship.

Access

The general public is welcome to visit the site during open farm time and work parties. Check the Zenger Farm website for up-to-date information. Call to schedule an educational group visit or to sign up for a class. The wetland and farm are visible from the Springwater Corridor between SE 111th and 122nd Avenues. If you don't plan to visit the farm itself, indirect access is via the nearby Springwater Corridor, which passes along the northern boundary of the farm next to extensive wetlands.

How to Get There

BY CAR: From Interstate 205 take the Foster Road exit and head east. Go through the traffic light at SE 110/111th Avenues. You will pass a large warehouse complex (Foster 205 Commerce Center) on the left. Zenger Farm is the next property on the left. Look for a red farmhouse with solar panels. If you reach the traffic light at SE 122nd Avenue you have gone too far. **BY BIKE:** Springwater Corridor head east to 122nd Avenue. Take 122nd south to Foster Road, turn right (west) onto Foster, and then turn right into the farm. The Springwater Corridor to the north provides visual access to the farm and direct access to the wetlands downslope of the farm. **PUBLIC TRANSIT:** TriMet buses 10 and 71 both stop a block away from the farm on Foster at 116th Avenue. TriMet bus 14 and the MAX Green Line will get you as far as SE Foster and 94th Avenue. From there you can catch the 10 eastbound at 94th and Foster or the 71 eastbound at 96th and Foster. MAX Green Line to Foster Road and ride your bike east on Foster to the farm. For a less busy route, get off at the Harold and 92nd Avenue stop and ride east on Harold to 122nd Avenue. Turn right on 122nd, right on Foster, and right into the farm.

By Alice Froehlich

More information: Portland Bureau of Environmental Services; Zenger Farm

› Refer to map on page 257

Beggars-Tick Wildlife Refuge

LOCATION: West side of SE 111th Avenue between SE Foster Road and SE Harold Street, immediately north of the Springwater Corridor, Portland **ACTIVITIES:** Hiking, Birding, Wildlife viewing **FACILITIES:** Parking, Unpaved trails **FEES AND REGULATIONS:** No pets **HIKING DIFFICULTY:** Easy **HIGHLIGHTS:** Diverse wetland native plant community and associated wildlife in an urban setting; Winter and spring waterfowl; Dragonflies throughout the summer and early fall **PUBLIC TRANSIT:** TriMet buses 10, 71

This small twenty-one-acre wetland is owned by Metro and managed by Portland Parks & Recreation. The refuge is named after two yellow-flowered plants in the sunflower family (*Bidens frondosa* and *B. cernua*) that bloom in late summer and fall. Beggars-tick is named for its barbed seeds that stick to people's clothing and the fur of passing four-legged mammals.

Beggars-Tick Wildlife Refuge is predominantly a wetland with three plant communities: shrubland dominated by spirea or hardhack (*Spiraea douglasii*), willow (*Salix* spp.), swamp rose (*Rosa pisocarpa*), and beggars-tick; emergent marsh in the heart of the wetland with a thick mat of smartweed (*Polygonum* spp.); and a willow swamp that surrounds the other wetland communities. In the late fall, winter, and early spring, much of the wetland is essentially a large, shallow pond providing habitat for migratory and wintering waterfowl. Most of the wet areas dry by late spring, exposing mudflats that are quickly occupied by emergent plants until flooding resumes in late fall. In addition to providing wildlife habitat, the refuge stores stormwater and removes associated sediment and pollutants.

The marsh and its wildlife are not easily viewed from the road, and annual flooding makes this area relatively inaccessible during the winter and early spring. However, during the dry season the habitat mosaic and vegetative screening offers excellent opportunities to closely observe the plant and wildlife communities and their relationships.

The emergent marsh is best accessed from the north parking area just off of SE 111th Avenue. When flooded, a variety of waterfowl is easily observed—the bright white and black bufflehead ducks are especially visible. At its driest in late summer, the vast bed of smartweed blossoms is visited by tens of thousands of honeybees and other pollinators. Abundant swallows and dragonflies hunt above the wetlands.

Although it is most profuse in the southern half of the refuge, the shrubland is best accessed from the north parking area in late summer. Hummingbirds, warblers, flycatchers, and other songbirds are seen and heard here. Careful observers may see green herons stalking prey along the edge where the shrub habitat borders the marsh.

The forested wetlands are dominated by willow, black cottonwood (*Populus trichocarpa*), and red alder that buffer the east and west boundaries of the refuge. Here is where you may see or hear marsh and Bewick's wrens; black-capped chickadees;

bushtits; several species of warblers; red-tailed, Cooper's, and sharp-shinned hawks; and a variety of songbirds.

Access

Year-round, though limited. One viewing area has shoulder parking for four to five vehicles on the west side of SE 111th Avenue, one quarter mile north of SE Foster Road. The other access includes a short loop trail, beginning at the junction of SE 111th and the Springwater Corridor; there is room for four cars at this parking area.

How to Get There

BY CAR: Head east on SE Foster Road, turn left (north) onto SE 111th Avenue (the road to the south at this intersection is SE 112th Avenue); proceed to either of the two designated parking areas west of SE 111th. **BY BIKE OR FOOT:** Springwater Corridor to SE 111th. **PUBLIC TRANSIT:** TriMet bus 10 (Harold Street) line stops at 111th and Harold on weekdays only; the 71 stops near 111th and Foster Road. Both lines connect to the Lents Town Center where MAX Green Line light rail and other bus lines converge.

By Ralph Thomas Rogers and Elaine Stewart

> **Refer to map on page 257**

Hold On To Your Cats!

Cat predation accounts for nearly 40 percent of the sixty thousand injured wild animals brought to Audubon's Wildlife Care Center over the past twenty years. The list contains over one hundred species and includes songbirds, woodpeckers, small hawks, owls, and a variety of mammals. Of all the types of wildlife treated at the Care Center, birds injured by cats have the lowest chance for survival—less than 17 percent compared to 60 percent for those that are shot, poisoned, or hit by a cars.

While habitat loss remains by far the single biggest threat facing wildlife populations, secondary threats such as cat predation still have significant impacts. The outdoors is not necessarily good for cats either—each year more than forty thousand cats are delivered to Oregon shelters.

Unlike many communities where cat advocates and bird advocates view each other as enemies, in Portland they have achieved what the *New York Times* describes as a "rare détente." Groups such as the Feral Cat Coalition of Oregon and the Audubon Society of Portland are working together to raise awareness of the plight faced by wildlife and cats when cats are allowed to roam free. How can you help? Please spay and neuter your cats and don't let them roam free. Consider converting your cat to indoor living or letting it out only in an enclosure or on a leash. It's good for cats, and it's good for wildlife!

—Bob Sallinger

The Shire:
Johnson Creek Canyon

I KNOW ONE PLACE ON EARTH like the back of my hand. It is a wilderness in the middle of the city with a creek running through it. At one end is Errol Heights, aka Felony Flats, birthplace of Gary Gilmore, a notorious serial murderer. At the other end is an upper-class neighborhood defined by the Reed College campus, substantial homes, and dense deciduous trees more like an older Connecticut suburb than a Portland neighborhood. It is a unique geological space, defined by ridges on the north and south ends. The small creek, named after William Johnson (not related), is twenty-four miles long and joins the Willamette River on its way to the Columbia River. My great-grandfather, Tideman Johnson, homesteaded along the creek in 1880. He bought eighty acres for $1,000 in gold coins. He didn't know the creek had his last name. When he died in 1912, Johnson Creek in the lower reach was known as Mill Creek.

Tonya Harding, the notorious skater, and Phil Knight, founder of Nike, lived in the watershed. The northern branch of the Beat Poetry generation was conceived there. Not a mint condition stream. One writer called it the "Chevy Impala of creeks"; on the other hand, David Duncan dedicated his novel *The River Why* "to the diseased body of Johnson Creek."

My family's pioneer home is on the south ridge along a busy road. The road wasn't always so busy. When my older sisters were teenagers, their entertainment was waiting for a car to go by, hoping the drivers might be teenage boys. The road became busy and dangerous as the city grew.

There is a long winding trail that leads through the forest down to the meadows, wetlands, and floodplain of the creek. The traffic noise disappears and you enter another world. It is always dark in the forest. The floodplain of the creek is the only place lit by the sun. A family friend, biologist Eugene Kozloff, told us that our forest for several months of the year had the same vegetation yield as the Amazon rainforest. Before white settlers arrived, it probably looked like Jurassic Park: ancient towering western redcedars and skunk cabbages the size of Volkswagens. During my childhood years in the 1950s, the creek still supported a vigorous fish population. If we dropped a line in—usually a willow branch, fish line, lead weight, hook, and earthworm—we inevitably caught a native trout. In the fall we could catch returning salmon in our hands as they desperately tried to return to the upper watershed to spawn and die. We didn't know any better.

We had names for the landscape: The Swimming Hole, Pilgrim Rock, The Trestle, The Butt (butte), The Waterfall, The Swamp, Buzzard Bait's Shack. We built forts,

rafts, dams, a dangerous but exhilarating rope swing, tree houses, contraptions to catch wild things (we didn't know any better), the cave dug by hand in the side of an unstable hillside. There was an interurban streetcar that ran through the canyon. We played chicken on the trestle. One friend lost. He fell from the trestle and was paralyzed from the waist down. I saw him twenty years after his fall in a wheelchair on the bus. He hadn't aged. On weekends and all summer we spent entire days in the canyon. We returned to the comfort of our middle-class homes, filthy, with torn clothes, nursing nettle stings and bruises and cuts from glass in the creek.

In the summer and fall there were wild berries, apples, and pears from tamed and wild trees—and my father's bountiful vegetable garden. On warm summer evenings we might set up camp alongside the creek, pull together our food from the wild (including native fish and crawfish), set a bonfire, cook our meals, and pretend we were the Last of the Mohicans. Of course we might as likely wander down the streetcar tracks to a supermarket, where a couple of dollars would yield sacks of Hostess cupcakes, potato chips, penny candy, and soda pop in a can.

If I walk through the canyon now, as an old man, I can stop every ten feet and tell a different story. That's where we found a dead octopus. The tree is gone, but that's where we found the skeleton of a man hanging by a rope. That's where Phil caught twenty-five carp in an afternoon (a sign the creek had become too warm to support native fish). That's where Mary, a teenage sweetheart who made all her own clothes, told me we were no longer going steady, and she was in love with a drummer from Paul Revere and the Raiders. Under that oak, the only one in the canyon, Huck gave me his white-handled knife in the shape of a sea lion head. See that cedar stump? My father told me that is where my great-grandfather's guardian, the magical and inept white beaver, lived. And that tallest of Douglas fir trees over there is the one Johnny Crawfish climbed and had to be rescued by Zeke, the obnoxious crow. I still have the trap my sister's boyfriend in high school used to catch muskrats, weasels, and river otters. There was a fallen tree where I went to talk to God. It was a Douglas fir that had toppled from the roots, leaving a gigantic hole on the side of the hill. Its roots towered above me. I built a flimsy lean-to out of boards and boughs from the tree. The God who could topple this giant like it was a toothpick was maybe powerful enough to help me win over perfect, red-haired Cathy, or at least help her remember my name when she passed me in the hallway at school.

My father spent his life taking care of the place. While one of his closest friends, poet William Stafford, created lasting monuments on paper, my father's legacy was our place. One of his pride and joys was a Japanese garden. A Japanese garden in the jungle? Like creating a Zen meditation gazebo at the super bowl. Talk about futility. One summer when I was bored I created a nine-hole miniature golf course in a seasonal wetland. Yes, I should have known better.

After I went away to college, leaving my father and uncle and mother in their retirement years, things deteriorated. With encroaching urbanization, evil forces dominated. The canyon became like Mordor in *The Lord of the Rings*. The creek died. First there was nothing but warm-water species, then nothing at all, as though an evil spell had been cast. Invasive species took over: English ivy, Himalayan blackberries. During the day, motorcycle gangs ran wild through the woods and along the abandoned streetcar tracks; at night drug and alcohol parties ran all night. The sounds of males running on speed and testosterone drowned out the sounds of wildlife.

In the early 1990s, when my father and uncle died, I moved back to the homestead. The forces of darkness were strong. My house was robbed; my life threatened. For a while I was forced to hire a security guard. The followers of Mordor almost won.

There are turning points in one's life, where one decides to stay put or flee. The American way, as Gary Snyder has noted, is to flee. If conditions don't suit you, move on. I decided to stay. In 1984 I got together with friends including Ethan Seltzer, Barbara Walker, and Greg Macpherson, and we started the Tideman Johnson Corridor Committee, aka, the Johnson Creek Marching Band. Our playful name reflected our sense of futility. At the time, the prevailing attitude toward Johnson Creek was to euthanize it; best to put it out of its misery by encasing it in stormwater pipes. Our group merged with an effort spearheaded by Walt Mintkeski, and in 1990 the Johnson Creek Corridor Committee was created, which evolved into the Johnson Creek Watershed Council. At the same time, the Springwater Corridor trail was created—a critical element in the evolution of efforts to save the watershed. The trail brought thousands of people biking along the creek, witnesses to the creek's value as a community resource. I had an epiphany in a classroom of third-grade stream stewards, from the same school that the serial murderer attended. With accuracy and passion they told me about the creek and why and how to save it. Amazing. We have collectively created a place that will continue to thrive. The forces of Mordor don't stand a chance.

In my shire, I can go for days without seeing much wildlife. But last night I was first entertained by three coyotes. They were happy and talkative in that Coyote kind of way. I watched them as they danced in front of my house. Then, standing on my deck, I heard something chewing on jewel weed under the deck. I shined my flashlight into the dark. It was a beaver the size of a sumo wrestler in a fur coat. Well, big anyway. While I watched him trundle back to the pond, a great horned owl flew overhead. I could hear his wings. The next morning I watched my regular bunny rabbit enjoy the dawn and saw that mama duck was there with six new windup offspring sharing the pond with a great blue heron.

I have traveled the world, but I always return to the canyon, my place on earth.

By Steve Johnson, illustration by Allison Bollman

Heron Marauders of Tideman Johnson

THERE IS ONE SUMMER the herons in these parts still talk about. It was in the early days of the restoration of Johnson Creek, before there was a formal watershed council and the memory of Portland's Bureau of Environmental Services as a sewerage agency was still fresh in the minds of bureaucrats. As citizens, all we knew was that we wanted to get salmon back into the watershed. There was the welcome wagon approach: restore it and they will come, but it felt like naturopathic medicine to us—holistic but slow. So for a while we went with introducing hatchery stock. On Tideman Johnson farm, across from the park, the Friends of Tideman Johnson Park built a hatch box,

and Dennis Wise with the Oregon Department of Fish and Wildlife brought eggs and sometimes fingerlings. The herons remember the fingerlings.

One day, we had a Boy Scout troop helping us move four- to six-inch coho into a small pond we called the storage brook. The small fish were not to go into the bigger pond because there was no tree cover, the water was warmer, and there was no way for them to get to the main stem of the creek. But you know ... those scouts wanted to put some in the bigger pond. They put in four or five hundred before we stopped them. Within days the word went out. Sometimes I had as many as four great blue herons walking the pond. Talk about easy pickings! I came home one day when a heron, we'll call him Zeke, had a big coho stuck in his neck and couldn't fly. I sat in the car listening to *A Prairie Home Companion* so he could digest his lunch in safety.

With the narrow, long, and colder pond that ran in front of my house, we had a different problem. We stocked it with thousands of fingerlings. Green herons immediately discovered this treasure trove. I sat on my deck and watched them. They would sit on branches, quietly dive down, and snag a fish. Over and over. The only thing in the way of their feast was gorging. If they ate too much they would literally fall off the branch. So I decided to stake down a gigantic web of black nylon over the entire pond. Again, I watched from my deck. No problem, if you're a green heron. You just fly down onto the netting, which then falls below the water surface, snag a fish and fly back to your branch.

Okay, so I pulled the netting tight, staking it down at multiple points until it was as taut as a trampoline. And then I waited. And waited. Finally, a green heron leaped from a branch—pond bound—and to his surprise the black netting didn't give. He bounced off the webbing and flew back to his branch, pondering what had gone wrong. I carefully circled around in back of him. He was lost in thought, and I was able to get within shouting range, and said, "Gotcha!" We had one of those interspecies moments. Eye contact. Then he flew away. I knew it was a pyrrhic victory. He would be back.

Many of the salmon in the storage brook did escape to the main creek, but the green herons feasted all summer. By summer's end, all salmon but one were gone.

By Steve Johnson, illustration by Virginia Church

Reed College Canyon

LOCATION: On the Reed College campus, Portland, bordered by SE Cesar Chavez Boulevard (east), SE Woodstock Boulevard (south), SE 28th Avenue (west), and SE Steele Street (north) **ACTIVITIES:** Hiking, Wildlife viewing **FACILITIES:** Unpaved trails **FEES AND REGULATIONS:** Pets on leash; Reed College campus is private property but birders and nature enthusiasts are always welcome. Please return the courtesy **HIKING DIFFICULTY:** Moderate (Trails can be wet and muddy in winter and uneven at any time of year.) **HIGHLIGHTS:** Rare glimpses of wildlife in the center of a residential area; Beavers and coyotes call the canyon home; Over 80 different avian species sighted; Green and great blue herons in the shallow waters of the lake and creek; Occasional Cooper's hawk swooping overhead; Late spring excellent opportunities to view nesting waterfowl as well as migrating steelhead in the lake **PUBLIC TRANSIT:** TriMet buses 75, 10, 19

Lying at the heart of the beautifully manicured Reed College campus, the Reed College Canyon remains an island of untamed nature in the center of an urban area. Essentially untouched from the 1930s to 2000, the canyon has been the focus of an ambitious habitat restoration project for the past decade. This work has restored the canyon to its "natural" state while improving opportunities for visitors to appreciate its beauty.

The canyon was formed by a number of springs located in the eastern portion of the lake, which constitute the headwaters of Crystal Springs Creek. The springs form a shallow lake that feeds into a fish ladder, and then descends to become a swift-flowing creek that slows through a meadow, passes under a new bridge at SE 28th Avenue, and reaches the Crystal Springs Rhododendron Garden located just to the south. Eventually, this water will enter the Willamette River before finding the Pacific Ocean via the Columbia. Pacific lamprey in the lake and returning salmon prove that there is uninterrupted passage between the headwaters and the ocean.

The canyon was donated to Reed College in 1910. At that time, the college intended to develop its real estate holdings along traditional lines—Tudor Gothic buildings, sculpted grounds, and formal gardens. Prohibitive costs, however, led the trustees in a different direction. The result is that the canyon was never developed nor manicured, and in 1913 it was declared a wildlife refuge by the state of Oregon. It still holds that status today.

The most widely used stretch of the canyon is the upper lake loop, which takes visitors on a gentle walk along maintained trails that are only occasionally interrupted by swampy vestiges of the springs underfoot. Side trails may lead you out of the canyon and onto the college grounds, but for the most part the trail is easy to navigate.

Douglas fir, big-leaf maple, red alder, and western redcedar form the tree canopy, while shrubs such as red elderberry, Oregon grape, and black hawthorn, along with herbs including trillium, Pacific water parsley, hardtack, skunk cabbage, and stinging nettle are common in the understory. Wildflowers abound in spring (over fifty different species have been identified in the canyon). Among the more common ferns are sword and bracken. Also, look in the drier areas for the somewhat uncommon gold-back fern.

More than eighty bird species, including great blue and green herons, belted king-fishers, and seven different species of warbler (orange-crowned, yellow-rumped, black-throated gray, Townsend's, MacGillivray's, Wilson's, and common yellowthroat) have been sighted in the canyon. This is also a good place to call for western screech-owls. Cooper's hawks are frequent guests, swooping low overhead, scouting for prey. In recent years, bald eagles have perched in trees overlooking the canyon, though they are apparently content to remain as visitors, not residents.

In addition to birds, the canyon is home to a diverse array of other wildlife. Fallen trees lining the lake show the telltale marks of resident beavers. Coyotes are occasionally glimpsed, furtively making their way through tall grass at the lake's edge. River otter and muskrat have also been sighted in the canyon. The damp underbrush of the southeast side of the canyon is home to the terrestrial *Ensatina* salamander. Nesting ducks guide their young across the lake. Mallards are obvious, but wood ducks, American wigeons, buffleheads, lesser scaup, common mergansers, green-winged teals, and ruddy ducks are here as well. In winter look for hooded mergansers.

Restoring the Canyon

Watershed planning efforts over the years have repeatedly identified Crystal Springs (especially its headwaters) as a high priority for restoration in order to benefit steel-head, cutthroat trout, and coho salmon spawning and rearing habitat. The Oregon Department of Fish and Wildlife's sampling of Crystal Springs in 2001–2002 gave the creek the second highest score for supporting fish populations of all the tribu-taries sampled in Portland. Species observed by ODFW in its study included lamprey, longnose dace, speckled dace, redside shiner, largescale sucker, cutthroat trout, coho and Chinook salmon, rainbow trout, steelhead, and prickly, reticulate, and riffle sculpin.

Reed College began restoration of its lake and canyon in 1999. It has achieved a number of objectives, including improving the observed diversity of wildlife, by man-aging invasive species and restoring native plant communities throughout the site and increasing potential habitat for salmon and other resident fish by providing effective fish passage (via a fish ladder) to Reed Lake. The Johnson Creek Basin Protection Plan identifies Reed Lake as "the only naturally occurring pond (or lake) remaining in the inner-city area." The project has also improved access to one of the few remaining wildlife habitats within city limits

The Reed Canyon is a local treasure—a carefully managed wilderness in the heart of the city.

Crystal Springs Creek is a natural jewel, though you might not know it by simply looking at a map. This modest 2.7-mile tributary to Johnson Creek in inner Southeast Portland is a unique mix of cold, clean, consistent, spring-fed water that creates ideal conditions for several species of native fish listed as threatened under the federal Endangered Species Act—coho and Chinook salmon and steelhead trout. The confluence of Crystal Springs and Johnson Creeks is near the Willamette River, making this habitat especially beneficial for salmon, which must return from the ocean to their exact birthplace. Other animals living here include beavers, bats, otters, turtles, green and great blue herons, killdeer, wood ducks, warblers, and lamprey, to name a few.

Crystal Springs originates from underground sources in two unlikely locations—Reed College and Eastmoreland Golf Course. The two forks of the creek converge in the public golf course just beyond Crystal Springs Lake and the Crystal Springs Rhododendron Gardens, and then flow under SE McLoughlin Boulevard into Westmoreland Park and through residential neighborhoods until joining Johnson Creek in Johnson Creek Park. The substantial amount of publicly owned land surrounding Crystal Springs Creek fosters community and city partnerships that protect and enhance the creek.

Crystal Springs is surprisingly pristine, but human intervention over the years has impacted water quality and the ability of fish to reach the spawning grounds in its headwaters. Recognizing the value of this natural resource, Reed College has been actively restoring Crystal Springs and the surrounding habitat since 1999.

The best way to view Crystal Springs Creek Watershed, which is relatively small and surrounded by publicly accessible areas, is on foot.

—Maggie Skenderian and Rowan Steele

Access

The canyon at the center of campus can be reached from any of the college's parking lots; the most convenient is the west parking lot along SE 28th Avenue. From there a short walk east along Botsford Drive will bring you between the Reed physical plant and the sports center. Walking in the direction of the physical plant's loading dock, you'll come to a land bridge, which affords a good view of the fish ladder. As you continue along the path, you'll have a choice of heading west, in the direction of the lower stretches of the creek, or east, which will take you on a loop trail around the lake. A map of the canyon can be found at the Reed College website. Though the college maintains the path, you should expect to encounter uneven footing, wet and muddy trails, and occasional foliage overgrowth in the path. Drier, summer months offer the best trail conditions. The upper reaches of the canyon are populated by a number of springs that saturate the ground and cause trail conditions to be less than optimal. Sturdy shoes are recommended.

How to Get there

By car: McLoughlin Boulevard (99E) to Bybee Boulevard and follow Bybee east. At the Woodstock Boulevard stop sign turn left onto 28th Avenue. The next right-hand turn is the Reed College parking lot recommended (across from the Crystal Springs Rhododendron Garden) for access to the canyon. From SE Cesar Chavez Boulevard (39th), turn onto SE Steele Street, headed west. Turn left onto SE 28th Avenue and park in the west lot. Additional parking areas are located along Woodstock Boulevard and Steele Street. **By bike:** The best access is to approach the campus via SE 28th Avenue, turn east onto Botsford Drive, and use one of the many bike racks located at the campus center at the top of Botsford. **Public transit:** TriMet bus 75 runs along SE Cesar Chavez Boulevard; 10 stops near Reed's north parking lot on SE Steele Street; 19 runs along SE Woodstock.

By Zachariah Perry and Bob Sallinger

More information: Reed College

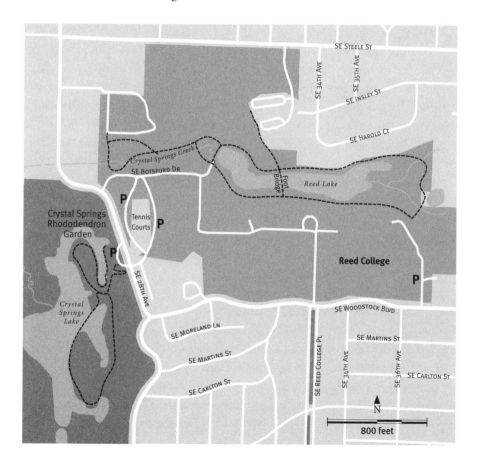

To Know a Salmon

DARK. WET. COLD. I finally relax. I'm just where I want to be. I'm starting here and I'll die here, but it is not my beginning or my end. Generations before me took their first and last swim right in this place. If I am fortunate, my offspring will do the same. This sense of place, this home, has left an indelible mark on my species' DNA. We've been around for over four hundred million years.

The changes in how rain falls on the land in Portland are like timelines on paper, but really, it's the river. This river connects the drops, brings the groundwater out of its deep hiding place, gathers lesser friends together and authors the history of this land, word by word, line by line, drop by wet drop. And salmon, my ancestors and I, are its Rosetta Stone. To know a river here, you must know the salmon.

And where is here? Closer than you think. Just off SE Tacoma Street onto SE 21st Avenue, three trees have fallen into Crystal Springs Creek. Most days, the trees' shadows prevent you from seeing my hiding spot. In the shadows, it's hard for predators to spot me too and I have a resting place from fast water. When I'm older, I'll return here, die along the banks, and give the saplings nutrients to grow tall and, hopefully, one day fall over to again provide refuge to my grandchildren's grandchildren. Salmon are always thinking to the twenty-fifth generation. From what I can see by the plastic bottle suffocating the caddis fly nymph below me, most people act for today. Don't get me wrong, I do too. But my kind is so close to extinction that each swish of my tail must get me back here so I can keep the species alive. It's a heavy burden to bear. Despite having hundreds of siblings, I'm here alone. My journey will take me downstream to the ocean, and then I'll retrace my strokes to return upstream to spawn.

I'll remain here for a while, mostly behind the protective hug of this tree. The water that runs through the culvert is very fast so it's hard for me to swim upstream. But when I can, there's a bounty of food. My first year consists of: wake up, don't get eaten, find food, rest where the water's not too fast or too warm, then do it again. Now, the days are getting shorter; the sun is lower on the horizon. Finally I'm big enough, about the size of a human hand, to point my head downstream for good. Something tells me to stay close to the edge and take my time.

Whoa, it's hot and hard to breathe. My stream suddenly doubled in size but instead of being refreshing, the water is too warm and lacks oxygen. Rocks and other pointed objects poke and scratch my scales. I hope an otter claw or an osprey talon isn't near. Suddenly, the river gains speed. I don't have the strength or energy to swim against the current. I need a place, any place, to rest. Instead, the river doubles in size again.

A very big fish is approaching, mouth open. He wasn't there a minute ago, I swear. I think I'm lunch. I can't hide. I'm disoriented, and my fins don't work correctly. Relief, it's only a carp. He's not from around here, but he knows where I am, the Willamette River. And I'm headed in the right direction to the Pacific Ocean. Ahh, the ocean. My nerves tingle, destination confirmed. The tingling tells me there's more. "Toxins" in the river, says the carp. That explains the fog and lethargy I'm feeling.

Salmon are lucky; we quickly move out of this river. The carp live here every day eating, breathing, and swimming in it.

In the Columbia River, I can smell something new, but this one feels right. For days on end I swim downstream toward that smell. Each day the smell and I grow

stronger. I find some great hiding places in the river, complete bed and breakfasts. I'm changing. Smolting in salmon terms. I'm used to living and breathing in freshwater, but that smell that's been steadily pulling me is the salt water from the ocean. A change in salt concentrations between my cells and the water around me can spell trouble. It's a phenomenon called osmosis and salmon are built so we neither explode nor desiccate when the salt concentrations change, which is a good thing. As long as we have enough time and the right conditions to adjust, we thrive. I'll go through it again when I return for my journey upstream.

For now, I'm off to the great big ocean. As a coho, I'll stay close to the continental shelf and then head north to Washington and Vancouver, British Columbia. My cousins, the Chinook and sockeye, are more adventurous and travel far into the open ocean. All of us eat plankton and smaller fish while avoiding the whales, sea lions, squid, and nets that kill us. Three years go by. Just like the unidentified cue to turn downstream, I now know to head back.

It's like I never left. I turned my nose to the freshwater, knowing exactly my destination. I've had friends come and go in the ocean, but there are many today by my side. We made it here because we started in healthy rivers. I don't need to look for food. I fattened up in the ocean for this trip. The big river is the same, hot and hard to navigate. This time I'm bigger and not as scared. We don't need to stay as close to shore on our return trip. Just follow the cold water upstream toward home. The river is quite low. We wait and wait and wait. The skies finally darken, the rain falls, and the freshet comes. It is time.

I make the last turn, the water getting cooler and cleaner with each new tributary. I expect to have to navigate a vicious culvert to get to my old friend the tree, but it's not there. Instead there's just cold water cascading over gravel. Applause at my return. And now instead of one tree to welcome me, there are dozens. A party in my honor. The plastic bottle is gone, replaced by cottonwood leaves floating on the surface. The dark house on the bank that warmed the rain as it fell on the roof is gone, replaced by numerous saplings and bushes. Evidence that humans do think beyond today.

I dart when I hear a splash, remembering my nemesis the otter. But the splash sounds different. More like a rock concert ... literally rocks tumbling over each other. I look out of my hiding place. It's a male salmon slapping his tail on the rocks. It is the best pick up line I've ever heard. And it works. I have borne my burden well. My species will survive, and I'm hopeful that of the nearly one hundred eggs I lay, we will have a single offspring. Once the eggs are buried in the cobble, we drift to the shore one last time. Feeding the bugs that will feed our children, and the roots of the tree that will save our species. Our timeline is the river's timeline, and we will go on.

By Kaitlin Lovell, illustration by Virginia Church

Crystal Springs Rhododendron Garden

LOCATION: SE 28th Avenue, north of SE Woodstock Avenue across from Reed College campus and adjacent to Eastmoreland Golf Course, Portland **ACTIVITIES:** Hiking, Wildlife viewing **FACILITIES:** Restrooms, Parking, Paved and unpaved trails, Picnic area/shelter, Interpretive signs/info **FEES AND REGULATIONS:** Small entrance fee Thursday through Monday, March 1 through Labor Day; Hours dawn to dusk daily; Pets on leash **HIKING DIFFICULTY:** Easy **HIGHLIGHTS:** Fantastic waterfowl watching in winter; Spectacular rhododendron and azaleas abloom in spring **PUBLIC TRANSIT:** TriMet 19

At only seven acres, this manicured, highly managed garden nearly surrounded by Crystal Springs Lake has an outstanding collection of rhododendrons, azaleas, and other lesser-known ericaceous plants as well as many companion plants and unusual trees. The Portland chapter of the American Rhododendron Society co-founded the park with Portland Parks & Recreation in the 1950s as a rhododendron test garden. During the past several years, the gardens have been completely renovated with rockeries, waterfalls, and extensive ramps and boardwalks to accommodate wheelchairs. Yet brambles and unkempt willows, what to some gardeners may seem an offensive eyesore, still remain on the left as you walk across the low bridge that crosses the pond.

While most of the site is a lovingly tended and truly beautiful garden, the messy-looking rough patch of shrubs, submerged logs, and emergent marsh vegetation that you see from the bridge is excellent wildlife habitat. Look for a gang of wood ducks. Green herons have nested here in the past as well. You might see their small, stick platform tucked in among the overhanging branches.

Winter is absolutely the best time to bird the "rhody gardens," when flocks of waterfowl and gulls congregate on and around the artificial lake that is fed by Crystal Springs Creek. The official checklist cites ninety-four species of birds. Great blue and green herons are on the list as are myriad ducks which include lesser and greater scaup, redhead, ring-necked, northern pintail, and blue-winged teal. It's also one of the few urban sites that you can count on seeing ruddy ducks and canvasbacks. Scan the golf course for American and Eurasian wigeon that graze on the grassy fairways and greens. (The Eurasian's

Please Don't Feed the Ducks

Please don't feed the waterfowl at our parks and natural areas. Although done with the best of intentions, providing handouts for ducks and geese can actually cause them great harm. Many of the foods that people feed to waterfowl, such as bread, are low in nutrients and can cause developmental and digestive problems. It is best to enjoy ducks and geese at a distance and let local populations adjust to the available natural food sources. Don't fear for the ducks and geese—they have wings for a reason.

—Bob Sallinger

cinnamon head and golden crown contrasts with the white crown and gray head with green eye stripe of the American wigeon.)

Virtually all of Portland's gulls have been seen here—mew, ring-billed, California, herring, Thayer's, western, and glaucous-winged.

In spring, migrant warblers are attracted to the lush vegetation. The gardens are ablaze in a forest of color at peak bloom generally in April and May. If your intent is birding, you may want to avoid the weekends as it is crowded. About the only residents in summer are a few squirrels and mongrelized mallards hanging around for a hand-out. However, this gorgeous garden is nice for a cool walk along the lake and under the evergreen rhodies.

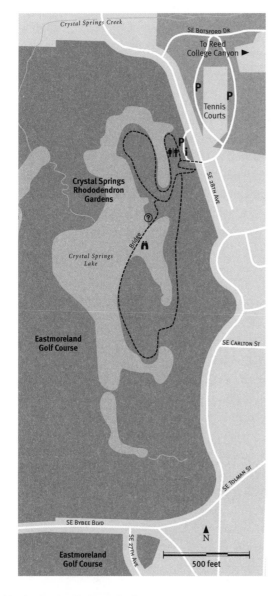

The fairly extensive upland forest attracts red-breasted nuthatch, chestnut-backed chickadees, brown creeper, and warblers. Depending on the time of year, you'll also see or hear Swainson's, varied, and hermit thrushes and American robins. Not a bad assemblage for a garden!

How to Get there

BY CAR OR BIKE: SE McLoughlin Boulevard (99E) to SE Bybee Boulevard and follow Bybee east. At the Woodstock Boulevard stop sign turn left onto 28th Avenue. The next left-hand turn is the parking lot. From SE Cesar Chavez Boulevard (39th), turn onto SE Steele Street, headed west. Turn left onto SE 28th Avenue for about a mile and you will see the parking lot and entrance on your right. **PUBLIC TRANSIT:** TriMet bus 19 stops near corner of SE 28th and SE Woodstock, just one block south of the garden

By Mike Houck

Columbia Slough Watershed

THERE ARE MANY QUESTIONS surrounding the Columbia Slough, such as "How do I pronounce it?" or even "What is it?" The answers: slough rhymes with blue, and the Columbia Slough is the long, slow-moving, largely manmade channel of water that flows through the Oregon side of the Columbia River's historic floodplain. More frequently, folks who have lived in the area ask, "Isn't it polluted?" While the slough has suffered from detrimental human impacts over the past one hundred years, it is still a beautiful, shaded wildlife haven in the middle of the city. Over the past several decades, government agencies, businesses, nonprofits, and citizens have worked to improve water quality and habitat in this fifty-square mile urban watershed. When you're looking for a quiet place to soak up nature after a busy day, it takes only a few minutes to drive or bike to a favorite spot along the slough.

The Columbia Slough Watershed is not only an important natural resource, it's also home to over 158,000 people. The slough's 4,200 businesses provide 88,000 jobs in what has become Oregon's largest industrial corridor. It's also home to over 175 species of birds, 26 species of fish, and 131 species of plants. The conspicuous juxtaposition of city and nature makes the slough unique.

At nearly nineteen miles in length, the Columbia Slough is best explored by kayak or canoe. The slough has been divided into upper, middle, and lower sections, which are marked by the cross levees at NE 143rd and NE 18th Avenues. The two upper segments are managed by the Multnomah County Drainage District, which prevents the waterway from flooding businesses, residents, and Portland International Airport. The more natural Lower Slough is directly connected to the Willamette River at Kelley Point Park near the confluence of the Willamette and Columbia Rivers.

The Upper Slough, from Fairview Lake downstream to the NE 143rd Avenue levee, is a narrow, twisting waterway with plenty of wetland flats, overhanging willows, and creek dogwoods, and mysterious nooks and crannies. In places it feels as if you are paddling through a green tunnel of leaves and water. If you're looking for seasonal migrants such as willow flycatchers or cedar waxwings, Big Four Corners is an excellent place to find them. This is a place where each corner often reveals a new wildlife sighting, so paddle quietly to avoid scaring animals before you see them.

The Middle Slough, from the NE 143rd Avenue levee to the NE 18th Street levee, is quite different in character. It's wider than the Upper Slough and has more ponds and side channels. There are also wetland benches that have been installed to help with water flow and to create wildlife habitat. Here, you may have close encounters with fallen trees, beavers, turtles, and Air National Guard training flights. If you paddle on a summer weekday you can wave hello to all the industrial workers enjoying their lunch along the slough's banks.

Downstream from the NE 18th Street levee to its confluence with the Willamette River at Kelley Point Park, the slough is wider and deeper, has some muddy beaches, and is influenced by tidal action. The Lower Slough passes by the former St. Johns Landfill, which is now restored to upland prairie habitat for western meadowlarks and streaked horned larks. It also passes by Smith and Bybee Lakes Natural Area, one of the largest urban wetlands in the United States. Paddlers are likely to see nesting bald eagles, osprey, red-tailed hawks, and great blue herons all along the Lower Slough.

If you're not inclined to paddle, you can also bike or hike along the slough. Portions of the 40-Mile Loop trail have been completed in the watershed, including the paved path along Marine Drive and the Slough Trail near Delta Park, and another spur off Airport Way. A number of parks and greenspaces are also available to birdwatchers, botanists, and nature-loving kids throughout the watershed.

The Columbia Slough has been dramatically altered over the past 150 years. Yet even with significant negative environmental impacts, wildlife biologists note that the slough is a critical wildlife corridor for animals looking to get from the Sandy River to the Willamette River. The slough provides a ribbon of green through a grey urban maze for turtles, deer, coyotes, muskrats, otters, frogs, salamanders . . . and people.

By Melissa Sandoz

A Brief History of the Columbia Slough

THE COLUMBIA SLOUGH'S quiet water and its dynamic floodplain ecology sheltered and fed Native Americans for thousands of years. Native settlements were located on high ground above current-day Columbia and Sandy Boulevards. Seasonal camps provided access to fish and fowl of all kinds. This historic slough and other sheltered waterways located in the powerful Columbia River's floodplain facilitated safe trade and travel.

Members of the 1805 Lewis and Clark expedition complained about the noise generated by the thousands of waterfowl, as Clark's diary attests:

> I [s]lept but verry little last night for the noise Kept [up] during the whol of the night by the Swans, Geese, white and Grey Brant Ducks ... they were emensely noumorous, and their noise horid.

By the 1850s, the Hudson's Bay Company's Fort Vancouver–based fur trade was supplanted by white settlers "proving up" on donation land claims. Ancient flood-deposited soils, now largely covered by industrial development, once allowed a wealth of agricultural products for the new immigrants. Huge sloughside conifers were floated and towed by oxen to downtown Portland by Lewis Love, purportedly Portland's first millionaire. From 1919 to 1921, settlers built levees to prevent annual floods south of the Columbia River. This profoundly affected the character of the floodplain. The elimination of spring freshets changed vegetation, prevented fish migration, and dried out lakes and ponds. Flood prevention and the opening of the interstate bridge to Washington State in 1917 prompted further non-agricultural development.

Sloughside sawmills created millions of board feet of shingles, which were floated in and out of the Lower Slough. Stockyards and meat processing plants, near what is now the Expo Center, fostered a vital meatpacking industry that established Kenton, a company town, built by the Armour and Swift companies. However, the "awful offal" resulted in such foul waters that mill workers went on strike to protest conditions.

Vanport City, once Oregon's second largest city, existed on land now occupied by Portland International Raceway, Heron Lakes Golf Course, and East Delta Park. Vanport was built in nine months and housed one hundred thousand World War II shipyard workers, Portland's first large population of African American residents, and returning servicemen and Japanese internees. But Vanport disappeared in only a few hours during the catastrophic 1948 flood. After the flood, levee strengthening and raising resulted in subsequent commercial and industrial development across the area, though the former Vanport site remained free of buildings for years.

For birds and wildlife, the slough's location along the Pacific Flyway and the east-west Columbia Gorge–Coast Range wildlife corridor is a critical migratory route. The human migratory counterparts—freeways, the transcontinental railroad, Port of Portland, and the international airport—all share the Columbia Slough corridor. Tree and shrub habitat can be as narrow as twenty-five to fifty feet in areas, making the slough the slimmest of lifelines. In an effort to expand the wildlife corridor, Portland's Watershed Revegetation Program, along with private landowners, have replaced invasive species with more than 1.2 million native plants. The revegetation program has literally transformed more than forty miles of streambank.

Today's Columbia Slough Watershed encompasses one of the largest urban wetlands in the country at Smith and Bybee Wetlands. Designated an Important Bird Area, the wetlands also provide twelve hundred acres of greenspace in the city.

A part of the Columbia River–Willamette River estuary, the lower nine miles of the slough provide a rest stop for the little backward-swimming migrating young salmon that need food and shelter as they travel to the Pacific. The notion that salmon used the slough was regarded as laughable by many until a 2009 fish sampling by federal fisheries scientists identified seagoing coho and Chinook salmon and lamprey nine miles up from Kelley Point Park—literally at the levee floodgates. The fish come from the upper reaches of the Columbia River and the headwaters of numerous Willamette tributaries. New Portland Bureau of Environmental Services projects include placing fish-friendly large wood and logs on beaches and reopening long cut-off floodplain channels to fish. Interestingly, three of the seven native northwest mussels, some of them relatively scarce, also live here in the fluffy, muddy bottom sloughs.

For birds, it's "location, location, location." Nearly every year, Audubon Christmas bird count teams working the Columbia south shore win the prize for the most bird species identified in the metro area. From the top of Rocky Butte to the lowlands and springs of Big Four Corners, Whitaker Ponds Nature Park, and the Vanport and Smith and Bybee wetlands, birds flock and nest in abundance. Western painted turtles, red-legged frogs, Pacific chorus frogs, and northwestern salamanders and their egg masses are found not only on undeveloped land, but in a surprising variety of Portland's stormwater facilities as well.

It is, perhaps, this new partially urbanized habitat with its improving water quality, and 1.25 million native trees and shrubs that provide hope for both wildlife and people. This precious green and wild oasis—home to salmon, otter, sea lion, osprey, beaver, mussels, school children, workers, and families—is easily accessible by bus, light rail, foot, or bike.

By Susan Barthel

Columbia Slough
Big Four Corners Natural Area

Tucked away amid warehouses in outer Northeast Portland lies Big Four Corners Natural Area, more than two hundred acres of quiet sloughs, cottonwood forest, willow wetlands, clear cold springs, and some of the largest remaining Oregon white oak trees in the city. This natural area, owned and managed by Portland Parks & Recreation and Portland's Bureau of Environmental Services (BES), is bisected by NE Airport Way and crisscrossed by multiple branches of the Columbia Slough. As there is a limited, informal trail system through this area, paddle access is the best way to experience this site.

From the **launch** ❶, paddle east (upstream), to the left as you face the water from the launch. Slough water levels allow access year-round, but June is a great time to visit, when water levels are highest and the forest is alive with birdsong.

Although the Columbia Slough has suffered from altered hydrology, contamination, and habitat degradation, decades of work by the City of Portland and its partners have largely restored this area of the slough to its native floodplain forest habitat. Black cottonwood and Oregon ash dominate the canopy here. Red-osier dogwood, Pacific ninebark, red-flowering currant, snowberry, Douglas spirea, and a variety of willows make up the understory. Otters are sometimes spotted in this channel; great blue herons perch in the trees overhead; long-toed salamanders lay their eggs in small; quiet ponds; and myriad songbirds sing in the forest. On a typical spring day listen, for Swainson's thrushes, yellow warblers, western wood-pewees, brown creepers, Bullock's orioles, and many more.

Heading east, paddle under NE Airport Way and continue to a junction where a slough **channel branches off to the north** (left) ❷. Turn left here and you are in the heart of Big Four Corners Natural Area, where four arms of the Columbia Slough come together. Turn right at the next junction and continue up the northeast channel for a side trip along a forested reach that ends at a Multnomah County Drainage District **pump station** ❸ below the Marine Drive levee. The pump station moves water from the slough to the Columbia River during winter storm events, to control flooding on this historic floodplain. This site is the original "head" of the Columbia Slough and its historic upstream connection to the Columbia River, prior to levee construction in 1915.

After exploring this dead-end slough arm return to the "four corners" intersection and bear left at both junctions to continue south on the main stem of the Columbia Slough. After you pass under NE Airport Way a second time ❹, the habitat opens up

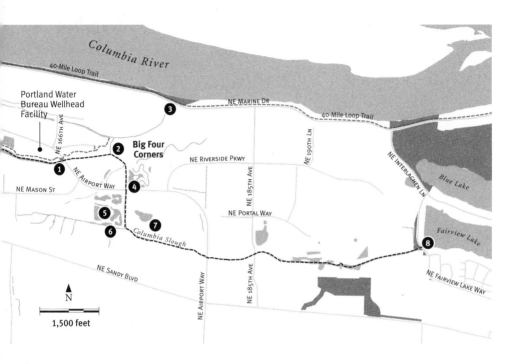

on your right where a twenty-five-acre scrub-shrub and herbaceous wetland lies west of the slough **⑤**. A variety of wildlife uses the wetlands throughout the year, including state-sensitive species like red-legged frog and western painted turtle. Portland Parks & Recreation and BES are planning a restoration project here that will improve hydrology and water quality and will enhance wetland habitat for sensitive wildlife species.

South of the wetland is a forested slope with several springs that supply the wetlands and slough with cold, clear water. Alice Springs **⑥** is named for Alice Blatt, a citizen activist who played a lead role in protecting the area from development. As elevation increases, the vegetation community transitions here to a forest of western redcedar, red alder, and big-leaf maple. Although Alice Springs is not accessible for recreation, you can see the small, narrow springs channel entering the Columbia Slough from the west (on your right), as the main slough turns ninety degrees to the east. This channel brings cool, clear spring water into the main slough, helping to lower water temperatures and improve water quality.

As you paddle east up the Columbia Slough, you will pass a scrub-shrub wetland on the north **⑦** that is home to willow flycatchers. South of the slough is a forested slope with some of the largest Oregon white oaks in the city; the darker green crowns of the large oaks are sometimes visible from the water.

The slough continues east, passing first under Airport Way and then NE 185th Avenue, where you leave the City of Portland and enter the City of Gresham. The reach east of 185th is known for its population of native freshwater mussels, with names like winged floater and Oregon floater. Throughout the Columbia Slough look for mussel middens where raccoons and otters have paused on the banks to dine, and have left a pile of shells behind. A short distance east, you'll dead-end at **Fairview Lake 8**, the primary source of water for the Columbia Slough. At a casual pace the round trip will take one and a half to two hours. Minimal current and quiet, flat waters provide a good opportunity for families and novices paddlers.

How to Get There

BY CAR: To find the launch dock, turn south at the intersection of NE 166th Avenue and NE Airport Way (16550 NE Airport Way) into a Portland Water Bureau facility access road to a small parking lot where there's an interpretive kiosk and trail to the launch.

By Dave Helzer

Otter City

OF THE FIFTY-ODD MAMMALS that call Portland home, perhaps twenty are regularly, if infrequently, seen. Of these, the most delightful is surely the North American river otter. These "amphibious" mammals are among the most graceful swimmers in the animal kingdom, and the mere glimpse of a river otter, slipping and gliding through one of our urban waterways, is guaranteed to elicit a smile—or a gasp—and make any day worthwhile. The first wild otters I saw in Portland had taken what I thought was a surprising detour up the Balch Creek drainage into Forest Park. They were swimming around the Audubon Society of Portland pond, which was big enough to allow them to display a little of their aquatic flair. It was a dazzling sight, and while I don't remember if I gasped, I do remember that it was an unforgettable natural history moment.

Otters are mustelids—members of the weasel clan—and like many of their family they are drawn to water. But of all their kin (except for their maritime cousin the sea otter) river otters are the most water dependent, and are rarely found more than a short distance from a lake or permanent stream. In the Portland area they can be found in many of the region's larger watersheds, including the Columbia River (and Slough), the Willamette, Tualatin, and Clackamas, and the area's larger lakes. Forays into some smaller drainages are not uncommon. River otters seem to be quite sensitive to water quality so perhaps we should regard it as something of an undeserved blessing that they are relatively common in Portland's waterways.

As top predators in their realm, otters, like other predators, were probably never historically abundant, but there were certainly enough of them in the years following European contact that—thanks to their possession of a luxuriant pelt—they became a mainstay of the early American fur trade. Their beautiful pelage may have made fabulous fur coats but, combined with human development, it sentenced river otters to a catastrophic population decline in the eighteenth and early nineteenth centuries, as hundreds of thousands of skins were dispatched to Europe. Happily, otter populations have rebounded considerably throughout their range in recent years, due to improved habitat management, reintroduction schemes, and controls on otter harvest (although Oregon and Washington still classify them as furbearers and permit trapping).

At four feet or more in length, river otters are among the Northwest's largest weasels; only the wolverine and sea otter run bigger. In addition to their size, they are easily recognized by their long, dark brown, weasel-like form with a robust, tapered tail making up a third of their total length. Otters could perhaps be confused with

other semi-aquatic mammals, but the rodents—beaver, nutria, muskrat—are chunkier and slower. The otter's mustelid cousin—the mink—is half the otter's size, and while it is a strong swimmer, it can't compete with the otter's lithe grace.

Otters like to live in mud banks beside ponds, rivers, and other permanent waterways, where they make use of tunnels—made often by beaver and nutria—in which they can shelter and den. Access to water is key because, although they won't pass up an avian or mammalian snack (molting ducks, mice, and occasionally young beavers are particular favorites), they feed primarily on underwater invertebrates and fish. And for fishing they are magnificently adapted. For starters, they can remain under water for up to four minutes, and their swimming ability is astonishing. One account compares their movement in the water to that of a "flexible torpedo," able to swim "either forward or backward, with astonishing grace and power." Their aquatic agility and the ability to put on bursts of speed of nearly seven miles per hour, make catching fish a snap. It is thought that they feed primarily on the slower-moving non-game fish, but they certainly won't turn down a young or sluggish salmonid.

When they aren't eating, it seems that otters spend much of their time playing. Otter play is proverbial, with much of their activity centered on "slides"—slick, muddy slopes perfect for slipping, sliding, and splashing into the water. Otters will use these primordial "water parks" over and over again. John James Audubon's experience is typical: "They glided down the soap-like muddy surface of the slide with the rapidity of an arrow from a bow, and we counted each one making twenty-two slides before we disturbed their sportive occupation."

Otters can be active day and night, but human presence tends to push them toward a more nocturnal existence. That, along with their tendency to live underground and feed under water, makes finding otters a matter of persistence or good luck ... or both. Easier to find is their sign, which is frequently visible alongside Metro-area waterways. Their tracks are relatively large (three and a quarter inches or more); their five toes generally show claw marks; and sometimes a faint trace of webbing between the toes is visible. Their droppings (sometimes called spraints) are distinctive as well. "Spraints" are often moist and can be indistinctly formed, even flattened. Since they come from a riverine predator they contain bones and scales as evidence of the otter's piscivorous diet, and they are frequently deposited as markers in conspicuous places. While looking for otter sign, keep an eye out for slides as well.

Spraints

With *spraints*—a word that still gets somewhat regularly used—we go back to the delightful world of medieval natural history, when animals collected in *gaggles* and *cetes* and *murmurations*, and when deer deposited *fewmets*, boar deposited *lesses*, and otter deposited *spraints*. Comparing this rich vocabulary of ordure with our own makes clear how much we have lost!

While actual numbers are hard to come by, otters are not rare in metro-area waterways. Still, I always experience finding evidence of their presence—not to mention glimpsing a live otter—as something of a gift. My last otter sighting was from the deck of a boat docked near the Sellwood Bridge. I was chatting with friends when an otter popped its head above the water—a real conversation stopper. The otter looped around the moorage in its graceful, effortless way for a minute or more, then it headed for the bank, bounded up the slope for a few leaps, and disappeared into the blackberry. I've been keeping my eyes open for it ever since.

By Bob Wilson, illustration by Elayne Barclay

Nadaka Nature Park

LOCATION: East Wilkes Neighborhood, NE Pacific Street, between NE 175th and 176th, Gresham, OR **ACTIVITIES:** Hiking, Wildlife viewing, Nature-based play area **FACILITIES:** Unpaved Trails **FEES AND REGULATIONS:** Pets on leash **HIKING DIFFICULTY:** Easy **HIGHLIGHTS:** A quiet neighborhood nature park; Great destination for a stroll, casual birding, and tranquility **PUBLIC TRANSIT:** TriMet bus 25

This twelve-acre mix of mature Douglas fir and open meadow habitat is located along NE Glisan Street, just west of NE 181st Avenue and north of the Rockwood neighborhood in the heart of west Gresham. The park has been a catalyst for rejuvenating the neighborhood and improving access to nature in one of our most nature-deficient areas.

Gresham acquired the ten-acre Nadaka ("Na-Da-Ka" or "Nature Day Kamp") property in 1995 from Camp Fire USA with funds from a 1990 voter-approved open spaces bond. However, lack of funds and connectivity with nearby parks limited access. For twelve years, Nadaka sat idle with an eight-foot chainlink fence surrounding it limiting access to one small opening at NE Pacific Street and NE 175th Avenue.

Lee Dayfield happened upon Nadaka several years ago while walking her dog, Tule. She saw a large forest surrounded by houses, hiding in broad daylight. From that moment she knew Nadaka would be a special place. In 2007, Lee and other Wilkes East neighbors became inspired by Nadaka's potential. They pulled ivy, organized cleanups, wrote grants, planted native plants, and introduced it to as many people as they could.

Entering Nadaka, prepare to be swept into a tranquil and sweet-smelling forest. Douglas fir, big-leaf maple, Pacific dogwood, vine maple, and hazelnut predominate. Still lower salal, sword fern, Oregon grape, and other native shrubs flourish thanks to ambitious invasive species removal. In May or June, yellow-rumped warblers can be seen feasting in the tall Douglas firs, while a variety of year-round residents—Pacific and Bewick's wrens, spotted towhees, song sparrows, and bushtits—abound in the understory.

On the mulched path to the right of the entrance off NE Pacific is a pair of painted turtle rocks, relics of the camp still maintained by Camp Fire USA. On the main pathway follow the quarter-mile loop trail, which leads to a meadow at the park's south end. Lee and her neighbors' efforts led to a collaboration with nonprofits, Metro, the City of Gresham, and East Multnomah Soil and Water Conservation District to acquire two more acres south of Nadaka which will eventually connect the natural area to NE Glisan Street and the Rockwood Neighborhood.

Access

The Neighborhood Park with community garden, orchard, rain garden, nature-based play area, and other facilities will be located on the two-acre lots south of the Nadaka

Nature Park off Glisan. The Glisan entrance is the Rockwood Neighborhood's "front door" to Nadaka.

How to Get There

BY CAR: The southern entrance to Nadaka Nature Park is located adjacent to St. Aidan's Episcopal Church at 17405 NE Glisan Street, Gresham. This location is about 300 yards west of 181st Avenue, one block north of the MAX Blue Line stop at Burnside and about 1 mile south of exit 13 on Interstate 84. **PUBLIC TRANSIT:** TriMet bus 25 from Gateway Transit Center out NE Glisan to Rockwood.

By Jim Labbe and Lee Dayfield

More information: Wilkes East Neighborhood Association; City of Gresham

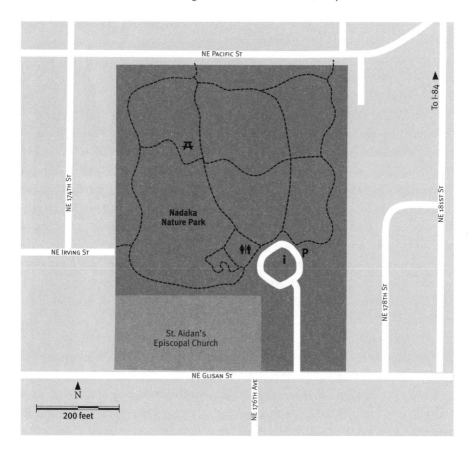

What Color Is Green?

WHEN JOHN CHARLES OLMSTED wrote in his 1903 Report of the Park Board that urban parks foster "healthfulness, morality, intelligence, and business prosperity," he spoke to the hopes of an audience eager to improve the social health of Portland's rapidly growing population. The idea that nature provides essential therapeutic benefits inspired the late-nineteenth-century urban parks movement in the United States. Diverse interests and cultural values came together and spawned an enthusiasm for urban parks and open space at a time when Americans were converging on cities. Between 1880 and 1920, the U.S. witnessed enormous and unprecedented growth in large cities. New concentrations of people, poverty, and political unrest fostered a broad consensus about the positive effects of urban parks for public health and "civilizing" urban populations. Olmsted and his contemporaries alleviated diverse anxieties about a growing urban working class and advanced the notion that distributing the benefits of parks, playgrounds, and nature in the city to all social classes would promote a larger social harmony.

Today, with almost 80 percent of U.S. citizens living in cities, a growing body of research in a variety of disciplines—from biology to environmental psychology to landscape architecture—documents what early urban parks advocates knew intuitively: nature has positive health effects, both physically and mentally, and urban greenspaces can make us healthier, happier, and probably safer and smarter as well. The link to physical health—particularly asthma and obesity—has become most evident. The Centers for Disease Control now strongly recommends improving access to places for physical activity such as biking or hiking trails to reduce the risk of cardiovascular disease, diabetes, obesity, selected cancers, and musculoskeletal conditions.

An abundant and diverse range of research also links access to nature to measurable differences in psychological health and happiness of humans. Richard Louv's *Last Child in the Woods* and his more recent book, *The Nature Principle* cite the numerous studies documenting that exposure to natural environments enhances children's cognitive development by improving their awareness, attention, reasoning, and observational skills. This influence is particularly acute in children growing up in socially or environmentally stressful settings. For example, one study found a strong relationship between near-home nature and self-discipline and confidence in inner-city children, particularly among girls. In the coming decades, we may well find that adequate access to nature is among the basic necessities for people to effectively learn, grow, and thrive in an equal-opportunity society; and as essential to urban dwellers as affordable housing and transportation.

Thanks, in part, to Olmsted's generation, the Portland-Vancouver area has one of the best regional systems of parks, trails, and natural areas in the country. More than many places, we have refined the vision and reality of nature in the city and have led efforts to foster more ecologically sustainable urban landscapes.

But when viewed at the neighborhood scale, there are significant inequities in access to parks and nature. These disparities matter to our social and cultural well-being as well as to future conservation. The Coalition for a Livable Future's *Regional Equity Atlas* found that 64 percent of the Portland metro population inside the region's urban growth boundary lives within one quarter mile of a natural area, and just under half lives within one quarter mile walking distance from public parkland. The atlas also found that those living beyond one quarter of a mile from a park or natural area tend to be lower income and people of color. If natural landscapes contribute to both individual and community health and opportunity, not everyone shares in these benefits in our region. In a region that prides itself on livability, the distribution of environmental good from neighborhood parks and nature and the distribution of negative environmental factors, such as brownfields and freeway pollution, represent important Environmental Justice issues.

Portlanders are beginning to take positive steps to address these disparities, steps that are remaking the perception and reality of nature in the city. The voter-approved 2006 Regional Natural Areas Bond Measure included a $15 million capital grant program prioritizing improved access to nature in low-income communities. The City of Portland followed Metro's lead by targeting portions of its local share to improving access in park-deficient neighborhoods in east Portland. In a number of cases, these efforts have dovetailed with those of nonprofit, affordable housing developers to create affordable, walkable communities that integrate nature into the built environment.

As the *Regional Equity Atlas* has documented, most of these park- and nature-poor neighborhoods are currently home to a higher percentage of people of color, many of whom are low income and recent immigrants. Environmental justice advocates remind us that these communities of color make up an increasing percentage of the overall population and thus potentially a growing portion of the future conservation movement. Hence, building leadership and relationships with communities of color to recover nature and ensure equitable access in perpetuity will be critical to the success of the urban greenspaces movement in the coming century. These efforts are essential to achieving an ecologically sustainable and socially just metropolitan region.

By Jim Labbe

Whitaker Ponds Nature Park

Location: Columbia Boulevard and NE 47th Avenue, Portland **Activities:** Hiking, Paddling, Wildlife viewing, Birding **Facilities:** Portable restrooms, Limited parking, Unpaved trail, Covered gazebo, Docks, Interpretive info **Fees and Regulations:** Restricted hours 5 am–midnight; No pets; No fishing or wading; No boating on the ponds; Park outside the gate, Stay on designated trails, the east pond is a wildlife protection area with no public entry **Hiking Difficulty:** Easy **Highlights:** Transformation from junkyard to park; Two freshwater ponds and a black cottonwood forest; Waterfowl, beaver, birds of prey; Dock for canoe and kayak access to Whitaker Slough **Public Transit:** TriMet bus 75

Whitaker Ponds Nature Park is just north of Columbia Boulevard, tucked in around construction equipment lots, metal recycling businesses, and the airport. Acquired in 1994, organizations, agencies, and countless volunteers have transformed this former junkyard into a peaceful oasis of nature in the heart of Portland's industrial district. During its restoration back to a lush natural landscape, over two thousand tires were removed.

The nearly twenty-five-acre park is home to two ponds, an ecoroof-covered gazebo, and a black cottonwood forest, which has been enhanced over the past fifteen years by the planting of thousands of native plants. A wildflower meadow near the entrance on NE 47th Avenue supports local pollinators in summertime, and the Lewis and Clark Garden near the gazebo highlights different plant communities. The park is frequented by many animals, including downy woodpeckers, rabbits, beavers, garter snakes, osprey, dragonflies, river otters, and wood ducks. In February, park visitors may spot fuzzy gray owlets from the great horned owl's nest in a bare cottonwood tree. And in May, bird enthusiasts can enjoy the feisty territorial spats between individual rufous hummingbirds as they establish who has rights to which red-flowering currant bush. A sloping ramp leads down to an observation dock on the west pond, from which visitors can see fish, frogs, and water bugs. A second dock for canoes and kayaks is located on the north side of the park on Whitaker Slough. Paddlers can launch from the park and travel west on Whitaker Slough to reach the main stem of the nineteen-mile Columbia Slough, but no fishing or paddling is allowed in either of the ponds.

The park and its facilities are the result of many collaborative partnerships between the City of Portland, Metro, the Columbia Slough Watershed Council, and many community members. Portland Parks & Recreation manages the nature park, and the Columbia Slough Watershed Council has offices onsite. The council regularly offers educational and recreational activities at the park in conjunction with the Bureau of Environmental Services and Portland Parks & Recreation.

Access

The half-mile loop trail is quite flat and surfaced with bark chips and gravel. Bike racks are located inside the entrance near the west pond. Vehicles are encouraged to park outside the entrance, as the vehicle gate may close without warning. A smaller adjoining pedestrian gate is always open during park hours.

How to Get There:

BY CAR: Follow Columbia Boulevard to NE 47th Avenue and go north approximately a quarter mile (or travel north on NE 42nd Avenue across Columbia Boulevard where it turns into NE 47th Avenue). The entrance to the park is on the right. **PUBLIC TRANSIT:** TriMet bus 75 makes a stop at the corner of NE 47th Avenue and Columbia Boulevard. Visitors can walk north along NE 47th to the park entrance

By Melissa Sandoz

More information: Portland Parks & Recreation; Columbia Slough Watershed Council; City of Portland Bureau of Environmental Services

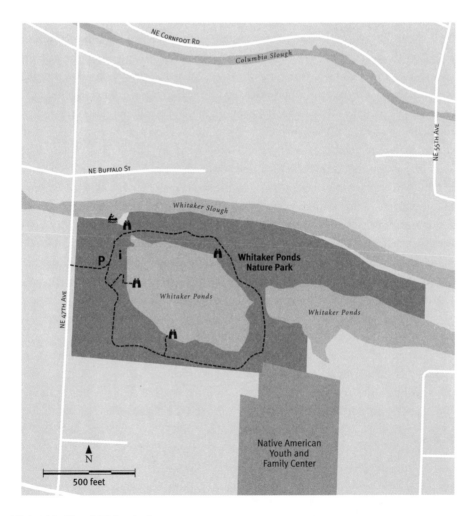

God's Dog Rides MAX:
Urban Coyotes

ON A BLUSTERY WINTRY DAY IN 2002, a coyote casually wandered though the open doors of a Portland International Airport MAX train and curled up in a window seat—just like any other traveler bound for the city. He had been spotted earlier in the day hunting rodents along the airport runways and later was seen darting in and out among the trains parked at the airport light rail station. Airport security was quickly summoned, and he was peacefully captured and released back to the remotest wilds of the Columbia Slough surrounding the airport. While his mode of travel was a bit unorthodox for his species, his destination was not—coyotes have been making their way into our urban interior for quite some time now.

Coyotes (*Canis latrans*) are members of the dog family. *Canis latrans* means "talking dog," a reference to the fact that coyotes have more vocalizations than any other North American mammal except humans. Navajo sheepherders once referred to this incredibly intelligent, adaptive animal as God's dog. Native American cultures traditionally have revered and appreciated coyotes for their cunning and adaptability—bestowing upon them a central role in their cosmology.

Post–European settlement America has not been so kind. For the better part of two centuries, coyotes have been among the most persecuted animals on the North American continent. Federal government trappers still kill tens of thousands of coyotes each year on rural landscapes in the name of protecting livestock. Despite what has been described as a war on coyotes, these canines have not only survived but flourished.

Today, there are more coyotes than at any time in history, and their range has expanded from the western two thirds of the United States to nearly all of North America. Prior to the 1940s in Oregon, coyotes were considered primarily an eastside animal, with sightings west of the Cascades relatively rare. However, in large part due to the removal of other, larger predator species and clearing of forests, they are common today throughout the state.

Sightings in and around Portland began in the early 1980s and have increased dramatically over the past thirty years. While most frequently observed near natural areas, coyotes are also occasionally seen in neighborhoods and even deep in the urban interior. It is a common misperception that coyote sightings in and around Portland have become more frequent because we have overdeveloped their habitat and they have nowhere else to go—this axiom is true for many species, but not for the coyote. They come to our city of their own volition, drawn by easy food sources, plenty of cover, and the absence of natural competition. They appear on our urban landscape not because we took habitat from them, but rather because, unlike most larger mammals, they are able to find sustenance on the urban landscapes we have created. Portland is not alone in experiencing the phenomenon of the urban coyote. Coyotes have established themselves in cities across North America.

Coyotes can be found living alone, in pairs, or in packs of up to eight animals. Unlike wolves, coyotes do not typically hunt in packs, so you are most likely to see only one or two individuals at a time, although there may well be more around. Packs will patrol their territories against incursions by other coyotes. Coyotes will take advantage of a wide variety of natural and manmade structures for dens including burrows, downed trees, thick blackberry brambles, culverts, and crawlspaces. Mating typically peaks in February, with young born in April. Litters tend to range from four to seven pups but have been known to exceed ten pups. Like wolves, only the alpha male and female in the pack reproduce, but coyotes are compensatory breeders. If pack structure is disrupted, all members of the pack will begin to breed and produce larger litters—an adaptation that has helped the species withstand even the most intensive levels of lethal control.

Coyotes are true omnivores. While the most common staple in their diet is small rodents, they will also eat rabbits, birds, reptiles, amphibians, bugs, carrion fruit and vegetables, garbage, compost, accessible pet food, and small free-roaming pets—a diversity of food sources that makes our urban landscapes a veritable smorgasbord. They play an important role in controlling other urban wildlife populations that otherwise tend to explode. Studies have shown that rodent populations can increase five to six times following coyote removal. In Chicago, research indicates that coyotes may prey on up to 40 percent of urban and suburban Canada goose nests.

While coyotes are most active between dusk and dawn, they can be seen at any time of the day. Unlike the MAX train coyote, most coyotes are quite shy and secretive. There are far more coyotes around our urban landscape than people realize. For the most part, they simply choose not to be seen. They are, however, curious and will sometimes observe human activity from what they perceive to be a safe distance.

Sadly, the coyote's reception in the urban landscape has not been much better than that received by his rural brethren. It is the risk to humans and pets that garners the most attention—fears that the local media has only been too willing to exploit with a steady succession of "jaws and claws" stories about coyotes. In fact, the risk to humans from coyotes is very small. Thick, dense fur can sometimes make coyotes appear larger than they really are. In Oregon coyotes typically weigh between twenty and thirty pounds. In the entire recorded history of North America, there have been two documented killings of humans by coyotes. There has never been an unprovoked attack documented in Oregon. Attacks that have been documented nationwide have usually been associated with coyotes that have been habituated to food handouts and have lost their instinctual fear of humans. More people are killed each year by dogs, cows, horses, bees, and jellyfish than have been killed by coyotes over the past two hundred years.

Yes, coyotes will take unattended cats and small dogs. The solution is to keep house pets indoors and monitor them closely when they are outside. Free-roaming pets easily become lost and face a wide array of other hazards including cars, poisons, disease, or attack by other animals. Regardless of whether coyotes are present or not, the life expectancy of an outdoor cat is less than two years, less than a fifth of the life expectancy of an indoor cat. Methods used to control coyotes on urban landscapes, including traps and poisons, are indiscriminate and can kill both non-target wildlife and the very pets they are being employed to protect. More importantly, new coyotes quickly replace those who have been removed—even at the highest levels of control,

there is no reason to believe that the next time you open the door and let Fluffy loose that a new coyote will not be wandering through the area.

One thing is certain—coyotes are here to stay. Let us greet this survivor not with fear and loathing, but with appreciation for the important niche it fills in our urban ecosystem, for its fascinating life history, and most of all for its incredible ability to persevere under the most difficult of circumstances.

By Bob Sallinger, illustration by Allison Bollman

Streaked Horned Larks

Visitors to open spaces in North and Northeast Portland might have the opportunity to see a particularly rare songbird that only occurs in the Pacific Northwest: the streaked horned lark (*Eremophila alpestris strigata*). Males are identifiable by a bright yellow face, distinct black stripes on the throat and cheek, a brick-red color on the back and head, and small, black, horn-like feather tufts. Once common from British Columbia to southern Oregon, the lark's population has plummeted due to alteration of river floodplains and loss of 99 percent of its nesting grassland habitat. Recent surveys indicate that there may be as few as three thousand streaked horned larks left in the wild.

Streaked horned larks nest and raise their young on the ground in sparsely vegetated grasslands. Faced with near complete loss of their native habitat, they cling to existence on some of our wildlife refuges and, somewhat more surprisingly, on undeveloped, industrial landscapes, including the vacant, grassy areas surrounding Portland International Airport, which represents one of the last strongholds for the streaked horned lark in northern Oregon.

In recent years there has been a focus on creating more habitat for this species at Portland natural areas—as it is likely that the streaked horned lark will be listed under the Endangered Species Act in the near future. Be sure to watch for this distinctive little bird and to listen for its delicate, high-pitched song, often performed in flight.

—Dave Helzer and Bob Sallinger

Heron Lakes Golf Course

LOCATION: 3500 N Victory Boulevard, Portland
ACTIVITIES: Golf, Birding **FACILITIES:** Restrooms,
Parking, Unpaved fairways and paved golf
cart trails, Interpretive sign, Snack bar, Golf
store **FEES AND REGULATIONS:** No pets; Golfers
have priority **HIKING DIFFICULTY:** Easy **HIGH-
LIGHTS:** Great blue heron nesting colony
mid February to June; Birding at Force Lake;
Golf; Vanport Wetlands, an 80-acre restored
Port of Portland wetland; 2,000-acre Smith
and Bybee Lakes Natural Area, off N Marine
Drive **PUBLIC TRANSIT:** MAX Yellow Line TriMet
bus 16

Between 1942 and 1945, 650 acres of the Columbia River floodplain were transformed into a city of 40,000 people, 9,000 dwellings, and 19 miles of streets. On May 30, 1948, a break in the levee at N Portland Road set loose floodwaters that wiped out Vanport, which was then Oregon's second largest city. In 1960, Portland Parks & Recreation purchased this property, and in 1970, built the eighteen-hole West Delta Park Golf Course. Nine holes were added in 1986 and the course was renamed Heron Lakes after Portland's city bird, the great blue heron. Nine more holes were added in 1992. Ironically, while the course was renamed to honor the great blue heron, the original eighteen hole course—where the blue herons nest—was named Green Back, which is the smaller green heron, while the newer course was named Great Blue. Jesse Goodling, long-time course manager, has done a great job of increasing wildlife habitat on the course and reducing the use of herbicides and pesticides. Portland's Bureau of Environmental Services revegetation program has also restored the wetlands that extend from Force Lake to the black cottonwood grove in which the great blue herons nest.

As you drive or cycle down N Force Avenue you'll see Force Lake on the right. It's worth a stop, especially in winter, to scope out the lake for wintering waterfowl. Great blue herons work the wetland edges on the quieter northern side of the pond. I've seen American bittern here as well. The weedy patch on the opposite side of N Force Avenue attracts American goldfinches, house finches, and other seed-eating birds.

Just past the golf course entrance, on the right, is a small parking lot with interpretive signs that provide the history of the city of Vanport and the Vanport Flood. There's also a wildlife interpretive sign, although the vegetation has grown so dense around the lake that you'll have to make your way to the nearby fairway to actually see Force Lake.

To view the heronry, walk from the interpretive parking area along the access road, or drive to the golf course maintenance yard and park there—make sure you're off the access road to the clubhouse. Walk around the right-hand side of the maintenance yard and take a left. You will see a paved golf cart path in front of you. Check that no one is teeing off and walk along the cart path or on the grass behind the maintenance shed. Just behind the #2 tee take a very short right to the next paved cart path, which passes between two greens. Then take a left on the paved cart path and walk past the #5 tee. You will see a small grove of trees ahead and to the right. Walk through the grove until you come to a small restroom shed. Just past the restroom, walk over a small grassy swale and you'll see several large cottonwood stumps. Keep to the right, skirting along the wetlands until you come to the large stand of black cottonwoods on your right. Before the trees leaf out, the heronry is clearly visible.

This is a safe place to bird without interfering with golfers at the 7th tee. The heron colony is in a large stand of black cottonwoods behind the tee. You might bring a portable chair and simply sit, waiting for adult herons to glide lazily to their nests as they return from feeding forays at nearby Smith and Bybee Natural Area or Force Lake. It's amazing to watch herons as they deftly thread their expansive, six-foot wingspan among a tangle of cottonwood limbs and settle into loosely constructed stick nests high up in a constantly swaying tree.

When young are in the nest, a cacophony of bill clacking, guttural squawks, and elaborate neck and plumage displays greets the parent. Although herons nest communally, they brook no intrusion on their individual nests. During early courtship the male proffers a twig to the waiting female. They both tug for a few seconds, then she ritualistically takes it and weaves it into the nest, and the male is off again, frequently being chased by crows and a mixed flock of violet-green and tree swallows.

Other attractions, in addition to the herons, are the nearby shrub-scrub wetlands and cottonwood forest, which are excellent for birding. The forest resonates with bird songs. Dazzling yellow and black American goldfinches snatch seeds out of teasel flower heads. The melodious, flute-like songs of Swainson's thrushes echo from behind blue elderberries where cedar waxwings, black-headed grosbeaks, and downy woodpeckers gather seeds and insects. The cottonwood canopy is alive with black-throated gray, orange-crowned, and yellow-rumped warblers, and the marsh buzzes with the common yellowthroat's "witchity, witchity" call. An occasional marsh wren may scold an intrusive red-winged blackbird. The numbered nest boxes affixed to trees along the course attract both violet-green and tree swallows. This is one of the few places I can count on hearing the unique "fitz-beew" of the willow flycatcher, which may be perched on a nearby willow twig.

Access

For access to the heronry, park at the maintenance shed, and make sure that you're off the access road to the clubhouse.

How to Get There

BY CAR: From downtown Portland Interstate 5 northbound, exit 306B and take the off-ramp to the traffic light and turn left. Pass under I-5 heading west and get into the right turn lane. At the stop sign turn right. Drive past Vanport Wetlands on your left and past the entrance to the MAX Expo stop and the entrance to Expo Center. Keep straight until you come to the stop sign at N Force Avenue. Take a left and drive to the entrance to Heron Lakes Golf Course on your right. The clubhouse and parking is another quarter mile if you want refreshments or a restroom. **PUBLIC TRANSIT:** TriMet bus 16 stops on Marine Drive next to the Expo Center. The MAX Yellow Line stops near Vanport Wetlands and the Expo Center. It's about a mile walk to the maintenance yard, where it's another half mile to the heronry.

By Mike Houck

More information: Heron Lakes Golf Course; Portland Parks & Recreation

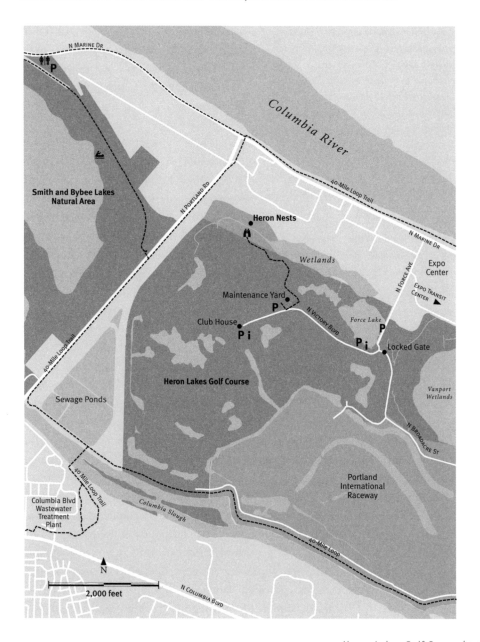

Smith and Bybee Wetlands Natural Area

Location: 5300 N Marine Drive, Portland **Activities:** Hiking, Wildlife viewing, Canoeing, Kayaking, Photography, Fishing, Metro education programs **Facilities:** Restrooms, Parking, Paved trails, Picnic area/shelter, Canoe/kayak launch, Bike racks, Drinking fountain, Interpretive signs **Fees and Regulations:** Hours dawn to dusk; Fishing; No powerboats (except electric trolling motors); No pets or biking; Contact Metro for group program use **Hiking Difficulty:** Easy **Highlights:** Designated an Important Bird Area by the National Audubon Society; 100 species of birds regularly seen; Winter waterfowl and raptors; Spring neotropical migrants; The largest population of western painted turtles in Oregon April, May, and June; Other wildlife abounds; Large stone carvings of natural subjects located around the parking area and at the canoe launch installed as a public art project funded by the construction of the nearby Wapato Jail **Public Transit:** No direct service

"I can't believe we're in the middle of Portland!" These words fit Smith and Bybee Wetlands to a T. Although it is large at 1,800 acres, the natural area is surrounded by warehouses, Port of Portland terminals, the old St. Johns Landfill, and other industrial sites, making it one of the biggest secrets in town. The Interlakes Trail, less than a mile long, provides the only pedestrian access. The rest of the natural area can only be seen by boat, which provides some of the best wildlife viewing.

People are amazed at the wildlife that can be seen here. Mammals include coyote, black-tailed deer, beaver, nutria, muskrat, river otter, mink, long-tailed weasel, cottontail rabbit, raccoon, opossum, voles, moles, shrews, and bats. Evidence of the very busy beavers is easy to find and coyote scat on the trail is a common sign of their presence.

Bird life is abundant and almost all water birds from the region can be seen at one time or another. Winter is great for waterfowl and birds of prey. The songbird migration through the riparian woodland in the spring is outstanding. Just about every migrant seen in the metropolitan area shows up at Smith and Bybee, and there are some birds that are much more conspicuous at the lakes than in most of Portland, such as the house wren and yellow warbler. Singing American goldfinches ring the meadow along the trail during May. The larger nesting birds include bald eagle, osprey, red-tailed hawk, great horned owl, great blue heron, Canada goose, and pileated woodpecker. In late summer white pelicans have become regular visitors, and fall brings great egrets, sometimes in the hundreds, along with thousands of shorebirds.

The western painted turtle may be the most famous resident at Smith and Bybee Wetlands since turtles are rare in the region. The healthy population of these beautiful reptiles is probably the largest in the state. Western painted turtle numbers have plummeted in the last few decades, and they are classified as sensitive, one step away from protection under the Endangered Species Act. Monitoring the turtles and enhancing their habitat is a goal of the management plan for the natural area. They are easy to see from the trail at Turtle Turnout on any warm, sunny day in April, May, and June.

The ultimate Smith and Bybee experience is paddling by kayak or canoe in the lakes. The paddling season is actually fairly short because the water level in the lakes varies greatly with the seasons. The best time for boating is from March through June. By July most years the low water level and rapid aquatic plant growth make paddling very difficult, if not impossible in places. The canoe launch is at the end of the entrance road, one third mile past the parking area. There is a painted area on the road where you can stop to unload your boat and gear. After unloading, drive to the turn-around at the end of the road and then drive back past the loading area and park in the painted spaces on the side of the road.

Wildlife spotting on the water is best late in the day and close to shore, especially when paddling between the lakes. The last few hours before sunset are the best for seeing mammals, but remember that Smith and Bybee Wetlands closes at dark. A great

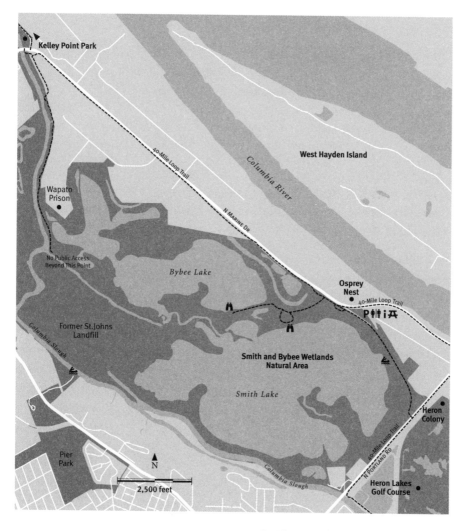

Not the Place to Leave Your Alligator

I have sort of a strange question. We have this pet alligator, and I was thinking Smith and Bybee Lakes would be a good place to let him go.

So began one of my all-time favorite phone calls to Audubon's Wildlife Care Center. It would have been almost funny if the caller was not serious. In fact, our landscape is full of escaped and abandoned pets that compete with native wildlife. Perhaps the most common feral species is the housecat. However, the list also includes domestic ducks and geese; imported turtle species; peacocks; ferrets; exotic fish; prairie dogs; hedgehogs; and yes, even the rare alligator. It is a misdemeanor in Oregon to release a domestic animal into the wild, and it's also inhumane and ecologically destructive. Many exotic species are now banned in Oregon because of their impact on native wildlife. If you can no longer keep your pet, please find it a new permanent home or take it to a shelter.

—Bob Sallinger

introduction to paddling at the lakes can be found by joining one of the free, guided paddle trips led by the Friends of Smith and Bybee Lakes. For those that do not have their own boat, Metro offers fee-based public paddle trips in spring.

Access
At less than a mile, the level, paved Interlakes Trail is the only trail into the natural area and begins where you turned into the entrance road from Marine Drive. From the parking lot, walk along the paved 40-Mile Loop trail, which parallels the entrance road. There are two wildlife-viewing platforms on the trail. The site is best seen by canoes or kayaks March through June—launch one third mile past the parking area at the end of the entrance road.

How to Get There
By car or bike: From downtown Portland, north on Interstate 5; exit #307 (Delta Park–Marine Drive); take the left fork of the exit road, following the sign for Marine Drive West. Loop under I-5; at the large intersection, turn right and go west 2.2 miles on W Marine Drive, past the Expo Center and past the lighted intersection at N Portland Road, proceeding north up and over the railroad tracks. Watch for the Smith and Bybee sign on your left as you come down off the railroad overpass. **Public transit:** No direct service. MAX Yellow Line Expo Center Station (end of the line), is within 2.2 miles on the Marine Drive bike path.

By James L. Davis

More information: Metro

Tracking Mammals

EVERYBODY LOVES TO SEE WILD MAMMALS. Watching a river otter, a beaver, or a coyote going about some everyday part of its life is a special thrill. Wild mammal spotting, however, is difficult; not like bird watching. It's no mystery why there are many more birdwatchers than other nature hobbyists. Birds are the most conspicuous animals on earth. There are so many different kinds of birds and they are active, colorful, and noisy. And, like us, most are out during the day.

Wild mammals, however, are a completely different story. As much as we love to see them, it's really tough to get a look at many, let alone actually watch them go about their normal lives. There are less than half as many diverse kinds of mammals as there are birds in the world. What's more, half of all mammals are rodents, and a quarter are bats. Since these mammals are mainly small, dark-colored, and nocturnal, it is no wonder there aren't mammal-watching clubs like there are for birds. Even the big mammals are mainly nocturnal, and all are generally secretive and stay out of sight of people. Given all this, how is it possible to know the mammals that live in a particular area?

The key to discovering mammals is to become a super nature detective. Mammals leave myriad kinds of evidence of their presence and these signs all become clues in a mystery to solve. The general term "tracking" is used to describe the study of animal signs in order to identify the animal and figure out what it was doing. Tracking is more than identifying footprints, however. Other clues or signs to look for include scat (feces), trails, burrows and nests, chewing or digging marks, feeding debris, fur, food caches, rubbings or scratching on trees, and even smells. To be able to put all the different clues together to identify which mammal was there, it is important to have some basic knowledge of the mammals living in the area and their natural history—their preferred habitat, diet, activity periods, and behaviors. All these clues help the tracker build a case for the identity of the animal. But tracking doesn't end with identification.

More exciting and complex than identifying the animal—the real detective work—is interpreting all the evidence to learn what the animal was doing, where it was going, and even why it behaved the way it did. People develop a whole new awareness of animals and their lives through tracking. In essence, skilled trackers learn to think like the animals they study. Tracking is "whole brain" learning using all of your senses. Tracking greatly increases your observational skills and awareness of the world around you. It is not surprising that many naturalists experience some of their most profound connections with the natural world through tracking.

How to Start Tracking

Fortunately, there is a tracking renaissance taking place in the Pacific Northwest. Tom Brown's books on tracking started a national revival of interest in tracking and nature awareness. Jon Young (mentored by Tom Brown) established the Wilderness Awareness School in Washington State, which is going strong. In Portland, Tony Deis started Trackers Earth, offering an amazing range of programs for many ages and interests. Some of the region's agencies and organizations, such as the Audubon Society of Portland, Metro Regional Parks and Natural Areas, Tualatin Hills Parks & Recreation District, and Cascadia Wild also offer programs on tracking and naturalist skills. Sometimes it takes a little tracking to track down the trackers, so you may have to just do some searching on the internet to find current information.

Tracking usually focuses on mammals, but other animals also leave evidence behind. There is now a tracking book completely devoted to birds and even one for insects! But the most important thing is "dirt time." Remember, just as with bird watching, the best way to understand and appreciate mammals is to get out into nature and experience the real thing.

By James L. Davis, illustration by Virginia Church

Books for Tracking

Many experienced trackers still recommend starting with a classic: *Tom Brown's Field Guide to Nature Observation and Animal Tracking* by Tom Brown Jr., with Brandt Morgan. Or some recommend the new *Animal Tracking Basics* by Jon Young and Tiffany Morgan. For a pocket guide to tracks and scats, James Halfpenny's *Scats and Tracks of the Pacific Coast* is very handy. A recent addition specifically focused on our region is the excellent *Wildlife of the Pacific Northwest: Tracking and Identifying Mammals, Birds, Reptiles, Amphibians, and Invertebrates* by David Moskowitz. After some experience you may be ready for the encyclopedic *Mammal Tracks and Sign: A Guide to North American Species* by Mark Elbroch.

Kelley Point Park

LOCATION: North Portland Peninsula, off N Marine Drive at the confluence of the Columbia Slough and the Willamette and Columbia Rivers, Portland **ACTIVITIES:** Hiking, Biking, Boating, Fishing, Wildlife viewing **FACILITIES:** Restrooms, Parking, Paved and unpaved trails, Interpretive info, Picnic area, Dock, Canoe/kayak launch **FEES AND REGULATIONS:** Hours 6 am to 9 pm; Pets on leash **HIKING DIFFICULTY:** Easy **HIGHLIGHTS:** Best views of the Columbia River ship traffic in the metro area; Sandy beaches; Access to the Lower Columbia Slough and the confluence of the Willamette and Columbia River; Unique views of Sauvie Island and a large operating grain elevator **PUBLIC TRANSIT:** TriMet bus 16

Kelley Point Park is named for Hall J. Kelley, a New Englander who, according to Portland Parks & Recreation, was one of the most vocal advocates for Oregon in the first half of the nineteenth century. Kelley's effort to establish a city where Kelley Point Park now stands failed. However, his advocacy of Portland over Oregon City and Sellwood was more successful.

The one-hundred-acre park occupies land that was historic Pearcy Island and the now-filled Columbia River floodplain. The Port of Portland deposited Columbia River dredge sands here to facilitate marine industrial development. The land that Kelley had envisioned as a city is now merely the peninsula's northwest tip.

The Port of Portland transferred Kelley Point to Portland Parks & Recreation in 1984. There is handy access to sandy beaches at the mouth of the Columbia Slough. Treacherous currents here have claimed the lives of several people in recent years, so be careful if you decide to take a dip.

Kelley Point Park encompasses a majestic black cottonwood forest, historic sites, a canoe and kayak launch, and rich wildlife habitat. In spring, the black cottonwood forest is alive with yellow warblers, brown creepers, and Bewick's wrens. Remnant fruit trees from the old Biddle estate are riddled with parallel, ladder-like sapsucker holes. Coyotes, deer, beaver, osprey, and great blue heron are frequent visitors. A great horned owl has nested near the launch in recent years. In May and June, flocks of band-tailed pigeons sometimes congregate at the mouth of the Columbia Slough, feeding on grain spills at the terminal across the slough. Recently, flocks of Eurasian collared-doves, a newly arrived non-native species, have also appeared in this area.

From the last parking lot, you can stroll along paved paths that give wonderful views of the Columbia River and Port of Vancouver as ocean-going freighters pass by. Watching longshoremen unload car carriers at break-neck speed is an entertaining spectacle. Osprey, double-crested cormorants, gulls, and Caspian terns are common.

Access

Parking: Off N Marine Drive, Kelley Point Park Road, just inside the entrance road on the left is the canoe/kayak launch site and parking for eight vehicles. The launch gives direct access to the Columbia Slough and provides a striking view of a "large wood" aquatic habitat improvement project. Farther along Kelley Point Road a paved path from the first parking area provides excellent access to sandy beaches. Beware of treacherous currents and deep holes, however. You can walk to the tip of the park from here along a paved path. The second parking area has access to the most popular paved paths, restrooms, picnic areas, and the best views of the Columbia River, the tip of undeveloped West Hayden Island, the Port of Vancouver, and Port of Portland's Terminal 5. An interpretive sign marking the Lewis and Clark Expedition is located at the confluence of the Willamette and Columbia Rivers.

How to Get There

By car: From downtown Portland Interstate 5 to Marine Drive. Continue on Marine Drive west to Kelley Point Park Road. **Public transit:** TriMet bus 16

By Susan Barthel, illustration by Virginia Church

More information: Portland Parks & Recreation; Columbia Slough Watershed Council

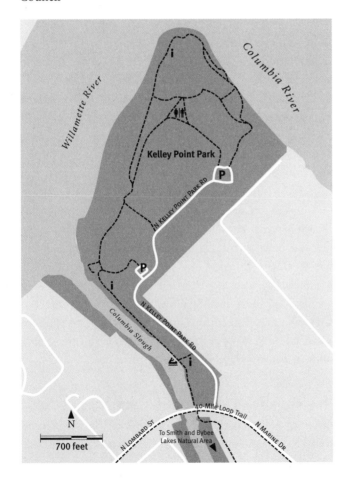

The "Jail" Trail

From Kelley Point Park there is a pleasant, paved 1.3-mile out-and-back trail along the north side of the Columbia Slough that starts across from the Kelley Point Park road entrance and can also be accessed behind the city-owned sewer pump station. Constructed by the Port of Portland, the trail's first third travels along the edge of a wooded wetland mitigation area. At the railroad bridge underpass, it hugs the riparian edge of the lower Columbia Slough. Willow, cottonwood, and ash plantings have greatly increased the riparian habitat on this reach of the slough. After about a mile you enter the two-thousand-acre Smith and Bybee Wetlands Natural Area, where you'll get your first view of the expansive wetland. You'll also be able to see the top of the not-yet-opened Wapato Jail in the distance.

Mudflats emerge during low water both in the wetlands and along the slough. Birds are numerous. The trail ends now at a cul-de-sac at the North Slough. Metro is planning a future bridge connection to North Portland and the 40-Mile Loop trail. The ash forest to the east is strictly for wildlife and off limits to hikers and birders.

Hard Drinkers:
Freshwater Mussels

STREAM CONSERVATION IN THE PACIFIC NORTHWEST seems to revolve around salmon: reengineering channels to add logs and meanders, planting trees to shade and cool the water, creating bioswales to filter and slow storm flows. These are all worthwhile actions, but for many people in urban or suburban neighborhoods, salmon occupy distant streams and rivers, not the neighborhood creek. So what does lie beneath the ducks in your local creek? Freshwater mussels, for one.

Mussels may not have the charismatic flair of fish leaping waterfalls on an epic journey, but they are an integral part of a healthy stream—and the life of salmon and mussels are intimately intertwined.

Ranging in length from one to eight inches, freshwater mussels are bean shaped, may be covered in concentric ridges and furrows, and range in color from yellow to brown to black. They can be mistaken for rocks, which is one reason why these animals tend to go unnoticed. Mussels are filter feeders that clean huge quantities of water—a single mussel can filter eighteen gallons (seventy liters) or more every day—as they feed on detritus, bacteria, algae, and diatoms. A dense bed of mussels can filter enough water to purify a stream. This helps to maintain clean water and support the teeming life of a healthy creek.

However, mussels would not be able to do this without the help of fish. An adult mussel can move short distances by dragging itself along with its muscular foot, but it is essentially a sedentary creature. To overcome this lack of mobility, larval mussels, called "glochidia," attach themselves to the gills or fins of fish. We don't know the host fish for all of the different mussels occurring in the Portland region, but those we do know include salmon, steelhead, various species of native and nonnative trout, sculpin, and stickleback. The young mussels remain on the fish for a few weeks and then drop to the creek or lake bottom, where they bury themselves in the substrate. In this way, mussels can recolonize disturbed areas or expand into new areas.

This may appear to be a one-way relationship, but work by Valery Ziuganov, a Russian scientist studying mussels and salmon in the Varzuga River of northern Russia, illustrates the way in which these two very different animals help each other. Ziuganov found visibility near a dense mussel bed to be twenty times greater than away from the bed. In this clearer water, light penetrated more deeply, increasing algal growth. Algae were consumed by aquatic invertebrates, which in turn were eaten by juvenile salmon. In addition, the clear water allowed fish to more easily find their prey. In the Varzuga, salmon populations were robust in part because large populations of mussels maintained good water quality.

There are only a few species of freshwater mussels in the Portland region. I wish I could be more precise, but there is discussion within the scientific world about how to separate some species or whether they are separate species at all. Historically, mussels were identified by shell shape. The advent of DNA sampling has proven this to be an unreliable method, and as a result the classification of mussels is in a pickle. The most recent thinking is that the western pearlshell (*Margaritifera falcata*) and western ridged mussel (*Gonidea angulata*) are valid species. It gets more complicated when we start talking about the floaters (genus *Anodonta*). One pair of species, the Oregon floater (*Anodonta oregonensis*) and the western floater (*Anodonta kennerlyi*), will probably be combined into a single species in the future. Researchers have discovered that a second pair, the California floater (*Anodonta californiensis*) and the winged floater (*Anodonta nuttalliana*), may in fact be half a dozen species, of which only one occurs in Portland!

Confused? Don't worry, long names and debates over what to call which mussel don't affect their importance in local creeks, nor do they alter the impacts on their habitat that are jeopardizing their survival.

Freshwater mussels can live as long as a human. The western pearlshell typically lives for sixty or seventy years, with some known to break the century mark. The western ridged mussel may live twenty years, and the floaters have a much shorter life of around ten years. Imagine how your neighborhood has changed in the past sixty years (was it even there?), and you'll have an inkling of the changes that occur during the life of a mussel.

We are fortunate that our mussels avoided the industrial-scale exploitation that beset mussels in the eastern United States, mainly because their shells are thinner than their eastern cousins. Beginning in the 1850s, two major industries were based upon mussels, resulting in entire streams in the Midwest, East, and Southeast being stripped of their mussels by pearl hunters seeking their fortune or button manufacturers seeking thick-shelled species from which to stamp pearl buttons. These days, more buttons are made from plastic, but freshwater mussels remain in demand by the pearl industry, though not for producing the pearls themselves. Pieces of shells are placed inside marine oysters as seeds to stimulate the formation of pearls.

In the Pacific Northwest, mussels were eaten by indigenous peoples, as evidenced by the shell middens found along some rivers. Sturgeon, river otters, muskrats, and raccoons eat mussels. The major threats to local mussels are from changing water conditions and creek environments. Nationally, freshwater mussels are one of the most endangered groups of wildlife. As filter feeders, mussels are exposed to chemical pollution, lack of oxygen, and increased sediment. In the Pacific Northwest's major rivers, dams and water extraction have been significant factors in mussel declines, along with declines in the native fish species needed as hosts by the mussel larvae. In your neighborhood, problems are more likely to come from housing and business developments than dams. Culverts under roads and trails act as barriers to fish movement and runoff from impervious surfaces creates fluctuation in water, oxygen and sediment levels. In addition, lawn chemicals, motor oil, and copper from roofs and car brakes are common suburban pollutants. These changes have had chronic effects on mussel populations, and since European settlers arrived, mussels have been eliminated from portions of rivers and even entire watersheds.

This is where the work to conserve salmon intersects again with the life of mussels. Efforts to protect salmon and improve their habitats will also benefit mussels, which are a major part of a healthy ecosystem. To quote the Russian scientist Ziuganov: "Thus, pearl mussels and salmonids form an important symbiotic community in which each species finds optimal conditions for survival. The protection and restoration of these valuable species is therefore interdependent, and the conservation of either one will benefit both."

The next time you are by your local creek, look past the ducks into the water and imagine the life supported by unassuming but hard-working—and hard-drinking—mussels.

By Matthew Shepherd

Lower Columbia River Watershed

The Columbia is the largest river flowing into the Pacific Ocean from North America. It is 1,243 miles long, capturing water from large areas of British Columbia, Washington, Oregon, Idaho, and even parts of Montana, Wyoming, Nevada, and Utah. Its watershed covers an area more than twenty-four times the size of Massachusetts. It flows from Canadian snowfields to high-desert grasslands and slices through two magnificent gorges, one in central Washington and our more familiar Columbia River Gorge National Scenic Area between Washington and Oregon. The Columbia goes on to create a tremendous estuary where the freshwater meets the sea.

Native Americans lived along her banks for over ten thousand years before Lewis and Clark's amazing 1805–1806 expedition to the Pacific. In the footsteps of the Corps of Discovery came fur traders, immigrant farmers, cattlemen, industrialists, and wind-surfers, many of whom still share the big river. The United States and Canada have transformed the Columbia into a workhorse for hydroelectric power, transportation, and irrigation. Abundant water and cheap electricity helped settle the West. We now wish we had been more careful with both.

As the Columbia pours out of the narrow confines of the gorge, it opens up into a broad floodplain near the Sandy River. On a summer day, follow the Columbia fifteen miles east of Portland to visit the Sandy, which begins as ice on the west side of Mount Hood and reveals its glacial origins with its silty, cold water. Near Interstate 84, hundreds of people swim from the banks of the Sandy on hot afternoons. Unfortunately, swimming in the Willamette and Columbia closer to Portland is limited, due to industrial and sewage pollution. The Sandy River scene is classic Pacific Northwest, where hardy Oregonians, along with their dogs, lounge on a gravel bar of a glacial river instead of a tropical beach.

Unbeknownst to most of the swimmers, thousands of fall Chinook salmon are making their way up the Sandy—a remarkably productive fishery so close to an urban area—to spawn in tributaries pouring off Mount Hood. Columbia River salmon are born in freshwater streams, grow to finger size in the river, pack on fat in the nutrient-rich Pacific Ocean for most of their adult life, and then return to their natal streams to spawn and die. The great upstream runs of salmon, full of ocean protein, have sustained rich tribal fisheries for thousands of years.

As the big river flows downstream from the Sandy, a series of low-lying islands—Government, Hayden, Sauvie, and Bachelor—create important wildlife habitat in wetlands and mixed forests. The broad valley also hosts fertile farms and the river's largest settlement at Portland and Vancouver. Salmon fishing is popular in the Columbia as well as in the Willamette, where boats dot the rivers seeking spring Chinook, fall Chinook, and coho.

At the west end of Marine Drive in Portland, next to massive parking lots for imported cars and containers, you can launch a canoe into the Kelley Point Park Slough and quickly reach the Willamette's confluence with the Columbia. To me, the confluence of two rivers is a special place—"where water comes together with other water," as Northwest writer Raymond Carver wrote. This major confluence is a good place to feel the industry and pavement of the city slip behind you as you paddle between the lovely Kelley Point on your right and Sauvie Island on your left.

While paddling on the mainstem Columbia or glancing down at the river from the Interstate 5 or Interstate 205 bridges, consider that hundreds of thousands of salmon swim by here each year, either leaving or returning home. Today salmon populations are just 3 percent of the millions of salmon that were in the Columbia at the time of Lewis and Clark. Thirteen populations are officially listed as threatened with extinction. Dams, overfishing, habitat destruction, and poor water quality all contributed to this stunning collapse. Despite the challenges, there is great hope as people recognize the economic and social imperative of saving the salmon. Our region is taking action to restore salmon habitat and improve water quality. Is it enough? Columbia River communities will continue to participate in this story as the big river flows on.

By Brett VandenHeuvel

Government Island

Location: Columbia River between river mile 111 and 119, just north of Portland International Airport **Activities:** Hiking, Paddling, Boating, Fishing, Wildlife viewing **Facilities:** Restrooms, Unpaved trails, Campground, Picnic area/shelter, Dock, Canoe/kayak launch, Interpretive signs/info **Fees and Regulations:** Much of the interior of the five-island complex is not accessible to the public; Camping is restricted to two weeks; Fires must be extinguished when not attended; Pets on leash **Hiking Difficulty:** Easy **Highlights:** Spectacular wildlife viewing opportunities for the adventurous **Public Transit:** None

Government Island is a bit like the land that time forgot. It is a place where coyotes stalk the beaches at dawn and black-tailed deer swim between islands at sunset. Beavers fell cottonwoods as big around as VW Bugs and drop them in a futile attempt to dam the mighty Columbia. Prehistoric-looking great blue herons with crooked necks and heavy wing beats flap in and out of their rookery bringing food to their croaking, beak-clacking, three-quarter-grown young. Recently fledged peregrine falcons "cack" from nearby trees, demanding food from their parents. A convocation of nearly a dozen bald eagles, some full adults with their telltale white heads and tails, and many still showing the brown mottled coloration of juveniles, feast upon a Canada goose on the beach only to find themselves doing battle with a bold raccoon whose hunger has overcome his common sense. These are the scenes that await you on Government Island.

True urban adventure is just one adrenaline-driven canoe trip away. At over 2,200 acres the site is actually a small archipelago of islands anchored by massive, elongated Government Island in the center and surrounded by the much smaller Tri Club and Lemon Islands to the west and McGuire and Ackerman Islands to the east. Prior to dams and dredging these islands were a shifting mosaic of vegetated alluvial sandbars, often partially submerged, which made passage of the river by larger ships nearly impossible. Because of periodic inundation, Native American use of the islands was probably limited to hunting and fishing forays rather than permanent encampments. However, as Neil Young says, "the aimless blade of science" has left the islands, like the river itself, relatively stagnant both in terms of geography and hydrologic cycles. For now mapmakers can rest relatively assured that their delineations will be mostly accurate.

The fact that the island remains in a natural state at all is amazing. It was originally given the name Diamond Island by Lewis and Clark, who camped there on November 3, 1805, and hunted ducks, swans, and geese by moonlight from a canoe. The U.S. Government laid claim to it in 1850 for "military purposes" and to raise hay for livestock. Later the island was used for private cattle grazing and agriculture.

More recently it could easily have morphed into a community of high-end condominiums and boat marinas. Worse yet, at one point it was targeted to serve as the third runway for Portland International Airport—which purchased the island in

1969—a feature that would have stretched across the narrow channels separating the island from the mainland, turning much of the island into deforested tarmac. However, the very thing that most threatened the island is ultimately what served to save it. Public opposition, and financial constraints caused the Port of Portland to abandon the runway project and noise and safety regulations associated with the nearby airport precluded most forms of development. Instead, the Port used Government Island as a mitigation site to compensate for natural resource impacts from the airport just across the channel, thus ushering in an era of restoration.

In March 1999, the Port of Portland signed a ninety-nine-year lease with Oregon State Parks to manage Government Island as part of the state park system. The combined island interiors include more than 800 acres of cottonwood forest, 600 acres of meadow, 500 acres of wetland, and the 432-acre Jewett Lake, which is mostly off limits to the general public. However, state parks has installed two massive boat docks for use by the general public on the north side of the island. Restrooms are located on Government, Lemon, and McGuire Islands, and overnight camping is permitted below ordinary high water (the vegetation line) around the perimeter beaches and in limited upland areas where picnic tables have been provided for visitors. Trails along the north sides of Lemon and Government Islands facilitate day hikes where access is allowed. Canoers and kayakers can find solitude by following the shoreline to places where powerboats do not congregate.

The combination of Port and state park restoration efforts is slowly improving the ecological health of the islands, which, like most urban natural areas that have not been actively managed, have become infested with reed canarygrass, blackberry brambles, thistle, teasel, Scot's broom, and other invasive species. State parks recently removed a remnant herd of cattle from the island and barged them to the mainland.

Wildlife and Airports

Portland International Airport (PDX) has one of the most innovative wildlife management programs of any airport in the United States. Beginning in 1996, the Port of Portland moved away from lethal control strategies employed by most airports to control local wildlife populations that might pose a risk to air traffic. The Port began working with state and federal wildlife agencies, private consultants, Portland Audubon, and others to develop an innovative Wildlife Hazard Management Plan. Focusing on research, monitoring, and management of nearby wildlife habitat and wildlife populations, the plan reduces safety concerns while protecting native wildlife populations. For example, they learned that removing local nesting birds of prey, as is still done today at many airports, actually increases risk to airplanes by creating a vacuum that new birds of prey quickly fill. The nesting birds know the landscape and avoid airplanes while also patrolling their territories to keep inexperienced birds of prey away. Today, many elements of the PDX plan are now being copied at airports across the United States.

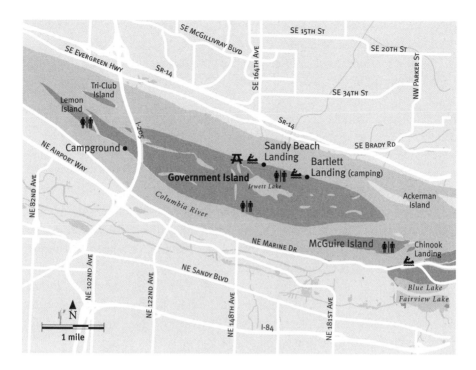

Unfortunately, two bulls escaped the roundup and remain at large. Longtime Government Island Ranger John Cowen notes that fortunately "rubbing two male cows together does not produce more cows" so when these lone fugitives succumb to the vagaries of age or the jaws of coyotes, the era of cattle grazing will finally be over.

Owing to its size, diverse mosaic of habitat types, and relative inaccessibility, it stands today as one of the metro region's true biodiversity hotspots. A variety of sensitive status wildlife species including western painted turtles, red-legged frogs, bald eagles, peregrine falcons, pileated woodpeckers, willow and olive-side flycatchers, western meadowlarks, horned grebes, red-necked grebes, buffleheads, and purple martins can be found on the island. The shallow-water habitat surrounding the islands provides critical habitat for federally listed juvenile salmon and steelhead to rest, forage, and escape from predators as they migrate to the ocean—an especially important feature in an otherwise heavily developed stretch of the Columbia River system.

In 2003, the Audubon Society of Portland designated Government Island as an Important Bird Area, one of only ninety-seven such sites in Oregon and approximately two thousand sites nationwide. In 2010, the Port of Portland, Audubon, and the City of Portland developed an innovative agreement that will result in the restoration of three hundred acres of grassland habitat on the island to provide habitat for streaked horned larks, a rapidly disappearing species and a candidate for listing under the Endangered Species Act. Wildlife populations on the island are closely monitored to ensure that restoration activities do not create wildlife hazards for flights arriving and departing from the nearby airport.

For the non-motorized naturalist, reaching the island is no mean feat and should not be attempted by inexperienced paddlers. The Columbia moves fast and strong near the islands and your journey will take you near shipping lanes and through waters that can be heavily traversed by powerboats. Pilings, channel markers, and other obstructions create unpredictable currents that can spin you and sink you without warning. Be diligent; take some time as you paddle to enjoy the osprey that nest on the pilings and channel markers that line your journey.

Motorboaters tend to congregate along the northern side of the island, so the southern portions lend themselves to greater solitude and wildlife viewing opportunities. The narrow channel between McGuire and Government Islands is serene, and the beaches provide spots to picnic or camp. A nice base camp can be created here for further boat- or beach-based exploring.

For the patient, quiet, adventurous traveler, Government Island can provide some of the best wildlife viewing in the metropolitan region. Please respect the areas that have been set aside for some of the region's most sensitive and imperiled wildlife species, pack out what you bring in, and keep dogs on leash at all times.

Access

Much of the interior of the five-island complex is not accessible to the public. There is a hiking trail on the north side of Government Island, and beaches below ordinary high water allow public access.

How to Get There

BOAT ACCESS ONLY: Public boat launches are located in Oregon at Chinook Landing and the 42nd Street Gleason Boat Ramp and in Vancouver at Vancouver Clark Public Park and Camas-Washougal Marina. The Chinook Landing boat ramp is the closest to the islands with a travel distance of less than a half mile to the eastern tip of McGuire Island. Circumnavigating the entire complex exceeds fifteen miles.

By Mary Coolidge and Bob Sallinger

More information: Oregon State Parks

Sauvie Island

SAUVIE ISLAND WAS FORMED one million years ago during the Pleistocene Epoch, when sediment was carried down the Columbia River with rains and snowmelt and was deposited at a ledge of large rocks. Through those aeons, soil accumulated in minute increments, and the ledge became the island's northern end. Each year the inundation continued, with annual freshets layering mud and sand, to a depth of thirty to fifty feet. Eventually the earth was shaped into soft, rolling contours, peppered with dozens of lakes and ponds. The resulting island is a river-bottom landscape unique in the West.

The island lies at the confluence of the Willamette and Columbia Rivers, a mostly narrow body of land approximately fifteen miles long and four miles wide, almost identical in size and shape to Manhattan Island. But Sauvie's twenty-four thousand acres are much differently settled—home to about five hundred households of humans and three hundred species of wildlife. The southern half of the island is graced with fertile farmland, sprouting farm markets and U-pick berry and flower businesses that produce bountiful, luscious harvests.

The twelve thousand acres of the northern half are managed as a Wildlife Area by the Oregon Department of Fish and Wildlife. Aimed at preserving and developing habitat for wintering waterfowl, the island is a major stop on the Pacific Flyway, and its land and waters are host to astounding wildlife spectacles.

On Sauvie Island, the seasons unfold with magnificent flourish. In spring, trees and wildflowers burst into bloom, and avian courtship dances are choreographed in the sky. The wild roses of summer sweeten the air, and scrumptious trailside blackberries tempt with thoughts of whipped-cream topped cobblers. Fall, like spring, brings the great Flyway migration, and a landscape speckled in brilliant golds and scarlets. Winter reveals nests in bare branches, ponds newly created with each rainy day, and once in a while, a carpeting of snow, daintily etched with the tracks of wild creatures.

A winter birdwatcher's journal might show on various days twenty-one bald eagles, a flock of a thousand snow geese, two hundred fifty sandhill cranes, eight hundred Canada geese, and seven hundred pintail ducks. A morning jaunt to a few favorite spots might turn up rough-legged hawks, red-tailed hawks, northern harriers, dozens of songbirds, bufflehead, ring-necked and wood ducks, and a pair of American kestrels.

Native to the island was the Multnomah tribe of the Chinook Indians. At one time they numbered about two thousand, living in villages of cedar longhouses. The distinguished people of the tribe were "flatheads," derived from the custom of tying newborn babies to a flat board with a piece of wood across the brow, pressuring the skull to flatten in a continuous line from crown to nose.

They lived barefoot and bare legged, clothed in animal skins and cedar bark. One of the food mainstays was wapato, a wetland tuber with arrow-shaped leaves also known as arrowhead or wild potato. Roasted fresh on embers, dried and stored, or traded, wapato were harvested by the tribeswomen, who waded out alongside a canoe and dug with their toes to find and loosen the mud-bound bulbs. Small patches of wapato can still be found today along some of the island lake shores.

Wapato Island was the name given by Lewis and Clark, who literally put the place on the map during their explorations of 1805 and 1806. Over the next decades, the native population weathered outbreaks of diseases, including smallpox and tuberculosis brought by the white man. Then in 1828, a horrifying epidemic of a fever known as the ague swept across the land and within three years all the Indians had died.

By 1916, the island came to be named for Laurent Sauvé, a French dairyman working for the Hudson's Bay Company at Fort Vancouver. Four hundred head of cattle were swum across the Columbia River from the fort to produce butter and cheese that the company sold to Russian settlements in Alaska.

The island was resettled in the 1850s, when immigrants arrived and divided parcels based on the new Donation Land Act, which allowed a married couple to claim 640 acres. A number of working farms on the island today can be traced back to pioneers that set out from Missouri across the Oregon Trail.

The farming tradition continues across the southern half of the island, protected from flooding by surrounding dikes. The twelve-mile loop of Gillihan-Reeder-Sauvie Island roads is a popular bike route, a flat road past scenic farm fields with a stunning backdrop on a blue-sky "Four Mountain Day" of Mounts Hood, Adams, St. Helens, and Rainier.

The northern wildlife area is one of a few remaining vestiges of something akin to the region's original wetlands, with twenty-one lakes as well as streams, sloughs, channels, and the meandering Gilbert River. It's a paddler's paradise. Boat ramps are sited at Oak Island, Gilbert River, and Steelman Lake. There's also the Old Ferry Boat Ramp with access to the Multnomah Channel, and St. Helens boat ramp with access into Cunningham Slough and Lake. The possibilities for gunkholing are endless and likely to result in sightings of a multitude of great blue herons, belted kingfisher, and maybe a beaver, osprey, or bald eagle. Beaver-gnawed trees dot the shorelines, the remains finely sculpted with hundreds of tiny, chiseled curves.

Along the Columbia River are some of the metropolitan area's finest sand beaches, with one section clothing-optional. Crowded in summer or a gorgeous day in any season, the miles of beaches also offer serene strolls in the off-season or under gray skies.

Because the Sauvie Island Wildlife Area was purchased and is maintained by hunting license fees and firearm taxes, one of its main purposes is to provide public hunting. Much of the wildlife area is off limits to birders and naturalists during hunting season, typically from October 1 to mid-January. To keep the enormous flocks of geese from devastating early farm crops, closures at some sites may extend until April 15. While continuing to provide hunting opportunities remains a high priority, a new management plan for the wildlife area developed in 2009 recognizes the importance of managing the refuge for both game and non-game species, and prioritizes maintaining healthy wildlife populations over other uses.

By Donna Matrazzo, illustration by Elayne Barclay

More information: Oregon Department of Fish and Wildlife

Visiting Sauvie Island

To get to the island sites, Sauvie Island Bridge is approximately ten miles northwest of downtown Portland on Highway 30.

A parking permit is required to park on state refuge land. Permits, for the day or all year, can be obtained at the small Sauvie Island grocery next to the bridge. They can also be bought at the convenience store in Linnton if you arrive at the island early in the morning before the Sauvie Island store opens.

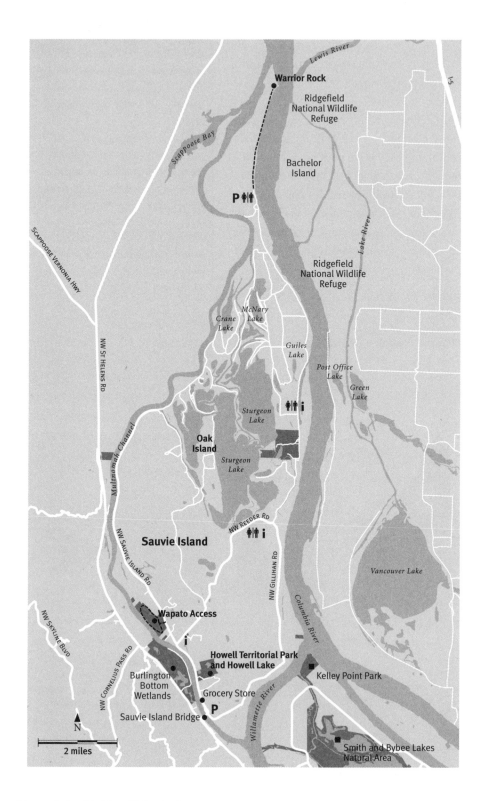

Lewis River

Warrior Rock

Ridgefield
National Wildlife
Refuge

Scappoose Bay

Bachelor
Island

SCAPPOOSE VERNONIA HWY

P ♦♦

Lake River

Ridgefield
National Wildlife
Refuge

NW ST HELENS RD

*McNary
Lake*

*Crane
Lake*

*Guiles
Lake*

*Post Office
Lake*

*Green
Lake*

*Sturgeon
Lake*

♦♦ i

**Oak
Island**

Multnomah Channel

*Sturgeon
Lake*

NW REEDER RD

♦♦ i

Sauvie Island

NW SAUVIE ISLAND RD

NW GILLIHAN RD

Vancouver Lake

Columbia River

NW SKYLINE BLVD

Wapato Access

i

NW CORNELIUS PASS RD

**Howell Territorial Park
and Howell Lake**

Kelley Point Park

Burlington
Bottom
Wetlands

Grocery Store

P

Sauvie Island Bridge

Willamette River

N

2 miles

Smith and Bybee Lakes
Natural Area

I-5

Howell Territorial Park and Howell Lake

LOCATION: NW Sauvie Island Road, approximately one mile north of the Sauvie Island Bridge; Bybee-Howell House at 13901 NW Howell Park Road **ACTIVITIES:** Hiking, Wildlife viewing **FACILITIES:** Restrooms, Parking, Trails, Picnic area/shelter, Interpretive signs/info **FEES AND REGULATIONS:** Restricted hours; No pets allowed **HIKING DIFFICULTY:** Easy **HIGHLIGHTS:** Excellent winter waterfowl watching at Howell Lake wetland; Large oak trees provide good views of forest birds, especially the white-breasted nuthatch; Barn owls near the fir trees; Historic Bybee-Howell House **PUBLIC TRANSIT:** TriMet bus 17

The graceful and authentically restored Bybee-Howell House, centerpiece of Howell Territorial Park, is Sauvie Island's only remaining house built by Oregon Trail homesteaders. In 1873, the Bybees sold the property to John and Joseph Howell, who founded a successful dairy farm on the site.

Today the ninety-three-acre park showcases Oregon's cultural and natural history in a pastoral setting that features an agricultural museum and a fruit orchard planted with cuttings from historic nineteenth century trees. Seven oak trees in a pasture comprise a remnant of the savannah-oak communities historic to island uplands. The stand of Douglas fir trees to the north of the house is a great place to look for barn owls. Even if you can't find the barn owls themselves, look for their pellets, which can be found all over the ground.

Howell Lake is actually a freshwater wetland. The two dominant plant species are reed canarygrass and soft rush. Wapato—the wild potato that was an important food source for Native Americans—still grows along the eastern edge. One of the few places west of the Cascades to spot yellow-headed blackbirds, the lake is home to dozens of species of birds, including green-winged teal, wood ducks, great blue herons, American coots, and common mergansers.

Large white gourds suspended from high posts near the lake provide nesting sites for purple martins, a sensitive species that once nested mainly in tree cavities.

A section of the Gilbert River defines the park's eastern boundary, and the site also contains other large natural wetlands and small mixed deciduous forest areas. Combined, these create good habitats for a multitude of species, such as California quail, barn owls, ring-necked pheasants, and reptiles like the western fence lizard.

While California ground squirrels are the most visible mammal, readily seen scurrying

Owl Pellets

Many raptors eat their prey whole. However, they are unable to digest certain body parts, such as fur, bones, beaks, feathers, insect exoskeletons, and claws. They concentrate these parts into oblong pellets in their stomach, which are then regurgitated. Pellets on the ground are often the most obvious sign of raptors roosting or nesting overhead. Dissecting pellets can be a fun activity to do with kids and a great way to learn about what the birds of prey are eating.

—Bob Sallinger

about the meadows and trees, other mammals frequently spotted are black-tailed deer, red foxes, coyote, and beaver.

Access

Visitors can roam the grounds surrounding the restored 1858 Bybee-Howell House, orchard, and fir grove. Groups can reserve areas of the park for picnics and events.

How to Get There

BY CAR, BIKE OR HIKE: From Sauvie Island Bridge follow NW Sauvie Island Road for approximately one mile and turn right on Howell Park Road. **PUBLIC TRANSIT:** TriMet bus 17 to the parking lot beneath the Sauvie Island Bridge, approximately one mile to the site

By Donna Matrazzo, illustration by Virginia Church

More information: Metro

> **Refer to map on page 320**

Oak Island Trail

LOCATION: At end of Oak Island Road, nearly seven miles from the Sauvie Island Bridge **ACTIVITIES:** Hiking, Wildlife viewing **FACILITIES:** Restrooms, Parking, Unpaved trails **FEES AND REGULATIONS:** Parking fees; Restricted hours; Pets on leash **HIKING DIFFICULTY:** Easy **HIGHLIGHTS:** The wooded oak habitat is resonant with birdsong from dozens of species **PUBLIC TRANSIT:** TriMet bus 17

Old oak trees, with their gnarled branches and corrugated trunks, line the trail and shape a wonderful woodland shelter for a multitude of bird species. Oak Island is no longer an island but a narrow peninsula jutting north between Steelman and Sturgeon Lakes.

This is a place where naturalists like to "pish"—throwing out a "pschee-pschee" sound that many birds seem to regard as a distress signal, which then lures them out in the open to check out the scene.

Frequently seen birds include song, white-crowned, and golden-crowned sparrows, and the occasional white-throated sparrow in winter; western scrub-jays, white-breasted nuthatches (an oak forest specialty), brown creepers, golden-crowned and ruby-crowned kinglets, black-capped chickadees, and in spring many species of warblers. Their various songs and sounds overlap and harmonize to fill the air with rich melodies, pierced by the sharp, flirty whistle of red-winged blackbirds. Years ago, you could count on seeing Lewis's woodpeckers on Oak Island, but the starlings and house sparrows seem to have pushed them out.

From the tree-lined woods, the trail opens up to a wide meadow. Beyond it are the waters of Wagonwheel Hole and Steelman Lake, with the thousand-foot Tualatin Mountains in the background. Bald eagles are regularly seen in these oaks in winter, and northern harriers sweep low over the fields, harrying their prey.

The next long stretch of trail traces the shoreline of Sturgeon Lake. Here great blue herons, sandhill cranes, Canada, cackling, and snow geese, and many species of ducks feed and flourish with the seasons. A solitary bench sits facing the lake and the view beyond—the Cascade Mountains and their snow-capped volcanoes stretching across the horizon.

Hunting Closures

In addition to closing part of the wildlife area to non-hunters during hunting season, Oregon Department of Fish and Wildlife also alternates hunt and non-hunt days throughout the season. The birding experience can be quite different depending on which day you choose.

For a seasonal schedule: Oregon Department of Fish and Wildlife

Access

The flat, grassy trail leads directly from the parking lot, with signs for the nearly three-mile loop. Currently the area remains closed from October 1 through April 15.

How to Get There

BY CAR OR BIKE: From the Sauvie Island Bridge follow NW Sauvie Island Road north for approximately 2.5 miles. Turn right at the junction with NW Reeder Road and continue about 1.2 miles to Oak Island Road. Turn left and follow the paved road for three miles to the end of the pavement and the entrance to the Sauvie Island Wildlife Area. Continue on the paved road for half a mile, where you'll come to a four-way junction. Continue straight ahead and at 0.4 mile you'll come to the trailhead. **PUBLIC TRANSIT:** TriMet bus 17 to the parking lot beneath the Sauvie Island Bridge; then approximately 6.7 miles to the trailhead.

By Donna Matrazzo

More information: Oregon Department of Fish and Wildlife

> **Refer to map on page 320**

Wapato Access Greenway State Park Trail

LOCATION: NW Sauvie Island Road, approximately three miles from the Sauvie Island Bridge **ACTIVITIES:** Hiking, Biking, Horseback riding, Fishing, Wildlife viewing **FACILITIES:** Parking, Unpaved trails, Picnic area/shelter **FEES AND REGULATIONS:** Restricted hours; Pets on leash **HIKING DIFFICULTY:** Easy **HIGHLIGHTS:** Excellent birding year-round, particularly outstanding during the winter months when abundant bald eagles join many other extraordinary species **PUBLIC TRANSIT:** TriMet bus 17

Once a well-kept secret, Wapato Access Greenway, formerly known as Virginia Lake, has grown in popularity in recent years. Oregon State Parks has invested in trail and parking lot improvements, habitat restoration, and interpretive signage. Now the small parking lot overflows on sunny days.

One of the park's most interesting features is the seasonal lake, which is rich with abundant and extraordinary birds in winter. Water levels fluctuate noticeably from day to day. Locals recall ice skating on the lake in years past. A viewing blind near the southern end of the lake provides a concealed spot for waterfowl watching.

The park is managed as a natural area with the trail curving past wildflower meadows, an upland forest that contains mostly big-leaf maple, western redcedar and western hemlock; and a coniferous forest of Douglas firs. In spring and early summer, sweet-scented wild roses, bursts of lupine, and tall golden stalks of mullein stipple the landscape, while August transforms the path into blackberry-picking heaven.

One trail spur leads to Hadley's Landing, a floating dock on the Multnomah Channel. Wapato Park is part of the Willamette River Greenway, and a portion of the trail follows the Multnomah Channel, with views of the Tualatin Mountains beyond.

Birding is excellent year-round. Listen for sora and Virginia rails, and keep an eye out for red-breasted sapsuckers and belted kingfishers. Songbirds present include bushtits, red-breasted nuthatches, Bewick's and Pacific wrens, American goldfinches, ruby-crowned kinglets, and western tanagers. The frog chorus is raucous in spring. Brush rabbits are commonly seen; rarer are sightings of coyote, fox, and black-tailed deer.

Access
An unpaved path makes a two-mile loop around a seasonal lake.

How to Get There
BY CAR OR BIKE: From the Sauvie Island Bridge follow NW Sauvie Island Road north to the junction with NW Reeder Road. Continue on Sauvie Island Road for one half mile. **PUBLIC TRANSIT:** TriMet bus 17 to the parking lot beneath the Sauvie Island bridge, then three miles.

By Donna Matrazzo

More information: Oregon Parks and Recreation Department

Warrior Rock Lighthouse Trail

LOCATION: At the far northeastern end of the island, approximately 15 miles from the Sauvie Island Bridge **ACTIVITIES:** Hiking, Horseback riding, Fishing, Wildlife viewing **FACILITIES:** Restrooms, Parking, Unpaved trails **FEES AND REGULATIONS:** Parking fees, Restricted hours, Pets on leash **HIKING DIFFICULTY:** Easy **HIGHLIGHTS:** One of the loveliest Columbia River beaches in the Portland-Vancouver region; Views of Ridgefield National Wildlife Area across the river; The lighthouse is an enticing locale for a picnic lunch **PUBLIC TRANSIT:** TriMet bus 17

In October 1792, after learning of the Columbia River from Boston voyager Robert Gray—captain of the *Columbia Rediviva*, for which the river was named—British Lieutenant William Broughton, as part of a naval expedition led by Captain George Vancouver, was dispatched to explore the great river. As legend has it, when Broughton landed with his crew—purportedly the first white people to step foot on what is now Sauvie Island—one hundred fifty warriors of the Multnomah tribe of Chinook Indians paddled up in two dozen canoes to greet them. Indians from another river tribe accompanying Broughton explained his mission, and the islanders welcomed the men, who stayed to trade and slept there that night. Thus, Warrior Rock was named to mark the occasion.

The spot is marked today with the Warrior Rock Lighthouse, a charming outpost near the northern tip of Sauvie Island. The most interesting way to hike there and back is to follow the forest trail in one direction and walk along the beach heading the opposite way. There may seem to be a few spur trails heading inland. Ignore them and take the route that parallels the shore.

Through the woods, black cottonwood trees abound; in summer their white fluff scatters along the path. River views are framed by the trees, with glimpses of immense barges and ships piloting up and down the Columbia, sometimes almost silently, followed by a swooshing sound as their wakes wash with force against the eroding banks.

Wild roses, herbs, and blackberries tangle beyond the path. At dusk on clear days, the tangerine orb of the sun glints brilliantly through the trees, while casting "magic hour" coloring on the woods across the river.

Near the lighthouse are the remains of a small house. The roof and walls long ago destroyed by fire, but a stone fireplace and chimney remain, giving testament to a measure of the remote island life of a lighthouse keeper.

A stroll along the Columbia's shore can take on the personality of the day's weather. Sometimes the river is calm, shrouded in fog. On other days, scudding clouds and wind whip the water into white-capped breakers. Tracks of raccoons, great blue herons, and shorebirds lace the wide, sandy beach.

Access

The trail is a six-mile round trip over fairly level ground. Options include following a mostly grassy roadbed or walking along the sandy shore of the Columbia River. Cows graze in the area and cow pies spatter the trail. Unlike most of the Sauvie Island Wildlife Area, which is closed during the hunting season (typically mid-October through mid-April), this area remains accessible, although people are hunting there until the end of January.

How to Get There

BY CAR OR BIKE: From the Sauvie Island Bridge, follow NW Sauvie Island Road northwest for approximately 2.5 miles; right at the junction with NW Reeder Road and continue 4.3 miles to its junction with Gillihan Road. Continue north on NW Reeder Road; at 6.1 miles the pavement ends. Follow the unpaved road another 2.3 miles to the parking lot; the trail begins at its northeast corner. **PUBLIC TRANSIT:** TriMet bus 17 to the parking lot beneath the Sauvie Island Bridge; then 15 miles to the site.

By Donna Matrazzo

More information: Oregon Department of Fish and Wildlife

> Refer to map on page 320

Raptor Road Trip

Every winter one of our region's great spectacles begins to unfold. Eagles and other raptors, along with thousands of sandhill cranes, several races of Canada goose, hundreds of thousands of ducks, snow geese, tundra swans, and other birds congregate on Sauvie Island.

While one can reach any of the hot raptor spots on the island by bicycle, during the cold winter months a warm car is preferable for a raptor road trip.

Out of hundreds of field trips, a winter's day afield on Sauvie Island looking for raptors, sandhill cranes, and waterfowl is a favorite. When the sky is clear, or even if it's misty, you can see forever. Using a spotting scope is even better as you can spy birds on distant treetops or far across fields, lakes, and wetlands. The sunrise over Mount St. Helens and Mount Hood isn't too shabby either!

Start the trip at **the grocery strore ❶**, just across the Sauvie Island Bridge. The store will not only supply you with hot coffee and Jo-Jos or wonderfully unhealthy fried chicken legs, it also sells day or seasonal parking passes, which are required to park on state land.

From the store head due north along NW Sauvie Island Road, past Metro's Howell Territorial Park and make a stop at the **Oregon Department of Fish and Wildlife headquarters** to look at maps and to orient yourself. For wintering songbirds you might stop at **Wapato Lake**, but for raptors strike out for the favorite bald eagle "flyout" stakeout on the Sauvie Island dike road at the **Columbia-Multnomah County line**. There are very few places to park and it's illegal to park on the side of the road, so look for a couple of turnouts on the right-hand side. Try to walk onto the dike road a half hour before sunrise to make sure you're there before the eagles start flying from their old-growth forest roost onto the island.

Around the last week of October, eagles come from as far away as British Columbia to congregate at a variety of sites throughout the West. They are all heading to their favorite winter roost, where they will loaf around and feed on whatever prey is handy. In this case, the winter roost happens to be in federally owned, Bureau of Land Management old-

Guided Raptor Road Trip

For a deluxe, guided raptor experience with expert naturalists to spot birds for you, the annual Raptor Road Trip can't be beat. Each February, Audubon Society of Portland, Oregon Department of Fish and Wildlife, and Metro staff and volunteers gather on Sauvie Island with spotting scopes, binoculars, and hot chocolate, coffee, and treats. All you have to do is show up and follow the Raptor Road Trip route for a raptor and waterfowl extravaganza.

growth forest to the west of Sauvie Island in the headwaters of Dairy Creek in the Tualatin Basin. In addition to the warmer overnight forest lodging, the hordes of over-wintering ducks and geese attract them here during the cold months. Ever the opportunists, bald eagles will pretty much feed on whatever is closest at hand and easiest to procure. In areas like the Skagit in Washington, Glacier National Park in Montana, and the Chilkat in Alaska, they feed on dead, river-chilled salmon. At Sauvie Island, it's dead or injured waterfowl.

At dawn, if you look west toward the Tualatin Mountains, you will see small dark specks on the horizon. In just a few minutes it's clear you're looking at eagles. With surprising speed they glide, usually without a wing beat, close overhead as they commute to their diurnal roosts on the island. Sometimes they fly solo and sometimes in small groups, occasionally locking talons and wheeling about in what appears to be a game. Other times they make a beeline for the island. If it's a warm winter, it's not worth taking the dike flyout side trip as the eagles rarely fly back to their roost at night, instead preferring to hang out on the island.

Once the flyout show is over, turn around and head back to NW Reeder Road and out to the locked gate on Oak Island Road. As you drive the road, scan the fields to the right for sandhill cranes and the wetlands for waterfowl. Once you've reached the locked gate, look in the treetops for merlin, peregrine falcons,

Eagle Spotting

Is it a golden eagle or a bald eagle? An adult or a young eagle? While some people report seeing golden eagles on Sauvie Island, more often than not what they are seeing are young bald eagles, which take five years to get their white head and tail. Young bald eagles can be identified by large amounts of splotchy white feathers on their chest and underwings. An adult golden eagle, which lacks the white head of the bald eagle, has no white on its body and an immature golden eagle has squarish white wing "windows," not the splotchy white of an immature bald eagle.

northern harriers, red-tailed hawks, the occasional rough-legged hawk, and both immature and adult bald eagles. While walking back from the gate, we usually scare up a host of songbirds, including spotted towhees, golden-crowned sparrows, song sparrows, and less frequently a white-throated sparrow. But it's raptors we're after and they abound in this area. Oak Island always has large numbers of eagles and other predatory birds.

Now, retrace the route back to NW Reeder Road and head to **Coon Point**, where an elevated dike provides an amazing panorama for spotting-scope views of eagles at their nest in the far distance ❷, a great blue heron colony ❸, flocks of two hundred or more sandhill cranes in the distant agriculture fields ❹, and sometimes thousands of tundra swans and other waterfowl at the south end of Sturgeon Lake ❺. There are also port-a-potties at Coon Point.

Keep an eye on the large farm fields and you are virtually guaranteed to see a northern harrier flying low, harrying prey. Harriers, formerly called marsh hawks, have owl-like facial discs, which amplify sound so that they hear voles and other small mammals scurrying in the grass ahead. A white rump patch, slightly up-tilted wings, and low-flying behavior are sure signs you've got a harrier. Follow one for a few minutes, and it will invariably pounce on something. If successful, it will often fly to the nearest fence post to enjoy its meal.

This is also a great place to see merlins—small, dark falcons that winter in Oregon but breed up north. Merlins are one of three wintering falcons, along with kestrels and peregrines, that you are likely to see on the island.

In recent years, Audubon has worked with Oregon Department of Fish and Wildlife to remove willows, reed canarygrass, and other vegetation that had grown around the wetlands in the foreground. This was done to create mudflats for migrating shorebirds and inadvertently has made viewing wintering waterfowl easier.

The second to the last stop, more for waterfowl than raptors, is at Oregon Department of Fish and Wildlife's **birding blind 6**, 2.8 miles north at the intersection of NW Reeder Road and NW Gillihan Loop Road. As you drive there, keep an eye out for a large eagle nest and a new great blue heron colony on the left, but always be careful to look for cyclists and oncoming cars of course!

If it's not a hunt day, you can count on a variety of ducks, swans, and oftentimes snow geese on the shallow lake in front of the blind. Waterfowl include ring-necked ducks, lesser scaup, ruddy ducks, northern shovelers, bufflehead, gadwall, and mallards. Pied-billed grebes and hundreds of American coot use the pond as well. If it's a hunt day you'll see very few ducks on the pond. Important information for coffee drinkers: there's a port-a-potty here.

The last stop is **Rentenaar Road 7**, another two miles north on Reeder Road on the left. Rentenaar is a favorite stop for sparrow devotees or for a diversion from viewing raptors. Check out the thick Himalayan blackberry hedges along both sides of the unpaved road for Harris's sparrows, white-throated sparrows, and our common song, fox, and golden-crowned sparrows. If it's only raptors you're after though, head straight to the end of a usually very muddy drive and an equally muddy parking lot (wear appropriate footwear). From the parking lot, head up on another dike to scope out the surrounding fields and treetops. This is usually a great spot

A Feast in the Mud

Shorebirds are long-legged and long-billed birds built to pick worms, insects, and crustaceans out of the mud and shallow water. A few species, such as the spotted sandpiper and killdeer breed here, but nearly two dozen species pass through the area on their incredible migration from the sub-Arctic to Central and South America. The mudflats that they depend on to survive are rapidly disappearing due to development and reduction of seasonal flooding. Restoration projects like the one at Coon Point ensure that these very cool, long-distance migrants will continue to have places to stop, rest, and forage.

—Bob Sallinger

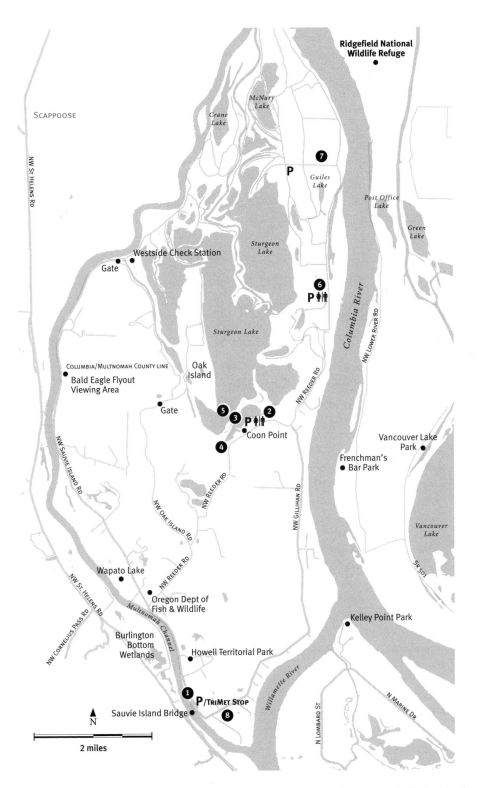

Ridgefield National
Wildlife Refuge

SCAPPOOSE

NW ST HELENS RD

McNary
Lake

Crane
Lake

P **7**

Guiles
Lake

Post Office
Lake

Green
Lake

Sturgeon
Lake

Columbia River

NW LOWER RIVER RD

Westside Check Station

Gate

P **6** 🚹🚺

Sturgeon Lake

NW REEDER RD

COLUMBIA/MULTNOMAH COUNTY LINE

Oak
Island

Bald Eagle Flyout
Viewing Area

Gate

5 **3** P 🚹🚺 **2**

4

Coon Point

Vancouver Lake
Park

Frenchman's
Bar Park

NW GILLIHAN RD

NW SAUVIE ISLAND RD

NW REEDER RD

NW OAK ISLAND RD

Vancouver
Lake

SR 501

Wapato Lake

NW ST. HELENS RD

NW CORNELIUS PASS RD

Oregon Dept of
Fish & Wildlife

Multnomah Channel

Kelley Point Park

Burlington
Bottom
Wetlands

Howell Territorial Park

Willamette River

N LOMBARD ST

N MARINE DR

1 P/TRIMET STOP

Sauvie Island Bridge

8

▲
N

2 miles

for the large, dark-plumed, dusky Canada geese, which winter here from their breeding grounds on Alaska's Copper River Delta. The dusky Canada goose is imperiled due to the 1964 Alaska earthquake that uplifted its nesting grounds, making them accessible to foxes and other predators. Hunters are trained to distinguish the relatively rare dusky from other races of Canada goose. When too many duskies are shot, the hunting season is closed down; so good identification ability is a highly valued hunting skill.

If there's time to scope for wintering loons, drive another three or four miles to the road's end and check out the Columbia River. Loons aside, finish off the raptor road tour in a loop by heading back to NW Reeder and NW Gillihan Loop Roads. Continue south on Gillihan Loop, keeping an eye on either side of the road for more sandhill cranes, and in the wetlands on the left-hand side ❽ for waterfowl, including green-winged teal and American and Eurasian wigeon, which like the shallow, muddy water margins and grassy fields. Northern harriers frequent the grassy fields as well.

Hawk Spotting

Is it a red-tailed or a rough-legged hawk? Our abundant red-tailed hawks can be found on Sauvie Island year-round, although they are present in larger numbers during the winter. The red-tail has a dark-light-dark pattern (brown head, whitish breast, and dark belly band). It also has telltale white scapulars (or shoulder blades) when viewed from behind, and the adults have the classic rusty-red-orange tail. Rough-leggeds, which winter here in small numbers from their arctic nesting grounds, have an eagle-like white head and chest, and big black splotches, or wrists, on the underside of their wings. They also have a distinct white rump, much like a northern harrier. Rough-leggeds will sometimes hover like an American kestrel.

—Mike Houck

For true fanatics, one last stop can be had on the return trip at **Howell Territorial Park**, off Sauvie Island Road on Howell Park Road about a mile after the bridge. James Francis Bybee moved to Oregon in 1847 and built the historic farmhouse that still stands on this property in 1856 after striking it rich in the California Gold Rush. The 120-acre park is a nice place for a picnic, and the stand of Douglas fir trees to the north of the house is a great place to look for barn owls. Even if you can't find the barn owls, look for their pellets, which can be found all over the ground. Wander to the back of the property to look for more waterfowl on Howell Lake and for red-tailed hawks, harriers, and kestrels hunting over the farm fields.

How to Get There and Distances

BY CAR AND BIKE: From downtown Portland, travel approximately 10 miles northwest on Highway 30 to the Sauvie Island Bridge. From the Sauvie Island store to the bald eagle fly-out it's 8 miles. From the store to Oak Island, if you skip the fly-out, it's 6.8 miles. From Oak Island to Rentenaar Road it's another 11.3 miles and back to the bridge is also about 11 miles. All told, if you do the entire trip, including the bald eagle fly-out, it's

51 miles round-trip. If you skip the bald eagle fly-out, the on-island trip is about 30 miles.

By Mike Houck and Bob Sallinger, illustration by Virginia Church

More information: Oregon Department of Fish and Wildlife; Metro; Audubon Society of Portland

Winged Winter

BY FEBRUARY, EVEN OLD MAN WINTER has grown a bit morose, with lichens sprouting on his sleeves and slugs in his sodden pockets. Yet, with hunting season and the rush of the holidays behind us, late winter is the perfect time to grab a raincoat and head out to see the ducks, geese, and other winged migrants that converge on Portland's ponds and lakes each year.

The Pacific Flyway

Our winter visitors come from boreal ponds rimmed with stunted spruce, prairie potholes, or arctic waters where clouds of mosquitoes quickly give way to ice. Bufflehead, northern pintail, lesser scaup, northern shoveler, green-winged teal, American wigeon, gadwall, tundra swan, cackling geese—birds of every size and feather—funnel south and west from Alaska and Canada along the Pacific Flyway. This broad migration route has been used by generations of waterfowl traveling from nesting to wintering grounds and back again. The birds fly day and night guided by the sun and stars, by landmarks such as mountains and river valleys, perhaps even the white stag beacon of our *Portland Oregon* sign in Old Town, as well as by magnetic fields. Theirs is an ancient navigation system that rivals our own GPS systems and has only recently yielded to scientific study.

However much we understand the mechanics of migration, there is still something mystical about a skein of geese in a clear, cold sky. Even boisterous Canada geese, known to raise the hackles of many a park manager, seem transformed in their seasonal flight. These large "honkers" are, in winter, joined by the smaller cackling geese, which despite their name, seem much more mannerly. Snow geese from as far away as Siberia home in on the Columbia River, stopping at Ridgefield National Wildlife Refuge and Sauvie Island to rest and feed. Whether settling in for the duration or simply passing through, geese seem to tug at something in our own restless spirit.

Nature's Buffet

During winter, resident Canada geese, mallards, and wood ducks that frequent our waterways share their table, so to speak, with an assortment of dabblers, divers, and fish eaters. The majority of our wintering duck species are dabblers or puddle ducks, such as American wigeon, green-winged teal, and the striking northern pintail with its creamy white neck. On a clear day in February 2010, volunteers with Metro's waterfowl monitoring program counted over five hundred pintail using the recently reclaimed wetlands at Gotter Prairie. Even greater numbers can be seen at Jackson

Bottom Wetlands Preserve. Pintail and other dabblers feast primarily on aquatic vegetation by tipping head down and tail up, an efficient, if undignified, feeding strategy. You will see most dabblers near the margins of small ponds and lakes, such as the Crystal Springs Rhododendron Garden, where pondweeds, grasses, sedges, and emergent vegetation are most plentiful.

Diving ducks, such as lesser scaup and canvasback, submerge completely when feeding, collecting roots and tubers that dabblers can't reach or snatching small mollusks and crustaceans from lake sediments. Diving ducks tend to select larger water bodies, such as those found at the Tualatin River National Wildlife Refuge, where there is sufficient depth for feeding and adequate space for taking off and landing. Unlike dabblers, whose broader wings let them drop into or flush out of small, enclosed ponds, divers need a running start to get airborne. Thus, they are usually found toward the center of a lake and may be wary of disturbance.

Common and hooded mergansers, with their striking black and white plumage, are in a class unto themselves. Their long, narrow bills have serrated margins that allow them to catch and hold the small fish on which they feed almost exclusively, although crayfish, frogs, and dragonfly nymphs are on their menu in season.

Scoping Out the Action

Whether you visit a regional park such as Commonwealth Lake, a state or federal landholding like Sauvie Island or the Ridgefield refuge, or a Metro-owned natural area such as Smith and Bybee Lakes, binoculars or a spotting scope will help you truly appreciate the diversity and beauty of our winter waterfowl.

Optics bring into focus the jewel-green crescent encompassing the eye of the male green-winged teal, the stiff tail of the ruddy duck, the white-banded bill of a ring-necked duck, or the soft, subtle markings of the gadwall, a species increasing in the Portland area—according to Harry Nehls, the go-to guy on Oregon birds. Even with the naked eye, beginners can learn to distinguish a bufflehead from a hooded merganser, while more advanced birders spot the Eurasian wigeon among its American kin or flock to see the occasional errant smew.

Preserving Our Wetlands

Despite our rainy winters, puddle ducks can't just plop down in the middle of Main Street to rest and feed. Likewise, a flooded field may look enticing during a storm but can leave ducks high and dry when the water recedes. Wintering ducks and geese require bodies of fresh water of adequate depth and permanence, with vegetated borders and protection from predation and disturbance. Portland is fortunate to have many such areas, as outlined in this book, which contribute to the relative stability of our waterfowl populations.

Wetland preservation and restoration efforts, even when not directed specifically at waterfowl, benefit migrant and resident birds, as well as fish, amphibians, snakes, turtles, and mammals. The U.S. Fish and Wildlife Service, the Oregon Department of Fish and Wildlife, Metro, city and county agencies, the Audubon Society of Portland, Ducks Unlimited, local Friends groups, civic-minded corporations, and others have played an important role in preserving and restoring healthy wetland ecosystems.

When winter's short, dark days and incessant rain drive you to your local bistro or watering hole, brush the lichen from your sleeve and raise a glass to the many dedicated scientists, volunteers, advocates, and administrators who have helped keep the winged in Portland's winter.

By Connie Levesque, illustration by Elayne Barclay

Ridgefield National Wildlife Refuge

LOCATION: Refuge entrances are located north and south of old town Ridgefield, Visitor Contact Station at 1071 South Hillhurst Road, Ridgefield, WA **ACTIVITIES:** Hiking, Paddling, Boating, Fishing, Wildlife viewing, Hunting **FACILITIES:** Restrooms, Parking, Unpaved trails, Visitor center, Picnic area/shelter, Canoe/kayak launch (from Ridgefield Marina), Wildlife viewing structure, Interpretive signs/info **FEES AND REGULATIONS:** Entrance fees; Restricted hours, dawn to dusk, various units are subject to seasonal closures; No pets **HIKING DIFFICULTY:** Easy **HIGHLIGHTS:** One of the best places in the region to view wintering waterfowl; Substantial population of dusky Canada geese is of special note; Over 200 bird species; River otters, beavers, and red fox **HISTORIC SITE:** Replica Chinookan Plankhouse **PUBLIC TRANSIT:** No direct service

The mild, rainy winter climate of the lower Columbia River Valley provides an ideal environment for migrating and wintering waterfowl that travel through the Pacific Flyway west of the Cascade Mountains. The Ridgefield National Wildlife Refuge offers extensive resting and feeding areas for migrating birds on the many sloughs, ponds, and shallow lakes bordering the edges of the lower Columbia River. Each fall, ducks, geese, and swans leave their northern nesting areas and migrate down the Pacific Coast to escape the Alaskan winter. By late fall, up to two hundred thousand waterfowl can be found between Portland and the mouth of the Columbia River. The most conspicuous species are mallard, northern shoveler, American wigeon, green-winged teal, northern pintail, Canada and cackling goose, and tundra swan.

Over two hundred species have been identified throughout the various seasons. Sandhill cranes, shorebirds, and a great variety of songbirds stop at the refuge during spring and fall migrations. Several waterfowl species remain on the refuge to nest; they are joined by songbirds such as marsh and house wrens, bushtits, warbling vireo, several warblers, and all of our area's swallows. Year-round residents include mallards, cinnamon teal, great blue herons, and red-tailed hawks. Black-tailed deer are the largest mammal on the refuge. Coyote, fox, raccoon, skunk, beaver, river otter, and brush rabbit are occasionally seen. It is common to see nutria, a rodent native to South America and introduced into the Columbia River basin in the 1930s, burrowing and feeding along dikes and ditch banks.

An Alaskan Earthquake Creates a Refuge

A violent earthquake that rocked southern Alaska in 1964 played a role in establishing the refuge. Repeated shock waves lifted the Copper River Delta six feet, changing, in a matter of minutes, the only area where dusky Canada geese had been nesting for centuries. Willow and alder trees invaded the higher, drier land, replacing marshy meadows that had once been goose nesting habitat. The resulting shrub thickets provided perfect cover for brown bears and coyotes, allowing them to approach nesting geese unnoticed. This altered habitat and increased predation greatly reduced

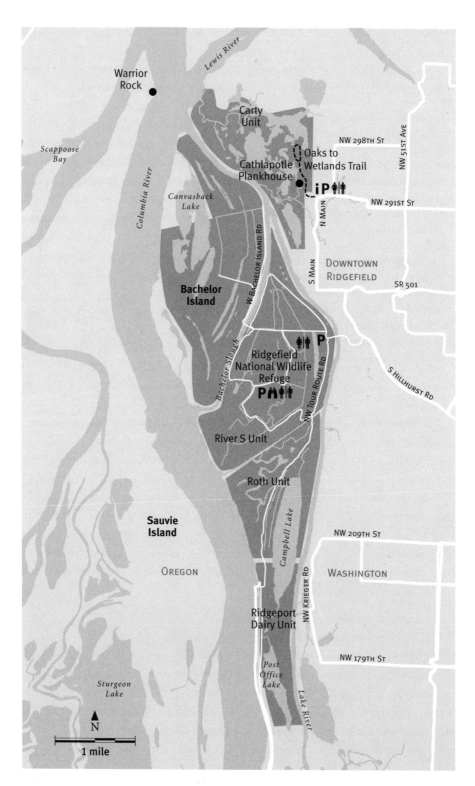

Warrior
Rock

Lewis River

Scappoose
Bay

Columbia River

Carty
Unit

Oaks to
Wetlands Trail

Cathlapotle
Plankhouse

NW 298TH ST

NW 51ST AVE

N MAIN

i P

NW 291ST ST

Canvasback
Lake

W BACHELOR ISLAND RD

S MAIN

DOWNTOWN
RIDGEFIELD

SR 501

**Bachelor
Island**

Bachelor Slough

Ridgefield
National Wildlife
Refuge

P

NW TOUR ROUTE RD

S HILLHURST RD

P

River S Unit

Roth Unit

**Sauvie
Island**

OREGON

Campbell Lake

NW 209TH ST

NW KRIEGER RD

WASHINGTON

Ridgeport
Dairy Unit

NW 179TH ST

Sturgeon
Lake

Post
Office
Lake

Lake River

N

1 mile

their opportunity to successfully hatch and raise their young, resulting in a decimated population.

Migratory waterfowl must endure the good and bad years on wintering grounds and summer nesting areas. When either the winter or summer habitat is disrupted, the other becomes much more important. Dusky Canada geese spend the winters along the lower Columbia River and in Oregon's Willamette Valley. While wildlife managers were unable to change the geology of the Copper River Delta, they could ensure that the geese and other species had secure wintering areas. Public lands were acquired to secure critical winter habitat that was at risk of development to aid in recovering and supporting the dusky geese and numerous other species. Thus, the result was the establishment of the Ridgefield National Wildlife Refuge in 1965, along with three other refuges in the Willamette Valley.

Unfortunately, much of the unprotected species-rich habitat along the lower Columbia River has continued to shrink due to diking, draining, filling, and development of floodplains and associated wetlands.

Agriculture for the Birds

The 5,218 acres of marshes, grasslands, and woodlands are characterized by two types of refuge management: natural and agricultural. Preservation of the natural Columbia River floodplain is the management objective on both the Carty and Roth Units. When snowmelt from the mountains swells the Columbia each spring, these units are flooded until the river level drops again. Basalt outcroppings on the Carty Unit form knolls above the high water level. These knolls are wooded with ash, oak, and Douglas fir and are covered with brilliant wildflowers in the spring. The knolls become extremely dry in summer, in contrast with the lush greenery of surrounding marshes. The Roth Unit is flatter and forested with cottonwood, ash, and willow. Cattle graze on parts of these units to maintain short-grass pastures preferred by many waterfowl for loafing and feeding.

The River "S" Unit and Bachelor Island, on the other hand, are protected from flooding by dikes around their perimeters. Pumps regulate the amount of water to each pond and lake to foster the growth of aquatic waterfowl food plants and to create resting areas for the birds. Grasslands are grazed by cattle, and grass is mowed or cut for hay or silage. These actions result in the short, green browse preferred by Canada and cackling geese when they arrive in the fall.

With the combination of natural and agricultural environments, waterfowl populations on the refuge have peaked at thirty thousand geese and forty thousand ducks. Research was conducted on the refuge to evaluate the effectiveness of various methods for reducing reed canarygrass, a highly invasive non-native species. Results have contributed to knowledge about this widespread, problematic species.

A History Thousands of Years Old

The mild climate and abundant fish and wildlife made the Ridgefield area attractive for human occupation long before recorded history. It was only recently discovered, after the U.S. Fish and Wildlife Service and Portland State University began exploring the area in 1992, that the refuge contained the site documented in 1806 by Lewis and Clark as one of the largest Chinook Indian villages along the lower Columbia River. This village, Cathlapotle, was occupied by at least 1500 A.D. Other locations on the refuge predate Cathlapotle, and presumably, predecessor villages encapsulate thousands of years of human occupation. Today, a full-scale replica Chinookan Plankhouse has been constructed on the refuge's Carty Unit. It was built using archaeological evidence from the Cathlapotle archaeological site and serves as a tangible link to those who lived here in the past. The Plankhouse is a unique site for the interpretation of the natural and cultural heritage preserved on the refuge. The exterior of the Plankhouse can be seen year-round during daylight hours. It is staffed for visitation from early April to early October on weekend afternoons. (Seasonal schedules and special events are posted online at the Friends of the Ridgefield National Wildlife Refuge website.)

Cathlapotle Village

Captain William Clark described the first encounter with the Cathlapotle People as the Expedition passed the settlements on November 5, 1805:

I observed on the Chanel which passes on the Star'd Side of this Island a short distance above its lower point is Situated a large village, the front of which occupies nearly 1/4 mile fronting the Chanel, and closely connected, I counted 14 houses (Quathlapotle nation) in front here the river widens to about 1-1/2 miles. Seven canoes of Indians came out from this large village to view and trade with us, they appeared orderly and well disposed, they accompanied us a fiew miles and returned back.

This "large village" was in fact one of the largest on the river, with an estimated nine hundred inhabitants, as recorded by Lewis and Clark when they returned to trade and visit on March 29, 1806.

Access

Ridgefield National Wildlife Refuge Auto Tour Route and Carty Unit Hours: Daily from 6:30 am to 6 pm (automatic entrance gate hours). The refuge is open every day during daylight hours. Closing times for the automated gate system are posted on the gates at the refuge entrances. Should you be locked in behind the gate, you may call the Ridgefield Police Department at 360-887-3556, and a police unit will be dispatched to your location. River "S" Unit: Auto Tour Route is a one-way, 4.2-mile loop on a graveled road (the first mile of the road is two-way). It is open daily to vehicles during daylight hours. It is also open to foot traffic between May 1 and September 30 during the non-hunting season. The Kiwa Trail is a 1.2-mile pedestrian loop trail open May 1 through September 30. It is the only walking trail available on this unit. The path is compacted gravel accessible to wheelchairs and strollers. The trail passes through an understory of Oregon ash trees and between open wetland areas. Between May 1 and September 30 only, visitors may also walk the Auto Tour Route. Observation Blind: An observation blind overlooking Rest Lake is located close to the halfway point on the Auto Tour Route just before arriving at the Kiwa Trail parking lot. This shelter is covered by a stand of Oregon ash trees and has cut-out windows where spotting scopes and cameras can be set up for close-up views of wildlife. The Carty Unit is open daily to foot traffic only during daylight hours. It is the location of the two-mile Oaks to Wetlands Loop trail. Although maintained, this trail is undeveloped. Many parts of the trail are uneven, rocky, steep, narrow, and may become slippery when wet. Sturdy shoes should be worn and caution should be used to avoid contacting poison oak on some parts of the trail.

How to Get There

By car: From Portland and Vancouver, Interstate 5 north to the Ridgefield exit and take NW 269th Street west (Route 501). To get to the River "S" Unit, before reaching the town of Ridgefield, take a left onto S 9th Avenue, which becomes S Hillhurst Road. Turn right onto S Refuge Road and proceed to the driving loop road. To get to the Carty Unit, drive into Ridgefield and take a right onto N Main Avenue and drive north, crossing over G Creek, and look for the gravel parking lot on the left 1.1 miles north of Ridgefield. **Public transit:** No direct service

By Eric Anderson

Rodent Extraordinaire

FOR HUMANS, THE SOUND OF WATER TRICKLING over stone invites quiet contemplation, if not the urge to relieve one's bladder. For beavers, flowing water triggers an entirely different reflex—it compels them to build, to mend, and to plug the leak in an otherwise sturdy bulwark. In this regard, beavers are not unlike human children, who given sticks or rocks and a sufficient lapse in parental supervision, invariably set out to divert a stream.

Beaver dams were once common on small, perennial streams throughout much of North America. An estimated sixty million of these industrious rodents were thought to exist prior to European settlement, but the animals were hunted nearly to extinction in the 1800s, driven by the demand for their thick, soft fur. Fortunately, sufficient numbers hung on as our tastes changed. Beavers have earned our sometimes grudging respect as fellow shapers of the environment, and are now an important part of the urban landscape.

B Is for Beaver

With its distinctive flattened tail and toothy grin, every school kid knows the beaver. In 1969, Oregon selected the beaver as its state animal. It graces the back of our state flag, is mascot to our sports teams, and is recognized in numerous place names for creeks, buttes, and towns, including the oft-maligned Beaverton—so called, according to Lewis A. McArthur in *Oregon Geographic Names*, "because of the existence nearby of a large body of beaverdam land ... sought for by pioneer settlers because of its productivity."

The American beaver (*Castor canadensis*) is the largest rodent in North America and the second largest rodent worldwide, surpassed only by the capybara of South America. Beavers range from three to four feet in length, including their tail, and tip the scales at thirty-five to sixty-six pounds. Despite their heft, it's likely few Oregonians have ever seen a beaver in the flesh, given their mostly nocturnal habit. Unfortunately, many of us have seen their slimmer counterpart, the nutria. Introduced to Oregon as a fur-bearer around 1937, this South American import escaped from captivity and has made itself at home in Oregon's waterways. You can often see nutria (*Myocastor coypus*) grazing along the grassy banks of our urban streams, accompanied by three to six young, which can be born throughout the year.

In contrast, the beaver breeds only once a year, usually in January and February. Three to five young, called kits, are born four months later. The kits are fully furred at birth, with incisors in place and ready to gnaw within a month. As in the adult, the lips of young beaver close behind their front teeth. This allows them to grasp and manipulate branches underwater. Beavers are territorial and mate for life, but share their pond with the young from previous litters until they're one to two years old. Family colonies cooperate in food-gathering and dam-building activities, but exclude other beavers from their territory with small mounds of mud and plant materials on which they secrete a pungent oil called "castoreum." Beavers in western Oregon often dig their dens in the banks of streams rather than constructing a traditional lodge. They may also den under logs and stumps.

Whatever their housing option, beavers are active year-round in Oregon. With our relatively mild winters, they rarely have to contend with their pond or stream icing over. In colder climates, beavers stash the branches of alder, willow, cottonwood, and other deciduous trees at the bottom of their pond to assure a ready supply of bark during inclement weather. Beavers also eat ferns, grasses, and aquatic plants, but gnawed-off stumps of trees and shrubs are the surest sign that a hungry beaver lives nearby.

Wetland Architects

Ponds and wetlands formed by beaver activity are valuable assets in the urban environment. Healthy wetlands help control flooding, filter pollutants, and provide habitat for fish, amphibians, birds, and other wildlife. However, the beaver's habit of felling trees can lead to conflict with property owners, whose carefully designed landscapes may be transformed overnight. With proper management, beavers can thrive in The Intertwine network as eager partners in maintaining our urban wetlands and waterways. To discourage gnawing, valuable trees and other plantings can be fenced off or wrapped with sturdy mesh. Plantings of native, but less favored, species such as cascara, elderberry, Indian plum, twinberry, or ninebark will encourage beaver to look elsewhere for a midnight snack. Blocked culverts and flooded roads can be remedied with flow diverters and other measures that prompt beavers to build their dam in a more convenient location—and build they will, compelled by the sound of flowing water.

The next time you contemplate a burbling brook, think of this extraordinary rodent. Look for signs of beaver activity at Smith and Bybee Lakes, Koll Center Wetlands, Jackson Bottom Wetlands Preserve, or in ponds and streams near you.

By Connie Levesque, illustration by Evelyn Hicks

Sandy River Watershed

THE SANDY RIVER and its tributaries gather water from over five hundred square miles. The Sandy cascades for over fifty miles from its origin at Mount Hood's Reid Glacier at six thousand feet to near sea level at its confluence with the Columbia River near Troutdale. Voluntary removal of the forty-seven-foot Marmot Dam in 2007 returned the Sandy to its natural, free-flowing condition after nearly a century of being dammed for hydropower production.

Its larger tributaries include the Zig Zag, Bull Run, Little Sandy, and Salmon Rivers. More than ninety tributaries like Gordon, Ramona, Whiskey, Badger, Otter, Bow and Arrow, Tumbling, and Arrah-wanna Creeks contribute their waters to the Sandy.

Below the former dam site at Alder Creek, and before the confluence with the Bull Run River at Dodge Park, the Sandy flows through the Sandy River Gorge with its rugged, high bluffs, deep-green pools, and rapids. By the time the Sandy reaches The Nature Conservancy's Sandy River Gorge Preserve, Indian John Island, and Oxbow Regional Park, the river has begun to meander along its lower gradient run to the Columbia River. At the confluence, it drops much of its sediment load onto the 1,400-acre Sandy River Delta. The accumulated sands at the Sandy's mouth prompted Lewis and Clark to name it Quicksand River when they stopped there on November 3, 1805, noting that the local Native Americans called it *Ye-ki-oo*.

The Sandy's abundant riffles, pools, side channels, and smaller tributaries are home to an amazing array of native fish, including Pacific and western brook lamprey, steelhead, rainbow trout, coho salmon, spring and fall Chinook salmon, cutthroat trout, mountain whitefish, redside shiner, white sturgeon, and smelt. Mammalian inhabitants include Roosevelt elk, black-tailed deer, cougar, bobcat, and black bear.

One of the most significant human uses of the Sandy River watershed is for drinking water. The City of Portland was successful in persuading President Benjamin

Harrison to establish a 139,520-acre Bull Run Reserve in 1892. In 1895, a large conduit, built to divert water from the Bull Run River to Portland, was completed at a site now occupied by the city's Headworks Dam. In 1911, a second conduit was added to carry water to Portland. A succession of projects, including a check dam at Bull Run Lake in 1915, the Headworks Dam in 1922, and construction of the two-hundred-foot-high Ben Morrow Dam (also called Bull Run Dam No. 1) means that Portland now has storage capacity of seventeen billion gallons of drinking water. Historically, one negative consequence of these actions was that the Bull Run River literally ran dry during summer periods of high demand and low precipitation. Recent listings of steelhead and salmon as threatened under the Endangered Species Act has led the City of Portland to commit to a fifty-year habitat conservation plan for the Bull Run system that will ensure guaranteed flow in the lower Bull Run at all times of the year and invest in restoration actions to recover salmonids throughout the Sandy River system.

The reach from Dodge Park downstream to Dabney State Park was designated as a federal Wild and Scenic River in 1988, and was one of Oregon's first scenic waterways. The old river terraces and eight-hundred-foot-high slopes are covered with late-succession native forest, including a true old growth forest of Douglas fir, western redcedar, and western hemlock. Black cottonwood and Oregon white ash are festooned with lichens, mosses, and ferns. It's impossible not to compare this reach of the river to the Olympic Peninsula's verdant rainforests when you peer down into the Sandy River Gorge or walk silently on lush green moss carpets at Oxbow Regional Park.

By Steve Wise

Oxbow Regional Park

LOCATION: 3010 SE Oxbow Parkway, Gresham, OR ACTIVITIES: Hiking, Biking, Paddling, Boating, Fishing, Wildlife viewing, Camping, Horseback riding, Swimming, Picnicking, Nature programs FACILITIES: Restrooms, Parking, Unpaved trails, Park office and Ranger station, Campground, Picnic area/shelters, Paved boat ramp, Canoe/kayak launch, Interpretive signs/info FEES AND REGULATIONS: Entrance fees and camping fees, annual pass available, Parking, Hours 6:30 am to sunset, No pets HIKING DIFFICULTY: Easy, Moderate, Difficult HIGHLIGHTS: Paths through old-growth forest; Wild salmon spawning in the river; Animal tracking. Inspiring nature classes and field trips; Short drive from Portland and easy camping with the kids; Easy day trip for that feeling of wildness where you could maybe, just maybe, see a bear PUBLIC TRANSIT: No direct service

Like Alice tumbling down the rabbit hole, visitors who descend the long steep road into Oxbow Regional Park will find a lovely and sometimes magical world awaiting—a place you must travel a little longer to get to than many but well worth the extra distance. At the bottom lies an emerald river canyon, where trails wander under towering trees and the wild animals (including rabbits) are abundant. One of the crown jewels of our regional natural areas, Oxbow is a 1,200-acre park in the heart of the Sandy River Gorge. It features an old growth forest; the Sandy River, which is a designated Wild and Scenic River; plentiful habitat for fish and wildlife; and tempting recreation opportunities.

Oxbow was developed as a park in the mid-1960s. It's about twenty miles east of downtown Portland and a popular spot for picnics. It can be busy on summer weekends, but those in search of peace and quiet will always find it. Whether you're listening to the splash of wild salmon or spotting elk tracks in the old growth, Oxbow offers opportunities for in-depth experiences of nature one might expect to find only in more remote wilderness. To explore Oxbow's wilder side, plan on spending several hours or a full day, and return during different seasons. Camping, hiking, kayaking, or just sitting on the riverbank are great ways to experience the park.

Oxbow's history is tied to the Sandy River, which tumbles down from its headwaters on Mount Hood, and slowing, forms the serpentine pattern called an oxbow that gives the park its name. As you travel down the park road, you are on a terrace deposited by the river during the last eruptive period of Mount Hood, over two hundred years ago. During this time, volcanic floods of sand and mud—lahars—poured down the river's course, burying entire sections of forest along the way. Amazingly, in the past few years several buried trees that were preserved (though not petrified) in the sand have been uncovered as the riverbanks have shifted. To view this ghost-forest, go down to the river on the trail from Picnic Area A and walk upstream along the sandbar to its tip. Look up at the bank to see the stumps sticking out of the sandy hillside.

Another good place to walk is in the 160-acre ancient forest, the largest accessible area of old growth near Portland, where many Douglas firs are seven hundred to eight hundred years old. The trail crisscrosses the road, and you'll notice that most of the larger trees are on the uphill side. Why? Because the aforementioned floods wiped out the trees closer to the river, while the trees on the next terrace up remained safe to continue growing. Tiny Pacific wrens sing from the undergrowth of ferns and wildflowers. Consider a visit in March, when the moss turns electric green and the trillium are in bloom, or during a rainy week in the fall to spot mushrooms. In any season you can look for nurse logs nurturing the next generation of western hemlocks, and snags (riddled with the work of pileated woodpeckers)—both key components of ancient forest ecosystems.

Wildlife observation, tracking, and birding can be very rewarding here, especially in the early morning and at dusk. Graceful Columbian black-tailed deer are abundant and accustomed to people, allowing for up-close views, and brush rabbits feed along the edges of the lawns. Good bets for birding include the old-growth trails and the floodplain trail, which loops through a cottonwood stand and then out to the water. Osprey grace nearly every bend in the river, and a pair often nests near Picnic Area A. Keep your eyes open for American dippers, common mergansers, and sometimes mink, river otter, or beaver along the river as well. There are also more elusive mammals: bobcat, red fox, coyote, Roosevelt elk, northern flying squirrel, spotted skunk, black bear, and the occasional mountain lion. Their tracks and signs give us insight to their presence. In fact, with lots of wildlife and lots of sand, Oxbow is known as one of the best places in the Northwest for practicing the art of animal tracking.

Stealthy Giants

It is a delicious paradox that you probably will not see the biggest animal found in the Sandy River Gorge. You'd think a whole herd of large, hoofed mammals weighing four hundred to a thousand pounds each would have a hard time being elusive, but these Roosevelt elk are masters at staying hidden. From tracks and occasional sightings, we know that the herd tends to spend more time at Oxbow in fall and winter and moves upstream in summer. You can look for signs of them along the river at the far ends of the park and on the floodplain loop trail. The two-toed hoof prints look like super-sized, rounded deer tracks. If you find them, look closely for more clues. Elk droppings are like the pellets of deer but larger, often with a little point like a chocolate kiss; in the summer they may look more like cow pies. Check for antler rubbings on the trees, bits of fur on the ground, and signs of thrashed vegetation from rutting males in the fall. You can also spot narrow elk trails in the ancient forest.

If you want to be sure to see live elk, go elsewhere, like the winter-feeding area at Jewell Meadows near the Oregon Coast. But the Sandy River elk will give you a different kind of pleasure: the fun of seeking something that is hard to find and that shiver you'll feel when you step over the fresh tracks of a giant beast that can disappear like a ghost.

Salmon are not usually on wildlife checklists, but at Oxbow they're stars of the show and a key reason to put a fall visit on your calendar. The Sandy River supports several seasonal runs of coho, Chinook, and steelhead whose lives are intricately tied to the health of the surrounding forest and watershed. Over the past twenty-five years, many Portlanders have come to think of the trip to Oxbow to witness the return of the wild fall Chinook to their spawning grounds as something of an annual pilgrimage—something that affirms our sense of belonging to this place. Weighing twenty to forty pounds, these fish are an impressive sight. They can be seen from late September through early November, when the fall rains bring them upstream in pulses to spawn. In recent years, the best viewing has been from the trail overlooking the river between shelters at Picnic Areas A and C. Salmon spawn in the riffles, where water is running over the rocks, not in the deep pools. Look and listen for the rhythmic splashing of the female salmon digging their redds (nests) with their tails. Viewing success varies

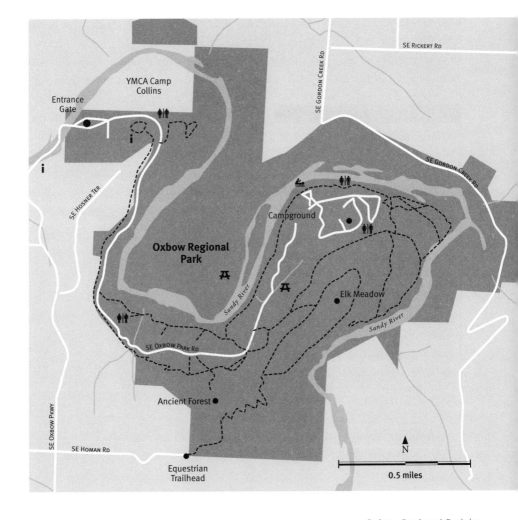

with the weather and river conditions; polarized sunglasses help. For the best bet at seeing the salmon, visit the park for Salmon Homecoming Days during the last two weekends in October, the peak of the run. Park naturalists will guide you to the best viewing spots.

Whether you participate in one of the park's excellent natural history classes or simply explore on your own, once you find yourself in the wonderland of Oxbow, you'll want to come back again and again.

Access

Fifteen miles of trails along the Sandy River and through riparian and upland forest (easy to moderate), and up to Alder Ridge (more difficult). Several loops are possible, and there are many places to park. A park map, available at the entrance, is required as trails are not signed except for occasional wayfinding letter markers.

How to Get There

By car: Interstate 84 east to Troutdale exit 17. Continue past the truck stops to the light. Turn right on 257th Drive, and go up the hill three miles. Turn left onto SE Division Street and continue 5 miles, following the signs for the park. Turn left onto Oxbow Parkway and proceed downhill 1.6 miles to the park entrance. **Public transit:** No public transportation to the park. Cyclists have been known to take MAX Blue Line to the end of the line in Gresham and bike the remainder of the route, but it's one tough hill at the end, and tougher on the way back up.

By Elisabeth Neely

More information: Metro; Oxbow Park Office

Native Aromas

There are two species of skunk that can be found in the region: western spotted skunk (*Spilogale gracilis*) and striped skunk (*Mephitis mephitis*). You are much more likely to see the significantly larger striped skunk in both open and forested habitats. They are active from evening to early morning as opposed to the less common, strictly nocturnal, spotted skunks found primarily in forested habitats. The two species do share the ability to spray a pungent musk accurately over long distances—the spotted up to six feet and the striped up to twenty! In fact, the striped skunk's scientific name means "foul odor." Regardless, I have always found skunks to be extremely reasonable creatures—leave them alone and they will leave you alone.

—Bob Sallinger

Crow Magic

IT IS LATE FALL AT OXBOW PARK. The Sandy River is rising, and you can catch the odor of dead salmon clinging in the air along the water's edge. Varied thrushes and golden-crowned kinglets are returning to the valley, and a black bear is leaving tracks on the sandy floodplain. The quiet rains have finally begun. Wild mushrooms and salamanders are poking their heads up from the wet leaves for a look around, and after a busy summer season with thousands of park visitors, I too, feel like I am resurfacing into the cool, damp calm.

At the height of the salmon's spawning season, we had one of those perfect school field trips here. Fifty second and third graders arrived from the city on a sunny day in late October. Led by volunteer naturalists, our groups headed off to explore. We saw spawning fall Chinook, spotted otter tracks, and a great blue heron, and listened as an impressive flock of more than forty crows flew back and forth, cawing raucously. They dipped and careened together along the tops of the trees above the river—a wild, peculiar ritual I have observed every fall. After lunch, I led my group along the water's edge. One girl was delighted to find a shiny black crow feather among the rocks, and I enjoyed her surprise at what I would have thought of as a common sort of treasure.

As we continued along the river, we passed a woman taking photographs. She pointed us toward a salmon that had just completed its life's journey, spawned and died, and washed up near the shore. It was hidden at the far end of the rocks where we would never have spotted it on our own. This salmon turned out to be perfect, still bright and silvery. When I pulled it up from the water and into the sunlight, the kids were drawn to its beauty. They all wanted to touch it and run their hands along its shining sides. As I set it back gently, I heard the kids laughing in wonder behind me. "What happened?" I asked. A boy had raised his arm to point at a falling, spinning maple leaf and, as if in response, the huge yellow leaf had floated right into his hand.

Creating Nature Clubs

If you're a parent, grandparent, or caregiver who would like to share outdoor experiences, or if you'd just like some moral support or an extra nudge to get out the door on a drizzly weekend, consider starting your own nature group. Whether or not we have children of our own, we're all members of a family—a larger kinship that extends to all the critters, large and small, that share nature with us. In that kinship we find comfort, health, meaning, and a pathway home.

—Richard Louv

To get started download the free Family Nature Club Tool Kit at the Children & Nature Network.

When it was time to leave we gathered in a circle, and I began describing our feelings of appreciation for the many different animals and elements of nature that had revealed themselves to us. The children responded with enthusiasm. As I gave thanks for the birds, I called out all that we had seen: the heron, geese, wrens. . . . When I mentioned the crows, that same big flock suddenly appeared in the opening above the clearing where we were sitting and swooped above us in a flurry of caws and flapping black wings! We all looked up, and the flock just as suddenly flew away. When we finished, I asked if anyone had anything else to add, and one child said, "I would like to give thanks to all our teachers." And so we did.

After the school bus had pulled away, and I was picking up the gear, I ran into that same photographer on the trail. I thanked her for telling us where to find the beautiful salmon that had so inspired the children. She said, "Oh, you're welcome. But the crows showed me where it was. Two of them were flying back and forth right above it."

It took a while for her words to sink in, but later, as I reviewed the day in my mind, I realized that the crows had somehow woven themselves through our trip from start to finish. As a flock of young children and their leaders had roamed the forest, explored a river in the warm fall sunshine, and greeted the returning salmon, the crows had accompanied us. With flight and sound and shiny feathers, they had revealed to us the magic inherent in the world. I thought of the child in the circle who had reminded us to thank our teachers. I was glad she had, for teachers come in many forms indeed. The familiar sound of crows cawing echoes a little differently now.

By Elisabeth Neely

Chronicler of Time:
The Bushy-Tailed Woodrat

OF THE MORE THAN THREE HUNDRED SPECIES of wild animals found in and around Portland, surely the most marvelous and least appreciated is the bushy-tailed woodrat. The word "rat" usually conjures images of the beady eyes and nearly furless, scaly tails of the black rat (*Rattus rattus*) and the Norway rat (*Rattus norvegicus*). These are both Old World rats that immigrated to the Americas with the first European settlers. Their nicknames: boat rat and water rat respectively, convey their propensity for water travel. While both species can be found in Oregon, the Norway rat is by far the more common and is the species most often observed nosing about our yards and neighborhoods.

By comparison, bushy-tailed woodrats (*Neotoma cinerea*) are native rats that have roamed North America since time immemorial. The U.S. Geological Survey estimates that their North American presence dates back as far as forty thousand years. These rats are far less visible and, anthropomorphically speaking, far more attractive than their Old World cousins. Ranging from reddish-brown to gray above with light-gray to pure-white bellies, woodrats can quickly be differentiated by their flattened, furred tails.

Bushy-tailed woodrats are distributed in open and forested habitats throughout Oregon and can be found locally in and around many of our larger natural areas, such as Forest Park, Oxbow Regional Park, Sauvie Island Wildlife Area, and the Tualatin River National Wildlife Refuge. They also occassionally find their way onto our developed

landscape. They are primarily nocturnal and, thus, are rarely seen. They can live alone or in harems of one male and several females. Woodrats are most conspicuous by their nests and their noisy, nocturnal ramblings. They will rapidly drum their feet when disturbed—a behavior that some biologists have speculated serves as an alarm system for other nearby woodrats. Predators that share the urban nightscape include great horned owls, weasels, bobcats, and coyotes.

Bushy-tailed woodrats construct open nests that are most commonly located in the cracks and crevices of cliffs and rocky outcroppings. However, they will also utilize hollow trees, tree branches, and manmade structures as well as any other protected available location. The nests are often used and expanded upon by generation after generation.

Woodrats are sometimes referred to as packrats or traderats, based on their propensity for collecting whatever items catch their eye as they forage for their primarily vegetarian diet. They are known to have a particular affinity for shiny objects and will sometimes drop one item to pick up something more enticing, perhaps swapping a fecal pellet or small twig for a shiny dime or your grandmother's antique wedding ring. Found items, ranging from bits of local flora and fauna to human artifacts, are stored in and around the nest and are eventually sealed into a solid mass by the woodrat's viscous urine.

To the homeowner who has the misfortune of sharing their abode with a woodrat, this habit of collecting is less than endearing. However, for scientists, woodrat refuse heaps, known as middens, have proven an invaluable source of anthropological and biological information. The inclination of successive generations of woodrats to occupy the same nest site, combined with their habit of amassing found objects, has allowed scientists to carbon date the continuous use of a desert woodrat nest in the southwestern United States and detail changes in the surrounding flora and fauna as far back as eight thousand years. In his epic poem "Mountains and Rivers Without End," the poet Gary Snyder entitles a section "Old Woodrat's Stinky House" and places a desert woodrat's nest somewhere between the occurrence of ice ages and the life of a bristlecone pine while providing a fantastic meditation on time.

During daytime rambles of our urban natural areas, keep your eye out for odd assemblages of natural and unnatural objects, especially among rocky outcroppings and in and around hollowed-out trees. Better yet, take a walk at night and listen for the nocturnal ramblings of this fascinating rodent. They can be found near the ground but are also able to climb high up the trunks of trees. Imagine them casting a wary eye above and below for nocturnal predators as they scramble about, searching for food and collecting relics of the world that surrounds them, inadvertently creating a catalog of our changing landscape for future generations to ponder.

By Bob Sallinger, illustration by Evelyn Hicks

Sandy River Delta

Location: Mouth of the Sandy River, near Troutdale, OR **Activities:** Hiking, Biking, Horseback riding, Fishing, Wildlife viewing, Seasonal duck hunting **Facilities:** Restrooms, Parking, Unpaved trails, Campground, Picnic area/shelter, Wildlife viewing structure, Interpretive signs/info **Fees and Regulations:** Dogs on leash on the Bird Blind Trail, No pets on grasslands and wetland areas on the eastern portion of the Delta **Hiking Difficulty:** Easy **Highlights:** Miles of trails leading through bottomland hardwood forests and past meadows and wetlands; Access to the confluence of the Sandy and Columbia River with miles of beach and mud flats; Dogs, horses, and bikes welcome; Maya Lin-designed *Bird Blind* commemorates the Lewis and Clark Expedition **Public Transit:** TriMet bus 81

The Sandy River Delta is a landscape on the mend. Nicknamed Thousand Acres, this parcel located at the confluence of the Sandy and Columbia Rivers is actually closer to 1,400 acres, making it one of the largest natural areas in the region. It is heavily used and well loved—don't come to the delta if your goal is to reconnect with your primeval forest spirit. Instead, bring the kids, the dog, and the mountain bikes, and have a grand old time exploring this mosaic of bottomland riparian forests, meadows, wetlands, and beaches. Experience the incredible effort that is being made to restore this landscape, but please keep any two-legged, four-legged, or wheeled friends to the well-worn trails and out of the fragile restoration areas.

The delta that greets visitors today is a far cry from the landscape experienced by Lewis and Clark when they passed by this site in November 1805 on their journey to the Pacific and again in April 1806 on their return home. Historically, the landscape was covered with thick bottomland hardwood forests. The Sandy River, which originates fifty-six miles to the southeast on the Reid Glacier of Mount Hood, split into two channels as it approached the Columbia River, carving out the large Sundial Island from the mainland. Captain William Clark gave the river the name Quicksand River when he attempted to wade across its shallow waters and found, to his "astonishment," the bottom to be a "quick sand and impassible." The expedition spent many days at this site, hunting the prodigious populations of deer, elk, bear, and "emence [sic] numbers of fowls flying in every direction."

The intervening years have not been kind to the delta. Much of the bottomland forest was removed during the twentieth century to make way for cattle grazing, and the Bonneville Power Administration placed gigantic power-line structures through the heart of the landscape. Most notably, in 1931 the eastern channel of the Sandy River was blocked by a 750-foot-long, 5-foot-tall dam made of wooden pilings, installed in a misguided attempt to support fish passage by increasing water flows in the remaining western channel. Seven years later, the dam was reinforced with riprap and raised to 10 feet. Today, little remains of the eastern channel. Except at the highest river flows, it is merely a series of stagnant sloughs, and Sundial Island, for all intents and purposes, has merged with the mainland. The eventual cessation of grazing led to an explosion of invasive blackberries, thistle, and reed canary grass that eventually carpeted the landscape.

In 1991, the delta was acquired by the Trust for Public Land and transferred to the U.S. Forest Service, ushering in a new era of restoration. Funded in large part by restoration dollars provided by the Bonneville Power Administration to mitigate for impacts to fish and wildlife caused by the federal hydropower system, the Forest Service and multiple partners including Friends of Trees, Ash Creek Forest Management, Ducks Unlimited, Portland Bureau of Environmental Services, and the Lower Columbia Estuary Partnership have been working for more than a decade to restore 600 acres of forest and 200 acres of wetland. The Forest Service is leveraging restoration dollars by allowing local farmers to cultivate 50- to 100-acre blocks for two years, after which the land will be replanted with native vegetation. Each farmer gets two years of crop harvest in return for leaving the land free of invasive species and ready for restoration. Perhaps most exciting, the Forest Service plans to remove the dam and restore the free-flow to the eastern channel of the Sandy River. When this happens, Sundial Island will once again live up to its name.

Visitors to the Sandy River Delta will find an extensive network of trails leading away from a paved access road and large parking lot. A few main trails are signed but a spider web of unofficial trails blankets the delta. It is easy to stay oriented however—the Columbia River to the north and Interstate 84 to the south provide easy frames of reference. It is hoped that many of these unofficial trails will be eliminated over time to allow for some larger intact habitat patches.

The Thousand Acres Road heads north from the western end of the main access road through stands of cottonwoods and past restoration meadows. Several spur trails to the west will take you to the banks of the Sandy River. A little over a half mile from the trailhead, the dirt road gives way to what appears to be large cobblestones. You are actually walking on top of the dam, and if you look through the thick vegetation on either side of the road, you will see the slough that was once the main channel of the Sandy. Readers of this book beyond 2012 may well find themselves at the trail's end staring across a flowing river to Sundial Island. Beyond the dam the trail continues another mile and a half through more cottonwood forest and meadows until it reaches the Columbia and a huge expanse of sandy beach.

At the eastern end of the parking area, the gravel Confluence Trail heads north across meadows to Maya Lin's *Bird Blind*. The *Bird Blind* is part of the Confluence Project, a series of seven art installations along the Columbia and Snake Rivers to commemorate the two-hundredth anniversary of the Lewis and Clark Expedition. The blind is on an elevated platform and composed of 129 vertical slats made from black locust. Each slat lists an animal observed by the expedition, the date it was seen, and its current conservation status. The installation is more about form than function—

an interesting spot to stop and ponder how many of the species seen by the expedition are in serious decline. However, its utility for watching birds is limited—trails run all around the outside and the vertical slats leave one with more of a sense of being in a birdcage than a bird blind. Beyond the blind, the trail drops steeply down to an extensive network of beaches and mudflats where the eastern channel of the Sandy once met the Columbia. This is a great place to look for herons, gulls, and shorebirds. For greater solitude and improved wildlife watching opportunities, take one of the many loop trails that head out toward the meadows and wetlands to the east.

While the Forest Service has worked to restore the delta, the area has simultaneously and quite literally gone to the dogs. Unlike most natural areas throughout the region, which either disallow dogs altogether or require that dogs be on leashes, the Sandy River Delta allows dogs to run free throughout most of the parcel, with the exceptions of the parking lot, along the gravel trail to the Maya Lin *Bird Blind*, and in the grasslands and wetlands area east of the Bird Blind Trail. The rules state that owners must carry a leash and keep dogs in sight and under voice control and they prohibit professional dog walkers from using the park for the dogs' "business" activities. However, far more could be done with signage to encourage dog owners to keep dogs out of the most fragile habitats and to reduce wildlife harassment by dogs.

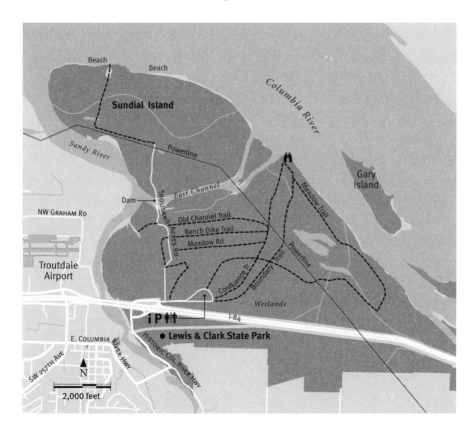

That said, restoration efforts are paying off at the delta. The birding can be outstanding. Look for red-eyed vireo, willow flycatcher, yellow-breasted chat, Swainson's thrushes, western bluebirds, orioles, meadowlarks, and lazuli buntings. In recent years, there have been sightings of yellow-billed cuckoos, a species considered extirpated from Oregon. Other rarities have included Lewis's woodpeckers. Go in the early morning before the dogs arrive to catch site of beaver and otter along the Sandy River or coyotes hunting in the meadows.

For people seeking a quiet contemplative nature experience, or for those who simply subscribe to the notion that habitat restoration sites and dogs probably don't mix, the Sandy River Delta is a place to be avoided. However, for a fun family outing, bikes and dogs in tow, with outstanding wildlife watching opportunities, the delta can't be beat. Just be sure to remember the amazing work that is going into restoring this landscape and treat it with kindness and respect.

Access
Several trails originate from the parking lot and access road.

How to Get There
BY CAR: Interstate 84 east to exit 18 near Troutdale. Loop back under the highway as though you are accessing the westbound onramp. Entrance to the Sandy River Delta is on the left. **PUBLIC TRANSIT:** TriMet bus 81 will take you to Troutdale. Exit at the Columbia Gorge Outlet Stores. Walk south 0.1 miles to the Historic Columbia Gorge Highway. Follow the Highway 0.9 miles east across the bridge over the Sandy River. Turn left and follow the Crown Point Highway north back under Interstate 84 for 0.7 miles until you reach the entrance of the Sandy River Delta.

By Bob Sallinger

More information: U.S. Forest Service

CLARK COUNTY WATERSHEDS

CLARK COUNTY WATERSHEDS are as varied as the communities through which the creeks and rivers flow. The Washougal River and Gibbons Creek, at the east end of Clark County, both begin in Skamania County at relatively high elevations, tumbling down into the Columbia River near Washougal, with Gibbons Creek flowing through Steigerwald Lake National Wildlife Refuge. Both creeks have rocky substrates, and the Washougal enjoys a robust run of salmon each year. The Lower Columbia Fish Enhancement Group has done a great deal of habitat enhancement on the Washougal River, and there is a hatchery just over the Skamania County line.

Lacamas Creek begins near the east side of Clark County and flows through Camp Bonneville, over three thousand acres of property owned by the United States Army. Lacamas Creek then flows west through rapidly developing farm and dairy land, picks up Fifth Plain Creek and China Ditch, turns south, and then west. It then reaches Lacamas and Round Lakes, two lakes originally carved by the Missoula Floods and deepened by a dam that directs water to the paper mill in Camas. Lacamas Lake is popular with water skiers and anglers, while the smaller Round Lake does not allow motorized boats and is almost completely surrounded by Lacamas Lake Park. Lacamas Creek then flows past the dam, through a forested area, and into the Washougal River.

Burnt Bridge Creek is by far the most urban stream in Clark County. Its headwaters, near Fourth Plain Boulevard and 164th Avenue, emanate from a wide wetland surrounded by housing developments and strip malls. Much of the creek was channelized to facilitate farming in the rich wetland soils. Since then, farms have been replaced by housing developments.

From its headwaters, Burnt Bridge Creek moves slowly through the suburbs and under Interstate 205, picking up Peterson Creek along the way. Much of the floodplain downstream of the freeway is owned by Vancouver and is a part of its long-term stormwater management plan. After the creek crosses Fourth Plain Boulevard in central Vancouver, it dives into a wooded canyon, crosses under Interstate 5, and adds Cold Creek, a small tributary. It then flows to Vancouver Lake through a wide floodplain that features housing developments on both bluffs.

Salmon Creek originates at 1,400 feet in east Clark County and flows due west to Lake River, draining a watershed roughly eighty-nine square miles in area. It receives water from several tributaries, including Mill Creek, Woodin Creek, and Curtin Creek. After dropping out of the hills on the east side of Clark County, it meanders through the center of the county and then flows into Klineline Pond and then Lake River and the Columbia River.

Whipple Creek, Flume Creek, Gee Creek, and Allen Canyon Creek comprise the west-slope creeks, which all start near Interstate 5 and flow through highly erodible, Missoula Flood–deposits and into Lake River and the Columbia. The west-side creeks feature some remarkable habitat frequented by raptors, beaver, and coyotes. Whipple Creek Park, Abrams Park, Mud Lake Park, and the Ridgefield National Wildlife Refuge all provide access to these remarkable creeks.

The North Fork Lewis River is joined by the East Fork Lewis River near the confluence with the Columbia. The North Fork flows between Clark and Cowlitz Counties and includes three dams with reservoirs that are popular with boaters and anglers. The East Fork begins high in the mountains of the Gifford Pinchot National Forest and flows undammed to the Columbia. As a result, it includes some of the best remnant salmonid habitat in the area. Lucia Falls, near the east end of the county, is thought to be the upper reach of salmon habitat, though steelhead regularly jump the falls and spawn upstream. The East Fork flows through rugged and rocky terrain that is popular with whitewater kayakers. As the topographic relief diminishes near La Center, the river becomes deep and wide. Moulton Falls Park, Lucia Falls Park, Lewisville Park, Daybreak Park, La Center Bottoms, and Paradise Point Park all provide easy access to this jewel.

By Gary Bock

Lacamas Lake Regional Park

LOCATION: 2700 SE Everett Street, Camas, WA
ACTIVITIES: Hiking, Biking, Paddling, Boating, Fishing, Camas lily field viewing **FACILITIES:** Restrooms, Parking, Paved and unpaved trails, Picnic area/shelter, Dock, Canoe/kayak launch, Interpretive signs/info **FEES AND REGULATIONS:** Pets on leash **HIKING DIFFICULTY:** Easy, Moderate **HIGHLIGHTS:** Waterfalls highlighting unique lava formations; Camas lilies in the spring; Three connected trail systems—trail access along three distinct water bodies with varying habitats; Non-motorized boating and fishing **PUBLIC TRANSIT:** C-Tran Line 92

Lacamas Lake Park became an instant jewel of the Vancouver-Clark Parks & Recreation regional park system when it was donated to Clark County in the 1960s by former paper giant Crown Zellerbach. Covering over 312 acres, the park hosts a six-mile network of scenic hiking and cycling trails that pass through dense forest and by three impressive waterfalls, as well as Round Lake and Lacamas Creek. At the south end of Round Lake, below the dam, Lacamas Creek becomes a cascading stream causing unique rock formations called The Potholes. Farther south in the central portion of the park, a bridge crosses the creek at Lower Falls, a picturesque spot that epitomizes the Pacific Northwest forested landscape.

There are many excellent birdwatching areas, and the spring-blooming camas lilies are an annual feature worth a visit. Upland forests support a variety of wildlife, including deer, wood ducks, western tiger swallowtail butterfly, beaver, osprey, bald eagles, kingfishers, and many others. Round Lake is a popular family fishing site, and the lake is stocked with bass, bluegill, and perch. Non-motorized boating is also allowed.

The park is considered the heart of a larger seven-mile ribbon of trails and greenways—connecting to Lacamas Heritage Trail to the northwest and to the Washougal River Greenway Trail to the southeast. The three trail systems combined travel along three distinct water bodies, offering varying habitats and scenery.

The Lacamas Heritage Trail is a 3.5-mile gravel, multiple-use trail located on the west side of Lacamas Lake and Lacamas Creek. It provides superb opportunities for watching birds, including the red-winged blackbird. Look for their cup-shaped grass nests showing in the reeds just above the water's edge. There are also interesting rock formations along the trail, as well as seasonal waterfalls. The southern portion of the trail is anchored by Heritage Park and offers picnicking, a boat launch, playgrounds, and toilets. The trailhead to the north at Goodwin Road also includes parking and restrooms.

The Washougal River Greenway Trail is 1.5 miles, anchoring the southeastern section of this larger trail network. Boardwalk sections of the trail pass through approximately 125 acres of contiguous greenway that includes several ponds, a 370-foot-high bridge that spans the Washougal River, and upland habitat. In addition to the trail, the greenway offers several small picnicking and seating areas, a primitive boat launch, and a connection to the recently renovated Goot Park. The greenway also supports fishing, kayaking and canoeing, biking, and swimming. Seasonally, the greenway is home to an array of fish and wildlife, including Chinook, chum, and coho salmon, as well as steelhead and cutthroat trout. Wildlife habitat in the greenway supports deer, raccoon, great blue heron, bald eagle, osprey, belted kingfisher, northern flicker, American goldfinch, black-headed grosbeak, pileated, downy, and hairy woodpecker, sharp-shinned hawk, wood duck, and many other species.

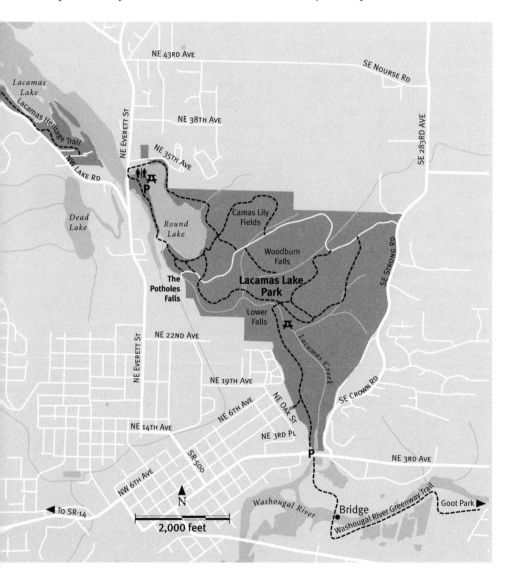

Access

There are multiple access points to Lacamas Lake Park: a trailhead parking lot on the southern tip of the park off of NE 3rd Avenue; and from the north by the Lacamas Heritage Trail through Heritage Park just north of NW Lake Road on the east side of NE Everett Street.

How to Get There

By car: From Vancouver or Interstate 205 take Lewis and Clark Highway (State Route 14) east and take the 6th Street exit to downtown Camas. Take a left (north) on State Route 500, which becomes NE Everett Street. Just north of NW Lake Road on the east side of NE Everett there is a parking lot on the northwest corner of Round Lake. **Public transit:** C-Tran Line 92 to Camas Transit Center; walk 0.75 mile to trailhead at NE 3rd Avenue.

By Lisa Goorjian

Swallow Tips

Two of our most common swallows present an identification challenge to beginning birders and, in some light, even to the more experienced. To distinguish the two, note the color on the bird's back, how much white it has on its face, and whether or not it has a white rump patch. A violet-green swallow has a green back, a large white arc over the eye, and a noticeable white rump patch. A tree swallow, on the other hand, has an iridescent blue back, crisp demarcation of white just below the eye, and no rump patch at all. They are both cavity nesters, which is why they are frequently seen in association with one another, although they are also seen in mixed flocks with barn, rough-winged, and cliff swallows.

—Mike Houck

Columbia Springs

Location: 12208 SE Evergreen Highway, Vancouver, WA **Activities:** Hiking, Nature study, Picnicking, Wildlife viewing **Facilities:** Restrooms, Parking, Paved and unpaved trails, Active fish hatchery, Interpretive displays, Native plant garden, Wildlife blinds, Wetland viewing platforms, Composting demonstration site **Fees and Regulations:** Daylight hours only; Pets on leash **Hiking Difficulty:** Easy, Moderate, Difficult **Highlights:** Historic fish hatchery built by FDR's Works Progress Administration in 1938; Rustic fish-rearing raceways and ponds; Fish observation and fish feeding pond; Hiking 100 acres of open space **Public Transit:** No direct service

Columbia Springs is a hundred-acre greenspace reserve of cultural and natural history hidden in an urbanizing area of Vancouver. At the center of Columbia Springs is a historic hatchery, built in 1938 as a Works Progress Administration project, the same federal project that gave us the facilities at Beacon Rock State Park and Timberline Lodge. The cold springs that supply the hatchery's fish-rearing raceways are also the source of water for a series of wildlife-hosting ponds and wetlands.

Though you might hear trains clattering on the nearby Burlington Northern tracks that parallel the Columbia River, the sounds that prevail are the ratchety calls of belted kingfishers, the "krik -kriks" of osprey, and the "groks" of the great blue herons that come to lunch here.

Hiking trails wind past two large ponds named East and West Biddle Lakes after Henry J. Biddle, an early resident and conservationist. Biddle, a Yale-educated engineer, naturalist, and botanist who built the trail that clambers up Beacon Rock, also included the purchase and donation of Beacon Rock in his conservation legacy.

While exploring Columbia Springs' trails you might spot wood ducks, osprey, great blue herons, or even a bald eagle. Look closer and you may see a well-camouflaged rough-skinned newt, a red-legged frog, or signs of otter or beaver. Education programs offered on-site include hands-on environmental education classes, a summer nature camp, and adult and teachers' workshops in sustainability and natural science.

At the east end of the parking lot is a short nature walk that features plants that were noted by the Lewis and Clark Expedition. At the west end of the parking area is an interpretive sign with the story of grist and lumber mills that were once located nearby.

Just north of the gristmill interpretive sign is access to the 0.3-mile Trillium Trail, which loops through a boggy area punctuated with boardwalks. Look for the giant leaves of skunk cabbage and wander through a young forest of red alder and big-leaf maple with an understory of Indian plum, snowberry, and salmonberry. In early spring, look for the blooms of the namesake trillium and the bright, yellow, spiky flowers of the skunk cabbage.

From the west side of the parking lot follow a paved trail west. A small hidden path on the right just after a section of steel posts and before the highway bridge leads to the Cedar Circle Trail. This trail winds though a layered forest of vine maple, red alder, and western redcedar that provides great habitat for diverse bird life. Look for spotted towhees, Bewick's wrens, and fox sparrows.

Heading east from the parking lot will lead you on a paved path to the hatchery. Operated by Washington Department of Fish and Wildlife, the hatchery raises rainbow and brown trout and steelhead. Steelhead eggs collected in the fall are grown to fingerling size in the small ponds and raceways before being transferred to other larger hatcheries. The rainbow and brown trout are grown to about eight inches and eventually planted in Clark County lakes.

At the east end of the hatchery buildings is a plaza with viewing scopes overlooking a small wetland area. Nearby are picnic tables under large cedars and two wetland-viewing platforms. Also nearby is a small, round fish observation pond where you can throw fish chow to the voracious trout.

Look behind the four long, fish-rearing raceways for the small, secret boardwalk trail that crosses the outflow from West Biddle Lake. Here you will notice the song of red-winged blackbirds and flowing water. You may also see small fish darting about.

Continuing to explore east, you will discover a stacked cordwood, octagon-shaped classroom with an ecoroof. Look out over West Biddle Lake from the platform next to the classroom and see if you can spot any waterfowl. Double-crested cormorants are often seen here in the late winter. A path loops around the north side of the lake and

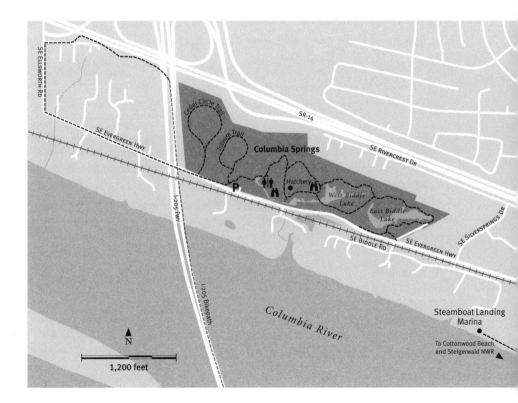

continues across a footbridge and through a meadow to a second larger lake called East Biddle Lake. Though manual eradication efforts continue, Himalayan blackberries are a late summer feast at the edges of this meadow. A path also follows the south side of West Biddle Lake past a ranch-style house that contains Columbia Springs offices. Follow this path past the house to link up with the formerly described path around the north side of the lake.

The Columbia Springs offices are adjacent to a backyard composting demonstration site, where visitors can see different composting bins and systems as well as the making of compost.

Access

Parking is at the public parking lot on the north side of Evergreen Highway just east of the underside of the Interestate-205 Bridge. Trails can be found at the east and west ends of the parking lot.

How to Get There

BY CAR: From Interstate 5 to State Route 14 heading east, take exit 5 (SE Ellsworth Road) and turn right toward the river. Turn left onto SE Evergreen Highway and go 0.7 miles east. From Interstate 205 take State Route 14 east to 164th Street. Exit. Turn right onto SE Evergreen Highway. Drive west. **BY BIKE:** From the bike trail that exits the I-205/Glenn Jackson Bridge, follow bike path signs to SE Ellsworth Road. Turn left on SE Ellsworth and ride one block south to SE Evergreen Highway. Turn left onto SE Evergreen and ride 0.7 miles east. **PUBLIC TRANSIT:** No direct service

By Jo Anne Dolan

More information: Columbia Springs

Hello, Chum

At a quiet bend in the Columbia River near Columbia Springs, cold springs bubble up near the river's shore. These sheltered springs provide ideal conditions for aerating salmon nests or redds. This small patch of riverside is managed as a conservation easement by the Columbia Land Trust, and hosts the largest known remaining chum salmon run in the mainstem of the Columbia River in Washington between Grays River and Bonneville Dam.

Chum salmon have some unique characteristics. Spawning males grow elongated, canine-like fangs and have bright, calico-colored markings. The name chum is thought to originate from the language of the Chinook people of the lower Columbia River, whose word *tsum* can be translated as calico.

In early December, The Circle of Life Salmon Celebration occurs. People gather to marvel at the tenacity of the salmon, and a Chinook tribal elder honors the salmon with a traditional prayer of song and drumming.

Cottonwood Beach

LOCATION: S Index Street and S 32nd Street, Washougal, WA **ACTIVITIES:** Hiking, Biking, Paddling, Boating, Fishing **FACILITIES:** Restrooms, Parking, Paved and unpaved trails, Picnic area/shelter, Dock, Canoe/kayak launch, Wildlife viewing structure, Interpretive signs/info **FEES AND REGULATIONS:** Pets on leash **HIKING DIFFICULTY:** Easy **HIGHLIGHTS:** One of the best places to access the Columbia River in Clark County; Sandy beaches; Spectacular views of Mount Hood; Lewis and Clark interpretation and sculptures; Trail connections to Steigerwald Lake National Wildlife Refuge and Steamboat Landing Park; Reed Island State Park, accessible only by boat, is easily reached by paddling from Cottonwood and is home to osprey, migrating and wintering ducks, and geese **PUBLIC TRANSIT:** No direct service

If you're planning on organizing a kayaking trip for eleven women ranging in experience from "I've never been in a kayak" to well-seasoned paddlers, Cottonwood Beach provides the perfect launching point. The sandy, shallow shoreline allows plenty of time for pre-launch instructions and proper fitting of equipment, and ensures a safe first-time trip for even the most inexperienced kayakers.

Once afloat, turn your sights to the east and head up the Columbia River into the slough dividing Steigerwald Lake Refuge and Reed Island State Park. It's a quick, easy paddle to the slough with little to no current to battle or waves to negotiate. Once in the slough, the water is shallow and easily navigable, allowing paddlers to sit back and enjoy the beauty and serenity of the refuge. Be sure to pack a lunch and enjoy the picnicking opportunities available on Reed Island State Park, a standout destination accessible only by water. There are plenty of birdwatching opportunities, and the view of Mount Hood on a sunny, clear day is breathtaking.

While Cottonwood Beach provides a perfect place to learn to kayak, it is not without allure for the more experienced kayaker. A quick paddle into the main waterway of the Columbia offers challenging tidal pulls, occasional high waves, and competition from motorized boats. When kayaking Cottonwood Beach, I prefer to drop a car at the Port of Camas-Washougal and, after paddling the refuge and soaking up all it has to offer, turn to the west and strengthen my skills via a paddle downriver to the port. River conditions vary providing for a fun-filled, challenging trip.

Although access to Cottonwood Beach from the parking lot of Captain William Clark Park is not easy (a kayak caddy is highly recommended to maneuver over the path that transverses the dike that separates parking from the beach) it is well worth the trip. On a sunny summer day, you may have to weave through the sunbathers and swimmers enjoying other amenities of the park, which include a three-mile walking, biking, and horseback trail, and covered picnic shelters.

Upon returning to the beach, check out the park's history at some of the Lewis and Clark Expedition historical interpretive elements, created in recognition of the park's namesake. On March 31, 1806, Meriwether Lewis and William Clark established a camp near Cottonwood Beach while they secured provisions for the return trip east through the Columbia River Gorge. This significant stay on their journey is celebrated throughout the park through interpretive panels and replica period pieces such as canoe sculptures and architectural structures.

Access

The main entrance is in Washougal at the intersection of S 32nd Street and S Index Street. Restrooms and parking are on the north side of the dike. A paved path travels over the dike. There are also parking areas along S Index Street at S 35th Street and S 37th Street with gravel paths to the dike trail and several informal paths down to the park and beach. The dike trail can also be accessed to the west at Steamboat Landing Park, and through an underpass trail beginning at the Pendleton Woolen Mills in Washougal and to the east at Steigerwald Lake National Wildlife Refuge.

How to Get there

BY CAR: State Route 14 (Lewis and Clark Highway) east to Washougal. There is a small parking area on S 15th Street (Steamboat Landing Park). The main entrance is south on S 32nd Street. **PUBLIC TRANSIT:** No direct service

By Cheri Martin

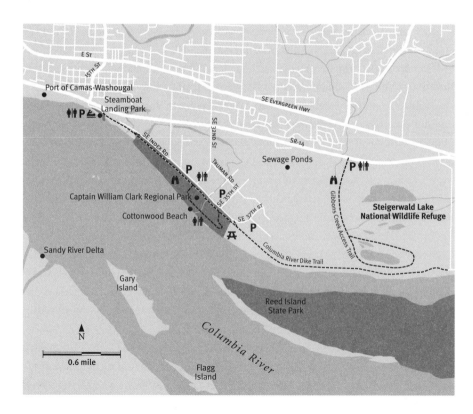

Steigerwald Lake National Wildlife Refuge

Location: East of 32nd Street and State Route 14, Washougal, WA **Activities:** Hiking, Wildlife viewing **Facilities:** Restrooms, Parking, Unpaved trails, Signs/interpretive info **Fees and Regulations:** No jogging, No bicycles, No horses or pets allowed on Gibbons Trail **Hiking Difficulty:** Easy **Highlights:** Wetlands boardwalks; Woodlands trails; Guided spring and fall hikes; Outstanding birding; Interpretive signs and art pieces **Public Transit:** No direct service

Steigerwald Lake Refuge, which is managed by the U.S. Fish and Wildlife Service, was established in 1987 to help mitigate the effects of constructing a second powerhouse at Bonneville Dam. The main purpose of the refuge is to protect and restore the wetlands and riparian and upland habitat to encourage wildlife and plant diversity.

The refuge is located at the western Washington Gateway to the Columbia Gorge National Scenic Area, and as such provides visitors with amazing views of the refuge wetlands, Mount Hood, and the beginning of the Columbia River Gorge National Scenic Area. While on the refuge, visitors may experience some excellent birdwatching. Steigerwald provides lingering habitat for birds flying both east-west along the gorge and north-south along the Cascades. Wilson Cady, an avid birdwatcher and long-time supporter of the refuge, says, "The refuge is like a Minute Mart operation at the busiest intersection of highways," during his many years of birding Cady has seen many rare birds at this location, including the black phoebe, white-faced ibis, and gyrfalcon.

In addition, the refuge's location is historically significant. In 1792, Lieutenant William Broughton, a member of the Vancouver Expedition—Captain George Vancouver's five-year exploration voyage of the Northwest—stood at Cottonwood Point and claimed the Columbia and all the land it drains for Great Britain. He then named Mount Hood for Admiral Hood, the sponsor of Captain Vancouver's endeavor. In 1806, Lewis and Clark camped at what is now named Captain William Clark Park nearby for a week, obtaining provisions for their return journey from Astoria back to St. Louis. In 1847, Joseph Gibbons brought cattle to an area on the refuge, built a cabin, and planted crops. In the early 1900s, stories had been told of row crops of potatoes a mile long. In the mid-1900s, the Steigerwald family operated a dairy herd in the Steigerwald Lake floodplain, keeping their cows in a large barn located west of the present-day Bi-Mart Store. Their dairy outlet store, shaped like a giant milk bottle, was on the corner of NE 37th Avenue and Sandy Boulevard in Portland. After several other configurations, it now sports a Budweiser beer sign. The Port of Camas-Washougal was established in 1935 but did not move into the Steigerwald Lake area west of the refuge until the Columbia River dike was completed in 1966. During the mid-1970s, the Roberts family operated a bean farm on a portion of what was to become the refuge. In 1984, Oregon Senator Mark Hatfield introduced legislation to create the refuge as partial mitigation for habitat lost during the construction of the Second Powerhouse at North Bonneville.

Since the opening of the Gibbons Creek Trail in June 2009, many visitors have taken the opportunity to visit this quiet place located at the mouth of the gorge, just outside the City of Washougal. Trail volunteers are sometimes present, offering information and answering questions about what the visitor may have seen. Some visitors have reported such exciting things as American bitterns bursting out of the marsh as they walked by, a turtle slowly walking across the trail, and Canada geese nesting in the top of a broken snag. Other times it is just a chance to "get away from it all," with gentle (sometimes forceful) Columbia Gorge breezes blowing through the leaves of the cottonwood trees, and listening to the songs and calls of the myriad of birds using the refuge.

Here is one description provided by a regular to the refuge: "Early mornings and just before dusk are beautiful times on Steigerwald Lake refuge for their own unique reasons. The early hours are peaceful and still, yet brimming with activity as wildlife awakens to the day. Looking from the trailhead across the refuge to the east, your eye follows the calm waters of Steigerwald Lake across open fields to cottonwood trees in the distance. Rising up from the horizon is a blanket of fog that blends into low lying clouds at the base of Mount Hood and the surrounding cliffs, the top of the mountain lit up by early morning sun. Sunset colors can shine in the mountain sky, with beautiful hues of orange, pink, and lavender, as birds circle in above your head to roost for the evening. Bird songs of all types float clearly across the calm night air as you walk a creekside path bordered by wild roses, Indian plum, and a host of other native plants."

Access

To protect wildlife throughout the rest of the refuge, public access to the Steigerwald Lake National Wildlife Refuge is provided on the Gibbons Creek Wildlife Art Trail. This 2.75-mile trail, opened in June 2009, has a connection to 0.5 mile of the Columbia River Dike Trail between the refuge and the Columbia River. The trail is graveled and compacted, with good access for larger-tired electrical-powered wheelchairs. The terrain is flat, except for two short approaches to the Columbia River Dike portion of the trail. There is a wheelchair-accessible restroom facility; parking for twenty cars; one RV vehicle; and two Americans with Disabilities Act parking sites. The trail is open from dawn to dusk with an automatic gate; open hours are posted on the gate. A portion of the trail along the north side of Gibbons Creek is closed from October 1 through April 30 of each year to protect waterfowl. Wintering birds use the wetlands and fields to the north of the trail for resting and feeding, and the closure ensures maximum protection from winter disturbance. The Gibbons Trail is for hiking and wildlife observation only. The Columbia River Dike Trail, however, does allow running, bicycling, horseback riding, and leashed pets.

How to Get There

BY CAR: From Portland: north on Interstate 205; east on State Route 14 toward Camas. Once past Camas and Washougal, be on the lookout for a large vertical sign marking the boundary of the Columbia River Gorge National Scenic Area on the right side of the highway at about milepost 16. From Skamania: Go west on State Route 14 towards Washougal. Drive past Evergreen Highway, which is a right turn (north) just before you reach the pastures of the Steigerwald Lake Refuge east of Washougal. **PUBLIC TRANSIT:** No direct service

By James R. Clapp

More information: Steigerwald Lake National Wildlife Refuge-Ridgefield National Wildlife Refuge; Columbia Gorge Refuge Stewards

> **Refer to map on page 368**

Bright Butterflies

MORE BUTTERFLIES MAY BE FOUND in Manhattan than in Vancouver. For a place of such natural charms and varied habitats, Vancouver supports a relatively poor butterfly fauna. This condition owes much to its position. Wet, cool, cloudy, forested, and off in a bio-geographical backwater, Ecotopia is less a butterfly utopia than a mollusk metropolis. We have no shortage of nectar or larval hostplants, but sunshine is numero uno: habitat unsunny much of the time means habitat less than prime for butterflies. Winter rot (of eggs, larvae, pupae, or adults, whichever stage hibernates) also limits their abundance and diversity. Yet, though we enjoy fewer butterflies than Los Angeles, Laramie, or Lynchburg, greater Portland is graced by a number of beautiful species, easy to spot, watch, and enjoy.

Winter Butterflies

The butterfly watching year actually begins with the winter solstice. Species that overwinter as adults, in hollow trees, or other shelters, commonly awaken to fly about on unseasonably warm days, so even midwinter offers the prospect of butterflies on the wing. These are the first to be seen in spring, tatty after their winter rigors. The mourning cloak, with its ragged, blue-spotted cream edges on chocolate-maroon wings, is the most conspicuous of the hibernators. Two relatives, the orange-and-yellow-striped Milbert's tortoiseshell and foxy California tortoiseshell fluctuate in numbers. During years when California tortoiseshells erupt by the many thousands in the Cascades, where their caterpillars strip ceanothus, they also invade the city. The related, russet-and-bark-colored satyr anglewing is most likely to be encountered in Forest Park and other sylvan city spots where nettles, their larval host plant, occur. Watch for its golden flash in forest glades. The rustier faun anglewing, or green comma, may be seen in the woodsy places its name suggests.

Spring Butterflies

Of the butterflies emerging freshly from their chrysalides in spring, two may be expected in almost any woodland clearing or roadside, the wilder the better. Sunny days in March and April see both the margined white and the spring, or echo, azure coming out, commonly so in years with mild springs. The indigenous margined white feeds as a larva on wild crucifers (mustard family) such as toothwort, unlike the garden-chomping European cabbage white. The linen males and lemony females have olive scaling on the veins below—quite lovely in their simplicity as they nectar on spring beauty or coltsfoot with echo azures. Clear lilac-blue and chalky white with

Clodius Parnassian

gray chevrons, the azures arise from lar-
vae that browse the flowers and buds of shrubs and trees
including dogwoods and ninebark. Oaks Bottom is a fine place to seek both the spring
and summer broods of azures, the species of blue most likely to occur in the city.

Soon another member of the white family, Sara's orangetip, emerges. One of our
prettiest butterflies, Sara flashes brilliant orange wingtips on white wings mottled
grass-green below. The buttery yellow female lays her eggs on various mustard
plants. At lilac time, Sara may be seen but seldom expected dancing through outlying
green and sunny spots including farm lanes and suburban open spaces. Two bits of
orange-peel flitting through the air, connected by a scrap of bright white, will be Sara's
orangetip—a springtime beauty well worth getting to know.

Spring/Summer Butterflies

May and June bring on the swallowtails, of which we are blessed with three species
and an odd but lovely cousin. The anise swallowtail, black with broad yellow bands,
uses dill, fennel, cow parsley, and other umbels (carrot family) as larval hosts. Males
haunt hilltops, where they joust and seek unmated females. Our two types of tigers
wander all over town. The black-banded, creamy pale tiger swallowtail feeds on alder
and ocean spray, while the lemon-yellow western tiger swallowtail, the more common
of the two, browses maple, willow, poplar, and other broadleafs. The western tiger is
our most dramatic city butterfly all summer long, as it soars down streets and glides
across glades, pausing to nectar on bramble or phlox. Big parks are good for it, but
your garden will do too. Untailed, utterly unlike other Oregon swallowtails except one
mountain relative, the Clodius Parnassian nonetheless belongs to the same
family. Ruby and coal spots set off the milky white, waxy wings, partially transparent
in females. Seek Parnassians about patches of bleeding heart, their larval hostplant, in
wilder parts of Forest Park.

Summer Butterflies

High summer belongs to bright members of the brush-footed family. Lorquin's admiral, a willow and ocean spray feeder, hang-glides all over Portland. Its jet-black wings, cream-banded and apricot-tipped, are unmistakable. The larvae and pupae mimic bird droppings, and the adults sometimes defend their territories against birds! Not closely related, the scarlet-banded red admiral (or red admirable) actually allies with the pinker painted lady and bright orange West Coast lady, all in the genus *Vanessa*. Their numbers fluctuate greatly depending on parasites, rainfall, and spring nectar in Mexico, since they mostly immigrate from the Southwest. The small, drab arrivals of early summer yield big, brilliant individuals in the next generations. Red admirables need nettles to breed on, painted ladies prefer thistles, and you can easily provide plenty of asters and other nectar plants in your garden for both. Watch for vanessas in open fields, along wood edges, or hill-topping crazily at sunset on Rocky Butte.

Another thistle-feeding brush-foot is the little Mylitta crescent. Clear orange with sharp black markings and only an inch across, Mylitta patrols roadsides or paths through vacant lots and meadows, gliding with an occasional flap. Paler but similar in size, ocher ringlets haunt Multnomah channel meadows where they flip-flop through tall grasses and their larvae graze.

As summer progresses, yellow tansy ragwort provides fodder for cinnabar moths, a European species introduced to fight this alien weed. Most people take the brilliant, day-flying cinnabar—scarlet and gun-barrel blue moths for butterflies.

Lorquin's admiral

pine white

Ragwort and the also-alien hawkbit furnish prolific nectar for late summer butterflies. Nearly every patch—and every bed of lavender—supports a cluster of woodland skippers in August. Skippers have hooked knobs on their antennae, stout bodies, short wings, and speedy, skipping flight. Woodlands, our commonest skippers by far, are tawny-gold with black dashes and pale patches. Grass feeders, they frequent unsprayed lawns, doing no harm but providing excellent company. Mylittas and woodlands keep company with purplish coppers, of the gossamer-winged family. Penny-brown male coppers flash metallic purple when the sun catches their wings just right, as they court bright orange, black-spotted females around dock and knotweed. Moist spots near meadows sometimes abound with coppers.

Summer/Fall Butterflies

Late summer finds pine whites, veined with red and black on white, floating around the crowns of Douglas firs. Their caterpillars resemble bundles of the conifer needles they consume. Now is the time also to watch for orange and clouded sulphurs streaking and spiraling together in courtship over alfalfa and red clover fields on Sauvie Island, in the Tualatin Valley, or out toward Sandy. Then, as nights begin to chill, the tortoiseshells and anglewings again seek winter shelter, yet come out to nectar and bask as long as the autumn rains hold off.

Did I say we have a poor butterfly fauna? It doesn't sound so bad in review. They may not compare so well to the prolific assemblage to be found in Cascade meadows and canyons, yet the region's butterflies offer variety, beauty, and fascination enough to recommend them to our notice. I urge you to go forth with wide-open eyes in search of the bright wings of summer, and of all the other seasons.

By Robert Michael Pyle, illustration by Elayne Barclay

Water Resources Center Wetlands

LOCATION: 4600 SE Columbia Way, Vancouver, WA **ACTIVITIES:** Hiking, Biking, Paddling, Boating, Fishing, Wildlife viewing, Nature study, Water events **FACILITIES:** Restrooms, Parking, Paved trails, Visitor Center, Picnic area/shelter, Dock, Canoe/kayak launch, Wildlife viewing structure, Interpretive signs/info, Backyard Wildlife Demonstration Garden, Nature play area, Student restoration projects **FEES AND REGULATIONS:** Hours dawn to dusk; Pets on leash **HIKING DIFFICULTY:** Easy **HIGHLIGHTS:** 50 acres of wetlands; paved biking trail; long stretches of beach; Spectacular views of Mount Hood and the Columbia River; Insight into the seasonal water and wildlife cycles of a dynamic wetlands; Backyard Wildlife Garden with 150 species of mostly native plants; Interactive exhibits, classroom lab, toddler-friendly Puddles Place, White Sturgeon Art Gallery; Wetlands teeming with wildlife; Bird watching out of the two-story windows overlooking bird feeders and secret ponds **PUBLIC TRANSIT:** No direct service

From the overlook at the Water Resources Education Center, you can see through wooded wetlands and across the Columbia River to Oregon. Eighty years ago, if you were standing on this spot, you would be swallowing a lot of river water and seeing river bottom. The Water Center wetlands slowly evolved from river bottom to riverine wetlands after Bonneville Dam was constructed in 1937. The towering cottonwoods, brushy willow, and pointed-leafed wapato did not and could not grow here before changing river hydrology slowed down the current and brought in more sediment.

As plants colonized the new land, so did wildlife. Over 150 species of birds, mammals, amphibians, reptiles, and invertebrates use this fifty-acre wetland habitat at some phase of their life cycle.

As the Vancouver wetlands emerged, much of the original extensive Columbia River wetlands on the Oregon shore were diked, filled, capped with an airport, and cut off from river access. Young salmon migrating downstream could no longer shelter in the braided-river side channels in Oregon. A salmon smolt heading to the ocean today has one off-channel resting and feeding option between river mile 112 at the I-205 bridge and river mile 106.5 at the Water Center wetlands—more than six miles without a place to rest or feed. Access to this inlet from the river is across a large area of shallows and over a sandbar that continues to enlarge. In 2010, the City of Vancouver and the Army Corps of Engineers re-cut a channel through this potential barrier so that young coho and Chinook salmon have continual access from March until the end of the spring freshet in late June.

The best viewing area, at the black wrought-iron overlook along a paved trail, gives a birds-eye view of the wetlands. From here you can watch dynamically changing water levels, from highest water in late spring when the geese and ducks are nesting to dry ground in early fall. On many sunny days in mid-spring, you can listen to red-winged blackbirds and watch painted turtles basking on the platforms built by a local eagle scout.

The healthy wapato colony also varies from year to year, depending on how successful flooding was in knocking back the competing reed canarygrass. The brush is thick and hides many birds; what you can't see you can listen to in season—songbirds, eagles, osprey, hawks, and shorebirds.

Come back in fall and watch the geese flocks settle in for the night; once the leaves fall off in winter, the over-wintering wildlife—beaver, muskrat, weasels, towhees, sparrows, Anna's hummingbirds, and occasionally a pileated woodpecker—are visible. If you have trouble visualizing how radically the water level changes, just look at the large signs next to you with photographs from winter, spring, summer, and fall seasons, framed by elegant silk paintings of the animals that are present during those months.

Walk or bicycle the trail east and south about a quarter mile to the river and you will skirt the edges of the riverine wetlands. The Water Center has worked with local schools and other volunteers to remove the invasive blackberries and ivy in the drier areas and replant with native plants. During the summer, you can watch an osprey pair raise their young on an installed platform. Turn your head slightly east and admire Mount Hood framed by the I-205 Bridge. Here you can also leave the paved trail and walk west along the long expanse of sandy beach that will take you to the south side of the inlet where the river enters through the newly dug-out channel. Use this season to look for beaver tracks and chew and signs of deer, muskrat, and other creatures. If you are really lucky, you might find one of the large native *Anodonta* mussel shells that mysteriously appear every so often. If you came back to this spot in a high-water season, you would need a boat. Water levels vary radically by season and moderately by time of day since this shoreline, like others up to Bonneville Dam, is influenced by ocean tides.

North of the road and paved trail is a seven-acre depressional wetland, a remnant of the pre-dam Columbia River floodplain lake. Soil cores taken by the University of Washington suggest that the lake sediments have been intact for a thousand years and show signs of burning. This wetland remnant has no general public access but is used

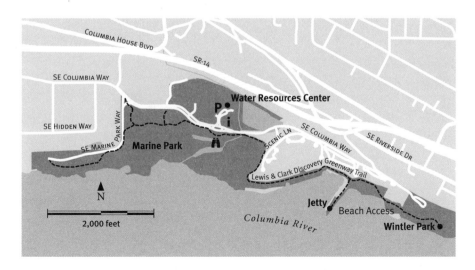

for educational programs. Red-tailed hawks have nested here for several years in a tall cottonwood at the edge. In summer you can stand in the Water Center parking lot and hear the shrieks of the fledglings crying for food.

Access

A fourteen-foot paved, multi-use trail, part of the longer Renaissance Trail, takes people to the Columbia River where they can walk along the beach. A dirt trail on the west side of the Water Center also goes to the river.

How to Get There

BY CAR: From Interstate 5 take State Route 14 to exit 1, bearing right. Under the railroad overpass, turn east (left) at the Columbia Shores intersection onto Southeast Columbia Way and continue about 2.5 miles. Follow the signs at the turnaround to the Center. From Interstate 205 take State Route 14 to exit 1 toward the Vancouver National Historic Reserve. Turn left onto Columbia House Boulevard and follow Columbia under SR 14 and the railroad overpasses to the Columbia Shores intersection. Turn east (left) and follow above from Columbia Shores. **BY BIKE:** From the Washington side of the I-205 bike trail, follow bike path signs to SE Ellsworth Road. Turn left on SE Ellsworth and ride one block south to SE Evergreen Highway. Turn right and ride about 2.5 miles west. Look for signs to Wintler Park that take you through neighborhoods. The paved trail to the wetlands begins there. Ride about 2 miles west to the wetlands. **PUBLIC TRANSIT:** No direct service

By Cory Samia

More information: City of Vancouver Water Resources Center

Vancouver's Discovery Historic Loop and Heritage Trees

Few places in the Northwest can claim as many historic and scenic attractions in such close proximity as Vancouver's Discovery Historic Loop. This 2.3-mile trail winds through Fort Vancouver National Historic Site, Officers Row, and downtown Vancouver, connecting to the Columbia River waterfront by Columbia Street on the west end and the Vancouver Land Bridge on the east. The walk can be completed in an hour, but more time is needed to do it justice. Along the way you can explore what makes this place special—an amalgamation of history, historic preservation, culture, and nature.

Old Apple Tree Park ❶ on Columbia Way is a good place to start, with parking available across the street at the west end of the Waterfront Renaissance Trail. The park was dedicated in 1984 to honor the oldest apple tree in Washington State. Planted in 1826 under the direction of Dr. John McLoughlin, Chief Factor of Hudson's Bay Company in Fort Vancouver, the tree still bears fruit today.

Continue east to the **Vancouver Land Bridge** ❷, where Northwest history, art, and landscape converge. Designed by Johnpaul Jones, of Jones and Jones Architecture in Seattle, in collaboration with artist/architect Maya Lin, the land bridge reconnects the terrain between the Columbia River and Fort Vancouver, long separated by railroad tracks and State Route 14. The forty-foot-wide overpass provides safe passage for pedestrians and bicyclists, along with lookout points and interpretive stations where visitors can enjoy the view and reflect on this region's unique past.

Native American-inspired artwork and native plant communities—woodlands, grasslands, and prairies—add to the experience. Images of basketry, vintage photos, interpretive panels, and the entry gate designed by Native American artist Lillian Pitt can be enjoyed year-round, while the landscape changes from season to season. Color is at its peak in spring when the wild roses, rhododendrons, and camas lilies bloom.

Lewis and Clark camped near the north end of the bridge in 1805, where **Fort Vancouver** ❸ was built twenty years later. As the base of operations for Britain's Hudson's Bay Company, the fort was the center of trade west of the Mississippi from Alaska to Mexico. It was also a place for Europeans to mingle with Native Americans, for whom this was an important tribal crossroad.

Today the 366-acre site is designated a National Historic Site operated by the National Park Service. You can enjoy a casual stroll around the grounds or explore the many layers of history represented at the site and surrounding area. Ten reconstructed buildings and an 1845 **heritage garden** are open daily year-round ❹.

Trees are the best monuments that a man can erect to his own memory. They speak his praises without flattery, and they are blessings to children yet unborn.

—John Boyle, Earl of Orrery, 1749

Vancouver's rich history is intertwined and rooted in trees. The city's founders as well as the native people depended on trees for shelter, warmth, and transportation. Trees have been used to mark property boundaries and as points of reference. Trees still provide us with many benefits, although they are not as easy to quantify and may not be immediately obvious. They mitigate stormwater runoff, improve air quality, reduce carbon dioxide, conserve energy, improve aesthetics, dampen noise, and provide wildlife habitat. Our relationship to trees may be less narrowly utilitarian than that of our forebears, but trees continue to sustain our lives and anchor us to our place, just as they did 150 years ago.

Vancouver's Notable Historic and Heritage Trees tour begins on the Columbia River at Waterfront Park on East Columbia Way. The tree locations are keyed on the map on the facing page. (HT indicates a Heritage Tree)

A **The Witness Tree**

B **Old Apple Tree** (*Malus* sp) (HT)

C **Officers Row and Centennial School Planting**

D **David Douglas' Fir**

E **Patrons Grove**

F **Centennial Cherries**

G **Mayor's Grove**, NW corner of Mill Plain and Fort Vancouver Way

H **Street Tree Arboretum**, McLoughlin Boulevard and Fort Vancouver Way

I **Black Walnut** (*Juglans nigra*) (HT), Arnada Park, at the dead-end of G Street

J **California Bay Tree** (*Umbellularia californica*) (HT), 401 E 22nd Street

K **Red Oak** (*Quercus rubra*) (HT), SW corner of Fourth Plain and Main Street

L **Norway Maples** (*Acer platanoides*) (HT), 117-127 W 24th Street

M **The Columbian Street Trees**

N **Old Apple Tree Offspring** (*Malus* sp) (HT), 1511 Main Street

O **Esther Short Park Trees** (*Conifer Grove*) (HT), 610 Esther Street

P **European Beech** (*Fagus sylvatica*) (HT), Esther and 6th Streets

By Charles Ray

More information: City of Vancouver Urban Forestry; Vancouver-Clark Parks & Recreation

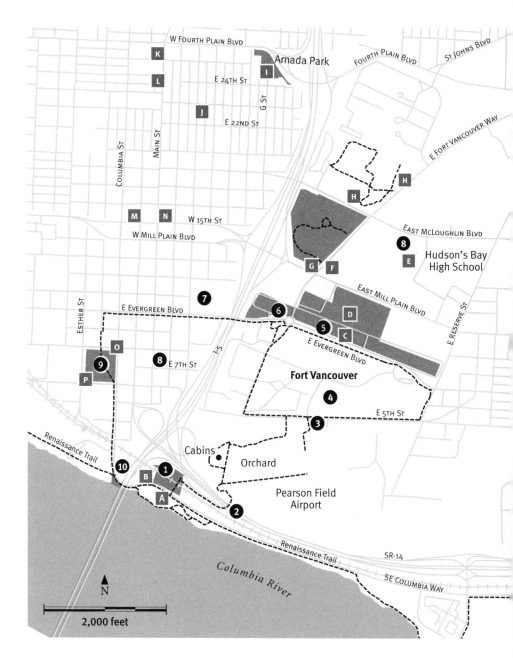

Discovery Historic Loop includes a leisurely stroll down **Officers Row** ❺, also run by the National Park Service. This is one of the oldest neighborhoods in the Northwest, composed of twenty-one perfectly preserved nineteenth-century homes. Ulysses S. Grant, George Marshall, and Omar Bradley were among the military notables stationed here. Information about "the Row" is available at the **Visitor Center** in the General O. O. Howard House at 750 Anderson Street ❻.

The last leg of Discovery Historic Loop takes you through downtown Vancouver, where the influence of the founding pioneers is felt in prominent structures such as **Providence Academy**, built in 1873 **7**. This was a hospital, school, and orphanage run by Mother Joseph, a Catholic nun and Northwest pioneer. You will also see fine examples of modern redevelopment, such as **Turtle Place 8** on Seventh Street, a former bus transit center that has been transformed into a quarter-block plaza dedicated to the "art" of recycling.

Of course, the focal point of downtown Vancouver is **Esther Short Park 9**, the oldest public square in the Northwest. Established in 1853, the park's Victorian rose garden, benches, drinking fountain, and lights all reflect the culture of the period. Major renovations, including a bell tower, glockenspiel, interactive fountain, and tulip garden were completed in 2001. The popular Vancouver Farmers Market—one of the region's largest—is held on Esther Street at the west end of the park every weekend from early March through October.

To complete the circuit, go south for several blocks on Columbia Street, passing the **Captain Vancouver Monument 10**. Back at the river you can continue your adventure east along the Columbia River on the five-mile Waterfront Renaissance Trail. It takes you by cafes, the Kaiser shipyards, Marine Park and wetlands, and Vancouver's Water Resource Center with exceptional views of Mount Hood and the Portland skyline in the distance. The trail ends at a pier that juts into the Columbia River and Wintler Park. The Renaissance Trail is a perfect place to appreciate the connection of history, culture, and nature all entwined.

By Kelly Punteney

Don't Miss This!

The Vancouver Land Bridge is part of the larger Confluence Project, which traces Lewis and Clark's journey in the Columbia River Basin through interpretive artwork by renowned artist Maya Lin. The ambitious undertaking was initiated in 2000 by a group of Pacific Northwest Native American tribes and civic groups from Washington and Oregon. Through the transformation of seven sites within the Columbia River Basin, the project aims to evoke the history of the Lewis and Clark 1805–1806 Expedition, highlight the changes it brought to the Pacific Northwest, and encourage action to preserve and protect our area's natural and cultural resources.

Burnt Bridge Creek Greenway Trail

Called the green jewel in the heart of Vancouver, Burnt Bridge Creek Greenway Trail truly is an amazing swath of green infrastructure. With a series of paved, shared-use trails, it continues for nearly eight miles past some of the best wild areas in Vancouver—from wetlands to heavy forest to open grassland. The location, right in the middle of the city, makes it all easily accessible from a number of different trailheads and many neighborhoods, either by foot or bicycle.

The dream started as part of Vancouver's even larger Discovery Trail, a project many years in the making that was the vision of Vancouver resident Dorothy Langsdorf and her troop of Girl Scouts in the 1960s. Searching for a substantive community service project, they developed a plan for a trail that would loop the community. They presented their proposal to the Vancouver Parks Commission and received a grant from *Reader's Digest* magazine to build the trail, which includes Burnt Bridge Creek. That award-winning effort gained national recognition and made history by helping launch the movement to develop Vancouver's urban trails.

Those new to Burnt Bridge Creek are amazed by the natural riches so close to the city. If you're approaching for the first time, park at the west end trailhead along Bernie Road where it meets **Fruit Valley Road** ❶. The sidewalk loops around just past the highway intersection to the signed official start of Discovery Trail. Those on foot can take a shortcut—a set of very steep cement stairs going directly from the lot down to the trail.

The wetlands in **Stewart Glen** ❷ provide excellent waterfowl habitat, and you may see lesser scaup, Canada geese, and mallards dabbling for aquatic plants. Hike the trail east along the south side of the creek and enjoy a forest that includes Douglas fir, western redcedar, big-leaf maples, salal, and vine maple. Scan the trees for robins, Bewick's and Pacific wrens, northern flickers, cedar waxwings, and spotted towhees. Several informal trails access the greenway from the northwest neighborhood, and you will often meet residents walking or biking along the trail. Continue east to where the trail meets **Hazel Dell Avenue** ❸. Walk south along Hazel Dell a few hundred feet and pick up the trail again on your left.

Now you access a bike- and pedestrian-only trail, which crosses over Interstate 5 on Leverich Parkway and into **Leverich Park** ❹. **The Ellen Davis Trail** ❺ (see page 391) takes off to the left just before entering Leverich Park, which features a large picnic shelter, a disk golf course, and trails along both sides of Burnt Bridge Creek. Leverich has plenty of parking and makes a great trailhead whether you're heading east or west.

Continue east along the trail through the park, crossing NE 15th Avenue and along NE 41st Circle and NE 18th Court to **Arnold Park** ❻, an undeveloped park that was originally slated for a housing development. The City of Vancouver saw the potential to conserve habitat and enhance water quality in Burnt Bridge Creek and purchased the property before any houses were built.

The paved trail picks up again at the end of NE 41st Circle and heads under Bonneville Power Administration (BPA) power lines. While the BPA easement limits the vegetation in the area, you will often see raptors hunting rodents in the meadow. Cross Saint Johns Boulevard at the signal and pick up the trail on the other side.

Continue upstream as the trail crosses under **State Route 500** ❼ and into **Burnt Bridge Canyon** ❽. The creek has carved a canyon perhaps seventy-five feet deep through this area, and the steep banks prevented development even during the era of lax environmental regulation. You will come upon the majestic sight of mature western redcedars towering over a forest floor filled with ferns. Listen for belted kingfishers as they patrol the creek looking for a snack, or search the undergrowth for salamanders during the spring. Linger in the forest for a while, and you will forget you're in the middle of the city.

As you come up out of the canyon, cross busy Fourth Plain Boulevard at the signal and continue southeast along the trail under the BPA power lines to **18th Street** ❾.

LBJ and the Discovery Trail

President Lyndon B. Johnson's message to Congress on February 8, 1965, was the inspiration for Dorothy Langsdorf and her Girl Scout troop to create the Discovery Trail. Because so many successful programs resulted from the speech, it became known as Johnson's Natural Beauty Message to Congress. LBJ spoke eloquently about the need for a national system of trails that would provide limitless opportunities for those who like to walk, hike, bicycle, or ride horseback. He cited the need for physical activity, both for fitness and for fun.

Once you cross 18th, the trail turns and follows the creek east across a broad floodplain punctuated by deciduous trees.

At Devine Road, a trailhead includes a parking area and restroom. This is the newest section of the trail and features a wide concrete path with plenty of space for the many bikers and walkers who use it daily. The floodplain is also unusually wide and provides habitat for beaver, coyotes, deer, and a wide variety of birds. Raptors often circle overhead looking for a meal. About a half mile from Devine, the **trail forks** ❿, with the left fork winding through a newly restored wetland habitat and ponds that also manage stormwater from the mall and car dealers to the north.

As part of the trail project, the City of Vancouver installed a signal that allows trail users to safely cross Andresen Road. On the other side of Andresen, you will find more stormwater and habitat ponds that host a variety of wildlife including frogs, fish, and ducks. The trail follows the creek east through scrubby vegetation such as spirea and thimbleberry and crosses under NE 86th Avenue. Note the many seeps that feed

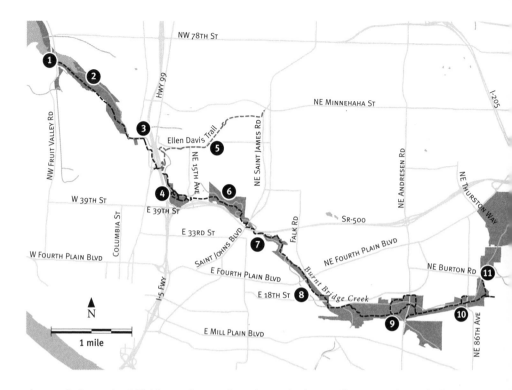

the creek from the hillside to the south and search the small, seasonal ponds for wildlife. The trail turns north and crosses a bridge over Burton Channel, which recently had an upstream culvert removed and habitat enhancement done.

Though the trail ends at **Burton Road** ⓫, the city continues to acquire property upstream to protect Burnt Bridge Creek and eventually extend the greenway. Many thousands of trees and shrubs have been planted to provide a lush canopy in the area and wetland enhancements are re-establishing the creek's natural water flow. The dream of a vibrant green infrastructure is alive and well in the heart of town.

Access

Stewart Glen Trailhead: NW Bernie Drive and NW Fruit Valley Road. (The western trailhead at Bernie Drive offers an expansive rock wall overlook perfect for watching wintering waterfowl as the creek ponds before entering Vancouver Lake to the west.) Leverich Park Trailhead: 39th Street north on NE Leverich Park Way. Continue north to the last parking lot on the left with trail entrance sign. Devine Road Trailhead: Devine Road just south of E 18th Street, Vancouver. NE Andresen Road: just south of 18th Street. Easternmost walk/bike-in location is at Burton Road, just east of 87th Avenue. On-street access: also includes Alki Road where the trail crosses the road; Hazel Dell Avenue just south of 59th Street; NE 15th Avenue; St. John's and State Route (SR) 500; Nicholson Road, just west of Falk Road; Fourth Plain Boulevard just east of

Falk; 18th Street just west of General Anderson; the most eastern access is Burton Road just east of 87th Avenue.

How to Get There
Stewart Glen Trailhead
BY CAR: From Portland take Interstate 5 exit 4, west on NE 78th Street, west on NW Fruit Valley Road, east on NW Bernie Drive. **PUBLIC TRANSIT:** From Vancouver take NW Fruit Valley Road, C-Tran Line 2; NE Hazel Dell Avenue, Line 6

Leverich Park
BY CAR: From Portland take Interstate 5 exit 2, east on E. 39th Street, north on NE Leverich Park Way. **PUBLIC TRANSIT:** From Vancouver take NE Hazel Dell Avenue, Line 6; NE 15th Avenue, C-Tran Lines 190, 173, 157, 134; E 39th Street, Line 3

By Gary Bock and Kelly Punteney

More information: Vancouver-Clark Parks & Recreation

Leave the Babies Alone

From our largest natural areas to our residential neighborhoods to the downtown hardscape, it is not uncommon to happen upon young birds and mammals making their first forays into the world during the spring and early summer. The first reaction may be to "rescue" them. Resist the urge!

Young birds often fledge (leave the nest) before they are able to fly. Many bird fledglings, from robins to red-tailed hawks, will spend extended periods, even several days, hopping about on the ground before they take to the air. The parents will periodically locate, feed, and provide them with guidance during this period—a critical part of their learning process.

Some species such as killdeer are precocial, meaning that they are able to move about and feed on their own almost from the time they hatch. They look tiny, fragile, and helpless, but they are mostly able to fend for themselves, relying on parents primarily for guidance and warmth. If you see a gosling or duckling wandering alone near a river or pond, leave it be and let it quack until mom returns.

Young mammals will often venture some distance from their parents. The parents are usually nearby but will likely stay out of sight if humans or other species they perceive as predators are in the area. Although young birds and mammals are highly vulnerable, their chances of survival are even lower if they are taken into captivity and then later returned to the wild without the training their parents would have provided. Young birds and mammals face hazards whether they are from our wildest landscapes or the inner city. The rule remains the same: if you care, leave them there.

—Bob Sallinger

Different Drummers

You can't walk for long in any forest, even the young, second-growth forests that are common around Vancouver, without being aware of decay, frequently in the form of broken, branchless, insect-ridden dead trees, or snags. It's sobering to look at the ruin of an eighty-foot Douglas fir, but these snags play a critical role in the forest ecosystem, providing lodging and feeding stations for many animals.

No bird has a more significant—or more intimate—relationship to snags than woodpeckers, who unintentionally turn snags into homes for chickadees, nuthatches, wood ducks, screech owls, flying squirrels, bats, and other animals as they drill for food and excavate their own nest cavities. No animals are better adapted for the job, either. Their X-shaped, zygodactylous feet and stiff tails make easy work of scooting up and down perpendicular surfaces. And it's a treat to watch them employing their long, chisel-like beaks, the perfect implement for tearing into trees in search of food and lodging.

Woodpeckers don't just use their beaks for feeding and nest building, either; they also use them in much the same way that songbirds use their voice—to declare territory and attract mates. The rapid staccato drumroll of a courting woodpecker is its springtime mating song.

Woodpecker feeding and breeding habits are fascinating to watch, but what can't be seen is just as amazing. Woodpeckers' tongues are longer than those of any bird. Barbed and sticky, they can be extended well beyond the length of their bills to probe for ants and wood-boring beetles. Woodpeckers have also evolved sophisticated structures for protecting their brain and eyeballs from the wear and tear of constant pounding. Altogether their suite of adaptations is among the most remarkable in the animal kingdom.

Resident Woodpeckers
Northern Flicker

Our most familiar woodpecker is the elegant northern flicker. Flickers are also our most "domestic" woodpeckers—domestic in the sense that of all our woodpeckers, they are the ones that are most likely to be found in neighborhoods and backyards. They are numerous and striking in appearance, sporting luminous, salmon-colored underwings and tails and a flashy white rump patch. And they are not at all shy. Consequently they are the most frequently seen woodpecker and the most frequently heard. Their extended "wick-wick-wick-wick" call can be heard throughout the spring, and for much of the rest of the year, they can be located by their ringing "kleear" call.

It turns out that flickers are also domestic in the more problematic sense, in that they are likely to use our homes for drumming sites and for constructing homes of their own. Flicker drumming is more likely to be irritating than destructive, but their drilling can occasionally cause some damage.

Pileated Woodpeckers

Pending the ambiguous resurrection of the ivory-billed woodpecker, the look-alike pileated is the largest of its tribe in North America. Up to a foot and a half long, all black and white except for the shock (or pileus) of bright red feathers on the top of its

head, it is also the woodpecker that most resembles Woody. The pileated is not seen as often as some metro-area woodpeckers, but its presence is noted in other ways. It is frequently detected by its voice, a wild outburst of sound, somewhat suggestive of a primordial flicker—a voice that Ira Gabrielson and Stanley Jewett (in *Birds of Oregon*) call among the most fit "to express the very spirit of the great western forests."

Just as striking as its voice are the vertical, rectangular gashes made by this woodpecker as it uses its two-inch bill to tear away large chunks of wood in a vigorous search for carpenter ants. The best sign of the presence of pileateds are these gouges, two or three inches wide and just as deep, that can extend down the side of a tree for several inches or several feet—as though someone has been busy with a hatchet. The region's forested hills are the stronghold of pileated woodpeckers, but they will also stray into river bottoms or anywhere else there is adequate habitat.

Hairy and Downy Woodpeckers

These small woodpeckers are very nearly twins in plumage, and similar in voice. Like other woodpeckers, they are mottled with black and white, and the males sport a splotch of red on the back of the head. But the downy and hairy can easily be separated from other woodpeckers by their clear-white to off-white backs.

The real trick is separating them from each other. The main difference between the two is their size, but although the hairy is nearly eight inches long and the downy only six inches, that distinction is hard to make in the field. The best way to tell these two apart is to examine their bills. The downy's slight, three-quarter-inch bill is less than the width of its head, while the hairy's sturdy, one-and-a-quarter-inch bill is equal to or greater than the width of its head.

Both downy and hairy woodpeckers call the Vancouver area home, but downys are far more common and, given their unwariness and their tendency to frequent backyards, they are easy to spot and frequently seen. Their springtime drumming and their distinctive "whinny" further call them to attention.

Hairys are uncommon in the metro area, as they are shyer and they tend to stick to forested regions. Still, they are regularly seen and heard by alert birders. Their raspy, low-pitched voice is reminiscent of the downy's but clearly distinguishable from it.

Red-breasted Sapsucker

The last of our resident woodpeckers is perhaps the most beautiful and certainly the most unusual. The red-breasted sapsucker's solid red head sometimes causes it to be confused with the red-headed woodpecker, which doesn't occur in the West; otherwise, it can be mistaken for no other bird. Shy and silent, it is a hard bird to find, but a glimpse of a sapsucker is one that will be remembered.

The distinctive thing about sapsuckers is that, while most of their family chooses to excavate in dead trees, sapsuckers drill in living wood, tapping the trees for their sap. The oozing sap is itself nourishing, but it also attracts insects, upon which the birds return to feed. These sap wells also tempt warblers, other woodpeckers, and even chipmunks to make unauthorized visits.

Sapsucker wells appear as small holes ranked in even rows, large numbers of them often on a single tree. Healthy trees are robust and resistant to sapsucker feeding. Still, extensive and long-term use of a single tree for sapsucker wells can weaken the tree, causing anxiety in arborists and orchardists. There are, however, a number of techniques that can be employed to reduce the incidence of sapsucker damage and provide another opportunity for practicing our intricate and important dance with urban wildlife.

Not many birds—or other animals for that matter—are more effective at shaping their environment than woodpeckers. That, of course includes environments we share with them and we ourselves shape. This occasionally gives rise to friction. But we haven't been at it—this getting along with woodpeckers—for very long, not in the Pacific Northwest at least. My hope is that with a little coaching and a bit of forbearance, we will learn to adapt our ways to those of the woodpecker and will continue to celebrate these essential residents of our forest home.

By Bob Wilson, illustration by Robin M. Jensen

Woodpecker Woes

An argument with a woodpecker generally starts over one of two issues:

> Territorial drumming is noisy, but unlikely to cause much damage, making it more of a nuisance than a real problem (although that can be hard to keep in mind at 5 am). It is also relatively easy to stop by finding the drumming surface—often a satisfactorily clangorous bit of flashing or gutter—and covering it with a bit of sound-muffling cloth or foam.

> The drilling that woodpeckers use to excavate a nest cavity can be destructive and usually requires a bit more patience and persistence to discourage, unless you actually are willing to share your abode with woodpeckers—unlikely, but think about it. Scare devices can often haze the woodpecker away from the area, and it is sometimes helpful to provide an alternative home by hanging a nest box adjacent to the drilling site. Of course, if the woodpecker appears to be drilling in search of food, your first step should be checking your siding for insect damage. Perhaps you owe the pecker a debt of gratitude for early warning of insect infestation. But that's another living with wildlife issue!

Ellen Davis Trail

This 2.4-mile roundtrip, ultra-urban trail follows paved paths, sidewalks, and graveled segments through a diverse terrain, including some steep climbs and switchbacks, as it connects Leverich Park and Burnt Bridge Creek Trail (see page 383) with the Ellen Davis Trailhead at Saint James Road. The route is well-known by neighborhood trekkers but can be a bit tricky for others. Vancouver-Clark Parks & Recreation has added new signage where the trail takes off from Burnt Bridge Creek Trail and NE 59th Avenue. The trail's namesake, Ellen Davis, who died in 1999, was a charter member of the Minnehaha Garden Club, the fifty-year-old Minnehaha Social Club, and the Vancouver Audubon Society. A memorial monument was dedicated in 2003 at the southwest trailhead, recognizing, her contribution to the trail as well as paying homage to her youthful mind and spirit.

The trail traverses a variety of environments, meandering along Burnt Bridge Creek through gardens, meadows, woods, and forest. The southern end begins just northwest of Leverich Park on the Burnt Bridge Creek Trail and crosses Burnt Bridge Creek at **Friendship Bridge** ❶. This wooden, Japanese-style bridge, constructed by Shin-Etsu Handotai America, makes an excellent stop for rest, and taking photographs. There is a large dedication stone with a marble plaque next to the bridge. From the Friendship Bridge, the trail follows along the **NE Ross Street sidewalk** ❷ on the southern edge of the **J D Ross Substation Complex** ❸, which serves as the hub of the northwest power grid for the Bonneville Power Distribution System. The towers supporting the high-voltage power lines offer dramatic photo opportunities. The area was once a propagation garden for plants used to landscape northwest power substations, including the Ross Complex and Bonneville Dam. Remnant plantings of birch, locust, cypress, and a variety of groundcovers can still be seen here. This was also a farm prior to construction of the complex. Seedling fruit trees and grapevines serve as living evidence of this earlier homestead, providing abundant food and cover for native birds such as cedar waxwings, song sparrows, house and purple finches, American robins, spotted towhees, and the ubiquitous starling. Northern flickers, along with hairy and downy woodpeckers, can also be seen here. Bullock's orioles and western tanagers frequent the Douglas fir and Oregon ash along Burnt Bridge Creek.

In early spring, daffodils are a surprising sight in this rather wild, meadow-like setting, yet a reminder that the property was once domesticated. The fragrance of spring-flowering locusts and violas fills the air, both remnants of earlier gardens. Western yew trees are also in view. In July and August (of most years) a wide variety of butterflies can be seen. Nettles beneath the locust trees provide a great food source for the larvae of the Milbert's tortoiseshell butterfly and wild mustard provides sustenance for the Sara's orangetip butterfly.

At **North Road** ❹ the trail heads north to NW 54th Street and then heads east to 22nd Avenue. It's then north a short distance up along a narrow road of nine **tight switchbacks** ❺. You'll get a workout on this stretch! Immediately at the top of the hill you will **enter a mixed forest** ❻. Keep an eye out for sharp-shinned hawks at the forest edge. A variety of songbirds, including chestnut-backed and black-capped chickadees, golden-crowned and ruby-crowned kinglets, Pacific and Bewick's wrens, spotted towhees, and dark-eyed juncos, also frequent the area. Swainson's, hermit, and varied thrushes, and American robins are common in early spring along with an abundance of several species of yellow, white, and purple violets, including *Viola glabella* and *V. sempervirens*. Next, follow an exposed and steep ascent under some power lines where the trail plunges into a thick forest. The trail splits just inside the forest of Douglas fir, wild cherry, large western redcedars, and the occasional big-leaf maple. Some of these trees, having lost their tops in a severe 1948 ice storm, have developed dramatic candelabra shapes. In one area there is a grove of over a dozen of these grand remnants of what was once an ancient forest. We are fortunate that the Bonneville Power Administration chose to save these trees as a splendid buffer to their complex.

Three plants here are a particular treat: inside-out flower, sweet-after-death or vanilla leaf, and carpets of *Geranium robertianum*. There are also patches of wild ginger—be sure to seek out their tri-tendriled, burgundy-colored blossoms, which hug the ground in the spring. You'll also find hordes of trillium and red and white baneberry, as well as western and starry Solomon plume, and helleborine (*Epipactis helleborine*)—a European orchid that was first found in the eastern United States in the 1870s but has steadily been making its way westward.

In the fall and spring, a great variety of mushrooms and lichens are in evidence, such as the diminutive bird's nest fungi and a variety of *Cladonia* sp., better known as British soldier lichen. Slime molds round out an astounding diversity of plant and animal life. Proceeding on, you will arrive at the **Saint James Road trailhead** ❼.

Access

Parking is available at the east end of the trail on the west side of Saint James Road, just south of NE Minnehaha Street; in the middle at the Ross Complex parking lot; or on the southwest end of Leverich Parkway, off NE 45th Street. The southwest end of the Ellen Davis Trail intersects the Burnt Bridge Creek Trail just south of the Interstate 5 trail overpass.

How to Get There

By car: To the west end take Interstate 5 north to 39th Street exit, and take E 39th east and immediately turn left on NE Leverich Park Way. There is a parking lot and restrooms. Walk north to the cul-de-sac at the end of NE Leverich Park Way where the Burnt Bridge Creek Trail (Discovery Trail) starts. The Ellen Davis Trail soon takes off to the right, heading east across Burnt Bridge Creek. To Saint James trailhead take I-5 North to NE 78th Street and head east on NE 78th to NE Saint Johns Road. Drive south on St. Johns Road and just beyond NE Minnehaha bear right onto what becomes NE Saint Johns Road. The trailhead is on the right next to the large power pole. **PUBLIC TRANSIT:** C-Tran from downtown Portland to BPA-J D Ross Park and Ride located on the Ellen Davis Trail

By Don and Sue Cannard

More information: Vancouver-Clark Parks & Recreation

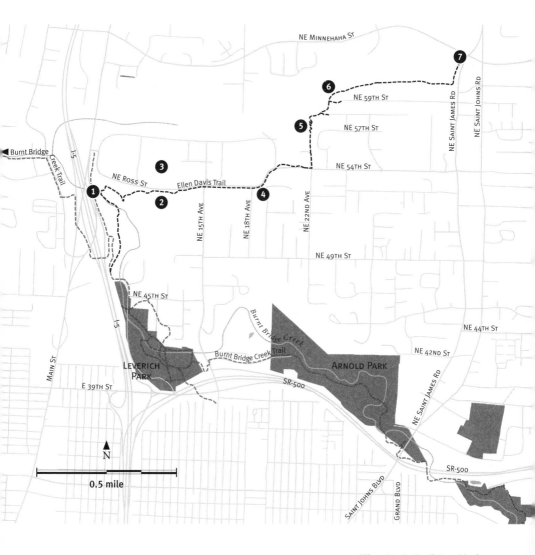

Salmon Creek Greenway

The 930-acre **Salmon Creek Greenway** includes extensive wetlands, mature Douglas fir, big-leaf maple, alder, and western redcedar forests, as well as black cottonwood, willows, alder, and the occasional stand of Oregon white ash bottomlands. Salmon Creek meanders between its canyon walls in a pattern typical of low gradient streams. The creek is also tidally influenced by the Columbia River where it enters Lake river. A 3.5-mile trail provides access to all of the habitats.

Once inside the park, at **Klineline Pond** ❶, cross a wooden pedestrian bridge over **Salmon Creek** ❷. Upstream, shallow, fast-moving water courses over gravels and larger rocks. Downstream, the water is quieter and deeper, but still swiftly moving. Across the bridge, you can fish, swim, picnic, or take a leisurely stroll. The pond is stocked with trout and is a popular fishing spot for people, double-crested cormorants, great blue and green herons, and both common and hooded mergansers. A backwater pond is also accessible by a pier where birds are abundant in spring and fall. Look for turtles in the hotter summer months. The "grooonkk" of the great blue heron and the "garooomp" of the invasive bullfrog are common sounds. A trail that begins at the north end of the pedestrian bridge in the parking lot heads both downstream (west) and upstream (east). If you head east, crossing under Interstate-5, the trail loops about three-quarters of the way around the **East Pond** ❸. This area, a reclaimed gravel pit, is dry and sparsely vegetated. In winter, waterfowl including Canada geese, mergansers, wigeon, bufflehead, grebes, and ruddy ducks rest and forage in the pond. Salmon and steelhead also use this area as a high-flow refuge.

If instead you head west on the trail that goes between the Klineline Pond and the **Sports Complex** ❹, you will end up at Salmon Creek and **open fields** ❺ where red-tailed hawks soar searching for voles, mice, and rabbits. Riparian buffers provide valuable habitat along this stretch of the Salmon Creek trail. Eventually, cedar will provide a wood recruitment source (fall into and around the stream providing complexity) that historically was important to the diversity, productivity, and stability of the creek and riparian area. There are also several snags in this segment that are important to birds for insect foraging, nesting, and roosting opportunities. Osprey, belted kingfisher, northern flickers, and the ubiquitous crow are common along this stretch of Salmon Creek.

Farther downstream, to the west, the greenway transitions to a passive recreation area. A large, roughly mowed field dominates the southern one third of greenway. Salmon Creek meanders away from the trail toward the north canyon wall shortly after the sports complex. At the apex of the ninety-degree meander, the creek laps against some large rocks, providing the unique, soothing sound I call laughing water. Take a deep breath, close your eyes, and feel the rhythm of the water as you relax and absorb nature's sounds around you. Watch for turtles in late spring and summer months as they sun on two platforms just short of a mile along the trail. In winter, waterfowl include Canada geese, common and hooded mergansers, American wigeon, bufflehead, pied-billed grebes, ruddy ducks, and spectacularly plumed breeding wood ducks. Local mammals include mink, raccoon, weasel, river otter, muskrats, and nutria, along with deer, coyote, and beaver. Even farther along the trail, the bottomland wetlands are home to rough-winged and violet-green swallows, red-winged blackbirds, and common yellowthroats. A massive habitat diversification and riparian re-vegetation effort includes dense plantings of rose, snowberry, spirea, red-osier dogwood, ocean-spray, willow, hawthorn, cottonwood, alder, Douglas fir, and western redcedar.

At mile 1.6, you can take a **loop-trail ❻** back to the Sports Complex along the base of the south canyon wall. Douglas fir, big-leaf maple, alder, and occasional mature cedars dominate the steep, south canyon wall. The understory includes sword fern, snowberry, elderberry, oceanspray, and other species. Along this side trail, as with much of the south canyon wall, sessile trillium (*Trillium chloropetalum*) can be seen growing among the sword fern around April Fools' Day. There are also many seeps

oozing from the canyon wall in this trail segment that, in addition to creating boggy trail
conditions, provide habitat for jewelweed,
horsetails, cattails, and spirea.

I prefer to continue west along the main
trail toward Lakeshore and 36th Avenue to
Cougar Creek, an important tributary that
provides year-round, relatively cool water to
Salmon Creek. A natural surface spur trail will
take you to **NW 119th Street** ❼, which is
another access point to Salmon Creek Trail.
Continuing west or downstream of the confluence of Cougar and Salmon Creeks,
you'll find a favorite spot for belted kingfishers and black-headed grosbeaks. Conifers
on the canyon wall attract golden-crowned and ruby-crowned kinglets, bushtits, black-
capped chickadees, and dark-eyed juncos.

The trail ends at **NW 36th Avenue** ❽, another jumping-off point. If you've
arranged for a shuttle on 36th, you're at journey's end. Before you go, turn around to
a grand view of snow-covered Mount Hood framed by the canyon walls. For those
heading back, all that's left to do now is to retrace your steps for the return ramble.
Savor the experience!

Kayaking Salmon Creek

While it's a steep climb down and
back up, it is possible to launch a
canoe or kayak at NW 36th Avenue
on the southeast side of the bridge.
A much easier access is at the Felida
Moorage and boat ramp at the west
end of NW 122nd Street and via
a short paddle north on Lake River
to the confluence of Lake River and
Salmon Creek.

How to Get There

BY CAR: Downstream: Take Interstate 5 north from Portland or Vancouver to the 134th
Street exit and proceed east on NE 134th to Highway 99. Continue east to NE Salmon
Creek Avenue and turn right (south) and drive to NE 119th Street. Turn right and continue until the NE 119th and NE 117th intersection. Continue west on NE 117th and
just after you pass under I-5 the entrance to Klineline Pond, Salmon Creek Park,
and the Salmon Creek Greenway Trail will be on your right. Midway: Follow the directions above but continue on NE 117th Street until it becomes NW 119th. Just past NW
11th Court on the right is Salmon Creek Trailhead, which will take you north to
Salmon Creek and the main trail. Upstream: Take the 134th Street exit off I-5 and proceed west on NE 134th until it becomes NE 139th and continue west. At NW 36th
Avenue turn left (south) and proceed just past NE Creekside Drive, which will be on
your right and look for the trailhead on the left. There is parking on the shoulder of
the road here. The trail entrance is just past the guardrail, on the left. **PUBLIC TRANSIT:**
C-Tran to Klineline Road and NE 117th, and walk .1 miles to the entrance.

By Patrick Lee

More information: Vancouver-Clark Parks & Recreation

Vancouver Lake Lowlands

When Portlanders want to see bald eagles and sandhill cranes, they invariably strike out for Sauvie Island. But those who live in North and Northeast Portland or Clark County know they have an option considerably closer at hand. For them, a Sauvie-like experience is a short drive or bicycle ride away.

Shillapoo Wildlife Area, Vancouver Unit

The Shillapoo Wildlife Area is an out-and-back trip at the end of La Frambois Road. If you brought your bike, a handy place to park your car is **Fruit Valley Park** parking lot off **Unander Avenue north of W 31st Street ❶**. Proceed by car or bike out La Frambois Road to the **sewage treatment ponds ❷**, which attract wintering waterfowl. I set up my spotting scope to look for ring-necked ducks, lesser scaup, ruddy ducks, northern shovelers, and bufflehead. Another quarter mile down the road is the Vancouver Unit of the Shillapoo Wildlife Area, a 450-acre Washington Department of Fish and Wildlife refuge. Don't bother going from mid-September through mid-March—it's closed all winter.

The refuge is primarily open grassy fields, wetlands, and huge, old Oregon white oak trees. As I drive along, I scan the open fields for short-eared owls—a rare sight in the metropolitan area—and the more common northern harriers, which fly low over grassy areas "harrying" their prey and listening for voles and mice with their slightly offset ears and sound-gathering, owl-like facial discs. If you're lucky you might see both short-eared owls and harriers crisscrossing the same field at dawn or dusk.

If you shy away from guns, be forewarned that there is a **skeet range ❸** about a mile from the entrance. The last time I visited the area skeet shooters were blasting away at clay pigeons, not the most serene experience I've ever had. But I find that the birding is worth the aggravation. At road's end I frequently park, making sure to put my permit in a conspicuous place on the dash, before heading out on the dirt path through the refuge's open fields and willow- and ash-riparian habitat. There is a simple graveled canoe and kayak launch here as well.

Vancouver Lake Park

More attractive by bicycle is a ride out Lower River Road to Vancouver Lake and Frenchman's Bar. Along Lower River Road on the right is **Elmer Rufner's Pond ❹**, which provides views of great egrets, blue herons, and myriad waterfowl. I find these marshes particularly impressive for their dominant native emergent wetland plants, including cattails, large-stemmed bulrush, and a mixture of sedges and rushes.

I also make sure to stop at the small parking area adjacent to the Vancouver Lake Flushing Channel. Vancouver-area birders report that incoming water from the Columbia River attracts hordes of birds that feed on the fish that get flushed into the lake. Local birders have observed loons and grebes, including red-necked and Clark's, here. During late summer or at low tide, the mudflats along the lake margins attract shorebirds, and during winter, thousands of gulls are drawn to the lone island in the distance.

Another 3.5 miles along, you can park in the small lot just beyond the intersection of Vancouver Lake Flushing Channel and NW Lower River Road. A second small parking area on NW Erwin O. Reiger Memorial Highway and next to **Vancouver Lake Crew boat storage** ❺ provides access to the Frenchman's Bar bicycle and pedestrian path that runs north to Vancouver Lake Park or west to Frenchman's Bar, a five-mile roundtrip. If I want to avoid cycling along Lower River Road, I'll load my bike on the car and start my cycle at the Frenchman's Bar path. It's heavily used by cyclists, runners, and walkers during warm weather. There are multiple access points, parking, and restrooms along the path, which is four miles long.

To get to Vancouver Lake Park, I ride north on the bike path or continue driving north on Reiger Memorial Highway. There are three parking areas with restrooms and great views of Vancouver Lake. It looks highly developed, but only thirty-five acres of the 234-acre park are given to more active recreation and picnicking. More than two miles of lakefront in the park offer birding opportunities and about every kind of recreational option you can imagine, including windsurfing, sand volleyball, and swimming in a roped-off area adjacent to a sandy beach. There are no lifeguards, however.

The lake gets its water from the flushing channel that connects directly to the Columbia River and from Burnt Bridge Creek, which flows from the east. Its maximum depth is fifteen feet and average is less than three feet. The island to the north is the result of early 1980s lake dredging by the Corps of Engineers. Lake River, which drains the lake from its northeast corner, can be canoed to Ridgefield and the Columbia River. However, it's a good idea to keep a sharp eye out for tidal levels and know whether the Columbia is running higher than the lake. Lake River actually reverses its flow into the lake for much of the year.

All six grebes commonly found in Oregon and Washington have been seen on the lake, although western and pied-billed are the most common in winter. Loons, gulls, and double-crested cormorants frequent the lake as well. Bald eagles can be seen in the cottonwoods surrounding the lake, and at least one active nest is within a mile of the lake. Several great horned owl nests can also be found in the trees surrounding the lake during early winter.

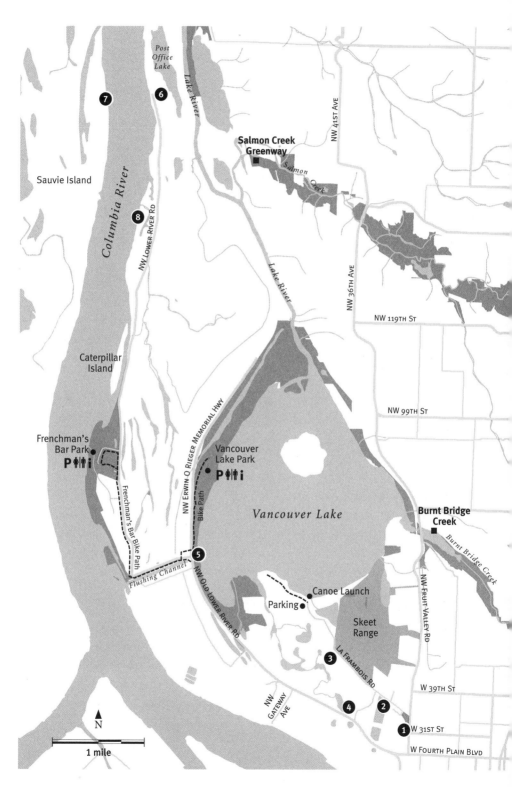

Frenchman's Bar Regional Park

To get to Frenchman's Bar Park, either ride or walk along the paved path or, if you're driving, continue west and then north on NW Lower River Road. Be sure to stop where the road takes a ninety-degree turn to the north. The bicycle path passes through here as well. There is easy access to a large sandy beach and the Flushing Channel.

The main entrance to Frenchman's Bar Park is a mile up the road on the left. Opened in 1998, Frenchman's Bar offers expansive views of Sauvie Island and ships plying the Columbia River. The fields south of Frenchman's Bar often have flocks of sandhill cranes, swans, and geese in the winter. Across the road is the state's Shillapoo Wildlife area. Check out the black cottonwoods for great blue heron nests. At one point this colony was 250 nests strong.

Ridgefield National Wildlife Refuge, Bridgeport Dairy Unit

I normally drive the additional six miles to get to Ridgefield National Wildlife Refuge if that's on my itinerary. NW Lower River Road dead-ends at an **informal gravel parking area ❻**, and a dirt path cuts through Himalayan blackberry patches and allows for a short hike. I take advantage of several turnouts en route that provide excellent views of open water and wetland habitat. Some of the best views of tundra swans, Canada geese, and waterfowl can be had from these viewing areas. And some of the best vistas of the Columbia River come into view as the road skirts along the main channel of the river. Across the river you can see **Willow Bar ❼** and the Sauvie Island Marina on the Oregon shore. Along the way, there are multiple osprey nests in trees on **Caterpillar Island ❽** across from the small marina and on utility poles lining the road. You might even see the relatively rare northern shrike, an exceptionally rare gyrfalcon, or an emperor goose.

How to Get There

By car: Shillapoo and Vancouver Lake Wildlife Area: Take Interstate 5 north, exit 1D, Fourth Plain Boulevard. Head west on W Fourth Plain through Vancouver. About two miles from I-5, turn right at the stop sign onto Fruit Valley Road and drive north 0.4 miles to La Frambois Road, which bounds the north end of Fruit Valley Park. Turn left (west) onto La Frambois, then after a quarter mile the sewage ponds are on the left. Another mile west on La Frambois is the entrance to the Wildlife Access Area. A fee is required, and there is no access mid-September to mid-March. Vancouver Lake Park: Follow the directions above, but at the stoplight at W Fourth Plain and Fruit Valley Road, continue straight (west) on Lower River Road (State Route 501). After about 3.5 miles you can either go left and continue on NW Lower River Road to Frenchman's Bar and Ridgefield National Wildlife Refuge or continue straight for 0.6 mile to Vancouver Lake Park. Frenchman's Bar Regional Park and Bridgeport Dairy Unit of Ridgefield National Wildlife Refuge: Instead of continuing north on NW Reiger Memorial Highway to Vancouver Lake Park, turn left and continue on NW Lower River Road.

Frenchman's Bar Park is 1.8 miles past the junction on the left. The Shillapoo Wildlife Area is another 2.7 miles past Frenchman's Bar on the right. The Bridgeport Dairy Unit of Ridgefield National Wildlife Refuge is at the gate about six miles north on Lower River Road.

By Mike Houck, illustration by Lynn Kitagawa

More information: Vancouver-Clark Parks & Recreation; U.S. Fish and Wildlife

Golden Purifiers

HOW CAN YOU NOT LOVE the turkey vulture?! It is a bird without pomp or pretense. While other birds strut and preen, sing and soar, the turkey vulture wobbles awkwardly in flight, goes prematurely bald, poops on its own legs to stay cool, and vomits when it gets nervous. It doesn't sing. When necessary it hisses, but mostly it doesn't say anything at all. It is the original "bird nerd," and it goes about its business de-putrefying our landscape and suffering the slings and arrows of a society that often fails to appreciate the role of death in sustaining life.

Turkey vultures (*Cathartes aura*) can generally be found in the Willamette Valley from March until October, although in recent years they have been increasingly documented staying later and returning earlier. In the metropolitan area, they are a common sight soaring over the Willamette and Columbia Rivers and above our greenspaces. Of course the classic turkey vulture sighting is of a group, or venue, of turkey vultures perched atop and around a dead critter lying in the middle of the road—the dominant birds feeding first while subordinates skulk nearby, waiting their turn.

Birdwatchers will often see swirling groups of turkey vultures, known as kettles, circling upward together on rising columns of warm air, or thermals. They use the thermals to lift themselves skyward with minimal energy. If you look closely, you will often see other species such as red-tailed hawks, bald eagles, and ospreys also rising on the same columns.

In flight, turkey vultures are easily discerned from other large, local species by the way they hold their wings in a dihedral (V-shaped) position and their tendency to rock back and forth from side to side. Their wobbly flight actually belies the fact that they are among the best gliders in the bird world, able to go for hours without flapping by riding thermals upward like natural elevators and then coasting gradually downward until they find another thermal. With wingspans that exceed five feet, turkey vultures are an impressive sight to behold.

Up close, adult turkey vultures are easily identified by their nearly featherless heads—gray when young and bright red as they reach sexual maturity. The lack of head feathers is an adaptation that allows them to immerse their heads in carrion without accumulating bacteria and debris on their feathers. They will often be observed perched on fence posts and tree branches with their wings extended, a position known as the horaltic pose. It is believed that this behavior serves multiple functions, including drying out the wings and exposing bacteria to sunlight. Where you see one turkey vulture, you often see many, since they form large, communal roosts and tend to scavenge in groups.

The roosts are believed to serve as "information centers," where vultures learn about new food sources by following one another.

Because of its hooked beak and raptor-like talons, the turkey vulture was long and incorrectly classified as a member of the raptor family and was often blamed for killing livestock. In fact, the turkey vulture is a true scavenger, now believed to be more closely related to the stork family. The vulture actually provides a great service to our ecosystem by perpetually searching the landscape for dead things and consuming the

remains of even the most contaminated animals. Turkey vultures' amazing digestive systems are able to process and neutralize botulism, anthrax, and cholera. The scientific name for turkey vulture, *Cathartes aura*, has been translated to mean "golden purifier" and "cleansing breeze."

Vultures nest on the ground, often in caves, among rock outcroppings, and in hollow logs and trees. They do not build a stick nest but rather lay their eggs directly on the ground, perhaps padded with a few dry leaves or woodchips. Both parents take care of the young in the nest, feeding them regurgitated carrion. It is amazing that any ground-nesting birds survive in our local natural areas with the hazards of natural predators and the added dangers of dogs, cats, and humans. It is particularly amazing that birds as large and conspicuous as turkey vulture manage to pull it off, especially given that their young are in the nest for nine to ten weeks.

Few animals have a more unique or charming defense mechanism than the turkey vulture. They are not at all aggressive birds, and given the choice between fighting and fleeing, they will simply leave. However, when cornered, the turkey vulture will sway back and forth, shifting its weight from leg to leg, and make a hissing sound akin to air escaping from a giant balloon. When all else fails, its face will exhibit a look of sad resignation. It will slowly lower its head toward the ground, swallow deeply, and then vomit up putrid gobs of whatever it last consumed. The display is completed by a quick shake of the head that clears the bird's mouth and spurts bits of half-digested opossum and road-kill squirrel like shrapnel.

Vultures' innate curiosity can sometimes be less than well received. The sight of vultures watching from overhead sometimes spooks people. This reaction reached an extreme when a group of vultures began perching on the ledge outside the windows at a local hospital. The patients were not thrilled by the spectacle of vultures staring at them through the glass. However, the vulture is not a harbinger of death—he keeps our landscape a cleaner, healthier place in which to live. Personally when my time comes, I can think of no more honorable or ecologically responsible way to become one with the universe than to be carried aloft in the belly of a vulture.

By Bob Sallinger, illustration by Lei Kotynski

Lake River to Bachelor Island

Lake River is a ten-mile slough connecting Vancouver Lake and the northern tip of Bachelor Island. It's a wonderful canoe and kayak route offering remarkable opportunities for wildlife viewing. There are two options to explore Lake River. If you want to focus on the Ridgefield National Wildlife Refuge and the Columbia River, the most convenient location is the boat ramp at the foot of Mill Street in Ridgefield, Washington. If you'd rather explore the upper Lake River and Vancouver Lake, put in at the Felida Moorage in Vancouver. Another option is to set up a shuttle, leaving one vehicle at either end of Lake River at these two boat ramps, and plan a one-way paddle.

Bachelor Island Loop

If you're out to explore Bachelor Island from Lake River, put in at the **Ridgefield boat ramp** ❶ and paddle downstream (north) past the tip of the River "S" Unit of the Ridgefield National Wildlife Refuge and around the northern tip of Bachelor Island, which (with the exception of the northwest corner) is also part of the refuge. Anytime you plan a paddle that takes you out on the Columbia River, be prepared for windy, choppy conditions. While the length of Bachelor Island is only three miles, the paddle from the Ridgefield boat ramp, around the island and back to Ridgefield via the slough is about ten miles. It's about a six-hour trip, so plan accordingly!

During your circumnavigation of Bachelor Island, you're guaranteed to see an abundance of wildlife, including great blue herons, an array of waterfowl, beaver, weasels, mink, and river otter. It's surprising how much easier it is to approach skittish wildlife in a canoe or kayak if you simply take the time to drift by quietly.

Bald eagles and osprey both nest in the area, the latter having increased in numbers dramatically in the past decade. You will also undoubtedly see many red-tailed hawks,

> **Eyes Open! Safety Tip**
>
> It's difficult to see Bachelor Island Slough on the return trip to Ridgefield, so keep a keen eye out for it. You don't want the sheriff's office out looking for you because you missed the entrance to Bachelor Island Slough!

northern harriers, and American kestrels. Most of the land is in public ownership, managed by either the U.S. Fish and Wildlife Service or the Washington State Department of Fish and Wildlife. Both agencies provide resting and wintering grounds for many of the waterfowl in the Vancouver Lake Lowlands and at Sauvie Island across the Columbia River.

As you paddle along Lake River, think of Lewis and Clark and the Corps of Discovery, who spent a restless, sleepless night due to the continuous noise of the geese, swans, and cranes. Cathlapotle was one of the largest Native American settlements on the lower Columbia River, with perhaps a thousand people living in long plankhouses fronting Lake River. Many of the flooded areas on the Ridgefield Refuge were sites for gathering wapato, a staple of the Native Americans' diet, along with salmon.

Continue your paddle along the **western shore of Bachelor Island ❷**, taking in views of Sauvie Island across the Columbia River. To the northeast is the largest nesting colony of great blue herons on the lower Columbia River, with over four hundred nests. These communal nesting areas are sensitive to human intrusion, so view the colony from the water. Viewing is best before the trees leaf out in mid-February, when the herons return to their nests in preparation to lay their eggs in early April. At the **upstream tip of the island ❸**, watch carefully on your left for **Bachelor Island Slough**, which is your route back to Lake River and the Ridgefield boat ramp.

Upper Lake River, Salmon Creek, and Vancouver Lake

If you paddle south from Ridgefield, upstream on Lake River, you'll come to the **mouth of Salmon Creek ❹**, on the left midway en route to Vancouver Lake. Salmon Creek is one of Vancouver's most significant urban waterways, and a paddle upstream will be rich in wildlife sightings. The 930-acre greenway includes extensive wetlands; mature Douglas fir, big-leaf maple, red alder, and western redcedar forests; and riparian habitat of black cottonwood, willows, alder, and Oregon white ash. Salmon Creek, being a low-gradient stream, has many meanders that add to the interest of an upstream paddle. If you continue your paddle upstream on Lake River, you'll find yourself at Vancouver Lake. From there you can either explore the lake or head back north on Lake River to the Ridgefield boat ramp. You should be mindful that Lake River either flows from or into Vancouver Lake, depending on tidal action and the relative level of Vancouver Lake and the Columbia River. Pay attention to the currents so you can time your return trip to Ridgefield with the current. Rather than return to Ridgefield, you can also arrange your own shuttle and simply take out at the **Felida boat ramp in Vancouver ❺**.

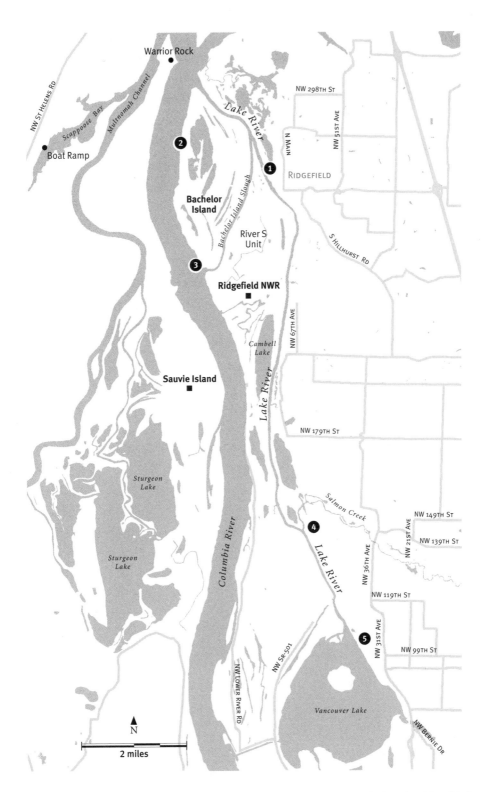

Warrior Rock

NW ST. HELENS RD

Scappoose Bay

Multnomah Channel

Boat Ramp

NW 298TH ST

NW 51ST AVE

N MAIN

2

Lake River

1

RIDGEFIELD

**Bachelor
Island**

Bachelor Island Slough

River S
Unit

S HILLHURST RD

3

Ridgefield NWR ■

NW 67TH AVE

*Cambell
Lake*

NW 179TH ST

Sauvie Island ■

*Sturgeon
Lake*

Salmon Creek

NW 149TH ST

*Sturgeon
Lake*

NW 21ST AVE

NW 139TH ST

4

NW 36TH AVE

Lake River

NW 119TH ST

Columbia River

NW 31ST AVE

NW 99TH ST

5

NW SR-501

NW LOWER RIVER RD

Vancouver Lake

NW BERNIE DR

▲
N

2 miles

How to Get There

BY CAR: Ridgefield Marina: From Portland take Interstate 5 north to the Ridgefield exit and take NW 269th (Highway 501) west into Ridgefield. Turn right on Main Avenue and proceed a short distance to Mill Street and turn left; proceed to the parking area. There is a coin-operated parking tag machine that takes quarters at the top of the boat ramp. A change machine is at the nearby restrooms. Felida Moorage: From Portland take Interstate 5 North to NW 99th Street exit and head west on 99th Street to NW 31st Avenue, and then head north on 31st to NW 122nd and turn left onto 122nd and proceed to the parking lot and boat ramp. Scappoose Bay Marine Park boat ramp in Warren: From Portland take Highway 30 about twenty-five miles west of Portland to Old Portland Road and turn right on Bayport Marina Lane.

By Don Cannard and Mike Houck

More information: Ridgefield National Wildlife Refuge; Washington Department of Fish and Wildlife; Vancouver-Clark Parks & Recreation

La Center Bottoms

LOCATION: East Fork Lewis River immediately upstream of La Center Bridge, Clark County, WA **ACTIVITIES:** Hiking, Paddling, Wildlife viewing, Picnicking **FACILITIES:** Restrooms, Parking, Paved and unpaved trails, Viewing blind, Interpretive signs, Canoe/kayak launch **FEES AND REGULATIONS:** 7 am to dusk **HIKING DIFFICULTY:** Easy **HIGHLIGHTS:** "Watchable Wildlife" site; Migratory waterfowl November through March; Coyotes; Canoe/kayak access for all skill levels **PUBLIC TRANSIT:** No direct service

The La Center Bottoms Stewardship Site is part of a habitat and greenway system that covers over 2,200 acres on the lower East Fork Lewis River. The East Fork Lewis River is Clark County's largest free-flowing stream. Rising in the Cascade Mountains near Cougar Rock, it flows forty-three miles through Skamania and Clark Counties and joins the North Fork just below Interstate 5 and Paradise Point State Park. The main Lewis then empties into the Columbia River just north of the Ridgefield Wildlife Refuge (see page 337).

The La Center Bottoms is located at the lower end of the East Fork Lewis (between river miles 3 and 4), where the basin has now expanded into a broad floodplain and the river has slower-moving, tidally influenced flows. The preserve covers 125 acres and is one of three state-designated "Watchable Wildlife" sites in Clark County. The property includes 3,500 feet of shoreline on the East Fork Lewis River and Brezee Creek, a small tributary that cuts through the north end of the property. The La Center Bottoms features a variety of habitat types, including emergent wetlands, floodplain/meadow, open ponds, and forested uplands. The expansive bottomlands, which dominate the site, attract a wide variety of migratory waterfowl, including Canada geese, wigeon, northern pintail, mallard, cinnamon teal, wood duck, bufflehead, bald eagle, osprey, and great blue heron. Especially watch for the large numbers of tundra swan that rest and feed in the bottoms and other nearby ponds and wetlands.

While the La Center Bottoms is a great place to visit the East Fork, it is just one feature in the larger greenway system. The lower greenway covers twelve miles and over 2,200 acres. Clark County owns and manages over 85 percent of the property, while other land managers include State Parks, State Fish and Wildlife, and the nonprofit Environmental Enhancement Group, which purchased an abandoned gravel mine with a vision for habitat restoration. Management emphasis on properties within the greenway ranges from habitat protection, with little public access, to fully developed parks. The bottomlands near La Center are state-designated priority habitat for large concentrations of migratory waterfowl and wintering bald eagles. The East Fork Lewis and its associated tributaries, side channels, and wetlands also provide critical habitat for federally listed coho, Chinook, chum, and steelhead.

The low-gradient stream system provides wonderful paddling and wildlife viewing for paddlers of all skill levels. Several miles of easy paddling are available on the East Fork Lewis, North Fork Lewis, Main Lewis, and Lake River (see page 407). The city of

La Center borders the La Center Bottoms to the north and provides restaurants, groceries, and other services.

Access

Quick and easy—mostly flat, paved pedestrian trail (two thirds of a mile long) borders the west edge of the property. The trail crosses Brezee Creek and leads to two viewing blinds that overlook the natural area and the extended greenway system. Access point for canoes and kayaks nearby, immediately west of the La Center Bridge.

Other sites: The greenway also offers public access sites at Paradise Point State Park, just upstream of Interstate 5, Daybreak Park, and Lewisville Regional Park, which was first developed by Works Progress Administration crews in the 1930s and provides hiking trails, open play meadows, picnic tables, and shelters. Well worth the visit, Lewisville is two miles north of Battle Ground via State Route 503.

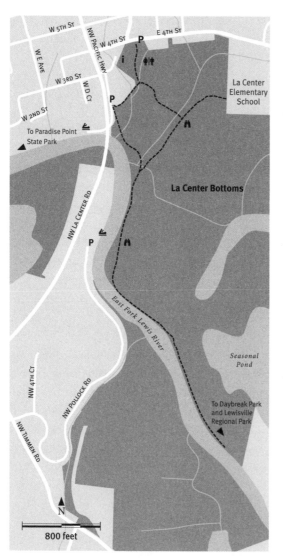

How to Get There

BY CAR: From Portland north on Interstate 5; exit #16 (319th Street); turn east on La Center Road and drive approximately 1.5 miles and take the first right after crossing the La Center Road Bridge. **PUBLIC TRANSIT:** No direct service

By Bill Dygert

More information: Vancouver-Clark Parks & Recreation; Clark County Legacy Lands

About the Contributors

Eric Anderson has worked multiple jobs with Ridgefield National Wildlife Refuge since 1994.

Bruce Barbarasch loves to wander the woods, waters, and wetlands of The Intertwine when he is not trapped at his desk as superintendent of natural resources for the Tualatin Hills Park & Recreation District,

Elayne Barclay has spent her entire life working with many kinds of wildlife, most recently propagating imperiled native butterflies at the Oregon Zoo.

Susan Barthel has worked on Columbia Slough watershed projects for the City of Portland and has organized hundreds of tours, events, and activities in and around the waterway since 1993.

Judy BlueHorse Skelton served as cultural student support specialist for Portland Public Schools Indian Education Program and is a faculty member at Portland State University, where she teaches Environmental Education Through Native American Lenses and Leadership for Sustainability.

Gary Bock is the executive director of the Vancouver Watersheds Council.

Allison Bollman is a Portland-based nature artist who also writes and illustrates graphic novels and picture books.

Eric Brattain is an educator and environmentalist who works on behalf of Fernhill Wetlands and its future as a place for human interaction with the natural world.

Matt Burlin is an urban planner and outreach coordinator for the Sustainable Stormwater Division of the City of Portland's Environmental Services.

Don Cannard has had a life-long interest in the environment and is founder of the Vancouver Audubon Society and cofounder of the three-hundred-mile Chinook Trail looping the Columbia River Gorge.

Virginia Church is a Portland artist who loves exploring local wild places.

James R. Clapp has been the refuge manager for Steigerwald Lake, Franz Lake, and Pierce National Wildlife Refuge—part of the Ridgefield Refuge Complex along the Columbia River—since 2001.

Matt Clark is the executive director of the Johnson Creek Watershed Council and is proud to work to protect and enhance the beautiful natural areas of the city where he grew up.

M. J. Cody is a food and travel writer and is the chair of Urban Greenspaces Institute.

Robin Cody is the Portland author of *Ricochet River, Voyage of a Summer Sun,* and *Another Way the River Has,* a collection of true Northwest tales.

David Cohen is the executive director of the Friends of Tryon Creek, a leading provider of innovative environmental programs focusing on children and community-based restoration efforts in Tryon Creek State Natural Area.

Mary Coolidge is the assistant conservation director for Audubon Society of Portland where she coordinates the Oregon Important Bird Area Program, manages metropolitan volunteer science programs, and is a 2010 Together Green Fellow working on a Lights Out Portland campaign to help make Portland a bird safe city.

Greg Creager works on habitat restoration and environmental outreach as a park ranger for Tualatin Hills Park & Recreation District.

James Davis, a naturalist at Metro, is the author of *The Northwest Nature Guide* and was Portland Audubon's first education director.

Lee Dayfield is a neighborhood activist working to improve Nadaka Nature Park by raising awareness, organizing cleanups to remove invasives, and improving access to the community.

John Deshler has made Portland's Forest Park his office since 2007, where he has conducted extensive research on the breeding biology and habitat selection of the small and mighty northern pygmy-owl.

Jennifer Devlin is an environmental program coordinator for the City of Portland's Bureau of Environmental Services and was formerly the director of education for Audubon Society of Portland.

Linda Dobson manages the Sustainable Stormwater Division for the City of Portland's Bureau of Environmental Services.

Jo Anne Dolan is the sustainability programs director at Columbia Springs when not exploring the wonders of Cascadia or creating urban wildlife habitat in her Northeast Portland yard.

Bill Dygert is a Vancouver-based consultant who specializes in the preservation and enhancement of fish and wildlife habitat and recreation lands.

Steve Engel is a naturalist and educator who lives in Portland.

Mike Faha is a founding principal of Portland-based GreenWorks, a landscape architecture firm that focuses on planning compact, livable communities that embrace and protect natural resources.

Toby Forsberg is a marketing professional, native Oregonian, and community activist residing in Gladstone, Oregon.

Nancy Fraser, born in Chicago, has been a volunteer at Audubon Society of Portland since 1975 and is a volunteer monitor, bander, and current president of The Prescott Bluebird Recovery Project.

Alice Froehlich is an outdoor educator who lives and works in beautiful Portland, Oregon.

Marshall Gannett is a geologist and Portland resident.

Martha Gannett is a graphic designer living in Portland, who enjoys urban wildlife and urban rambling.

Lisa Goorjian is a registered landscape architect who has worked as a parks, trails, and greenways planner and developer for Missouri State Parks and the Vancouver-Clark Parks & Recreation Department.

Peter Guillozet has developed and managed projects for the Washington Council of Governments and Clean Water Services and is an ecologist who strives to do more good than bad.

Rafael Gutierrez is a freelance cartographer specializing in print and web-based mapping.

Jane Hart is a senior project manager at Metro whose expertise is preparing trail master plans for regional trails throughout the Portland metropolitan region.

Stephen Hatfield is the stewardship director for the Forest Park Conservancy and lives in North Portland with his wife and two daughters.

William J. Hawkins III, architect, FAIA, is a board member of the Portland Parks Board and the National Association of Olmsted Parks and is the great-nephew of Colonel L. L. Hawkins.

Dave Helzer lives, works, and birds in Portland, where he is a terrestrial biologist who focuses on the Columbia River and the Columbia Slough with the City of Portland's Bureau of Environmental Services.

Evelyn Hicks is a Portland artist and illustrator.

Scott Hinderman is a natural resources park ranger for Tualatin Hills Park & Recreation District.

Mike Houck, executive director of the Urban Greenspaces Institute, has been engaged in urban park, trail, and natural area issues since founding the Urban Naturalist Program at Audubon Society of Portland in 1980.

Tom Hughes, prior to his current position as Metro Council president, served as mayor of Hillsboro, Oregon, and taught at Aloha High School.

Robin M. Jensen is a self-employed medical illustrator, part-time Audubon Society of Portland employee in the Backyard Habitat Certification Program, dedicated volunteer, and president of Friends of Marquam Nature Park.

Marie Johnson is a program coordinator at the City of Portland's Bureau of Environmental Services and delights in sharing her backyard with red-winged blackbirds from Fanno Creek.

Steve Johnson, PhD, is an adjunct professor in urban studies and planning at Portland State University and an international lecturer on sustainable community development and community engagement.

Nathan Kappen is an artist and resides in Portland, where he professionally practices landscape architecture and urban planning at Walker Macy Landscape Architects.

Lynn Kitagawa is a medical and scientific illustrator at the Portland VA Medical Center and an adjunct faculty member at Pacific Northwest College of Art's Continuing Education Program.

Lei Kotynski is a naturalist and wildlife enthusiast at heart, which makes her love of drawing from nature a passion.

Jim Labbe spent much of his youth exploring Northwest Portland's urban natural areas and has served as Audubon Society of Portland's urban conservationist since 2003.

Patrick Lee coordinates Clark County's Legacy Lands Program, which seeks to establish, restore, and maintain an interconnected system of parks, natural areas, trails, and open spaces within the region.

Ursula K. Le Guin has lived and written near Portland's Forest Park for the last fifty years or so.

Connie Levesque lives in Southwest Portland, has an MFA in creative writing, and lives in a house beset by urban vermin.

Jo Linden hails from the Rocky Mountains and now lives in Portland, where she is a novice naturalist and practicing massage therapist.

Richard Louv is the chairman and cofounder of the Children & Nature Network and is the author of eight books, including his most recent, *The Nature Principle: Human Restoration and the End of Nature-Deficit Disorder.*

Kaitlin Lovell is the manager of the Science, Fish, and Wildlife Division for the City of Portland's Bureau of Environmental Services

Melissa Marcum is the natural resources volunteer coordinator for the Tualatin Hills Park & Recreation District, and is currently focused on increasing and improving community involvement in the park district's natural areas.

David B. Marshall is a consulting wildlife biologist.

Cheri Martin, a native of Clark County, Washington, is the executive director of the Parks Foundation of Clark County and is an avid outdoor enthusiast who takes advantage of any and all opportunities to share her passion for kayaking and hiking with others.

Donna Matrazzo is a science writer and the author of *Wild Things: Adventures of a Grassroots Environmentalist* who has lived on Sauvie Island for twenty-three years.

Tom McAllister, native Oregonian, wildlife biologist, and OSU alumnus, was the outdoor editor of *The Oregon Journal* and *The Oregonian* daily newspapers for 40 years and then a naturalist/historian for Lindblad Expeditions.

Tammi Miller manages the office and technology systems at Audubon Society of Portland, where she enjoys introducing visitors to Ruby, a turkey vulture, and Aristophanes, a common raven.

Bill Monroe is a retired outdoor writer for *The Oregonian*, where he's contributed weekly columns for thirty years covering fishing, hunting, birding, and all other things wild.

Michael Murphy is a professor of biology at Portland State University and is the current editor-in-chief of *The Auk*, the quarterly journal of the American Ornithologists' Union.

Elisabeth Neely is an environmental educator who served as park naturalist at Oxbow Regional Park from 1997 to 2008; her current projects include teaching community-based nature education, parenting two children, and raising goats.

Jonathan Nicholas, a vice president at ODS, is a writer and raconteur who abandoned a very long and frequently wild-in-the-city newspaper career to try his hand at helping to reform health care.

Jonna Papaefthimiou is an urban planner and sustainability advocate.

Zachariah Perry is an Oregon native and has been responsible for formulating the strategy and implementing all aspects of the Reed College Canyon restoration since 1999.

Kendra Petersen-Morgan is a natural resource ecologist for Portland Parks & Recreation's City Nature West program, where she is responsible for the ecological management of Forest Park and thirty-four other natural areas on Portland's west side.

Sarah Pinnock has a degree in environmental science from Marylhurst University and has been the wetlands education specialist at Jackson Bottom Wetlands Preserve in Hillsboro, Oregon, for eleven years.

Ken Pirie, an associate with Walker Macy Landscape Architects, works on urban design, public lands, and campus planning projects across the West.

Kelly Punteney is a Washington State Parks commissioner, a board member of the Urban Greenspaces Institute, and the on-site manager of the Jane Weber Evergreen Arboretum and historic Stanger House in Vancouver.

Robert Michael Pyle, a naturalist, lepidopterist, and Guggenheim Fellow, writes essays, poetry, and fiction and does a little science along a tributary of the Lower Columbia River.

Charles Ray is the urban forester with the City of Vancouver, and is certified through the International Society of Arboriculture as an arborist and municipal specialist.

Meryl A. Redisch, a native New Yorker and formerly an urban park ranger in New York City, is the executive director of the Audubon Society of Portland.

Julie Reilly is a botanist, wetland ecologist, and habitat restoration professional who works for the Tualatin Hills Park & Recreation District.

Ralph Thomas Rogers is a retired regional wetland ecologist for the Environmental Protection Agency who lives near Goldendale, Washington and spends much of his time pursuing his lifelong passion surveying and studying dragonflies and damselflies of the Pacific Northwest and beyond.

Bruce Roll served for eight years as the assistant director for Whatcom County Public Works in Washington State, where he oversaw Watershed Management, Salmon Recovery, Marine Resource, River and Flood, and Solid Waste Programs before joining Clean Water Services.

Mike Rosen manages the Watershed Division for the City of Portland's Bureau of Environmental Services and is lucky to work with many enlightened biologists, arborists, and urban naturalists.

Emily Roth is the natural resource planner for Portland Parks & Recreation and enjoys walking, hiking, and bird watching in our urban natural areas.

Bob Sallinger is the conservation director for Audubon Society of Portland and lives in a park-deficient neighborhood in Northeast Portland with his family and an assortment of dogs, cats, chickens, goats, and pigeons.

Cory Samia, head weighed down by multiple hats, is an informal science educator, land protector, and herp lover who shares her experiences with many as she clomps through wetlands and watersheds.

Melissa Sandoz is the outreach director for the Columbia Slough Watershed Council and is a Northeast Portland resident with a background in environmental education, community stewardship, and ecological theatre.

Matthew Shepherd is a senior conservation associate at The Xerces Society for Invertebrate Conservation, has been engaged in wildlife conservation for a quarter century, and has a particular interest in insects and other invertebrates.

Mat Sinclair, executive director of Hoyt Arboretum Friends, has actively pursued the organization's vision of a true living museum through environmental education, stewardship, and understanding of the natural environment.

Jim Sjulin is the retired head of Portland Parks & Recreation's Natural Resources Program.

Sarah Skelly is a park ranger at Tualatin Hills Nature Park, where she manages a diverse array of habitats and trails and is passionately involved in the development and implementation of many nature education programs.

Maggie Skenderian is the Johnson Creek Watershed manager for Portland's Bureau of Environmental Services and lives in Southeast Portland, just a short bike ride from Johnson Creek.

Jonathan Soll has spent twenty-four years studying and practicing biodiversity conservation in the Pacific Northwest and is currently Science and Stewardship Division manager for Metro.

Kyle Spinks is a park ranger and has been working for the Tualatin Hills Park & Recreation District for ten years.

Kim Stafford is the founding director of the Northwest Writing Institute at Lewis & Clark College and the author of *The Muses Among Us: Eloquent Listening and Other Pleasures of the Writer's Craft.*

Rowan Steele is a recent graduate of Portland State University's Master of Urban and Regional Planning Program and organizer for the Crystal Springs Community Collaborative.

Adam Stellmacher is a natural resources technician with Metro and restores and maintains wildlife habitat on publicly owned natural areas.

Elaine Stewart is an ecologist with Metro who restores habitat and conducts applied research on publicly owned natural areas.

Sue Thomas is the environmental education specialist for Portland's Park & Recreation's City Nature Division and manages programs in all ten thousand acres of city parks.

Dawn Uchiyama is a landscape architect with the City of Portland, where she contributes to the city's Stormwater System Plan and Asset Management Program.

Carolyn Uyemura is a longtime volunteer and interpreter of the Tualatin National Wildlife Refuge and a member of the nonprofit group, Friends of the Refuge.

Brett VandenHeuvel is an avid river user, an environmental lawyer, and the director of Columbia Riverkeeper, where he works to protect and restore the big river.

Brian Vaughn is a natural resource scientist for Metro.

Amin Wahab is an environmental program manager for Fanno and Tryon Creek watersheds in Southwest Portland.

Brian Wegener is the advocacy and communications manager for Tualatin Riverkeepers and occasionally paddles the Tualatin River in his home-built cedar-strip kayak.

Wim Wiewel, prior to accepting the position of president of Portland State University in 2008, was the provost and senior vice president of academic affairs at the University of Baltimore, with degrees in sociology and urban planning from the

University of Amsterdam in the Netherlands and a PhD in sociology from Northwestern University.

Travis Williams has worked as riverkeeper and executive director of Willamette Riverkeeper since 2000 and he is the author of *Willamette River Field Guide*.

Bob Wilson still retains his fascination for the connection between the human and the wild after thirty-plus years of watching, and occasionally writing about, the plants and animals of our urban greenspaces.

Mark Griswold Wilson, an oak-savannah enthusiast, tends a camas prairie garden in his front yard and currently serves as the *Willamette River* ecologist for the City Nature Division of Portland Parks & Recreation.

Steve Wise, executive director of the Sandy River Basin Watershed Council, has worked for two decades on water, river, and ecosystem conservation and sustainability in the Pacific Northwest, Great Lakes, and elsewhere.

Index

Maps are indicated with bold type.

WILD IN THE CITY: EXPLORING THE INTERTWINE

Designed by Martha Gannett, Gannett Design

Maps by Rafael Gutierrez, Grafa Geographic Design

Cover photography by Nelson Photography (otters) and Mike Houck

Cover image composition by Jonah Sutherland

Typography by William H. Brunson, Typography Services

Printed by Data Reproductions Corporation